The Best of
Mainly for Students

Volume Two

Edited by

Phil Askham

and

Leslie Blake

A member o. .....u Business Information

First volume published 1993
This volume published 1999
ISBN 0 7282 03170

British Library Cataloguing-in-Publication Data
A catalogue record for this book is available from the British Library

Typesetting by Amy Boyle, Rochester, Kent
Printed and bound by Bell and Bain Ltd, Glasgow

Contents

CONSTRUCTION

ESTATE MANAGEMENT

ECONOMICS

PROFESSIONAL SKILLS

PLANNING/ENVIRONMENT

SURVEYING

VALUATION

Professor Nicholas Bourne Barrister; Assistant Principal, Swansea Institute of Higher Education

Ian Brookes Regional New Build Manager, Halifax plc

James Brown Barrister; Senior Lecturer in Law, South Bank University

Stuart Carvell Commercial Property Manager, Sheffield Hallam University

Steve Crocker Senior Lecturer in Planning, School of Urban and Regional Studies, Sheffield Hallam University

Robert Cumming Senior Lecturer in Planning, School of Urban and Regional Studies, Sheffield Hallam University

Karl Dalgleish Research Manager, Planning and Economic Group Ecotech Research and Consultancy Ltd

Monica Dawson Senior Lecturer in Law, School of Urban and Regional Studies, Sheffield Hallam University

Dave Egan Senior Lecturer in Economics, School of Leisure and Food Management, Sheffield Hallam University

Chris Gaskell BSc (Hons.) Urban Land Economics (First Class, 1998, School of Urban and Regional Studies, Sheffield Hallam University, Estates Surveyor, T & S Stores plc.

Rob Hetherington Economic Consultant, DTZ Peida Consultancy

Lynda Hinxman Principal Lecturer in Facilities Management, Co-Director, Facilities Management Graduate Centre, School of Urban and Regional Studies, Sheffield Hallam University

Austen Imber General Practice Surveyor, Rail Property Ltd., Visiting Lecturer, School of Urban and Regional Studies, Sheffield Hallam University

Ernie Jowsey Senior Lecturer in Economics, School of Urban and Regional Studies, Sheffield Hallam University

Dr Jon Kellett Senior Lecturer in Planning, School of Urban and Regional Studies, Sheffield Hallam University

Silviu Klein Barrister; Chief Executive, Specialist Engineering Contractors Group

Anthony Lau Chapel Hill, North Carolina, USA

Rosalind Malcolm Barrister; Senior Lecturer in Law, University of Surrey

Philip Marshall APC/CPD Studies, Beckenham, Kent (former Principal Lecturer in Valuation, South Bank University), London

Janine Midgley-Hunt Senior Lecturer in Law, School of Urban and Regional Studies, Sheffield Hallam University

Alan Morris Quantity Surveyor and Law Lecturer, Director Alan Morris Training, Visiting Lecturer in Law, Kingston University, South Bank University and University of Surrey

Martin Moyes Solicitor, Lane and Partners, London

Olu Popoola, South Lambeth, London

John Storr Senior Lecturer in Valuation, School of Urban and Regional Studies, Sheffield Hallam University

V Charles Ward Solicitor, Chadwell Heath, Essex

Thanks are also due to Chris Gaskell for providing the index and tables. Finally we would both like to thank the staff at the *Estates Gazette* for their continued support and encouragement.

Phil Askham and *Leslie Blake*, January 1999

Table of Cases

Table of Legislation

Circulars and Statutory Instruments

EU Treaties, Directives etc.

CONSTRUCTION

CHAPTER 1

Tree roots and foundation damage

First published in Estates Gazette February 6, 1993

The severe droughts of 1975 and 1976 caused considerable cracking in low-rise residential buildings. The extent of the problem can be measured in terms of the number of insurance claims for subsidence and heave damage in domestic buildings. Data collected by the Building Research Establishment indicate that there were more than 20,000 claims in 1976 compared with 4,000 in 1974 and 11,000 in 1977. High numbers of claims were also recorded for 1984 and 1989: 24,000 and 32,000 respectively, following dryer than average summers. The past two years have also been characterised by exceptionally dry springs and summers and it seems reasonable to expect further increases in claims as resultant damage becomes evident.

The question of tree roots and foundation damage has been considered before in "Mainly for Students" and the reader is referred to *Estates Gazette* Vol 201 p1094, Vol 202 p162 and Vol 254 p221. However, it is a subject to which it is well worth returning if only in terms of its obvious significance to surveyors carrying out domestic surveys and the ease with which potential problems can be overlooked, as evidenced by a number of negligence cases concerning this very problem.

One recent case serves to illustrate the danger. *Beaton v Nationwide Building Society* [1991] 38 EG 218, concerned a mortgage valuation. The valuer noted that there were cracks in the property indicating past structural movement. There were two large oak trees nearby, about 80 years old, but still growing. The valuer judged that the cracks were of long standing and failed to make any mention of the presence of the trees in his report. Further structural problems did occur and judgment went against the valuer, who was deemed not to have exercised due care.

Shrinkable clay soils
Where damage is the result of the presence of trees this is usually where they exist in areas of shrinkable clay soil. Trees cause clay soils to shrink by withdrawing water through their roots in summer. The amount of shrinkage will depend upon the type of clay soil, the type of tree and the weather as well as the amount of water in the soil. This shrinkage is usually confined to the top layer of the soil to a depth of about 1m to 1.5m, where tree roots are most active and where reduction in moisture content is accelerated by surface evaporation. Below these levels, moisture content is likely to remain more constant and changes in volume are usually insufficient to have a damaging effect.

Clay soils are those which contain a large proportion of very small mineral particles. As any gardener will know, they are characteristically smooth and greasy to the touch. When wet, clays are soft and sticky; when dried out they shrink and crack and become hard. Shrinkable clay soils commonly occur in the South East, south of a line drawn between the Severn and Humber estuaries, but this should be regarded only as a broad indication. They can occur anywhere in the country, even in areas dominated by lighter soil types. Furthermore, it is not unknown for clay to be used as fill on building sites and it can also exist as a subsoil under a thin layer of lighter soil. So, even where an area is not generally recognised for its clay soils, it is no guarantee that it is not present and that localised problems cannot occur. A further general indication of the distribution of clay soils can be provided by the Geological Survey and Soil Survey maps, but even at scales of 1:25,000 these will be insufficiently specific, with large urban areas unclassified. There can be no substitute then for detailed site investigation for absolute certainty.

Trees
Certain trees are more likely to cause problems than others as they make greater demands on the soil for water; oak, poplar, ash and willow are generally regarded as the worst offenders. Many cases involving tree-root damage are concerned with these species, but the surveyor should be aware that all vegetation draws water from the soil and it is not unknown for hedges, shrubs and even climbers to have a damaging effect. In fact, any vegetation on shrinkable clay soils, in close proximity to a building, boundary wall, drain or

paving on clay soils, should be regarded with suspicion.

It is generally thought that there is a "safe distance" between tree and building beyond which damage is unlikely to occur. This is often taken as the expected maximum height of the tree, but this should be regarded only as a rule of thumb. Houseowners should be conscious that new trees should be planted no closer than the recommended distance having regard to the likely maximum height of the species on maturity. *BRE Digest* 298 provides a table for the main species of tree, giving tree heights and recommended distances. This is based on data collected at the end of the drought in August 1976, when they examined a large number of properties which suffered damage at that time.

Again, as a rough guide for new buildings, it makes sense not to erect them on shallow foundations closer than the height of a nearby tree when mature. For groups of trees this distance should be increased to 1.5 times the maximum height. However, it is often the case that new building sites are cleared of trees and vegetation before building commences, so the surveyor who encounters a new building on clay soil should be wary that soil recovery after felling can be substantial and is not likely to be uniform. It may also take many years for the soil to recover to its full volume. In such circumstances foundation problems are equally likely to occur as a result of heave owing to the swelling of the soil as water content increases. Where clay soil exists and there is vegetation, or was in the past, then a necessary precaution for new buildings would be the provision of deeper foundations or pile and beam foundations to resist any future movement. Details of such precautions are outlined in Digests 240–242. In the absence of such precautions, the surveyor would do well to advise the client of the consequent potential danger of future damage, even where there is no actual evidence at the time of inspection.

Cracks

If cracking of any description is encountered on a survey, the surveyor must ask a series of questions. Is the damage due to foundation movement or some other cause? If foundation movement is suspected, is the movement the result of changes in the volume of shrinkable clay subsoil, heave or subsidence? Having established the cause, the surveyor must go on to consider the seriousness of the damage, and whether it is likely to be progressive, and, in any case, what the appropriate remedy might be. To answer these questions, the surveyor must have a detailed appreciation of the processes of shrinkage and swelling and the environmental circumstances encountered in a particular case, as well as detailed observation and recording of the actual defects manifested.

If damage is suspected to be from existing trees, this will be confirmed if cracks open up in the summer, particularly during drought, but tend to close in the spring following winter rainfall. Excavating close to the centre of movement will confirm the nature of the subsoil, the depth of foundations and the presence of tree roots.

Cracks should be well documented on a survey, the position of each one being shown on a sketch of the damaged walls, noting the differences between tensile, compressive and shear cracks, the direction of taper, width and frequency. These can be plotted both internally and externally on sketches of the various elevations.

Where possible, the age of the cracks should be determined. The occupants will often be aware of their first appearance, but dirt accumulation within the cracks is a good indication, new cracking normally having a clean appearance. The surveyor should also look for other signs of movement, tilt and bulge of walls, slope of floors and difficulty in closing doors and windows as well as consequent damage, how the serviceability of the building is affected in terms of draughts, rainwater penetration and even the fracture of service pipes.

The characteristics and concentration of the cracks should also be noted. Tree root damage is often characterised by damage to internal walls and partitions and ceilings as well as external walls, and is often more extensive on upper floors. Cracks tend to be concentrated in areas of maximum structural distortion as well as structural weak points such as door and window openings. All this will help to build up a picture of the nature of the distortion.

It will also be necessary to identify the materials used and the details of the construction as this will affect the way in which the rest of the structure responds to foundation movement.

Finally, the surveyor should ascertain the history of the site and building damage and record the age, species and position of all nearby trees and shrubs as well as the condition and position of nearby drains which are, if anything, more likely to suffer damage than the structure itself.

Extent of damage

In general terms, damage by cracking can be classified as affecting the aesthetics, serviceability or stability of the building. Some attempt has been made to categorise damage to walls in these terms as well as in terms of crack width (see *BRE Digest* 251).

Aesthetic damage affects only the appearance of the property, is generally negligible or can be repaired by decoration. Typically, cracks would be no more than 5mm in width. The second category concerns cracks of 5mm–15mm in width which may well be sufficiently serious to have further significance for the serviceability of the property. They may result in water penetration, the fracturing of service pipes and the jamming of doors and windows. Repairs would be limited to opening and patching any cracks and dealing with consequent damage. The final category is, of course, more serious, carrying with it the risk of collapse if left unattended. More extensive structural repair work will be necessary to elements of the structure. Any such categorisation is, of course, only indicative and it would be dangerous in the extreme to base diagnosis solely on the width of the crack.

What is of most concern is the cause of the crack and whether it is likely to be progressive. Cracks in the structure of a building arise because of differential movement in that structure associated either with the structure itself or the ground beneath it. Those associated with the structure include material shrinkage, corrosion or decay, differential thermal movements, poor design or workmanship.

Movement associated with the ground can, of course, occur from a number of causes other than ground subsidence and heave owing to the change in the volume of shrinkable clay soils. These include settlement and heave of floor slabs on poorly compacted in-fill, instability of sloping ground, movement in made ground, mining subsidence, movement because of nearby excavations, chemical attack on foundation concrete, erosion of soil particles by the passage of water; leaking water mains or fractured drains for example, unequal foundation pressures resulting from added extensions or areas of load concentration such as chimneys. These are all alternative possibilities which need to be considered before diagnosis can be confirmed.

Shrinkage and heave because of clay soils is, however, a major cause of damage to foundations. Where this is the cause the surveyor is likely to encounter three distinct situations: open ground away from major vegetation, buildings near existing trees and buildings on sites newly cleared of trees.

On clay soils where there is no nearby vegetation, seasonal foundation movements may well occur in buildings with foundations of less than 1m depth. Slight cracks may occur which open and close seasonally. Remedial measures will depend on the seriousness of the damage, but may range from ignoring minor movement to the necessity for complete underpinning. For buildings on sites newly cleared of trees, potential problems can be avoided by providing suitable foundations at the design stage. Where trees exist in close proximity to the building and further tree growth is likely, pruning to reduce moisture extraction is a better remedy than complete removal as the presence of the tree will have created a dry zone in the subsoil. If the tree is no longer present to continue drawing moisture from the soil, the clay could swell causing foundation heave which could produce more serious damage than has occurred as a result of the presence of the tree.

Where the trees are mature, seasonal shrinkage and swelling can be envisaged, but larger movements are unlikely to occur except in spells of exceptionally dry weather. Where trees are not mature, however, progressive foundation damage is more likely.

The surveyor should always be conscious of the effect of other local environmental changes. It would be more than embarrassing to recommend the repair of a leaking drain only to suffer further damage as a result of further root growth of existing trees whose fortuitous additional water supply is suddenly cut off.

In shrinkable clay soils, then, it is always necessary to diagnose the cause of structural cracks correctly and to be aware of the potential hazard of nearby trees and other vegetation and report these to the client. In no circumstances should it be said that further movement will not occur unless there is absolute certainty that this is the case.

Further reading

BRE Digests

Once again, the student can do no better than to refer to the excellent information provided by the Building Research Establishment, which should be regarded as essential reading by all practitioners involved in the surveys of buildings. The main

Digests concerned with cracking resulting from clay subsoil are listed below:

75 Cracking in Buildings;
240 Low-rise buildings on shrinkable clay soils: Part 1;
241 Low-rise buildings on shrinkable clay soils: Part 2;
242 Low-rise buildings on shrinkable clay soils: Part 3;
251 Assessment of damage in low-rise buildings;
298 The influence of trees on house foundations in clay soils

Contributed by Phil Askham.

CHAPTER 2

Underpinning solutions

First published in Estates Gazette 27 November 1993

In what circumstances is underpinning necessary and how may a suitable method be selected?

Underpinning can be defined as the construction of a new foundation which enables a load, bearing on an existing footing, to be carried at a lower depth. It is important to appreciate that underpinning is a potentially dangerous operation. Apart from stopping the progressive movement of a foundation, underpinning may be needed for other reasons. Underpinning may be undertaken so that the load-bearing capacity of the foundations can be improved. Building work adjoining a foundation, such as the formation of a basement leading to loss of lateral support, may also result in the need to deepen foundations.

In 1991 a Building Research Establishment report estimated that, during a period of some 15 years, the hitherto small-scale market for remedial underpinning had developed into an £80m pa market. Remedial underpinning in the UK is mainly carried out to domestic and other low-rise buildings. Each year up to 14,000 homes were thought to be disturbed by such work. The drought of 1975–76 led to extensive shrinkage of clay soils and much subsidence damage. BRE comments that this resulted not only in a considerable increase in subsidence insurance claims but also increased the sensitivity of surveyors acting for building societies and estate agents to cracks in houses.

While subject to debate, it is probable that some remedial underpinning now undertaken is not needed purely for engineering reasons. BRE suggests a number of reasons for this occurrence: pressure for a sale to proceed; insurers and loss adjusters seeking a solution with no further risk; consultants' conservative attitudes, protecting professional indemnity insurance; a conservative and commercial policy by specialist contractors and a defensive position adopted by some local authorities in the implementation of building control.

Greater awareness of cracks in properties and tolerance of them has resulted in owners becoming anxious when damage is slight, even when it is not likely to affect structural stability. Many surveyors will have encountered this anxiety, to perhaps a more limited extent, in the past. Both owners and potential buyers of domestic property expect freedom from cracking. BRE feels that expectation of this is likely to continue to rise. The amount of the investment in the property, its age and locality affect the level of expectation.

Underpinning is generally required only if further foundation movements causing damage need to be prevented. Its necessity or not should be based upon the probability of damage progressing to an extent that affects the serviceability of the building. At this point cracking and distortion affect wall functions such as weather tightness, fracture of service pipes and jamming of doors and windows. There is not, as yet, an unacceptable danger of collapse of some part of the structure (see broad categories of damage in *BRE Digest* 251).

In most cases, owners, prospective purchasers and mortgage valuation surveyors are concerned about what may be called aesthetic damage. A house sale may be put at risk by cracks 3mm wide or perhaps less. In reality, completely uncracked buildings are rare, which helps to put this development into perspective.

Reasons for structural cracking are numerous, but it is essential that a correct interpretation of causes should be made by inspection and assessment. Clay shrinkage and heave have been found to be the commonest cause of conditions requiring remedial underpinning. A diagnosis is frequently based only on an inspection of cracking. If the damage is comparatively severe this may be acceptable. However, BRE feels that this is not advisable where damage is Category 2 or less (see *BRE Digest* 251 for categories).

Investigation

Insight into subsoil conditions is needed if the possibility of progressive foundation movement is to be considered. Apart from desk studies, experience and local knowledge, an actual ground investigation is required. Confirmation of the reason for damage would be provided by a trial pits and, possibly, boreholes.

While crack surveys and site investigations should indicate the causes of damage, they may not prove that progressive movement is taking place. Probably the most useful technique for this purpose is to monitor levels, for example along the line of the damp-proof course. Such monitoring requires a surveyor's level and specially installed points. A level survey, along a damp-proof course, to estimate the amount of settlement or heave which has already occurred, is best achieved using a water level (see *BRE Digest* 344). Even when level monitoring is adopted the results may not be conclusive.

Specialist laboratory testing techniques are available for assessing the depth and degree of soil desiccation. These can be used for determining future heave. If the heave is likely to be slight, underpinning may not be required.

Underpinning is not the only method used for remedial purposes in cases of progressive foundation movement. For example, the cause may be removed. Though an apparently simple solution, this approach may not prove so in practice. The repair of a leaking drain, for example, may not prevent further movement because cavities could have formed in the subsoil which may affect the foundations for a number of years (see also "Tree roots and foundation damage"). Structural strengthening of the building is another alternative and may include resin bonding, brick stitching and corseting with a reinforced concrete beam at ground level. The subsoil may be strengthened by grouting, used as permanent underpinning or in conjunction with more normal methods.

Underpinning is the commonest way of halting progressive foundation movement. The general sequence of operations involves, prior to underpinning, the possible strengthening of the building by repairs to walling. Shoring may also be necessary to provide support. Removing loads from the foundation could possibly be in stages by "needling" passed through the wall to obtain temporary support. After the new foundations are formed and pinned up, any temporary support is removed.

Much of the underpinning carried out in this country is only partial in extent, although there is debate about its effectiveness. Where engineering practice is adequate, partial underpinning should be a success. Potential legal and insurance problems exist if semi-detached or terraced properties are underpinned, however.

Methods

Underpinning can be classified in two broad categories: "continuous", which employs mass concrete; and "discontinuous", in which either piers or piles are used.

The mass concrete form transfers the load from the existing foundation to its new bearing (Figure 1). In common with most forms of underpinning, success is especially linked to effective pinning up of the new and old work so that settlement is avoided. A gap of 75mm to 150mm is generally left between the new and old construction, which is filled later by ramming a mortar with low moisture content into the space.

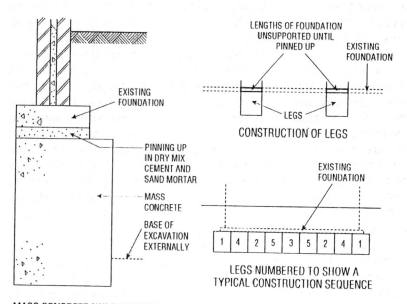

MASS CONCRETE UNDERPINNING

FIG. 1

The underpinning is carried out in narrow bays known as "legs" distributed equally along the length of the wall. The width of each leg can, with safety, generally be 1m to 1.5m. The number of legs which can be under construction simultaneously should generally be limited so that not more than 25% of the length of the structure to be underpinned is unsupported at one time. Careful underpinning may mean that disturbance to the building is minimised.

BRE estimates that mass concrete is used for more than 40% of the underpinning carried out. It is technically the easiest to construct and is well understood. The process is slow, however, and much hand excavation and concrete is required. High costs of excavation and the limited loadings generated by low-rise buildings result in mass concrete generally being used only up to depths of approximately 2m. In addition, it is appropriate only on clay where shrinkage or heave is fairly slight and an unaffected stratum exists within the 2m limit. Steps will be needed to isolate the underpinning from the effects of heave, such as a lining of thick polystyrene. A high water table could prevent the use of such underpinning, especially if the excavation is in poor ground conditions.

About 30% of underpinning employs a "pier and beam" technique: a reinforced concrete beam is cast in the wall just above or replacing the existing footing (Figure 2). The beam spans piers consisting of mass concrete poured into pits bearing at a suitable depth. Generally the beam is formed first. A series of "stools" are installed in holes cut along the proposed line of the beam. Stools made of steel and precast concrete are subsequently cast into the beam. If insufficient support for the stools can be obtained, reinforced concrete foundation pads bearing on the ground can be used.

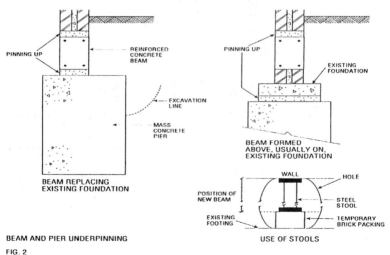

BEAM AND PIER UNDERPINNING

FIG. 2

After the stools are placed, the remaining brickwork or existing foundations are removed and the beam is formed. The top of the beam is pinned up to the brickwork above. The piers can then be excavated, concreted and pinned up.

Beam and underpinning is suitable for most ground conditions and is safer for the operatives than mass concrete methods. High labour costs, owing to hand excavation of piers, limit the depth to which it is generally used to under 4m. A high water table would lead to the consideration of an alternative method. It is particularly suitable for use in clay which is subject to shrinkage and heave. By using a polystyrene lining to the sides of the piers the building may be isolated from volume changes in the clay.

Other methods used for underpinning lowrise buildings were found by the BRE almost exclusively to involve piling. The systems may be a beam and pile method or simply entail piling. The beam and pile method is similar to beam and pier underpinning (Figure 3).

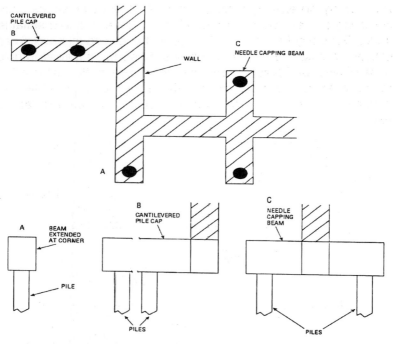

BEAM AND PILE UNDERPINNING

FIG. 3

Beam and pile is applicable where hand excavation to form piers is no longer economical, or at shallower depths where adverse ground conditions exist and hand excavation is precluded. It is suitable for almost all circumstances, but is most economical at depths over 4m to 6m. Beams are constructed in a similar way to those for beam and pier underpinning, but project at corners, junctions and other appropriate points. The extended portions act as caps to the tops of the piles. Piles used to form intermediate supports act through a needlecapping beam where access is available to both sides of the wall. Alternatively, a cantilevered pile cap is used so that internal access is not needed. Piles are usually 150mm to 400mm in diameter for low-rise buildings and are generally augured or bored and cast in situ. Smaller diameter piles may be driven. The system is safe, provided that the beams rather than the piles are constructed first.

Underpinning with piles (Figure 4) does not involve extensive beams: instead, transverse needles or cantilevered pile caps are used to transmit the loads direct to the piles. Alternatively, the piles may be installed through the existing foundations. Spans between piles are small (usually 1m or less) in low-rise buildings and small diameter or mini-piles are appropriate. Typical pile diameters are 75mm to 150mm: they are formed by driven steel castings filled with cement grout or are augured and cast in situ.

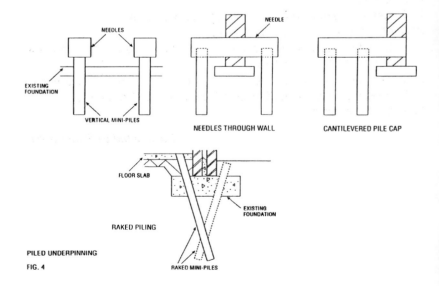

VERTICAL MINI-PILES

NEEDLES THROUGH WALL

CANTILEVERED PILE CAP

PILED UNDERPINNING

FIG. 4

RAKED MINI-PILES

Piles placed through existing foundations are formed at an angle and cast into the footing. The piles are placed alternately each side of the foundation at 1m centres, or less, dependent on the state of the footing and subsoil. Success depends on the capacity of the existing foundation to deal with the forces from the alternately sited piles.

The main application of these systems is generally where satisfactory ground exists at depths of less than 3m to 4m. Owing to the slenderness of the piles, they are not very suitable where clay shrinkage or heave exists or where the strength of the structure adjacent to the footing level is low. Labour content is small and piling is thus comparatively cheap.

Acknowledgement

The author is grateful for the help received from M S Crilly, BRE.

References

BRE Report (1991) Foundation movement and remedial underpinning in low-rise buildings Boden JB and Driscoll RMC "House foundations – a review of the effect of clay soil volume change on design and performance", *Municipal Engineer* Vol August 4 1987 pp181–213.
BRE Digests
251 Assessment of damage in low-rise buildings
313 Mini-piling for low-rise buildings
343 Simple measuring and monitoring of movement in low-rise buildings. Part 1: cracks
344 Simple measuring and monitoring of movement in low-rise buildings. Part 2: settlement, heave and out-of-plumb.
352 Underpinning.

Contributed by Paul Adams.

CHAPTER 3

Valuing the refurbishment potential

First published in Estates Gazette April 2, 1994

What factors need to be considered in valuing office buildings with potential for refurbishment?

Office specification

Advances in technology present developers with a problem: they cannot respond quickly to the changing demands of prospective tenants and the speed of technological change means that building specifications can become quickly out of date. At the present time the "state of the art" seems to be summed up by the concept of the intelligent office building, where heating, ventilation and security are controlled through a central building management system to minimise overheads and, particularly, energy costs. This enables the level of service provision to be adjusted automatically according to changes in the level of occupancy.

This requires provision of horizontal and vertical ducts, utilisation of ceiling voids capable of taking optical fibre cables and other communication systems, raised floors, with a minimum clear space of 150mm to 250mm, and total access to the underfloor area to provide maximum flexibility in the distribution of services.

Where IT use is paramount it has been said that each workstation requires 1kW to power a PC, printer and appropriate lighting. The need for flexibility demands that these must be capable of being moved. Floor voids may be used for power, data and telecommunication cables which need to be laid out separately and screened to prevent cross interference.

Heat gain from electronic equipment has become increasingly important. Air-handling equipment can be located in the ceiling voids to provide continuous air change, controlling heating and humidity as well as dust levels.

However, the present slump in commercial property values, combined with greater environmental awareness and the need for energy conservation, has brought about changes in perception of the desirability for such high levels of specification. To an extent this is market led and often locational and physical constraints will simply not stand the additional cost involved. At the same time IT requirements are constantly changing and recent technological developments are moving occupiers away from high floor loadings and substantial floor or ceiling voids. Concern over CO_2 emissions has intensified the attraction of low energy use and it is becoming increasingly desirable to maximise the use of natural ventilation and daylight to provide acceptable levels of comfort at comparatively low specification. Combine all this with an increase in the number of listed buildings and an increased emphasis on urban regeneration and conservation, and the consequence is that, in existing urban locations, refurbishment will often take precedence over redevelopment.

This article looks at the analysis of refurbishment options in respect of an actual building with particular emphasis on the role of the valuer.

Refurbishment options

With a given existing building there are, of course, a range of options from complete redevelopment to a cosmetic refurbishment. In every case, the precise extent of refurbishment or redevelopment will be determined by the building itself as well as its market.

Whatever the level of refurbishment, the broad valuation approach is the same. It is necessary to start with a detailed survey of the existing structure which must include an assessment of the whole volume of the building. This will obviously require drawing up existing floor plans, but also sections which take into account existing floor to ceiling heights. It will also be necessary to consider the nature and condition of the structure, in particular its floors and services and its overall potential for flexibility.

The detailed survey will reveal loading capacities of floors, service routes, their capacities and age. Wall and roof construction, insulation and the capacity for conversion, suitability for extension, formation of new staircases, lift shafts and window openings will all need to be considered at this stage.

The extent of the refurbishment will be determined by the relationship between demand, cost and value, so detailed market analysis must be undertaken. It is of little consequence to consider a low-cost refurbishment if the demand is for high-quality space. On the other hand, while the best conservation solution might be redevelopment behind the facade, this will fail miserably if rents in the area are inadequate to support the additional development cost. Costs might be controlled by a scheme which produces low floor to ceiling heights and a poor net to gross floor area, but the resultant building may be difficult to let.

It is assumed that the valuer will have a clear and close working knowledge of rent and yields from transactions recorded on the office data base. Inquiries will have been monitored so that market demand is clear. The valuer needs then to work with the client's building surveyor to understand the extent of refurbishment and the costs involved. At this initial stage it is likely that financial constraints will make a fully drawn and costed approach inappropriate. What is needed is an outline and approximate appraisal to determine the appropriate level of refurbishment which can then be costed in detail.

The value of the different levels of refurbishment will be determined for each option, but it is logical that any appraisal should start with a determination of the existing use value as it is quite conceivable that this will exceed any of the refurbishment alternatives.

The illustrations which follow concern a building which has a frontage of 25m and a built depth of 12.5m. The gross area of each floor is therefore 312.5m² and the net area 250m². Figure 1 shows a sample floor plan.

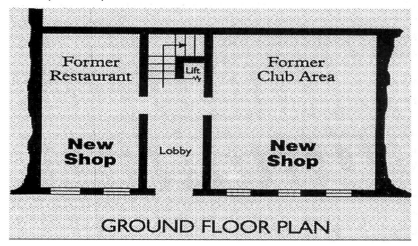

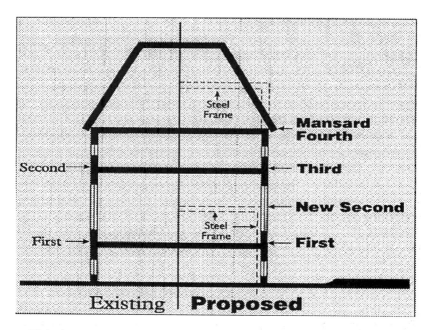

This is a typical stone and slate three-storey Victorian building with 100% site coverage. The previous use was probably a former gentlemen's club, recently converted cheaply to form offices which are now vacant. Interesting features of the building are the former ballroom at first-floor level, which has a ceiling height of 6.15m and which would therefore accommodate the introduction of an additional floor, and a lofty roof structure which could provide a further additional floor by means of a mansard roof approach. A section of the building illustrating present and proposed construction is shown in Figure 2.

The office rental levels in the locality are based on £135 per m² for prime space, £85 to £105 for secondary and existing use at £65. Prime office yields in the area are 8% to 9%.

For each level of refurbishment the residual approach is used to identify the value of the redundant building, but with each level of refurbishment it is necessary to have regard to the existing use value.

The appraisal which follows considers three alternative levels of refurbishment. The first example highlights a complete rebuild behind the existing facade, the second a refurbishment of the existing structure and, finally, a low-cost scheme.

Construction costs on a gross area basis are as follows:

New build	£540–£600 per m²
Complete rebuild behind facade	£540–£600 per m²
Refurbishment	£375–£475 per m²
Low cost works	£215–£325 per m²

Existing use valuation

Ground floor 250m² £65	£16,250
First floor 250m² @ £27.50	6,875
Second floor 250m² @ £11	2,750
ERV	25,875
YP in perp at, say, 13%	7.69
	198,979
Value, say,	£200,000

Example 2 Development appraisal

Offices 1000m² @ £135			£135,000pa
YP in perp @ 10.5%			9.52
			1,285,200
Less purchaser's costs of 4%			51,408
Value of completed development			1,233,792
Investment value, say,			1,234,000
Less costs			
Building			
1200m² @ £375	£450,00		
Professional fees, say, 12.5%	56,250		
	506,250		
Finance for 9 months			
@11% on 50% of cost			
506,250 × 50% = 253,125			
× (1.11)⁻⁷⁵–1 0.814	20,604	526,854	
Fees			
Letting 10% FRV	13,500		
Marketing, say,	12,000		
Investment sale costs 2%	24,680	50,180	
Profit			
20% of investment value		246,800	
Total development costs and profit			823,834
Surplus for land			410,166
Land price	1.00x		
Purchase fees	0.04x		
Finance			
9 months @ 11% of 1.04x			
(1.11)⁻⁷⁵–1 0.814	0.864x		

				1.1246x =	410,166
				x =	364,772
Land price, say,					£365,000

Example 3 Development appraisal
Ground floor

Showroom/Offices 250m² @ £130		£32,500pa
250m² storage @ £45		11,250
Total ERV		43,750
YP in perp @ 11%		9.10
		398,125
Less purchaser's costs of 4%		15,925
Value of completed development		382,200
Investment value, say,		280,000
Less costs		
Building		
600m² @ 215	£129,000	
Roof and stone cleaning, say,	30,000	
Professional fees, say,	12,000	
	171,000	
Finance for 2 months		
@11% on 50% cost		
171,000 × 50% = 85,500		
×(1.11)$^{.167}$−1 0.175	1,496	172,496
Fees		
Letting 10%	4,375	
Marketing, say,	3,000	
Investment sale costs 2%	7,600	14,975
Profit		
20% of investment value		76,000
Total development costs and profit		263,471
Surplus for land		116,529
Land price	1.00x	
Purchase fees	.04x	
Finance		
2 months @11% of 1.04x		
(1.11)$^{.167}$−1 .0175	.0182x	
	1.0582x =	116,529
	x =	110,120
Land price, say,		£110,000

Contributed by Stuart Carvell.

CHAPTER 4

Retaining existing facades

First published in Estates Gazette July 23, 1994

A recent "Mainly for Students" article dealt with the development value of buildings with retained facades. What are the technical considerations in such cases?

Building behind existing facades of structures and thus combining conservation with redevelopment has become common during the past 20 years. In the process designers and builders have been confronted with technical problems requiring solutions quite different to normal practice. The projects consist of the partial demolition of the structure and its rebuilding while the whole or a section of the original facade is protected, supported, restored and attached to the new work.

Much redevelopment of this kind has been to Victorian buildings in town centres. Each project needs careful scrutiny to identify its own unique limitations and possibilities. Usually the structures can be categorised as medium or large size, ranging from two to seven storeys in height. The retained facades tend to be of substantial load-bearing masonry. Late in the 19th century steel frames were used internally somewhat before their adoption externally. Framed exterior walls were not permissible in London, for example, until the 1908 London Building Act. The stock of buildings with exteriors worth preserving, but which are unsatisfactory internally, is considerable and it is to be expected that redevelopment of this kind will continue to be widespread.

As was pointed out in an earlier article, "Valuing the refurbishment potential", *Estates Gazette*, April 2, 1994, there are a range of refurbishment or redevelopment options for a given existing building, the extent of which will depend on the building as well as the market. Here, the alternatives which involve the construction of an entirely new building behind a retained facade will be considered. Apart from the legal restraints owing to listing, the extent of facade retention depends significantly on location. If the building is isolated the entire exterior facade of the building may merit retention while the interior and roof are demolished. An approach of this kind would be appropriate where the developer needs completely new accommodation not restrained in any way by the existing interior. In a case where the building is at the end of a block or on a corner only two or three elevations may be retained, the rest of the building being demolished prior to reconstruction. One elevation only may be retained where, for example, it fronts an important or interesting thoroughfare.

The statutory protection of buildings of architectural or historic importance is one of the main legislative constraints affecting the choice of alternatives. Listing such buildings gives protection against demolition or alterations which are not in keeping with the original construction, and as a consequence of the number of buildings listed there is often a conflict of views between conservationists and developers. While listing may include interior features, it is more commonly based on exteriors, hence the construction of a new building at the rear of a retained facade often represents a compromise.

Costs

A project involving facade retention may be little different in cost to one in which the existing building is entirely demolished and rebuilt. The cost of retaining the facade may well be similar to that of building a new facade. However, there could be a "time penalty" because the retained facade may cause obstruction to processes used by the builder to transfer components from the exterior. For example, new elements such as precast floor slabs may be difficult to position in the interior.

Some broad economic advantages may result from facade retention, however. Organisations such as financial institutions could pay higher sums to purchase or lease a building with architectural merits, but with the efficient office interior which often results from facade retention schemes.

Many buildings where facades are retained have storey heights greater than is customary in modern practice and additional floors can be created. Basement accommodation can be added by excavation below the existing structure and, at roof level, mansard construction may allow one or two extra floors. The creation of additional floorspace gives a corresponding increase in a property's value. In general, forms of redevelopment where a large part of the interior is refurbished tend to be the most economically attractive in the short term. The construction of a new interior behind a retained facade, although more costly initially than refurbishment, is often the most viable.

Criteria

The criteria for the design of a facade retention project include the following. The new structure behind the facade should, as far as possible, be concealed. The characteristics of a retained facade can be considerably influenced by what can be seen of the inside through its windows. It is desirable for the scale of the rooms behind the facade to reflect its design and the original purpose of the building.

If alterations have caused the loss of significant original features of the facade the project should include an accurate restoration of these features if it is feasible. A common example of such inappropriate alteration is the introduction of shop fronts at ground level. The building's new function may require a contemporary frontage which makes restoration or the retention of the existing frontage undesirable. If a modern ground-floor frontage is necessary its design should match the existing facade, particularly with regard to the windows.

New materials used in the construction of modern frontages or in replacement or restoration work to the retained facade should, if possible, be of the same material as the original. Failing this, careful matching should be attempted. Sometimes artificial materials can satisfactorily solve the problem which otherwise may be too costly both in material and craftsmanship.

Care is needed where projects include an extension beyond the retained facade to ensure that it is not dominant at the expense of the original. Side extensions may either match or contrast with the adjoining facade. Extensions at the rear pose fewer problems as there will not generally be a risk of intrusion.

Facade retention may involve keeping or reconstructing features which are typical of the building's original architecture or function. Chimneys, for example, may be retained, to indicate that a building's first use was domestic. Windows and doorways may be sealed off where not required, but "dummies" left on the exterior.

Features such as towers and spires which contribute not only to the building's appearance but also to the townscape should be retained or reconstructed where possible. The roof can be regarded as an extension of the facade and its retention may therefore be as important as the main facade. As many facade-retention projects include the formation of additional floors in the upper part of the building it may not be possible to retain the original roof or construct a replica. New roofs which will generally extend above the retained facade should be designed so that they do not reduce the effect of the elevation. Mansards can be used either set back or raked. Roofs of this kind are effective in masking the roof from close quarters, but are less satisfactory if significant viewpoints exist at a distance; careful design is needed in the latter case.

Technical considerations

The main technical problems typical of facade-retention schemes include: temporary support of the facade; tying back of the facade to the new works; avoidance of adverse effects to the facade resulting from foundation construction and avoidance of structural damage owing to differential movement between new and existing construction. Costs (see reference 2) can vary considerably depending on the scale of renovation and amount of strengthening needed. As an example, a cost range published in April 1993 quoted typical amounts as £440 to £1500m² of facade. The amounts given are within the range which could be expected for a new facade. The breakdown of items of costs given were: demolition and facade support 30% to 35%; underpinning 10%; tying back to new structure 5%, repairs and cleaning 25% to 30%; and windows 25%.

The temporary support system (Figure 1) must resist horizontal wind loads from any direction until the facade is permanently tied to the new structure. The supports tend to cause obstruction. Their positioning determines the type of obstruction created. Supports constructed solely on the interior tend to obstruct demolition and rebuilding. However, pedestrian walkways and traffic are not obstructed. Supports placed only on the exterior of the facade restrict pedestrians and traffic and for this reason may not be permitted. However, demolition and construction operations are not impeded if they are used. A system which is located partly externally and partly internally may, to some extent, impede both

Fig. 1   Temporary support systems: typical examples

(a) Flying shores and internal towers – supports located on interior

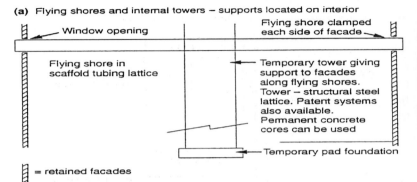

Window opening

Flying shore clamped each side of facade

Flying shore in scaffold tubing lattice

Temporary tower giving support to facades along flying shores. Tower – structural steel lattice. Patent systems also available. Permanent concrete cores can be used

Temporary pad foundation

⌷ = retained facades

(b) Vertical cantilever supported by portal frame – supports located on exteri

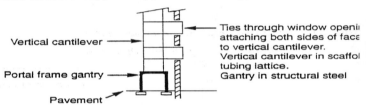

Vertical cantilever

Ties through window openii attaching both sides of facε to vertical cantilever. Vertical cantilever in scaffol tubing lattice. Gantry in structural steel

Portal frame gantry

Pavement

foot and vehicular movement as well as demolition and construction work.

A number of options exist when the actual form of the temporary support system is being considered (Figure 1). Among these are raking or flying shores; temporary internal towers or permanent concrete cores from which bracing can be undertaken either by flying shores or patent systems; and vertical cantilevers supported by portal frames at ground level. "Island sites", where all four facades are to be retained, can be supported by continuous horizontal girders bolted to the facade at each floor level around the perimeter.

All facade-retention schemes have in common the need to tie permanently the facade to the new structure at the rear. The ties must transfer lateral loadings, replacing the support which was provided by the original internal structure. Vertical loads from the new structure should not be transmitted to the facade by the ties. Any differential settlement between the new and existing structure must be able to occur without damaging the ties, the facade or the

Fig. 2   Connection of facade to new structure and dealing with differential movement

(a) Connections without provision for differential movement

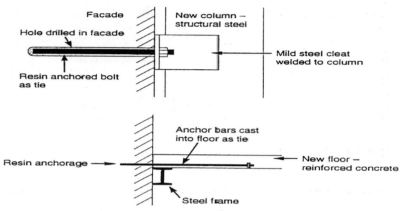

(b) Connection with differential movement provided for

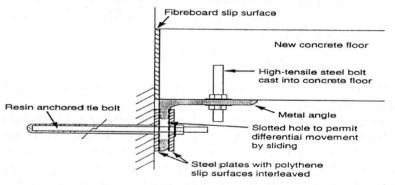

new structure, The ties must be long lasting and protected against fire and act to unite rather than separate parts of the facade.

Various types of tie have been tested for different facade constructions. Site "pull out" tests on the proposed fixings have proved very important. The use of resin anchored steel tie bars for these attachments is widespread and a rapid-setting resin mortar is used. Figure 2 illustrates three examples of attaching the tie bars to the new structure.

Resin anchorages in facades may be formed in a hole drilled in the facade, either with the aid of a resin capsule or by pumping in a pre-mixed resinous mortar. A typical capsule may be of glass or

Fig. 3   Foundation construction to minimise disturbance
adjacent to retained facade

(a)

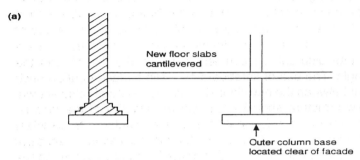

New floor slabs
cantilevered

Outer column base
located clear of facade

(b) Balanced base foundation

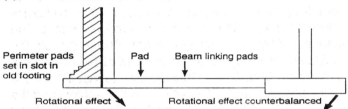

Perimeter pads
set in slot in
old footing

Pad

Beam linking pads

Rotational effect

Rotational effect counterbalanced

plastic containing the ingredients for the mortar. The action of
driving the tie bar into the hole breaks the capsule and mixes the
mortar. A pumped mortar into which the tie bar is set is appropriate
where the facade is porous with many cavities. As an alternative,
ties may take the form of a bolt which passes through the facade
and is secured with a plate on the front elevation. On the interior the
bolt is fixed to the structure in the same way as the resin anchored
ties. It is not, however, easy to conceal the ends of this form of tie
where exposed on a brick or stone elevation.

Allowance in the ties between the facade and the new structure
for any anticipated differential movement is best achieved by
avoiding a rigid joint. Rigidity here could cause damage and the
differential movement should be permitted to occur. Figure 2 shows
a method in which the steel angle linking the bolted fixings between
the facade and new floor slabs is provided with a slotted hole. The
slot allows differential movement to take place. Settlement of the
new foundations or heave of the facade foundations owing to the
removal of existing loads are two examples of such movement.

The bonding of the surfaces of the retained facade and the new
structure must be prevented if differential movement occurs.

Bonding is typically prevented by creating slip surfaces between the new and existing faces. Polythene, either in one or a number of layers, or a thin compressible layer of fibreboard, is suitable for this purpose. An alternative method is simply to leave a narrow gap at this point. Slip surfaces in polythene are shown in Figure 2 where they facilitate differential movement between the tie bar and the slotted angle. The use of fibreboard as a slip surface to allow such movement between the new floor slab and the facade is also shown. The new structure should not affect the stability of the facade. Problems may occur at foundation level in particular . The simplest method of avoiding disturbance near the facade may be to set back the new column bases and cantilever the floors to abut the facade (Figure 3). If new columns must be placed closely adjacent to the retained facade they will be placed on their base so that the load is discharged eccentrically, which results in a rotational effect. The effect is counteracted by constructing a beam which connects the base to an adjacent one (Figure 3), creating what is known as a balanced base foundation. If the structure and foundation of the retained facade can be proved, by survey, to be satisfactory and the loads balanced to those of the existing building, it is possible that it can be reused as a load-bearing element. The result is that perimeter columns are minimised and no provision is necessary for differential movement at the junction of the facade and the new work. The cost advantage could be worthwhile if this were possible.

References

1. Students are recommended to this very comprehensive view of the topic for further reading:
Highfield D, *The Construction of New Buildings behind Historic Facades*, 1st Ed E & F N Spon, London, 1991.
2. Kaminski M P, "Facade Retention – City Buildings Enhanced", Focus, Building Refurbishment and Property Appraisals, Campbell, Reith and Hill, April 1993.
3. Goodchild S L and Kaminski M P, "Retention of Major Facades" *The Structural Engineer*, Vol 67 No 8, April 18, 1989, pp131–138.
References 2 and 3 give views from the standpoint of consulting engineers, with much that is likely to be of great use to readers.

Contributed by Paul Adams.

CHAPTER 5

Contractor's loss and expense

First published in Estates Gazette September 16, 1995

In what circumstances may a contractor claim for loss and/or expense in a construction contract?

Damages are the normal remedy for a breach of contract at common law. In order to obtain damages, however, it is necessary to have recourse to litigation or to arbitration proceedings. Only a judge in the course of litigation, or an arbitrator acting in the course of arbitration proceedings, can award damages.

However, building contracts, and other contracts, find a way around this. They provide for the certification by the contract administrator of payments for "loss and/or expense" as an alternative to the protracted process of seeking damages in litigation or arbitration.

One therefore never goes far in construction work without meeting the phrase "loss and/or expense". The term is found in the express conditions of the building contract – most construction work of any consequence will involve a set of express conditions and it is there that reference will be made to "loss and/or expense".

Loss and/or expense, in the contractual conditions, is (mainly) concerned with situations where the building contractor is impeded by the employer in carrying out the construction work: if that happens, the contractor may be entitled to recover money from the employer as part of an ordinary payment under the contract for the loss and/or expense he suffers as a result. He will be able to do this to the extent provided for in the conditions, which recognise a number of causes; for example, where the contractor is impeded because of not receiving, in due time, instructions or drawings from the contract administrator: refer to clause 26.2 of the JCT Standard Form of Building Contract (JCT 80).

In such a case (and provided that required formalities have been carried out – see below) the contractor's loss and/or expense shall be ascertained and paid. As clause 26.1 of JCT 80 puts it: ". . . if and as soon as the Architect [contract administrator] is of the opinion that the direct loss and/or expense has been incurred or is likely to be incurred then the Architect from time to time thereafter shall ascertain, or shall instruct the Quantity Surveyor to ascertain, the amount of such loss and/or expense which has been or is being incurred by the Contractor; . . ." and payment shall be made.

This is a very significant provision of great assistance to the contractor, avoiding all the disadvantages that attend an action in the courts or at arbitration.

Formalities

There are normally certain formalities imposed upon the contractor in the contractual conditions. These are pre-conditions which he must observe in order to enjoy the benefit of the provision. The formalities amount, in essence, to: good practice; keeping the employer informed (in good time); and co-operating in the necessary ascertainment of the amount of loss and expense. Clause 26.1 of JCT 80 provides:

If the Contractor makes written application to the Architect stating that he has incurred or is likely to incur direct loss and/or expense in the execution of this Contract . . . because the regular progress of the Works or of any part thereof has been or is likely to be materially affected by one or more of the matters referred to in clause 26.2 (see above) . . . [then the contractor shall be entitled provided that] the Contractor's application shall be made as soon as it has become, or should reasonably have become, apparent to him that the regular progress of the Works or of any part thereof has been or is likely to be affected as aforesaid; and the Contractor shall in support of his application submit to the Architect upon request such information as should reasonably enable the Architect to form an opinion as aforesaid; and

the Contractor shall submit to the Architect or to the Quantity Surveyor upon request such details of such loss and/or expense as are reasonably necessary for such ascertainment as aforesaid . . .

The contractor must work within these formalities in order for him to have the right to have his loss and expense ascertained and paid under certificate of the contract administrator. If he does not do so then his right to payment under the conditions in respect of the delay (though not his right to damages at common law) will be forfeited.

Quantum

What is the quantum (amount) of loss which the contractor is entitled to recoup under a "loss and/or expense" provision?

The amount that can be recouped will be the same as in general damages at common law: see *Minter (FG) & Welsh Health Technical Services Organisation* (1980) 13 Build LR 1.

The starting point for any discussion of general damages in the law of contract is the important case of *Hadley* v *Baxendale* (1854) 9 Exch 341. Here, a distinction was made between general damages and special damages. General damages would be those damages which arose naturally from the breach of contract, while special damages would be those which covered everything in the reasonable contemplation of the parties when they entered into the contract:

Where two parties have made a contract which one of them has broken the damages which the other party ought to receive in respect of such breach of contract should be such as may fairly and reasonably be considered either (1) arising naturally, ie according to the usual course of things from such breach of contract itself, or (2) such as may reasonably be supposed to have been in the contemplation of both parties at the time they made the contract, as the probable result of the breach of it.

The distinction between general and special damages was explained further in a later case, *Victoria Laundry (Windsor) Ltd* v *Newman Industries* [1949] 1 All ER 997. At pp1002–3 the judge said:

Everyone, as a reasonable person, is taken to know the "ordinary course of things" . . . This is the subject-matter of the "first rule" in Hadley v Baxendale, but to this knowledge, which a contract-breaker is assumed to possess whether he actually possesses it or not, there may have to be added in a particular case knowledge which he actually possesses of special circumstances outside the "ordinary course of things" of such a kind that a breach in those special circumstances would be liable to cause more loss. Such a case attracts the operation of the "second rule" so as to make additional loss also recoverable.

Since direct loss and expense under the contract conditions is as comprised in the "first rule" here, it would appear to be the case that knowledge of special circumstances cannot be considered in the contract administration's ascertainment of loss and expense.

Keeping to the contract

The contract conditions provide, as we have seen, that the ascertainment of loss and expense is to be carried out by the contract administrator or quantity surveyor. It may be a matter of surprise, therefore, that we sometimes find the contractor doing the ascertaining, submitting his figures to the contract administrator for the contract administrator to approve. Here one finds, even today (where clients are very watchful of their consultants), that a contract provision is not being observed in the manner agreed.

There are a number of reasons which can be put forward to justify why this should be so.

It is argued that the contractor has all the information and is better placed than the contract administrator or quantity surveyor to work up the information into a claim.

It is also argued that, for the contractor to provide his information, which must then be produced (by the quantity surveyor) as a claim, then in turn to be contested by the contractor, is counter-productive. There may also be a feeling in some quarters that the contractor should not be encouraged to make loss and expense claims.

Yet all this is by way of taking liberties with what the parties have agreed: a perilous course, surely.

Disruption

It is clearly the case that not every delay to the contractor will cause the completion of the building to be postponed. The delay may not lie on the critical path for the job in question. Even so, there will often be loss and expense suffered by the contractor which has resulted from reduced productivity.

In such a case, provided the cause of the loss and/or expense is one of those specified, a payment for the recoupment of the loss and expense will be due to the contractor, in the same way as where the completion of the building is delayed.

Proven cost

For the ascertainment of loss and expense, proof of actual costs to the contractor will be needed. This can present problems: the contractor will have to prove what his loss and additional costs have been; while the employer now has to concern himself with the contractor's costs. The contractor's actual costs are not, in the normal way of any interest to the employer. The contractor will have tendered a price for his work. What lies behind that price is not of immediate concern to the employer.

Once, however, the contractor's loss and expense has to be paid the contractor's actual costs will now be important to the employer. It will be necessary for the employer to keep a check on the contractor's costs, now that he is having to pay them as they are incurred.

Two or more causes for delay

Contractual conditions stipulate for events as if they always happen tidily. But delays may arise in a less than tidy manner. There may be two or more causes of a delay running together. One may justify a loss and expense claim while the others may not. A question will arise as to whether the contractor is entitled to recoup his loss and expense.

The contractor's position will be decided by reference to the dominant cause. In order to be entitled to reimbursement he must show that the cause which allegedly qualifies for loss and expense is, as a question of fact, the dominant cause. This must be decided by applying common-sense standards; and just because a cause comes first in time will not necessarily mean that it is the dominant cause.

Employer's loss and expense

It may be a matter of surprise to readers that only the contractor's loss and expense is considered in this article: the employer's own loss on account of delay is not addressed. The reason for this is that the contractor and the employer normally recoup their losses and expenses in entirely different ways under the contract.

Contributed by Alan Morris.

CHAPTER 6

Railroad to ruin

First published in Estates Gazette October 18, 1997

Construction law laid down tracks almost 125 years ago with the rulings on the famous case, Sharpe v San Paulo Railway Co.

Some cases never age, and it is likely that, even 125 years from now, standard works on construction law will be citing *Sharpe* v *San Paulo Railway Co* (1873) as sufficient authority for half a dozen propositions. A glance at the table of cases in *Halsbury's Laws of England* and the various practitioners' books on construction law will show how useful the case still is to textbook writers and law lecturers, even though four generations of lawyers have passed on since the decision was first reported.

Railway boom

Nineteenth-century British engineers built railways not only in the UK but in every other inhabited continent. Until he was deposed by landowners and military commanders in 1889, Pedro II – a liberal and enlightened emperor – ruled Brazil for 55 years. During that time he abolished slavery and lessened the military's importance. He was also a patron of the arts and sciences and shared the enthusiasm of his age for building railways.

Among the railways which the emperor authorised was one from the important manufacturing town of Jundiahy (or Jundiai), 2,320ft above sea level, to the great port of Santos on the swampy plains of the Santos River. Between these two towns stood the city of Sao Paulo, known as the "heart of coffee land", rising from low alluvial plains to the tableland, 2,500ft above sea level. A "singularly healthful" city as an old edition of the *Encyclopaedia Britannica* happily proclaims.

The approximate distance from Jundiahy to Sao Paulo is 86 miles and from Sao Paulo to Santos, 49 miles.

Pedro II's government guaranteed a return on capital to shareholders of the company which was formed to build the railway. This guarantee was valid up to a capital of £2m. If the company required more capital, its promoters would have to raise it at their own risk and on the strength of their own guarantees. Naturally, therefore, the company's promoters did not want the cost of the railway to exceed £2m.

An English engineer and a Brazilian banker were among the company's promoters, which was eventually formed in England and named "the San Paulo Railway Company" (not, strange to say, "the Sao Paulo Railway Company" although the language of Brazil is Portuguese, not Spanish).

The English engineer was James Brunlees. Born in Kelso in the Borders in 1816, he had intended to follow his father as steward and gardener to a landed estate.

He was, however, captivated by the challenge of surveying and engineering and became swept up in the railway building boom of the 1840s and 1850s. He went on to build the railway tunnel under the River Mersey, the Avonmouth Dock at Bristol and Southend Pier. He became a natural choice to be one of the two engineers to the original Channel Tunnel Company.

In 1860, however, he was one of the promoters of a company which proposed to build a railway over the tableland, across the cataracts, down to the alluvial plains and across the littorals of south-eastern Brazil. Much more to the point, he was also to be the engineer.

Contract

Brunlees prepared a detailed statement of the nature and quantities of the various works to be executed. He submitted the statement to Sharpe & Sons, the proposed contractor, with the assurance that the details had been prepared with great care and might be relied upon as entirely accurate.

Sharpe & Sons made a tender to the promoters totalling £1.85m. Then and only then was the company formed. So Sharpe & Sons relied on Brunlees in making the tender and Brunlees and the other promoters relied on Sharpe & Sons in forming the company. The contract was signed between Sharpe & Sons and the San Paulo Railway Company on February 8 1860. But the contract price was less than £1.85m.

The contract contained some 95 clauses and 2 schedules: see below.

PRINCIPAL TERMS OF THE CONTRACT TO BUILD THE RAILWAY
* Principal stations to be built at Jundiahy, Sao Paulo, and Santos.
* Line-side stations to be built at seven other places.
* Walls and landing stages to be built at Santos Harbour.
* The railway to be constructed "on the model of good European lines".
* The engineer's certificates to be "binding and conclusive on the company and the contractor".
* The engineer's final certificate to be "final and conclusive on both parties without any appeal".
* Payment to be by such monthly instalments as the engineer should from time to time certify to be payable.
* The company was not "under any circumstances or on any account" to be liable to pay the contractor more than £1,745,000.
* The contractor was to execute all such other works as in the opinion of the engineer were necessarily or reasonably implied.

Contractor's problems

Starting the construction from Santos, the first portion of the railway was intended to be carried over the Casqueira river by means of an existing bridge. But the bridge was found to be insufficient and Brunlees required the contractor to build a new one of great magnitude and difficult construction. The contractor's claim for extra money was settled by granting it a considerable extension of time. (A supplementary contract was drawn up for this purpose.)

Shortly afterwards, the Cubatas River flooded and washed away a bridge which the contractor had built to the engineer's plans. Brunlees then required the contractor to rebuild the bridge greater than before and in a much more expensive manner. The contractor claimed £98,000 for this work, separate from the contract sum, eventually settling for £30,000.

Toward the completion of the work it became obvious that the proposed mode of conveying traffic up a mountain, called Serra, was wholly inadequate. Brunlees therefore prepared new plans which required 4 million cubic yards of earth to excavated – double the original calculation.

All that Brunlees was prepared to offer the contractor in return for this unforeseen work was savings in sidings, stations and other items – savings which were insufficient to compensate the contractor.

Completion

The contractor finished the work on October 1 1866. By then it was (to quote the law report) "in want of money", and in debt to one of Brunlees' associates, the banker (Baron de Maua) – another promoter of the company.

The contractor therefore assigned its interest in the contract to trustees, on trust for itself and its creditors (principally, for the benefit of Baron de Maua). The contractor then sued (among others) the railway company and Brunlees.

The contractor claimed that the final certificate did not comprise all the sums due and that it included deductions which ought not to have been made. It also alleged that it had been asked to do extra work and that it was entitled to extra payment for that work, independently of the original contract. Finally, it argued that it would amount to an act of fraud to withhold certificates for the work which it identified as extra work.

Rolls Court

The contractor's claim was tried in the Court of Chancery before the Master of the Rolls Lord Romilly (son of the famous prison reformer, Samuel Romilly). This particular court was therefore called the Rolls Court. Lord Romilly MR's judgment was reported in *The Law Times* (1873) vol XXVII p699.

He gave judgment for the defendants, observing as he did so, that

if contractors and railway companies can be bound by a document in writing between them, this is that case, and if they cannot they had better not enter into any contract at all, but have the work done by measure and value.

Lord Romilly MR also held that Brunlees, as engineer, had no power to alter the terms of the contract. His certificates were final, unless and until fraud could be proved, and there was nothing like fraud particularised in the contractor's claim against Brunlees.

Appeal

The contractor appealed to the Court of Appeal in Chancery: see (1873) 8 LR Ch 597. The appeal was heard by two Lord Justices, Sir William Milbourne James and Sir George Mellish.

James LJ neatly turned the tables on the contractor so far as its allegation of fraud was concerned. He noted that the company was formed on the basis of a guarantee from the Brazilian government and that it would be a "singular hardship upon the shareholders, almost a fraud upon them" if they found, after taking shares in the company, that they were to see the cost of the works go up "in consequence of some conversations between the contractor and the engineer".

There was no allegation that Brunlees had wilfully made miscalculations for the purpose of deceiving the contractor. If it did not want to rely on Brunlees' experience and skill as an engineer, it ought to have looked at the consequences and made calculations. What the contractor had done was to contract, for a lump sum, to build a line "from terminus to terminus complete".

James LJ upheld the finality of the engineer's certificates:

> The very object of leaving these things to be settled by an engineer is that you are to have the practical knowledge of the engineer applied to it, and that he, as an independent man, a surveyor, a valuer, an engineer, is to say what is the proper sum to be paid under all the circumstances.

Mellish LJ agreed. He observed that it was impossible to read the contract without seeing that the parties had, "with the greatest possible care" made the certificate of the engineer a condition precedent to the right of the contractor to recover any sum whatever under the contract.

Postscript

Sharpe & Sons no doubt sank into insolvency. Perhaps the Baron de Maua continued to prosper. Pedro II, deposed in 1889, died in Paris in 1891. Brunlees was granted the Order of the Rose of Brazil. In 1882–1883 he was the president of the Institution of Civil Engineers. In 1886 he was knighted after his work on the Mersey railway tunnel. He died in Wimbledon in 1892, aged 76.

But what of the case to which he was so unwillingly made a party? It is a story which will run and run. With each waxing and waning, and waxing again, of the tort of negligence, this case will need to be read afresh.

Are contractors really to have no remedy if they act upon negligent misstatements by architects, engineers, surveyors or valuers? And yet, if we cannot nowadays be so dismissive of alleged negligence and collateral contracts as those Victorian judges showed themselves to be, is there not a reluctant admiration for their love of finality, and in their ability to propound a decision which (for 100 years or more) prevented litigation rather than encouraged it?

Certainty, after all, is a sort of justice in itself. If negligence is to be given its head, and if contractual conditions are not going to be allowed to excuse it or to protect the person who allegedly committed it, what would then become of the finality of a final certificate or the decision of a valuer "acting as expert and not as arbitrator"?

"Let justice be done though the Heavens fall" is a fine maxim. But there are only so many hours in a day and only about 2,000 weekends in a working lifetime (even for young professionals). Any judgment which emphasises the sanctity of contract, the apportionment of risk and the finality of decisions made in good faith will find a ready following in any generation.

Contributed by Leslie Blake.

CHAPTER 7

The Housing Grants, Construction and Regeneration Act 1996 – a contractual revolution

First published in Estates Gazette November 15, 1997

The new Housing Act strengthens the rights of subcontractors – and best of all, challenges the unfairness of the old "pay when paid" system.

Part II of the Housing Grants, Construction and Regeneration Act 1996 came into force in April 1998. It deals with building contracts, and could go some way towards improving relationships in the construction industry.

The government has seen for itself the deterioration of relationships in the industry because it is a major procurer of construction services. The deterioration was particularly acute between main contractors and their subcontractors, and between subcontractors and their own "sub-subcontractors". The government has also been bombarded with complaints from small firms about the tactics of larger companies. Chief among these complaints were:

- lengthy payment periods;
- late payments;
- "pay when paid" clauses;
- unlimited set-off;
- unjustified discounts;
- late receipt (or non-receipt) of retention money;
- the high cost of arbitration and litigation.

"Pay when paid" clauses

The *bête noire* of subcontractors was the notorious "pay when paid" regime. These clauses deprived the subcontractor of his ability to establish a debt if his own employer had not yet been paid. Such arrangements also left the subcontractor with little or no protection against insolvency; not just the insolvency of his own employer, but also the insolvency of his employer's employer. Moreover, it is not uncommon for receivers to be called in when main contractors have, in fact, been paid and have received large sums for transmission to subcontractors.

All these problems, and others, were highlighted by Sir Michael Latham in the *Latham Report: Constructing the Team* (see Mainly for Students, March 4 1995).

Omissions from legislation

There has been disappointment among subcontractors that the 1996 Act does not introduce measures to protect them against the insolvency of the main contractor or the insolvency of the ultimate employer. The *Latham Report* recommended "mandatory trust funds for payment" in all construction work governed by "formal conditions of contract". Under these proposals, clients would have had to deposit money in a trust fund at the beginning of each stage. If the client afterwards became insolvent, this money would have been paid to the main contractor. If the main contractor was already insolvent, appropriate sums of money would have been paid (out of this trust fund) to the subcontractors. The same arrangements would also have covered retention money.

But if a contractor became insolvent after receiving money from this fund, but before he had had the opportunity or the inclination to pay his subcontractors, the Latham recommendations would not have changed this unsatisfactory situation. The subcontractors would have been unsecured creditors, joining others who would ultimately be paid a trifling percentage of their debt, if anything.

The previous government was reluctant to introduce the trust fund principle because of upsetting the well-established rule relating to the distribution of an insolvent person's (or company's) assets, although, in fact, some exceptions to these principles have already been enacted by Parliament in other areas of the law.

The 1996 Act also omits provisions for the payment of interest on late payments. But, the Late Payment of Commercial Debts (Interest) Act 1998 has introduced a statutory right to simple interest payable from the date that the debt was created.

The *Latham Report* also recommended that legislation should declare invalid any contractual provision which allowed the payer to set off any money owed to him under other contracts. This recommendation has not been followed. The government itself (being composed of many Departments, several of which might have had dealings with the same contractor) would have been one of the losers if such provisions had been enacted.

Scope of the legislation

Part II of the Act applies to written contracts which relate to "construction operations". This term is widely defined by section 105. Nevertheless, there are some exclusions from the scope of the legislation, including the manufacture of components and materials off-site if there is no element of fixing.

The legislation applies only to agreements to the extent that they are for "construction operations", in other words, the whole of a contract might not be subject to the Act. This might cause confusion, for example, where a steelwork fabricator enters into an agreement to manufacture steelwork off-site and also to do some design work in relation to the fixing of the steelwork (which is to be carried out by another contractor). In the event of a dispute, it will be difficult to separate those issues which relate to the design work (covered by the Act) and those issues which relate to the off-site fabrication (this being outside the Act).

Payment provisions

There are seven elements to the Act's provisions relating to payment:

- there will be a statutory right to be paid by instalments;
- contracts will have to have an "adequate mechanism" for determining what payments are due and when;
- contracts will have to specify a period for the discharge of due payments;
- contracts will have to provide for the giving of notice specifying the amount of an instalment payment and the basis of the calculation;
- there will be statutory restrictions on the right to withhold money;
- there will be a statutory right to suspend performance of the contract for nonpayment;
- there will be statutory restrictions on "pay when paid" clauses.

Instalments

The requirement (in s109) that contracts must provide for periodic payments is not particularly significant. Most forms of subcontract already include an entitlement to monthly payments. Indeed, at common law there is some authority to the effect that monthly payments can be implied in construction contracts: see *DR Bradley (Cable Jointing)* v *Jefco Mechanical Services* (1989) 6 CLD 7–21.

Even in cases where, previously, a right to payment by instalments would not have been included, the effect of s109 may be minimal. For example, a contract lasting 12 months could provide for the bulk of the price to be paid on completion and for nominal amounts (eg £5) to be paid at four-month intervals.

Nevertheless, the right to payment by instalments extends to "any work under the contract", so it seems that off-site work (including any design) will be covered in addition to on-site work.

The right to instalments will arise unless the contract states that the work will last for not less than 45 days, even if the number of days (eg less than 45 days) is wholly unrealistic. Furthermore, there is no requirement that the figure actually stated must reflect continuous working. For example, a contract (stated to last 30 days) may, in fact, be spread over six months. If the contract does not state the duration of the work the parties will be free to agree that it is likely to last less than 45 days.

"Adequate mechanism" as to payments

Section 110 of the Act requires construction contracts to have an "adequate mechanism" for identifying what payments will become due and when they will become due. This requirement is likely to be satisfied where the basis of the payment regime is the traditional measure-and-value approach. Nevertheless, the contract ought to make it clear which party has the responsibility for carrying out the valuation. In some standard forms of contract (and in many non-standard forms) it is not clear who has the responsibility for carrying out the valuation. Furthermore, contracts should clearly identify the event which qualifies as the due date for payment.

Section 110(2) requires the payer to provide a notice within five days of the due payment date, specifying the amount of payment and the basis upon which this amount was calculated. This is expected to be of immense help to subcontractors. It is not unusual for main contractors to forward cheques without indicating the work, or even the contract, to which those cheques relate. The new notice procedure will enable subcontractors to exercise the right of suspension for nonpayment and also to decide whether to dispute the amount or the basis of its calculation.

Period of discharge of due payments

Section 110(1)(b) requires the insertion of a further date in all contracts following the due date by which payment must be discharged. It is up to the parties to decide what that period of discharge should be, but weaker parties will have to put up with the periods stipulated in their subcontracts.

Statutory restrictions on rights to withhold money

Section 111 states:

A party to a construction contract may not withhold payment after the final date for payment of a sum due under the contract unless he has given an effective notice of intention to withhold payment.

To be an effective notice, it must specify the amount to be withheld and the ground(s) for withholding payment. Unfortunately, section 111 is not as clear as it could have been. Set-off may not be considered, technically, as a withholding of payment but rather as discharge of payment. Therefore it is regrettable that the drafting of section 111 was not made much clearer.

A notice set-off must not be given later than the prescribed period before the final date of payment, but the parties can agree what that period is to be. Assuming that the final date for payment refers to the last date by which any due payment must be discharged, the period prescribed for the notice of set-off could coincide with the final date for payment. This could be many weeks after the due payment date.

Right of suspension

The statutory right of suspension in section 112 was, not surprisingly, welcomed by many in the industry, especially by subcontractors. Before the right of suspension can be exercised the payee must ensure that:

- a sum is due;

- payment has not been made in full by the final date for payment (the date of expiry of the period of discharge);
- an effective notice of withholding payment has not yet been given;
- a notice of intention to suspend has been issued at least seven days before suspension, stating the ground(s) on which it is intended to suspend performance.

One concern is whether the statutory right to suspend can be excluded by express contractual provision. This would appear doubtful.

Restrictions on "pay when paid" clauses

The note in the margin in the Act refers to: "Prohibition of conditional payment provisions". The case against "pay when paid" regimes is overwhelming but, unfortunately, the Act may not go far enough.

There is an inherent ambiguity in the term "pay when paid" since it can be construed as relating to timing – so that payment to the payee is made when payment is received by the payer from the third party – or entitlement to payment so that payment is made only if payment has been received by the payer from the third party.

Cases in the US, Australia, and New Zealand suggest that the courts are reluctant to accept that payment entitlement can be wholly dependent upon receipt of payment from the third party unless very clear words are used to that effect. A "pay if paid" clause requires the payee to act as the insurer of the payer following nonpayment by the third party.

In the original draft of the Bill, pay when paid clauses were to be void. However, this was probably seen as conceptually difficult, since a pay-when-paid clause can be resurrected under section 113(2) when the third party becomes insolvent. Therefore pay when paid clauses are only "ineffective". The word is not a legal term of art and it remains to be seen how the courts will define it.

The Act does not actually refer to pay when paid clauses, but to contractual provisions which make payment "conditional on the payer receiving payment from the third person". It would be possible to reintroduce pay when paid arrangements by the back door by inserting other conditions, such as making payment dependent upon receipt by the payer of a certificate (which includes the relevant payment) issued by the architect or engineer engaged by the third party, the client or building owner: see *Dunlop & Ranken* v *Hendall Steel Structures* [1957] 1 WLR 1102.

Although a pay when paid clause can be resurrected on the insolvency of the third party, it would seem that there would be no reason why a payee could not still challenge the validity of a pay if paid arrangement and, if successful, obtain a *quantum meruit* for the work executed up to the time when the third party became insolvent.

Section 113(6) provides that the parties can agree alternative payment provisions if the pay when paid clause is ineffective. If such agreement does not take place, the Scheme for Construction Contracts will be applied.

Dispute resolution
The industry was united in its support for the statutory right of adjudication embodied in section 108 of the Act. It will, no doubt, help to reduce the incidence of "bread and butter" disputes such as valuation and set-off disputes which, under present arrangements, generally result in unfair settlements. For many in the industry the pursuit of arbitration proceedings is tantamount to commercial suicide.

The essential difference between adjudication and arbitration is that adjudication does not involve a final disposal of the dispute between the parties. It is a "stop-gap" procedure.

Adjudicators' decisions should reflect soundly rooted commercial commonsense rather than any detailed application of technical legal rules of construction.

There are two major concerns about the statutory adjudication provisions. First, there is the fear that the process of adjudication could become overproceduralised. If adjudication procedures are too lengthy and formalised, there is substantial scope for attacking the jurisdiction of the adjudicator.

Second, there is an absence of any express provision in section 108 dealing with the enforcement of adjudicators' decisions, although enforcement is dealt with in section 111(4) in relation to set-off disputes. Under section 111(4) the adjudicator's decision is to be construed as requiring payment not later than seven days from the date of decision or the date, which apart from the notice of set-off, would have been the final date for payment, whichever is the later.

Contributed by Silviu Klein.

ESTATE MANAGEMENT

CHAPTER 8

Unlawful eviction

First published in Estates Gazette January 22, 1994

To what extent does the law relating to the unlawful eviction or harassment of a tenant give rise to problems for a managing agent or valuer?

The Housing Act 1988 made considerable additions and amendments to the Protection from Eviction Act 1977 (PEA). Under PEA the criminal offences of unlawful eviction and harassment were already in existence and the Housing Act added to these the civil right to compensation for residential occupants who were unlawfully evicted or who were victims of harassment. This enables an occupier to bring an action for damages in the civil courts if his rights under the 1977 Act are breached. The occupiers protected by these statutes include tenants and licensees occupying premises as a residence.

Prior to statutory protection being given to tenants, tenants could bring actions only in contract or tort. An action in contract could be initiated for breach of an express term, for example failure to provide a service or facility, or for breach of an express or implied covenant for quiet enjoyment. The possibilities for an action in tort included trespass to land or nuisance. PEA, however, gave tenants additional causes of action in the form of unlawful eviction and harassment. Section 29 of the Housing Act 1988 creates an additional offence by adding section 1(3A) to PEA. This subsection relates to acts done by a landlord or his agent, which are likely to result in the residential occupier giving up occupation of the premises or which cause the residential occupier to refrain from exercising any right or pursuing any remedy in respect of the whole or part of the premises. It is now no longer necessary to prove intent. The test is now actual knowledge of the likely effect of the conduct or that the landlord, or his agent, has reasonable cause to believe that the conduct is likely to cause the residential occupier to give up occupation etc.

What is harassment?

PEA section 1(3A) loosely incorporates acts likely to interfere with the peace or comfort of the residential occupier (or members of his household) or the persistent withdrawing or withholding of services reasonably required for the occupation of the premises as a residence. This is not a closed net. It is open to the court to look at any new situation. It is also important for managing agents to be aware that harassment may arise inadvertently as a result of bad management. In *R* v *Yuthiwattana* [1984] Crim LR 562 the Court of Appeal held that the failure by a landlord to replace a lost front door key amounted to an act of harassment.

When acting for a landlord agents may, for example, wish to limit the number of keys issued to tenants. However, agents should consider the personal needs of tenants: for example, an elderly tenant may request an additional key to be given to a relative. Refusal may be construed as interfering with the "peace and comfort" of the tenant and thus constitute an offence under the statute. Section 11 of the Landlord and Tenant Act 1985 generally applies to periodic tenancies and fixed-term leases for less than seven years under which landlords are generally responsible for repairing the structure and exterior of the dwelling-house and for keeping the installations for the supply of water, gas, electricity, water heating, space heating and sanitation repaired and in good working order.

Under section 1(3A) of PEA persistently withdrawing or withholding services reasonably required for the occupation of the premises is specifically listed as falling within the definition of harassment if the landlord or his agent knows, or has reasonable cause to believe, that this conduct is likely to cause a residential occupier to give up occupation of the whole or part of the premises, or to refrain from exercising any right or pursuing any remedy in respect of the whole or part of the premises. Therefore, landlords or agents needing to withdraw services for valid reasons, such as carrying out essential repair work under section 11 of the 1985 Act, might consider, as a matter of good practice, keeping disruptions to a minimum, keeping the tenant fully informed and, if possible, giving the tenant notification of relevant dates.

Managing agents should be aware that the withholding of services or facilities may still constitute an offence even if the tenant has no contractual right to those services or facilities. This principle was established by the Court of Appeal in *R* v *Yuthiwattana* (*supra*) and was affirmed by the House of Lords in *R* v *Burke* (1990) 22 HLR 433. In *R* v *Burke* the landlord prevented one of the tenants who lived in the basement of a house from using the basement bathroom and lavatory by storing furniture in the bathroom corridor. He also padlocked the door of the lavatory situated between the ground and first floors thereby preventing the tenant from using it. He also disconnected a front door bell, which communicated with the basement. Although these actions did not constitute a breach of contract, it was still an offence as it was done with the purpose or aim of getting the tenants to leave.

Unlawful eviction
When can an occupier be evicted without court proceedings?

A residential occupier may be evicted without court proceedings if he falls within section 3A of PEA (as amended by the Housing Act 1988) and the occupation of the premises commenced post the Housing Act. In general, occupiers falling within this section are those sharing premises with the landlord or with a member of the landlord's family, provided that it is part of the landlord's main residence, or is accommodation in the same building as the landlord's principal residence (but not including a building which is a purpose-built block of flats) or if it confers on the tenant or licensee the right to occupy the premises for a holiday. (The other exemptions are not directly relevant to agents of private-sector accommodation.) Legal advice should be sought before attempting to evict occupiers appearing to fall within excluded categories in order to ensure that the occupiers are indeed within these categories and also that the mode of eviction does not infringe the law.

Under section 5(1A) of PEA (added by section 32 of the Housing Act 1988) periodic tenancies and licences must be determined by notice in writing not less than four weeks before the date on which it takes effect. Licensees are generally protected from unlawful eviction under the 1977 Act. However, in *Norris* v *Checksfield* [1992] 1 EGLR 159 the Court of Appeal held that a licence expressed to be terminable on the cessation of an employee's employment comes to an end without the requirement of any notice (following *Ivory* v *Palmer* [1975] ICR 340). As such, section 5(1A) of PEA does not apply since there is no notice which is relevant for the purposes of that subsection. This was not a periodic licence falling within section 5 of PEA; it was a licence for the period of employment.

Managing agents, having obtained a possession order against a tenant, should be aware of the order and the implications of *Haniff* v *Robinson* [1992] 2 EGLR 111. In this case a warrant for possession was obtained. However, before the warrant was executed by the bailiffs, the tenants were ejected from the premises. It was held by the Court of Appeal that this was unlawful eviction and damages were obtained. It is important to note, therefore, that a tenant cannot be evicted except by enforcement of the possession order by a bailiff executing a warrant for possession.

Section 27 of the 1988 Act introduced a new cause of action allowing a residential occupier to bring a civil action in tort against the landlord or person acting on his behalf rather than having to rely on a prosecution being instigated. Managing agents should note that agents, as well as landlords, can be prosecuted for their involvement in unlawful evictions and harassment of tenants, either as principal offenders or because they are aiding and abetting, counselling or procuring the crime. In the recent case of *Jones* v *Miah* [1992] 2 EGLR 50 the respondents, who each had a protected tenancy of a bed-sitting-room in a building, sued the appellants for damages pursuant to section 27 of the 1988 Act when they were evicted by the appellants, who had been let into occupation by the vendor landlords before completion of the sale of the reversion. The Court of Appeal considered the meaning of "landlord" and it was held that this term included purchasers who had moved into occupation between exchange of contracts and completion. The appellants became the owners of the leasehold term when they entered into their contract to purchase. The appellants satisfied the test (under section 27(9)(c) of the 1988 Act) of being the persons who, but for the residential occupier's right to occupation, would have been entitled to occupation of the premises.

In relation to the acts of an agent, in the recent case of *Ramdath* v *Oswald Daley* (T/A D & E Auto Spares) [1993] 1 EGLR 82, the Court of Appeal ruled that exemplary damages (which are awarded to punish a wrongdoer) cannot be ordered against a landlord's agent unless it is established that he stood to benefit from the eviction. Ordinary damages were, however, awarded against the agent.

Reinstatement

Reinstatement is one of the defences provided by section 27 of the 1988 Act. An offer of reinstatement (or actual reinstatement) may be a complete defence or it may reduce damages where:

(i) the conduct of the displaced residential occupier or a person living with him makes it reasonable to do so; or

(ii) if, before proceedings are begun, an offer of reinstatement was made and it was unreasonable of the residential occupier to refuse; or

(iii) if the tenant has already obtained alternative accommodation it would have been unreasonable to refuse.

The courts seem to be applying a liberal interpretation to the defence of reinstatement which is in the occupier's favour. In *Tagro* v *Cafane* [1991] 1 EGLR 279 the following points were clarified by the Court of Appeal. First, reinstatement does not consist in merely handing the tenant a key to a lock which does not work and inviting resumption of occupation of a room which has been totally wrecked. Second, a tenant has a right to decide whether to accept reinstatement. In *McCormack* v *Narniou* [1990] CLY 1725 the court held that, although the plaintiff had been reinstated in the premises, he was entitled to an award of damages including aggravated damages, reflecting the fact that there was an assault on the plaintiff's son, and exemplary damages, taking into account an attempt by the defendant deliberately to flout the law.

Role of the valuer

Amendments and additions made by the Housing Act 1988 to PEA substantially increased the damages payable under the Act. The basis for the assessment under section 28 is now the difference between the value of the landlord's interest with the occupier still enjoying the right to occupy, and the value of the landlord's interest without any such right. The date for the purposes of this valuation is the date immediately before the residential occupier left the premises. Under section 28(2) the whole building in which the premises are comprised, with its curtilage, is the premises which have to be valued.

By section 28(3) it is assumed, on valuation, that the landlord is selling on the open market to a willing buyer; that neither the residential occupier nor any member of his family wishes to buy;

and that it is unlawful to carry out any substantial development of any of the land in which the landlord's interest subsists or to demolish the whole or part of any building on that land. There have been two main cases which have addressed the basis of assessment under section 28. Neither is particularly helpful in this regard. In the first, *Tagro* v *Cafane* [1991] 1 EGLR 279, no surveyor was called for the defendant and in the later case of *Jones* v *Miah* [1992] 2 EGLR 50 Dillon LJ stated that none of the four professional valuers who were called to give evidence at first instance gave the judge any assistance at all.

In *Tagro* the surveyor revised his earlier valuation to take into account market conditions at the time of the hearing. Lord Donaldson MR pointed out that the valuation at first instance was wrong because it ignored the fact that the relevant time for the valuation was immediately before the residential occupier ceased to occupy the premises. Furthermore, the landlord's interest was a leasehold interest determinable on a month's notice subject to the Landlord and Tenant Act 1954 and, as such, his interest was potentially precarious. The Court of Appeal held, however, that in assessing damages under section 28 it must be assumed that a landlord can sell the property in the open market to a willing buyer; the section does not contemplate that the premises will be treated as virtually inalienable and having no value in consequence.

In *Jones* it was made clear that, where there is an immediate and a superior landlord and it is the immediate landlord who is responsible for the unlawful eviction, then the interest of the immediate landlord should be valued, not the freehold. It is of note that in *Tagro* the surveyor valued the freehold interest which was, as Lord Donaldson MR stated, "immaterial" because the appellant "was not a freehold owner". As the appellant had not called any valuation evidence, the court felt unable to lower the amount of damages to a more realistic figure, but accepted that the damages awarded were on the high side.

In *Jones* the premises comprised a restaurant on the ground floor and, on the upper floor, four bed-sitting-rooms. The Court of Appeal rejected the argument put forward by the appellants that the value of the goodwill of the premises should be taken into account. The court said that the goodwill of a business carried on in a property does not form part of the value of the freehold or relevant leasehold interest and as such is inconsistent with normal valuation practice.

In valuing the property subject to the right of occupation a similar line will be adopted as if valuing property for investment purposes. The nature of the tenancy held by the occupier needs to be carefully assessed. Rent Act 1977 tenancies offer greater protection than Housing Act assured tenancies because the grounds for possession are slightly wider under the 1988 Act. An assured shorthold tenancy offers even less protection as the landlord is guaranteed possession at the end of the fixed term. Therefore, the main criterion here is the length of the lease. Succession rights also need to be considered because a spouse, a cohabitee or a member of the deceased tenant's family may, in certain circumstances, succeed to the tenancy on the tenant's death. The tenant's age is another pertinent consideration: an elderly tenant living on his own will give a greater prospect for vacant possession than a younger tenant with a family.

The 1988 Act has increased, in some respects, the likelihood of an action being brought for unlawful eviction or harassment by allowing the occupier himself to bring an action. A residential occupier does not have to prove intent. Therefore, a managing agent must be aware of the possibility of harassment arising inadvertently, either through his own actions in managing the property and/or when advising his landlord client. To act as a deterrent to the unscrupulous landlord the amount of damages that can be awarded both for unlawful eviction and harassment has been substantially increased. In future, the chartered surveyor will undoubtedly play a greater role in such assessments.

Contributed by Monica Dawson and Janine Midgley-Hunt.

CHAPTER 9

The curse of the black spot: condensation and the law

First published in Estates Gazette April 1–15, 1995

What remedies (if any) does a tenant have if the house or flat which he/she is renting is severely affected by condensation?

Most tenants who experience condensation damage will be inclined, at first, to assume that the cause of this problem is a leaking roof, rising damp, defective plumbing, or some other example of a landlord who has disregarded his repairing obligations, or of a builder who has botched up his job.

In fact, complaints about dampness on the inner surfaces of dwellings are common. There may be a number of causes – not only the symptoms of disrepair, but also the presence of hygroscopic salts (which absorb moisture from the air) and, of course, condensation. The presence of black mould is a reliable sign that the cause of the problem is condensation from inside, not dampness from outside. This mould requires pure moisture to germinate and condensation is the most common source of this moisture, not water which has passed through the impurities of a wall.

What causes condensation?
Condensation is caused when water-vapour, normally present in the air, comes into contact with cold surfaces in the dwelling. If the air is cooled at this point, to the extent that it cannot retain its original content of water, some is changed into liquid water. The temperature of the air determines the amount of water-vapour which it can hold. Mould growth is a further cause of dissatisfaction for the occupier and it is found particularly on walls affected by condensation. This growth leads to the spoiling of decorations and clothing, a musty smell and a possible risk to health. While the

mould can be subjected to short-term toxic treatments, the problem will return unless the cause of the excess moisture is attended to. Condensation is an especial problem in tenanted dwellings, although it is frequent in all types of housing. Its occurrence depends upon a number of factors particularly: excessive moisture production; inefficient ventilation; lack of cavity-walls or other good thermal insulation; and the absence of sufficient heating in the home: see *BRE Digest* 297: Surface Condensation and Mould Growth in Traditional-Built Dwellings.

Moisture production
Water-vapour is produced in all dwellings by normal household activities, especially cooking, bathing, washing, drying clothes and using paraffin heaters. Unvented tumble-driers are a significant producer of moisture. If a building is troubled by condensation, heaters using paraffin (or unflued heaters using bottled gas) are best avoided because of the moisture they add to the property.

Changed social habits (such as the move away from Edwardian public baths and laundries and municipal bag-wash services to bathing and laundering at home) have added to the amount of moisture generated in houses and flats. Many homes are now less well equipped to deal with this moisture than when they were first built as a result of the modern movement towards lack of ventilation.

Lack of ventilation
Ventilation is the principal way in which water-vapour is removed from accommodation. Of late, however, with the decline in the use of open fires and the blocking up of fireplaces, dwellings have become less well ventilated. Better-fitting doors and windows and draught stripping have also reduced chance ventilation in the home.

Adequate provision for ventilation is needed in all houses and flats, particularly in kitchens and bathrooms where much moisture originates. Ventilation, however, inevitably leads to some loss of background heat in the general living space. It therefore adds to the tenant's heating costs and he or she may seal up ventilation blocks and keep windows tightly closed in an effort to save money. This is obviously going to be a temptation which is strongest among those who cannot afford to rent the best-quality well-insulated accommodation.

Thermal insulation
Improved thermal insulation reduces the risk of internal surfaces falling below the temperature (known as dewpoint) at which condensation can occur. The lowering of heat lost from the dwelling results in higher household temperatures. Occupiers then become more likely to use their heating systems for longer periods and in more rooms, because less money is spent on fuel. Yet, even if walls are adequately insulated overall, "cold bridging" (for example, at lintel level or in window reveals) may cause condensation and local growths of mould.

Condensation on single-glazed windows is often severe, running down to form pools of water on sills. Unless this is regularly mopped up, rot and corrosion may occur. Double glazing may not be the solution; it may be the cause of even more condensation and consequent mould growth because of tight-fitting replacement window-frames. Drainage of condensation from timber window-sills, through lined holes, is therefore worthwhile.

Heating
The provision of full central heating can eradicate condensation problems. In tenanted property, a low continuous background heat, under the landlord's control, can reduce condensation risks; arrangements for charging for this will, of course, be needed in the tenancy agreement.

The formation and control of condensation can be simply observed inside a car as an aid to clarification of all the above points. Moisture created by the breathing of the passengers may condense on the window glass. It can rapidly be dispersed by increasing the heating and opening the windows.

Who is to blame?
The problem of condensation is an intractable dispute between landlords and tenants. Landlords (including those in the public sector) tend to blame the lifestyle of their tenants, while tenants tend to blame the indifference or short-sightedness of their landlords. The matter usually comes to the attention of law centres, environmental health officers, or estate managers when the tenant's wallpaper, carpets, or clothing has suffered damage, or the children of the tenant have become ill because of dampness in the

home. In the case of public sector tenancies, the problem is usually allied to a desire to be rehoused in more modern accommodation. The search for blame is often a waste of time. A tenant is not to be blamed for being too poor to afford efficient heating or for drying his washing in the bathroom. The landlord is not to be blamed for the out-of-date design of a building, which was erected when ventilation was taken for granted and ordinary laundry was boiled in an out-house copper. Both the landlord and the tenant are equally to blame for a way of life which gives greater priority to parking spaces than it does to gardens for hanging out washing.

It is relevant to consider question of blame on the part of the tenant only if he has broken the express or implied terms of this tenancy agreement. Obviously a residential tenancy agreement cannot (without contradicting the essential nature of such an agreement) forbid the ordinary activities of making a home – the place where one eats, sleeps, and has one's being.

In so far as the tenant has an implied duty to take reasonable care of the landlord's property, this is not (of course) a duty to avoid fair wear and tear, or an obligation to lead an out-of-date lifestyle: see the dicta of Lord Denning MR in *Warren* v *Keen* [1953] 2 All ER 1118.

There are perhaps two situations in which a landlord may be blamed for condensation, or at least for the damage which it has caused. The first situation is where the condensation has been caused by some failure of the landlord to carry out his repairing obligations, eg to mend any windows which have rusted shut or to repair his own heating system if it has broken down. The second situation is where the condensation (however it may have started) has been around long enough to cause damage to the structure, to electric wiring or to anything else which it is the landlord's duty to repair. (In all residential tenancies which are periodic in nature, or which are for a fixed-term of seven years or less, the landlord has – whether he likes it or not – significant repairing obligations under section 11 of the Landlord and Tenant Act 1985. This statutory implied term dates back to the Housing Act 1961, section 32. Strictly speaking it does not apply to any tenancies created before October 24 1961, but the courts may imply a similar term at common law: see *Barrett* v *Lounova (1982) Ltd* [1988] 2 EGLR 54.) In *Staves* v *Leeds City Council* [1992] 2 EGLR 37 the Court of Appeal held that a local authority landlord was under an obligation to repair damage to the plaster in a flat caused by condensation. This was because the plaster (unlike wallpaper) was held to be part of the "structure" of the premises.

Modern dwellings

If a house or flat is a modern one it should not give rise to problems of condensation. It should have been designed with the good and bad habits of modern householders in mind. Even if the dwelling is insufficiently ventilated, it should be better insulated than older dwellings used to be. If, therefore, a modern home gives rise to condensation problems, that may betoken some fault on the part of the architect, builder and/or property developer. In such a case, a tenant of the dwelling may be able to bring an action under section 1 of the Defective Premises Act 1972, if the condensation has caused damage to the property or some disease or personal injury (eg bronchitis). It should be noted that section 1 of the 1972 Act does not concern itself with the repairing obligations of a landlord. If a tenant sues his landlord under section 1, this will be because that landlord was responsible for building or designing the dwelling or arranging for it to be built. For example, local authorities may be sued for defects in the housing stock which they have built themselves or which they have employed others to design, build, or otherwise provide for them: see section 1(4) of the 1972 Act.

A failure to carry out work which a reasonable builder or architect would have carried out is as much a breach of the 1972 Act as the inclusion of defective features or the carrying out of work which is shoddy. The test in both situations is whether the dwelling is "fit for habitation when completed". In *Andrews* v *Schooling* (1991) 23 HLR 316 the Court of Appeal held that the omission of a damp-proof course in a basement flat was a breach of the Act. Clearly, therefore, it will be open to a tenant to argue that the absence of adequate thermal insulation is likewise a breach of the statutory duty to build dwellings properly.

Plaintiffs under the Defective Premises Act 1972

The problem with the Act is that it allows a person to sue only if he or she has a "legal or equitable interest" in the dwelling. This obviously includes any freehold or leasehold purchaser of the dwelling (eg a local authority tenant who has exercised his "right-to-buy"). Existing tenants will also come within this category, although they are not so likely to be faced with the costs of repairing any part of the building. This burden normally falls upon the landlord: see section 11 of the Landlord and Tenant Act 1985, referred to above. Nevertheless, as we have already seen, a tenant must have suffered damage to his decorations, his books, his bedding, his furniture, and his clothing, not to mention his health.

Husbands and wives usually ensure that any tenancy agreement is in their joint names. Even if this were not to be the case, the Act would undoubtedly give a remedy to the wife or husband of the tenant, because he or she would be recognised to have an "equitable" interest in the dwelling. Sad to say, however, it is usually the children in a family who suffer various illnesses from dampness. They cannot normally be looked upon as people who have a "legal or equitable interest" in the dwelling and so they have to find their remedies outside section 1 of the Act.

Another, even more frustrating, defect in the Act (so aptly called the "Defective" Premises Act!) is the question of the limitation period. Because the statutory duty of the architect, builder, property developer etc is to provide a dwelling which will be "fit for habitation when completed", any cause of action under section 1 of the Act is stipulated to "accrue" on the date when the dwelling was completed (unless, perchance, the culprit subsequently returned to carry out remedial work). In either case the time-limit for bringing an action under section 1 is six years from the completion of the work in question. The Latent Damage Act 1986 (with its more sensible limitation period – 15 years, provided that the action was commenced within three years of the date on which the damage became reasonably discoverable) seems to have made no difference to this time-limit, because it is confined to actions at common law for the tort of negligence. Any broader interpretation of that Act would require the court to overlook the literal words used by the parliamentary draftsman in favour of a presumed intention by Parliament to benefit plaintiffs who wish to rely on the statutory duty in the 1972 Act. Such an interpretation is, no doubt, possible, but the whole sorry story of these two Acts of Parliament is an additional proof that statutory law reform is usually a curse, not a blessing.

In sum, therefore, a landlord may blame the out-of-date design for the presence of condensation in a house or flat and, even if he built or designed that dwelling, may escape liability under section 1 of the Act if the work was finished more than six years earlier. The most notorious examples of this defence succeeding are the two decisions of the Court of Appeal in *Quick* v *Taff Ely Borough Council* [1985] 2 EGLR 50 and *McNerny* v *Lambeth London Borough Council* [1989] 1 EGLR 81.

The pitiless nature of these decisions has led tenants and their advisers to look in other statutes and in other legal principles for an effective remedy against the ravages of condensation.

It follows from everything that has been written in the first part of this article that condensation in a house or flat may make that place unfit for human habitation. It may come as a surprise to many people who are unfamiliar with the history of the law of housing that there is no general duty (contractual or otherwise), which requires a landlord to ensure that residential accommodation is fit for habitation at any time.

This fact is implicit in such decisions on condensation as *Quick* v *Taff-Ely Borough Council* [1985] 2 EGLR 50 and *McNerny* v *Lambeth London Borough Council* [1989] 1 EGLR 81. The law is more generous to tenants, and their families, in cases where the landlord's negligence causes accidents: see *Rimmer* v *Liverpool City Council* [1984] 269 EG 319 and *Targett* v *Torfaen Borough Council* [1992] 1 EGLR 275.

The origin of this rule lies in that same deep well-spring of law-making which once moved someone, somewhere, to write or to say "caveat emptor" ("let the buyer beware!").

A tenant is equated with a buyer – he is, indeed, a "purchaser" of a legal estate in land even if his tenancy is a periodic one and his payment is rent. Accordingly, the common law of England has always taken the view that the maxim "caveat emptor" extends to a prospective tenant of a house or flat.

Furnished premises

In 1843, the courts recognised an exception to the "caveat emptor" rule. A landlord named Mr Smith rented out furnished premises, at 5 Brunswick Place, Brighton, to Sir Thomas Marrable. Lady Marrable subsequently found the premises to be infested with bugs and Sir Thomas gave notice to Mr Smith that he was giving up the tenancy. Mr Smith argued that Sir Thomas had no right to give up this tenancy because it had been agreed for a minimum term of five weeks and only five days had elapsed.

In subsequent litigation, it was held that Mr Smith had impliedly promised that the premises would be fit for habitation at the commencement of the tenancy, because the agreement was for a furnished letting: see Smith v Marrable (1843) 11 M&W 5.

This exception to the general rule was justified on the basis that a prospective tenant of furnished premises did not have unimpeded freedom to inspect those premises to see the nature and quality of everything that he was getting. (The topical relevance of this argument to building surveyors may be noted!)

As the rule in Smith v Marrable is a rule of common law, not a statutory provision, it is therefore possible for a landlord to exclude it altogether by means of an express term in the tenancy agreement. The Unfair Contract Terms Act 1977 does not apply to contracts which create, or transfer, any interest in land.

Whether or not a landlord of furnished accommodation attempts to "contract out" of the rule in Smith v Marrable, it is not, in fact, likely that he would stand by while condensation damages his own furniture and his own decorations.

This may be one of the reasons why so many complaints about condensation nowadays refer to public-sector houses and flats. It is in the public sector, more than anywhere else, that periodic tenants of unfurnished accommodation are nowadays to be found. It is therefore public-sector tenants who are likely to suffer damage to their furniture and decorations, and perhaps to their health, before the landlord's own property succumbs to any damage caused by condensation.

Slums

In 1885 Parliament attempted to deal with slum landlords. Section 12 of the Housing of the Working Classes Act 1885 extended the rule in Smith v Marrable to all houses (and parts of a house) rented to the "working classes" at low rents, even if the property was unfurnished.

In 1903 Parliament made it impossible for a landlord to "contract out" of this statutory implied term and in 1909 the scope of the landlord's duty was broadened. From then onwards, the landlord had to "keep" the premises in a habitable condition throughout the duration of the tenancy, not merely to provide them in a habitable state at the commencement of that tenancy.

This statutory implied term is now a dead letter. Parliament has failed to keep the legislation in step with the level of rents which the "working classes", and even unemployed people, can nowadays be expected to pay. The implied term as to fitness for habitation is now to be found in section 8 of the Landlord and Tenant Act 1985. The 1985 Act is, however, mainly a consolidating statute. The actual rent limits have not been changed since 1957. The section applies to tenancy only where the rent does not exceed £80 pa (in London) and £52 pa elsewhere. The rent levels are even lower if the tenancy was created before July 6 1957. Ground rents are excluded. Section 8 does not apply to fixed-term agreements of three years or more.

The Housing Acts

Parliament realised from the outset of its concern with slums and overcrowded housing conditions that the imposition of private contractual duties on landlords was not an effective answer to the problem. (How could tenants have enforced those duties in the days before legal aid?) Instead, Parliament chose to proceed by way of public law, giving statutory bodies the power to compel landlords to carry out repairs, irrespective of whether the tenants had any contractual right to complain about the conditions which they were enduring. (The phrase "unfit for human habitation" seems to have been coined, in this context, by the parliamentary draftsman who wrote the Artizans and Labourers Dwellings Act 1868.)

The modern criteria for deciding whether a dwelling is "unfit for human habitation" is to be found in section 604 of the Housing Act 1985, as amended (indeed, thoroughly rewritten) by the Local Government and Housing Act 1989, Part V of Schedule 9.

A dwelling may be unfit for human habitation (but not inevitably so) if it fails to meet one of the eight criteria listed in the revised version of section 604. Two of these criteria clearly have relevance to the problem of condensation (although thermal insulation is not mentioned in the section): section 604(1)(c), freedom from "dampness prejudicial to the health of the occupants"; and section 604(1)(d), adequate "lighting, heating and ventilation". For a case where a broken sash-cord made a house unfit for habitation, see *Summers* v *Salford Corporation* [1943] AC 283.

The principal purpose of section 604 of the 1985 Act is to allow local housing authorities to serve a "repair notice" on the "person having control of the house" requiring that person to execute specified works to make the dwelling fit for habitation. This method of dealing with unsatisfactory housing dates, as we have already seen, from 1868. One obvious problem, however, is that a local housing authority cannot serve a repair notice on itself (even if it wanted to do so): see *R* v *Cardiff City Council, ex parte Cross* (1982) 14 HLR 54.

This means that tenants of local authority housing accommodation cannot rely on section 604 unless there is a term in their tenancy agreement which makes an express promise about fitness for habitation. Such a situation arose in *Johnson* v *Sheffield City Council* (Sheffield County Court, February 15 1994) Legal Action, August 1994. In that case a local authority tenancy agreement expressly promised the plaintiff that his council house would be "fit to live in". This allowed the judge to consult the criteria listed in section 604, even though the case was being brought against (not by) a local housing authority. He then decided that the presence of condensation and the growth of mould had made the house "disgusting" and unfit to live in. He awarded damages to the plaintiff as follows: £3,000 general damages; £200 for extra heating; £500 for damage to curtains and carpets; £100 for extra decoration; and £430 interest.

Environmental health

The law of environmental health used to be known as the law of "public health" and, in earlier days, as the law of "sanitation". It obviously relates to much wider problems than the law of housing, but it has always largely overlapped with that subject, for obvious reasons. Indeed, the concern of Parliament with public health dates from the Nuisance and Disease Prevention Act 1848 – 20 years earlier than its concern with housing.

The most important part of environmental health law to landlords and tenants is the law relating to "statutory nuisances". A list of these nuisances is now to be found in section 79 of the Environmental Protection Act 1990 (as amended by section 2 of the Noise and Statutory Nuisance Act 1993). The most relevant of these nuisances to the problem of condensation is to be found in section 79(1)(a): "any premises in such a state as to be prejudicial to health or a nuisance".

Section 80 of the 1990 Act empowers a local authority to serve a

notice (known as an "abatement notice") on the person responsible
for the nuisance or, in the case of structural defects, on the owner
of the premises. This notice can require the person in question (for
example, the landlord) to execute works and to take such other
steps as are necessary to abate the nuisance or "to prevent or
restrict its occurrence or recurrence". There is an interesting
distinction between the service of an abatement notice under this
Act and the service of a repair notice under the Housing Act. An
abatement notice will come from an environmental health officer,
not from a housing officer.

He or she may therefore be willing to serve an abatement notice
on the housing department of the local authority, even though it is
the same local authority for which he or she works. It is an open
question whether this procedure falls foul of the prohibition in *R* v
Cardiff City Council, ex parte Cross (*supra*). Arguably that case
goes no further than saying that the housing authority cannot serve
a notice on itself and does not prevent another sovereignty (so to
speak) from doing so.

Even if an environmental health officer is not willing to serve an
abatement notice on the local housing authority, the Environmental
Protection Act 1990 contains a fall-back procedure which the
Housing Act 1985 does not contain. Section 82 of the 1990 Act
allows the tenant (or any other person "aggrieved" by the nuisance)
to apply to a magistrates' court for an order requiring the
appropriate defendants to execute the works or to take the steps
which are necessary to abate the nuisance. The court may also
impose a fine on the defendants at the time of making the order in
question. (This power must not be confused with the separate
power of the court to punish people who disregard abatement
notices made under section 80 or orders of the court made under
section 82.) Local housing authorities do not have any immunity
from proceedings brought by one of their tenants under section 82.

Compensation

Once a landlord has been fined for disregarding an abatement
notice, repair notice or an order made by a magistrates' court, this
amounts to a criminal conviction. This allows the court to make a
compensation order under the Powers of the Criminal Courts Act
1973. It has also been held that this power exists at the time of
making an order under section 82, even if the defendant is willing

to comply with that order: see *Botross* v *Hammersmith and Fulham London Borough Council The Times*, November 7 1994. In *Johnson* v *Hackney London Borough Council* (Wells Street Magistrates' Court, March 30 1994), Legal Action August 1994, a local authority landlord was ordered to pay £2,500 compensation (and £2,290 costs) to a tenant who had been badly affected by the lack of sound insulation in a council flat.

Damages

Leaving aside any right to compensation under the Housing Act 1985 or the Environmental Protection Act 1990 the tenant may, of course, have a right at common law to sue his landlord for the defective state of the premises. These rights can be summarised as follows:

(1) A right to sue for the tort of "breach of statutory duty" if the landlord negligently built, designed or otherwise provided the premises within the past six years: see section 1 of the Defective Premises Act 1972.

(2) A right to sue for damages for the tort of negligence if the landlord is responsible for an accident in the home or in the common parts of the building: see *Rimmer* v *Liverpool City Council* [1984] 269 EG 319 (glass which was too thin) and *Targett* v *Torfaen Borough Council* [1992] 1 EGLR 275 (inadequate handrail on dangerous steps).

(3) A right to sue for "breach of covenant" if the landlord is in breach of an express term in the tenancy agreement: see section 104 of the Housing Act 1985, which gives all public sector tenants the right to receive a "tenants' charter" containing information about the terms of their tenancies.

(4) A right to sue for "breach of covenant" if the landlord fails to comply with the repairing obligations contained in section 11 (or, in the unlikely event of it being applicable, section 8) of the Landlord and Tenant Act 1985.

(5) A right to sue for "breach of covenant" if the landlord fails to comply with any implied term recognised by the common law: see *Liverpool City Council* v *Irwin* [1977] AC 239; *Barrett* v *Luonova* (1982) Ltd [1988] 2 EGLR 54; and *Smith* v *Marrable* (1843) 11 M&W 5. (It should be noted that it will not be enough for an implied term to be reasonable in the eyes of the common law – it must be vital.)

FLOW CHART: LANDLORDS AND CONDENSATION IN HOUSES AND FLATS

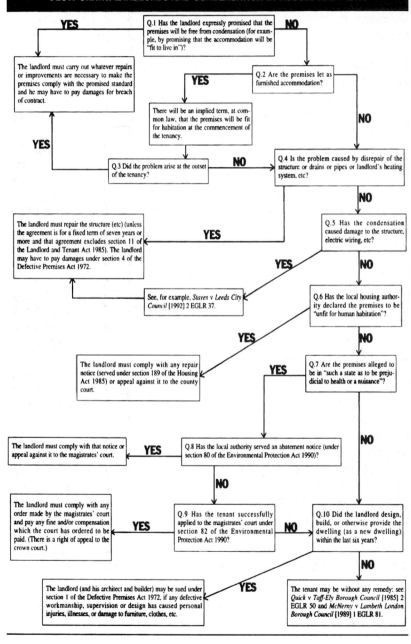

Q.1 Has the landlord expressly promised that the premises will be free from condensation (for example, by promising that the accommodation will be "fit to live in")?

YES → The landlord must carry out whatever repairs or improvements are necessary to make the premises comply with the promised standard and he may have to pay damages for breach of contract.

NO → **Q.2** Are the premises let as furnished accommodation?

YES → There will be an implied term, at common law, that the premises will be fit for habitation at the commencement of the tenancy.

Q.3 Did the problem arise at the outset of the tenancy?

NO → **Q.4** Is the problem caused by disrepair of the structure or drains or pipes or landlord's heating system, etc?

YES → The landlord must repair the structure (etc) (unless the agreement is for a fixed term of seven years or more and that agreement excludes section 11 of the Landlord and Tenant Act 1985). The landlord may have to pay damages under section 4 of the Defective Premises Act 1972.

See, for example, *Staves v Leeds City Council* [1992] 2 EGLR 37.

NO → **Q.5** Has the condensation caused damage to the structure, electric wiring, etc?

NO → **Q.6** Has the local housing authority declared the premises to be "unfit for human habitation"?

YES → The landlord must comply with any repair notice (served under section 189 of the Housing Act 1985) or appeal against it to the county court.

NO → **Q.7** Are the premises alleged to be in "such a state as to be prejudicial to health or a nuisance"?

YES → The landlord must comply with that notice or appeal against it to the magistrates' court.

Q.8 Has the local authority served an abatement notice (under section 80 of the Environmental Protection Act 1990)?

NO → **Q.10** Did the landlord design, build, or otherwise provide the dwelling (as a new dwelling) within the last six years?

YES → The landlord must comply with any order made by the magistrates' court and pay any fine and/or compensation which the court has ordered to be paid. (There is a right of appeal to the crown court.)

NO → **Q.9** Has the tenant successfully applied to the magistrates' court under section 82 of the Environmental Protection Act 1990?

YES → The landlord (and his architect and builder) may be sued under section 1 of the Defective Premises Act 1972, if any defective workmanship, supervision or design has caused personal injuries, illnesses, or damage to furniture, clothes, etc.

NO → The tenant may be without any remedy: see *Quick v Taff-Ely Borough Council* [1985] 2 EGLR 50 and *McNerny v Lambeth London Borough Council* [1989] 1 EGLR 81.

Section 4 of the Defective Premises Act 1972 refers to those situations where a landlord is under a duty to maintain or repair the premises. It does not list those situations, but leaves it to the tenant to show upon which express or implied term he is relying. (In most cases, the duty will arise under section 11 of the Landlord and Tenant Act 1985 and, as we have already seen, this section is not in itself wide enough to compel a landlord to carry out improvements to the design of the premises.)

Section 4 gives a right to sue for damage if the landlord's failure to comply with his obligations causes personal injuries or damage to any property (for example, furniture). This section extends to diseases and "any impairment of a person's physical or mental condition", as well as to accidents. The leading case on the assessment of damages against a landlord in cases of disrepair in houses and flats is *Calabar Properties Ltd* v *Sticher* (1983) 268 EG 697.

Section 4(2) requires the plaintiff to prove that the landlord knew, or ought to have known, of the defect in the premises. In most cases this will mean that the landlord will be in the clear if has not received prior notification of the defect and does not have any particular reason to suppose that an inspection of the premises is appropriate or overdue. However, complaints from other tenants on the same estate will be a clear indication that a general inspection should be carried out.

Section 4 does not merely give a remedy to the tenant, but also to members of his or her family and to "all persons who might reasonably be expected to be affected by defects in the state of the premises". This provision therefore abrogates the old common law rule which held that only a tenant could sue for breach of a repairing obligation: *Cavalier* v *Pope* [1906] AC 428.

In cases where damage or illness has been caused by condensation, section 4 of the Defective Premises Act 1972 does nothing to release the plaintiff from his obligation to prove that the landlord is responsible for the defect which has given rise to the problem. Nevertheless, the section does make it clear that bronchitis, asthma and other illnesses suffered by members of the tenant's family can be a legitimate head of claim under the 1972 Act.

Contributed by Paul Adams and Leslie Blake.

CHAPTER 10

Can you explain what is meant by the term "facilities management"?

First published in Estates Gazette July 8 1995

In the property world we are constantly introduced to new vocabulary and, if we are honest with ourselves, most of us use this new-found jargon without fully understanding the meaning.

"Facilities management is a distinct management discipline which is concerned with the overlap between 'people', 'processes' and 'places' in organisations."

Facilities management – a growing profession
There is a general consensus, among scholars, practitioners, commentators and observers of facilities management, that five principal factors have contributed to the growth of the discipline and the profession:

- information technology
- global competition
- high cost of space
- rising employee expectations
- cost of mistakes

Obviously the above will evolve and new factors will be introduced as the discipline continues to develop.

History and development of facilities management
Facilities management has been developing ever since the Industrial Revolution moved the workplace into the urban environment. In the past two decades, however, facilities management has gradually become more prominent in organisations and has grown considerably as a function and as a recognisable profession.

The regulation of modern, industrial working time is different from agricultural working days, which are based on the season and the weather. The nature of industrial tasks required rigorous discipline and the concentration of workers in one place. Thus, as the facility itself, being the container and focus of industrial production or administrative processes, gained central significance, systems for its planning and maintenance also grew in importance.

Whatever these early support functions were, and whatever they were called individually or as a group, they were the beginnings of what is now known collectively as facilities management. as the nature of commerce, technology, means of communication and production have changed, naturally the support requirements for organisations have also changed, becoming more sophisticated and technically and professionally demanding.

The early movement towards the concentration or workers in one confined physical environment, around either a fixed production system with its characteristic divisions of labour, and its parallels in the administrative office, education and health sectors, marks the first phase of the development of modern facilities management.

The origins of modern facilities management thinking lie in the movement towards scientific management, which related to these new systems of mass processing and production, largely instigated in the USA by pioneers like Taylor & Gilbreth and the turn of the century.

Facility planning became regarded as worthy of further research and consideration, based on the realisation of the link between space and function. In this regard, one may consider the publication in the USA in 1975 of a detailed annotated bibliography on planning educational buildings as a major early milestone in the modern facilities management history.

The second phase in the development of modern facilities management is merely 15 years old and is characterised by the eventual recognition of facilities management as a profession in the USA and the UK, initiated by the formation of the International Facilities Management Association.

The developments in the first and second phases of facilities management history owe much of their progress to the development of space planning and systems furniture in office-based activities. The discipline, however, goes well beyond the arena of office space planning.

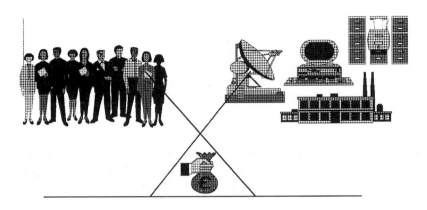

Conclusion

The British Institute of Facilities Management is at the present time producing a list of core competencies.

The illustration above shows that, increasingly, the facilities manager role in large organisations is seen to be one of a "strategic broker", co-ordinating and managing, people, machinery and contracts, etc in delivering a range of required support services. The essence of professionalism in facilities management is therefore best summarised as:

- being able to tune into the organisational objectives and values;
- being able to organise the provision of the type, quality and level of support required;
- having the ability to stay sensitive to the needs, attitudes and behaviour of people and knowing how to facilitate information exchange and co-operation.

The facilities management discipline, in its current form, is a relative youngster, but watch it like a hawk, because, as it matures and finds its way in the business world, we should be looking at an extremely exciting and challenging adult.

Further reading

Park A. *Facilities Management: An Explanation*. Macmillan, 1994.
Duffy F. *The Changing Workplace*. Phaidon, 1992.

Contributed by Lynda Hinkman.

CHAPTER 11

Houses in multiple occupation

First published in Estates Gazette August 31, 1996

What are the consequences to a landlord if his property is held to be a house in multiple occupation? What constitutes "multiple occupation" for the purposes of the law of housing?

Seldom has an article in this series been more appropriately entitled "Mainly for Students", for this is an article about students and their landlords, as well as about landlords and their problems.

Students, of course, very commonly have to share rented accommodation – three or four students together being the usual number. In many cases they will be strangers to each other until their need for affordable accommodation brings them together. They may be studying different courses, coming and going according to different timetables, squirrelling away their tins in different cupboards and storing their perishable food in different compartments in the fridge. Their common life may be confined to arguments about the telephone bill and to various rotas for housework and shopping, more honoured in the breach than in the observance. Does this lack of family ties, and their abiding together for the sake of convenience, therefore turn their shared accommodation into a form of "multiple occupation"?

The principal reason why a landlord does not want his house' to be labelled a "house in multiple occupation" (HMO) is because, even if it is in a good state of repair and not suffering from any "statutory nuisance", he may nevertheless be ordered to carry out expensive works, especially those relating to fire precautions and to

---

'An individual flat in a block of flats is a separate "house" for the purposes of this article: see *Weatheritt* v *Cantlay* [1901] 2 KB 285. But a house which has been converted into flats may still be a single "house", not a collection of "houses": see *Okereke* v *Brent London Borough Council* [1966] 1 All ER 150.

the means of escape from fire. In addition, his house may have a legal maximum number of occupants fixed for it, even if it could comfortably accommodate more.

In other words, a landlord may be required to spend more money on a "house in multiple occupation" (and to ensure that fewer people live there) than would be the case if he was planning to let that property to a single large household or to live there himself with his own family.

The legislation

The present law relating to HMOs is to be found in Part XI (sections 345 to 400) of the Housing Act 1985, as amended. It is this part of the 1985 Act which gives local authorities the power to make schemes, codes, and orders relating to HMOs and to serve notices on landlords.

The history of this legislation is rooted in the control of lodging houses. Until 1969, the phrase which was commonly used by parliamentary draftsmen was: "a house . . . let in lodgings . . . or occupied by members of more than one family".

Montagu Williams QC (1853–1892) wrote about some of these lodging houses in his book of reminiscences:

These places – which are most numerous in Shoreditch, Whitechapel, and Commercial Road districts – are simply and solely hot-beds of crime . . . Those in the neighbourhood of Flower and Dean Street, Weymouth Street, and other alleys and byeways of Spitalfields, often contain as many as 150 beds . . . The "singles", that is, beds for single men, are let at fourpence a night; the "doubles", for male and female, at eightpence. The rents paid for the buildings by those who farm them – some of whom are very well-to-do persons, living in the West End, and utterly regardless how their income is derived – are mostly very small; thus, crowded as these houses are every night of the year, they represent a very remunerative investment . . . New to his surroundings, and desperately eager to obtain food for his family, [the lodger] may glide at once, and almost imperceptibly, into the dishonest practices of those about him; or – and this is perhaps more frequently the case – he will resist the temptation for a while, but, at last, in face of the sneers and jeers of his disreputable companions, his moral courage will desert him. *Leaves of a Life* (1890)

By the mid-20th century, the purpose of the legislation was not so much to protect lodgers from racketeering, moral degradation, and the spread of disease, but more to protect working-class tenants from fire hazards and deficient facilities in dilapidated houses, where three or four families (all on the council-house waiting list) might share a single bathroom and wc.

The changing nature of family life has meant that, in practice, it has become less important to know whether the inhabitants of a house are members of the same family, but more important to know whether they are living together like a family. The phrase "occupied by members of more than one family" has therefore become out of date. A single large house may contain two or more generations of the same family, living (so far as they can) separate lives.

This was the situation in *Holm* v *Royal Borough of Kensington and Chelsea* [1967] 1 All ER 289. In that case the Court of Appeal held that the Housing Act 1961 did not apply in a house where a son and his wife lived on one floor and his father and mother lived separately in the other parts of the same house. Although there were two households, the legislation could not disregard the close relationship of consanguinity and affinity which nevertheless made them one family.

Because of this defect in the legislation, parliament amended the 1961 Act (and two other statutes also) in order to reverse the effect of *Holm*. Parliament did this by expressly coining the phrase "houses in multiple occupation" and using it as the heading for section 58 of the Housing Act 1969. This section made it clear that the relevant statutory powers (contained in that Act and also in earlier legislation) could be exercised in any case where a house was occupied by "persons who do not form a single household".

This statutory definition has been perpetuated in later statutes and section 345(1) of the Housing Act 1985 is the latest word on this matter:

In this Part "house in multiple occupation" means a house which is occupied by persons who do not form a single household.

It is no longer correct to argue that membership of the same family will prevent a house from being a "house in multiple occupation". But the question which has recently concerned the courts is whether members of different families (not living together as spouses) can, notwithstanding their independence as individuals, constitute a "single household" for the purposes of section 345(1).

Students and other sharers

The Housing Act 1985 does not contain any definition of the phrase "single household". In *Simmons* v *Pizzey* [1979] AC 37, the House of Lords held that this question was one of "fact and degree". It was held that a local authority had been correct to treat a hostel for battered women as an HMO, even though the residents took meals together and managed the house on a collective basis. The facts which seem to have been decisive with the House of Lords were the sheer size of the community and the short duration of each resident's stay, arising out of circumstances of utmost urgency, so that the house in which they dwelt was a haven, not a home.

In *Barnes* v *Sheffield City Council* (1995) 27 HLR 719 the Court of Appeal had to turn its attention to the way modern students share accommodation when studying away from home.

In 1990, Mr and Mrs Barnes bought a turn-of-the-century mid-terrace house at 494 Crookesmoor Road, Sheffield. They did it up and then let it to five students, from July 1990 to July 1991. In July 1991, three of the students left and they were replaced by three more. All five of the students were girls. The father of one of the girls reported the condition of the house to the local authority.

In May 1992 Sheffield City Council served three notices on Mr and Mrs Barnes. The first notice was a "repair notice", served under section 189 of the Housing Act 1985. It alleged that the house was unfit for human habitation and ordered the installation of roof lights in two of the attic bedrooms. This notice did not depend upon the house being an HMO.

The second notice was served under section 352 of the Housing Act 1985. This notice alleged that the house was an HMO and that it was not "reasonably suitable" for occupation unless specified works were carried out. These works were: the fitting of a larger worktop in the kitchen; the carrying out of improvements to the outside lavatory; and the total upgrading of the house for the purposes of fire precautions.

The third notice was served under section 354 of the Housing Act 1985. This notice alleged that the house was an HMO and that the maximum number of people it was fit for was four (not five), because one of the bedrooms was too small.

Mr and Mrs Barnes complied with the "repairs notice" and they also carried out some of the work referred to in the section 352 notice. By June 1992, the number of tenants had already fallen to four by virtue of the departure of the five girls and the arrival of four boys (also students). Nevertheless, Mr and Mrs Barnes appealed against the notices, arguing (among other things) that 494 Crookesmoor Road was not a "house in multiple occupation".

Appeals against notices
In the case of notices served under the Housing Act 1985, appeals lie to the County Court. The position is therefore different to notices served under the Environmental Protection Act 1990, where appeals lie to the Magistrates' Court, and to notices served under the Health and Safety at Work Act 1974, where appeals lie to an Industrial Tribunal.

In *Barnes* the County Court judge decided that the house was not an HMO and that, even if it had been, the work carried out by Mr and Mrs Barnes was adequate for the purposes of the fire precautions. The decision caused some disquiet among environmental health officers (who, in the main, have to enforce this legislation) and the Council appealed.

The Court of Appeal was at pains to abide by the ruling in *Simmons* v *Pizzey* and to reiterate that there was no "litmus paper" test for deciding whether a house was an HMO. Nevertheless, the Court of Appeal adopted the argument of counsel for Mr and Mrs Barnes and recognised nine factors which were relevant in deciding this question. The court made it clear that there was no order of priorities when considering these factors and that "the weight to be given to any particular factor will vary widely from case to case depending on the overall picture".

Barnes was a rare case where the factor which tends to weigh most heavily with the local authorities, ie the mode of living of the occupants, was, on the facts of that particular case, not so important in the eyes of the Court of Appeal. Nevertheless, Sir Thomas Bingham MR made it clear that it was not "by any means the least important of the factors" and could, in other circumstances, have been of considerable importance.

On the facts, the Court of Appeal identified a single household, not a multiple occupancy, at 494 Crookesmoor Road – although Sir Thomas Bingham MR thought that the boys had shown themselves to be "rather more communal" than the girls(!) Accordingly, the local authority's appeal was dismissed.

Only two further points might be added now by way of comment.

First, given that the paramount purpose of the modern legislation relating to HMOs is the prevention of fire, there is some sense in observing that house sharing by students is somewhat outside (or, at least, only on the borders of) this purpose. Houses shared by students do not normally contain separate cooking facilities in each room and the discipline of a shared kitchen is a significant safeguard against the risk of any fire from this source.

Second, the Court of Appeal did not deal with the common situation where private landlords accept nominations from the accommodation officer of a university, college, or students' union. Such a system cannot be equated with the use of an estate agent acting on behalf of the landlord, but neither can it be assumed that these students will always have arrived together as one group. Since, however, the selection of the group lies, in the first instance, with the accommodation officer, not with the landlord, it will be a reasonable position for the landlord to take that he has not created a house in multiple occupation. Nevertheless, the final categorisation will depend upon a proper consideration of all the factors which the Court of Appeal took into account in Barnes.

Is an house an HMO?
Indications and contra-indications

1) Did the occupants arrive as a single group, or were they independently recruited by the landlord or by an estate agent? (Arrival as a single group is a contra-indication.)
2) How many facilities and rooms are shared between the occupants? (Extensive sharing is a contra-indication.)
3) Are the occupants responsible for cleaning the whole house? (Responsibility for the whole house is a contra-indication.)
4) How many rooms can be (and have been) locked against other members of the group?("No-go areas" indicate an HMO.)
5) Who has the responsibility of filling vacancies if someone leaves? (Landlord's responsibility indicates an HMO.)
6) Who allocates the rooms? (Landlord's prerogative indicates an HMO.)
7) How many people, in total, are occupying the house? (Large numbers indicate an HMO.)
8) Is the group stable or does it fluctuate? (A fluctuating community indicates an HMO.)

9) What mode of shopping, cooking, eating, cleaning, and otherwise living together (or apart) does the group follow? ("Own-life" habits indicate an HMO.)

Contributed by Leslie Blake.

CHAPTER 12

Outlawing undesirable practices

First published in Estates Gazette March 8, 1997

The Estate Agents (Undesirable Practices) Order 1991 sets out various requirements which need clarification. Sale boards are also regulated by often complicated rules.

The undesirable practices order conjures up all manner of extraordinary images. A search through the EGi archive found a number of articles appearing in Estates Gazette in the early 1990s – a somewhat traumatic period for estate agency practitioners.

Faced with both a difficult market and the introduction of legislation aimed at regulating estate agency practice, unsuspecting agents became liable to committing offences which can result in heavy fines or even disqualification from practice.

The Estate Agents (Undesirable Practices) Order was one of a number of regulations introduced under powers conferred by the Estate Agents Act of 1979. The legislation had a long parliamentary gestation revolving around the need for regulation of estate agency practice.

Despite the Act, it remains the case that anyone can set up as an agent. The Act does, however, confer powers on the Director-General of Fair Trading to ban agents from practice in certain circumstances. The Act followed an increasingly bad press for estate agents during the 1970s, culminating in some less than complementary Which? reports. The introduction of the Orders in 1991 came after a review of the Estate Agents Act in 1988 by the Director-General of Fair Trading and the DTI review of estate agency in 1989.

Even today, parts of the Act have not been brought into force, principally section 22 which provides for the making of regulations to prescribe minimum standards of competence. However, since 1979, a number of Orders have been introduced to bring the other parts of the Act into effect. John Murdoch, in *The Law of Estate*

Agency and Auctions, describes this procedure as a system of negative licensing where, in broad terms, anyone can continue to practise as an estate agent until they breach the regulations.

Undesirable practices

The Estate Agents (Undesirable Practices) (No 2) Order 1991 is concerned with three areas:

* disclosure of personal interests;
* arrangement and performance of services; and
* other matters.

First, where an agent has a beneficial interest in property, or knows of a connected person who has an interest, they are obliged to disclose this to the client promptly and in writing. This would include the situation where an agent acting for a vendor wishes himself to purchase the property.

Second, it is illegal to discriminate against prospective purchasers on the grounds that they will not be accepting other services from the agent. Agents must advise clients if they intend to offer such services to prospective purchasers. Provision of other services, such as mortgages and insurance, has become an issue as a result of the growing involvement in estate agency by the big financial institutions.

Finally, other matters are concerned with misrepresenting the existence of offers, including the status of prospective purchasers. This means that an estate agent cannot, for example, claim that an offer has been received or that a purchaser is a cash buyer if this is not the case. In addition, all offers received must be transmitted to the client in writing unless the client has already indicated, in writing, that he does not wish to receive, for example, those below a certain price.

Other Orders

* The Estate Agents (Specified Offences (No 2) Order 1991 and (Amendment) Order 1992.
* The Estate Agents (Provision of Information) Regulations 1991.

Estate agents are obliged to advise clients as to the most appropriate method of selling or letting a property. In outlining the alternatives the agent must clearly indicate the differences in fee structure between methods.

They are also required to issue warning notices to the client whenever the terms "sole selling rights", "sole agency" and "ready, willing and able purchaser" are used.

These notices, which are specified in the Act, identify precisely when the liability to pay remuneration will arise. Where the precise remuneration cannot be specified at the outset, the estate agent must tell the client the basis of the calculation.

Estate agents must also provide information about any additional charges for advertising, sale boards and photographs and anything else not included in the basic commission. Any subsequent variations in the contract must also be provided in writing.

Estate agents will be acting sensibly when they ask clients for written confirmation that they accept these terms.

This information is outlined in the RICS publication, *Putting the Estate Agents Act 1979 and its orders and regulations into practice* – a guide which lists advice under 19 separate headings.

Accounts regulations

• Estate Agents (Account) Regulations 1981.

Clients' money, contract and pre-contract deposits must be paid into a separate client account with an authorised institution (bank or building society) and must be kept separate from all other moneys.

Interest on such deposits must be paid to the client. Estate agents are also obliged to keep detailed records which must be audited.

Controls

The Estate Agents Act and its Regulations are controlled through a combination of civil law and criminal prosecution. If an agent is shown to be in breach of the regulations and requirements, this could well render the contract with the client unenforceable, resulting in the forfeit of the whole or part of the fee.

Breaches, such as discrimination, which are criminal offences, may trigger the powers enforced by the Director-General of Fair Trading. This could lead to fines or banning orders which may disqualify the perpetrators from estate agency practice.

To apply this ultimate sanction, the director-general must first be satisfied that the agent is unfit to practise. A banning order prevents a person from undertaking estate agency work of the type specified in the order. The order can be either a total ban or one limited to certain types of geographical area.

The director-general can also issue warning notices in respect of non-criminal breaches or undesirable practices. Persistent infringement would then result in a declaration of unfitness to practise.

Trigger events include criminal conviction, discrimination or failure to comply with obligations under the Estate Agents Act. Any orders made under the Act have to be registered by the Director-General.

Property Misdescriptions Act

The Property Misdescriptions Act was passed in 1991, although it was not put into effect until 1993. Until the Act was passed, estate agents had been exempt from trades descriptions legislation. Now they are required to ensure that any statement made must be accurate. Statements may be oral as well as written and can include photographs as well as plans. The Act is enforced by local authority trading standards officers.

If an agent does make a misleading statement, he must show that he took all reasonable steps and exercised all due diligence to avoid committing an offence. The details of the legislation have been well documented elsewhere, and readers are referred to Murdoch's *Staying Afloat* (*EG*, April 3 1993).

Sale boards

Sale boards are controlled by planning legislation and not the Estate Agents Act. The erection of a board would, in normal circumstances, require planning consent but it would be absurdly impractical for consent to be required every time a sale board were to be erected.

There is therefore a system of deemed consent under section 222 of the Town and Country Planning Act 1990. This is controlled by the Town and Country Planning (Control of Advertisements) Regulations 1992 which set out specific and standard conditions. Standard conditions include the need for any advertisement to be in a clean, tidy and safe condition, to be displayed with the owner's permission and not to obscure road traffic signs.

Estate agents' boards fall under class 3 of Schedule 3 to the order covering "Miscellaneous temporary advertisements". The conditions for this class are summarised in Figure 1.

Figure 1. Sale board conditions

• Only one advertisement is permitted.

• Additions to the existing advertisement are limited to a statement to the effect that a sale or letting has been agreed or that the land and premises have been sold or let, subject to contract. The point here is that the board is advertising the property and not the agent selling or letting it. The words "subject to contract" must be included and the absence of this phrase or the addition of any other form of words would result in non-compliance. This means "Sale agreed" would seem to be in contravention.

• The board must be removed 14 days after the sale is completed or a tenancy is granted.

• Boards must not exceed $0.5m^2$ for residential use or development and $2m^2$ for any other use or development (these areas are increased to $0.6m^2$ and $2.3m^2$, respectively, in aggregate where two boards are joined together).

• The maximum projection from the face of a building is 1m.

• Boards must not be illuminated.

• No character or symbol should be more than 0.75m (8.07ft) in height or 0.3m (0.98ft) in areas of special control. Such areas can be designated by the local planning authority and will usually include national parks and conservation areas.

• No part of the board shall be more than 4.6m (15.1ft) above ground level or 3.6m (11.81ft) in areas of special control. In the case of the letting of part only of a building, the board must be positioned at the lowest point practicable.

To date there is no such thing as a telephone informer line to enable citizens to tip off the planning officer about suspected offenders, but can you spot any non-compliant boards in your part of the world?

This article has provided only the briefest overview of the principal controls affecting estate agency. This is a complex area of law, and readers are encouraged to refer to the guidance material produced by the professional bodies, as well as the thorough treatment of the subject provided in the two texts on estate agency law and practice referenced below.

References

Mackmin D, *The Valuation and Sale of Residential Property*, 2nd ed, Routledge, 1994

Murdoch J, *The Law of Estate Agency and Auctions*, 3rd ed, Estates Gazette, 1994

Contributed by Phil Askham.

ECONOMICS

CHAPTER 13

Current economic issues

First published in Estates Gazette December 12, 1992

Government economic policy has four main aims: control of inflation, a low level of unemployment, a reasonable balance of payments position and sustained economic growth. It is not often possible to achieve these goals all at the same time: there may be a "trade-off" between inflation and unemployment – for example, the famous Phillips Curve relationship (Figure 1).

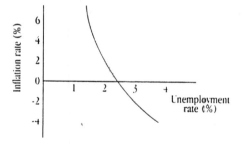

In the past it has not been possible in Britain to have sustained economic growth and a reasonable balance of payments position. Governments in the 1950s and 1960s had to "stop" economic growth because the balance of payments deficit was becoming too large. Once the deficit was reduced, controls on the economy could be relaxed and the economy could grow again. This became known as "stop-go policy" and it may be that Britain's weak trading position with the rest of the world is largely responsible for poor growth rates in most of the post-war period.

In the 1970s the Phillips Curve relationship had clearly broken down; there were high levels of unemployment and high inflation. This was termed "stagflation" by economists at the time – a combination of stagnation and inflation. Governments began to use tight monetary and fiscal policies to reduce inflation, even though in the short run this leads to lower output and higher unemployment (a "price worth paying"?).

The traditional trading picture of the UK economy is of a manufacturing exporter, importing raw materials and food and making up any deficit in the balance of payments with sales of "invisibles" – financial, shipping and insurance services – to the rest of the world.

In the 1980s this picture changed somewhat, with manufacturing industry declining, but the "gap" in the trade balance being made up by exports of North Sea oil. At the same time, deregulation of financial markets led to a great expansion of borrowing, much of which was spent on imported goods. The resulting deficit in the balance of payments has reached a record level in the 1990s and this put pressure on the value of the pound.

The level of the pound on foreign exchanges depends very much upon the trading position of the UK. The "price" of pounds in terms of other currencies depends on the demand and supply of pounds in foreign exchange markets. If we buy a great deal of imports, we supply a lot of pounds (to buy other currencies), whereas if we sell many exports, the demand for pounds rises as people in other countries buy them in order to buy our goods (Figure 2).

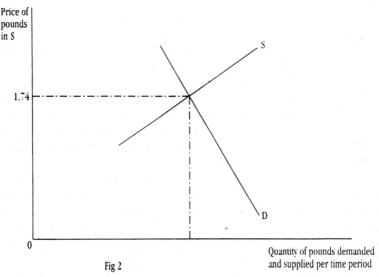

Fig 2

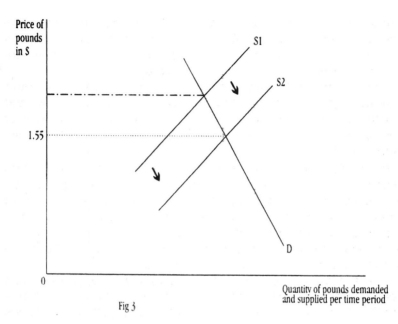

Fig 3

Thus a persistent balance of payments deficit means an oversupply of pounds to the foreign exchange market (Figure 3) . . . and the pound falls.

One way of offsetting this, at least temporarily, is to have high interest rates in the UK – because then people and firms overseas will want to invest here and to do that they need to change their currency for pounds, therefore increasing demand. But high interest rates are bad for the domestic economy, raising the level of interest payments which firms have to make and increasing mortgage payments so that customers have less "disposable income" to spend on goods and services. High interest rates slow down the economy and may cause a recession with output actually falling, rather than economic growth.

The Government in Britain has made inflation public enemy number one for the past 13 years, with "tight money" and a high exchange rate for the pound being part of the strategy to reduce inflation. The problem is that such policies will also lead to increases in unemployment and a slowing of economic growth. In addition, a high level of the pound makes imports cheaper and our exports more expensive, thus worsening the balance of payments.

The trade-off for a low rate of inflation has been a worsening of the other three main aims of Government economy policy! The battle to reduce inflation has led to higher and higher levels of unemployment. High interest rates, in particular, cause bankruptcies, redundancies and house repossessions as firms and families fail to keep up with their loan repayments. Unemployment has increased in this recession by 1.5m and is still rising. It looks set to exceed 3m by the end of the year. There are daily announcements of thousands of job losses: 4,300 job cuts were announced in the first three days of October; 1,220 firms per week are going bust, according to Dunn & Bradstreet[1].

Fixing the exchange rate within the Exchange Rate Mechanism of the European Community was thought to be a good idea as the economies of Europe "converged". Unfortunately, that convergence was not really evident and the weakness of the UK economy (in particular, the large balance of payments deficit) was prevented from lowering the value of the pound – "devaluing" – only by high interest rates and European central banks intervening to buy pounds. This process could not go on forever and on "Black Wednesday", September 16, Britain was forced to leave the ERM and to let the pound "float" – that is to allow it to find its own level on the foreign exchanges as dictated by the forces of supply and demand.

As the pound falls, or floats downwards, imports will cost more and this could prove inflationary! On the other hand, as imports become more expensive we may buy less of them; our exports will be cheaper and, so, we may sell more of them. This could improve the balance of payments and unemployment figures; the recession may end and economic growth may begin again. But watch out for that inflation figure! As inflation rises, the benefits of low export prices can be lost because UK firms' costs and prices increase. Inflation has other damaging effects on the economy – it creates uncertainty which causes businesses to curtail their investment plans; it leads to high "cost-of-living" wage demands; it reduces the value of savings and encourages borrowing because when the money is repaid it is worth less. Ultimately inflation can lead to a complete loss of confidence in the currency and then to economic breakdown – the most famous example of which was in Germany in the 1920s.

A further consequence of increasing unemployment is the strain on Government finances. Not only do people stop paying taxes when they become unemployed they also receive benefit payments from the state. A sort of "double-whammy" to state finances! The Public Sector Borrowing Requirement (PSBR) is the Government's "overdraft" and it will be more than the projected £32bn this year largely because of rising unemployment. This may mean that Government spending cuts are made in other areas and this in turn may actually increase unemployment. The recession could become a "depression", which is much more prolonged and much more difficult from which to escape.

As output falls then, obviously, economic growth rates slow down. Gross domestic product of the UK fell by 0.7% in the past 12 months, while industrial production dropped by 2.3%. It is no coincidence that the unemployment rate rose from 8.4% to 9.7% over the same period[2]. There is a tendency to overlook the importance of economic growth. Even at the modest average rates of around 2.5% pa achieved in Britain since the war, output will double in 28 years. This means that, ignoring any environmental or unquantifiable consequences, living standards could double within a generation. Young people could begin their married life with the standard of living that their parents have achieved by retirement age. Britain's boom-and-bust economy has not achieved consistent real growth over the past 13 years.

In previous recessions the housing market has also turned downwards. This happened in 1974–76 and 1980–83, with houses falling in price by 19% in 1975 and 10% in 1983. A downturn has followed the boom years of 1972–73, 1979 and 1988–89. This downturn follows a familiar pattern, but is exacerbated by the following: a sharp fall in the number of house purchases after 1988; a fall in house prices in nominal terms (ie not just a lower rise in prices than the inflation rate); and record numbers of repossessions in 1991 and 1992, partly because the real cost of borrowing remained very high. Falling house prices mean that owners' equity is reduced and the "wealth effect" from this means that people are less likely to spend on consumer durables etc because they feel less affluent. Negative equity (mortgages greater than the value of the house) is also a problem, preventing people, especially those in the South East, from moving either upmarket or with their jobs.

In this way the fortunes of the housing market affect the whole economy, which is why the Chancellor of the Exchequer has tried to stimulate housing with £750m provided in his Autumn Statement for the purchase of 20,000 repossessed homes. Recovery in the housing market may take rather longer than previously because of the large number of properties on the market and the loss of confidence in housing as an investment.

References
[1] Source: *Guardian* September 30 1992.
[2] Source: *Economist* September 1992.

Contributed by Ernie Jowsey.

CHAPTER 14

Government stock

First published in Estates Gazette April 17, 1993

Investment can be defined as the parting with the possession of money, in exchange for the prospect of future income, or a capital gain, or both. Investors are usually investors *per se*, that is, they are not interested in investing in a particular sector of the investment market, property for example, but merely in providing the balance of future income and/or capital gain which is appropriate to their personal needs and all other circumstances.

The major investors – the institutions, particularly insurance companies and pension funds – control the largest proportion of investment funds. They will hold a range of investments representing a portfolio which is balanced in terms of the particular requirements of the institution. Valuation surveyors are, of course, specifically concerned with property as an investment; but, because all investment vehicles compete with one another for the funds available, even the property investment market, which is normally perceived as requiring specialist appraisal, cannot be seen in isolation. Property values, like those of any other investment, are influenced by prices and returns in other competing investment sectors, in particular stocks and equities.

In one further sense Government stocks have developed an even greater significance for the valuer specialising in investment property. This importance has resulted from the increasing use of contemporary discounted cash flow – based valuation techniques. Such growth-explicit methods rely not on the traditional all-risks yield, which has little or no significance outside the world of the property investment valuer, but on internal rates of return such as the equated yield, which adopt, as their bench-mark, the market yields on fixed interest securities. These yields, because they are virtually risk free (apart from inflation risk), represent a point of reference against which other types of investment, with different levels and types of risk, can be compared.

For these reasons a knowledge and awareness of other investment markets, especially the fixed-interest security market, are of great importance to the valuer. Government stock or gilt-edged securities (gilts) are loan stock issued by the Government as a means of raising money to fund its activities. In addition, in recent years they have become an important instrument of monetary policy. The name gilt-edged arises from the fact that they represent the highest form of credit, backed as they are by the Government.

By 1919 the national debt had reached £8bn and remained at this level until the second world war. In the post-war era, with the extension of such Government functions as nationalisation and the welfare state, the debt continued to increase. This debt was financed largely by borrowing, most of which (75%) was achieved by the issue of marketable securities dealt on the Stock Exchange. The rest is made up of National Savings, Premium Bonds and Treasury bills. Clearly, then, a high level of public borrowing results in increased supplies of Government paper. With the current public sector borrowing requirement (PSBR) expected to reach £50bn, the Government needs to raise £1bn each week during the course of this year.

Stock is offered in exchange for a loan from the purchaser. In return, the Government promises to pay an annual rate of return and, in many cases, promises to pay back the original capital at a future specified date. These dated stocks are divided into three categories: shorts – with redemption dates in five years; mediums – five to 15 years; and longs – more than 15 years. In some instances redemption dates are not specified, but are a range of dates which gives the Government an option to enable repayment to be made at the most propitious time.

Stock can also be undated, in which case there is no promise to repay the capital, so that this, in effect, becomes a permanent loan. The Government can choose to repay undated stocks at any time and this would occur if interest rates generally fell below those paid on the stock.

The secondary market

One of the great attractions of gilts, apart from the security of income and capital, at least in absolute terms, is the high degree of liquidity. Existing stocks can be bought and sold quickly and cheaply through the medium of the Stock Exchange. This is known as the secondary market, as distinct from the market in issues of new stock made by the Government.

Stock prices are identified daily in the financial pages of the major newspapers, where an entry might appear as follows:

Tr 8.75% 97 108$^{9/16}$ 8.06 6.52

This is a short-dated Treasury stock paying interest at 8.75% and which will be redeemed in the year 1997. Its market price is £1,08$^{9/16}$ and its running yield 8.06% and redemption yield 6.52%. Some entries will also quote additional information including the high and low prices over the last year and price movements on the last day of trading.

So, what does it all mean?

The name of the stock usually refers to the purpose for which it was originally issued. Other names include "Exchequer", "Funding" and "Conversion", although "War loan" and "Consolidated" also appear in the titles of older, undated stock. The price quoted is the market price of a single unit of stock with a nominal value of £100. The market price of gilts is quoted in 30 seconds (the tick) of a pound. So in this case the price is £108.56.

The interest rate of 8.75% is the amount of interest payable on the nominal value, ie £8.75 each year, although with the vast majority of stocks interest is paid in two equal instalments. In this case, two payments of £4.375 each will be received on March 1 and September 1. The nominal, or running, yield is found by dividing this annual income by the price paid:

$$\text{Running Yield} = \frac{8.75}{108.56} \times 100 = 8.06\%$$

The redemption yield is the overall internal rate of return of the stock taking into account that the nominal value will be repaid on the last interest payment date, which is September 1997. It is assumed that the stock is held to maturity. In the case of dated stock with a range of redemption rates, the last possible redemption date is assumed for the purpose of calculating the redemption yield.

The internal rate of return, found by trial and error, is 3.26%. To find the redemption yield this needs to be multiplied by two, to adjust from six monthly payments to equate to the annual return, which is therefore 6.52%. The redemption yield takes account of the capital gain or loss when the stocks are redeemed.

Interest payments

Interest is earned day-to-day and, normally, interest due since the last dividend date is added to the cost of an investment or the proceeds of a sale. Thus, forthcoming interest is paid to the seller not the buyer. This is known as accrued interest.

Interest on gilts is liable to income tax and this is normally deducted from gilts held on the Bank of England Register. However, gilts held on the National Savings Register are paid without deduction and are therefore attractive to nontaxpayers. Gilts are exempt from Capital Gains Tax provided they are held for a minimum period of a year and a day.

Stocks are a fixed-interest investment and are regarded as secure because the interest and redemption payments are guaranteed. However, at times of high inflation, the real value of both income and capital is rapidly eroded. After the late-1970s, when inflation was running at high levels, the Government introduced index-linked stock to provide an income and redemption which is fixed in real terms by tying interest payments and the redemption to the Retail Price Index. Such stock was issued at low coupon rates of 2% to 4.5%, but the tie-in with the RPI ensured an inflation-proof yield. Index-linked stock was first issued in 1981. The low coupon might appear at first sight to be unattractive, but this represents the "real" return to the investor. Understandably, index-linked stocks tend to be more attractive at times of high inflation.

The primary market

New issues are bought by direct application to the Bank of England and issues are usually announced in press advertisements. The timing of the issue of new stock will depend on whether this is to cover a budget deficit or to finance the repayment of existing stocks. In the latter case, existing stockholders may be offered conversion into the new issue, sometimes with the incentive of a discount.

A new issue is opened by a prospectus which specifies the amount of stock offered, the interest rate and the repayment date. Anyone can apply for stock in multiples of £100. Any balance not taken up by public subscription is taken up by the Issue Department of the Bank of England, the National Debt Commissioners and other Government departments with funds in hand. This becomes known as the tap issue which is dripped into the market at a price adjusted to reflect market conditions. Naturally, the price at which the new issue is offered and the coupon have to be carefully determined, as these will influence the market price of existing stocks in the secondary market.

Several different methods of issue have developed during recent years. Issues can be made at a fixed price with the amount payable on application or in two or three instalments. Alternatively, issues are by tender at a minimum price. If such an issue is undersubscribed, it is allotted at the minimum price with the Bank of England taking up the residue. If the issue is oversubscribed then allotments are made at the lowest accepted tender with allotments above this price being made in full. More recently, issues have been offered by auction with no minimum price, where it is expected to sell the whole issue at what the market considers to be the going rate.

The coupon reflects the nature of the economy at issue. The oldest, 2.5% Consols, were issued in the last century. At the other extreme, 15.5% Treasury stock 1998 was issued in 1978 at time of strained Government finances and high inflation. Clearly, the Government is hardly likely to offer stock at prices which do not compete with the market, but, equally, cannot afford to make new issues so attractive that they cause a decline in values in the secondary market.

Market prices

Gilt prices are affected by normal economic and political factors as well as the normal laws of supply and demand but the main determinant of prices and yields is the redemption date. As a general rule, the shorter the date, the lower the yield. Naturally, as a particular stock nears its redemption date, the price will tend to move towards the redemption value, £100.

Low coupon stocks have market prices below the repayment level, but these appeal to higher rate taxpayers who are highly exposed to income tax on the interest payments received. The main attraction is the high capital gain potential of a stock with a low market price compared with the repayment. Consequently, on occasion the government will issue low coupon stock by tender at low minimum prices to cater for this sector of the market.

The major factor affecting the price, apart from supply and demand, is confidence in the economy and future economic outlook. At the present time, with interest rates falling and inflation at low levels, the price of stock has tended to rise with a consequent fall in yields.

Concern is currently being about the prospect of substantial gilt issues to finance the PSBR. Pension fund holdings of gilts remain low at around 5.7% of the total investment portfolio and the main institutions are not expected to increase this level. Part of the concern seems to stem from the Government's economic policy which, by stimulating growth, may push up inflation. This may, of course, result in a switch from fixed-interest to index-linked gilts. There is also a view that equities will out-perform gilts during the next 12 months. Even so, as pension funds mature and face the prospect of paying out more in pensions than they receive in contributions, gilts at least do offer the attraction of producing a higher income than other investments.

Footnote: To help in publicising the Government's campaign to sell more gilts, Post Offices will now be displaying free booklets to help take away some of the mystique and to encourage the smaller investor. Entitled *Investing in Gilts*, a guide for the small investor, it explains some of the basics of investing in gilts.

Redemption yield calculation

Coupon date	Cash flow	× PV @ 3.26%
Mar 93	(108.56)	(108.56)
Sep 93	4.375	4.24
Mar 94	4.375	4.10
Sep 94	4.375	3.97
Mar 95	4.375	3.85
Sep 95	4.375	3.73
Mar 96	4.375	3.61
Sep 96	4.375	3.49
Mar 97	4.375	3.38
Sep 94	104.375	78.19
NPV		0.00

$$\text{Accrued interest} = \frac{\text{Coupon} \times \text{No of days}}{365}$$

Contributed by Phil Askham.

CHAPTER 15

Yields and rates of interest

First published in Estates Gazette September 4, 1993

I am confused by the differences between yields and rates of return and find it difficult to distinguish between the internal rate of return and other discount rates. An article on the subject might help to clarify this.

The terminology surrounding the use of phrases connected with yields on investments, returns, rates of interest and discount rates causes students of valuation a great many problems. This should come as no surprise. The Jones Lang Wootton *Glossary of Property Terms* lists well in excess of 50 terms relating to investment and valuation which include the words rate, return or yield.

These three words "although not synonymous, are similar and tend to be used indiscriminately"[1] to describe the various ratios between income and capital value or cost. Their use by valuers is certainly imprecise and inconsistent to the point where identical phrases have been used to mean quite different things to different people. The student has no choice, if complete confusion is to be avoided, to come to terms with this multiplicity of definitions. Before becoming thoroughly exasperated, however, be advised that all is not completely lost. The glossary itself has gone a long way towards addressing these difficulties and, since its publication in 1989, has received widespread recognition as the source of the "correct"definition. It is therefore the ideal place for our confused student to begin.

An appendix to the glossary takes up this issue and provides a precise note of guidance on usage by drawing a broad distinction between yields, returns and rates. Yields are defined generally as annual percentage amounts expected to be produced by an investment. They are also used as the measure for the capitalisation of income in the specific context of investment valuation. The yield is therefore identified very much as a measure of market expectation. Returns (on capital) on the other hand, are defined as the annual percentage amount produced by an investment by reference to its cost or value. Returns can be distinguished from yields in that the value, on which they are based, is not necessarily a market value.

Rates of interest, finally, are simply the annual percentage amounts payable on borrowed money and are further used in the context of discounting to reflect the time value of money.

It is possible to take this general distinction a stage further by considering five broad areas of usage of the terminology of yields, returns and rates:

(a) the measures of the relationships between income and capital,
(b) terminology which is concerned principally with interest rates,
(c) the more sophisticated measures of investment appraisal used in discounted cash flow analysis, specifically the internal rate of return,
(d) the concept and application of discount rates,
(e) and, finally, the specific terminology which refers to stocks and shares.

This article will consider each in turn. The reader should be warned, however, that even this type of distinction can become arbitrary as the usage tends to overlap between these five broad areas. However, an understanding of the origin of a particular term should help to create a better understanding of the way in which it has been applied in practice.

Relationships between capital and income
Arguably this is where most of the initial confusion begins. To resolve this it is necessary to distinguish between the process of analysis or appraisal on the one hand and market valuation on the other. Valuation can be defined as the prediction of the most likely selling price of an investment, whereas appraisal is the estimation of investment worth, a more subjective assessment which takes account of the circumstances of a particular investor. So far as the investment method of valuation is concerned, what valuers are endeavouring to do is utilise the relationship between capital value and income to analyse market behaviour and thus make predictions about future patterns of behaviour. Here the valuer will

be concerned with "returns" as the ratio of annual net income to capital, expressed as a percentage and derived from the analysis of market transactions. There is a tendency to call this percentage the "yield" of the investment.

The years' purchase is the inverse of this yield for fully rented properties and is the amount by which net income is multiplied to arrive at the capital value. The yield for fully rented properties, derived from market analysis, is often referred to as the all risks yield. Used as a valuation tool this is really a discount rate which, when applied to the full rental value, will provide a capital value. This, then, is the discount rate which reflects "all the prospects and risks attached to the particular investment"[2]. Baum and Crosby provide some detailed thoughts on precisely what these prospects and risks are and conclude that "The initial yield is . . . a highly complex measure of the quality of an investment"[3].

The construction of this yield starts from a risk free or neutral rate obtainable in the investment market based on a notional investment assumed to be free of income or capital growth, liquid, free of operating expenses and money risk free. Fixed interest gilts come closest to this definition in that they are liquid, there is normally no capital or income growth and they have low management costs. Initial yields for property can then be derived from this base yield by adjusting upwards for risk, operating expenses and lack of liquidity, but downwards to allow for rental and capital growth. Be warned, though; while this type of analysis provides a theoretical basis for the determination of property yields, "the process of initial yield construction is dangerous and impossible to practise"[4].

Above all it should be recognised that "The all risks yield is a unit of comparison and not a rate of return"[5], so that its application in practice is nothing more sophisticated than a simple comparison valuation.

Of course not all property valuations are concerned with fully let freehold investments. More typical, especially in times of rental growth, or more familiar at the present time of rental decline, most investment properties will be between reviews and let at something other than the full rental value. Assuming the actual rent passing is less than the full rental value and that there will be a rent review at some time in the future restoring the income to that full value, it is necessary to be aware of other definitions of property investment yields.

The anticipation of a future reversion, to provide an increased income, might encourage an investor to pay a price for the investment which appears to be higher (ie based on a lower yield) than the going rate. This is sometimes referred to as the initial yield and is the initial net income divided by the purchase price. If upon reversion the rent does in fact increase, then of course the yield (or more correctly the return), in relation to the original purchase price, will also rise.

Students should also be aware of the following definitions which appear to be in common use:

Current yield is the remunerative discount rate appropriate at the date of valuation, assuming a property is let at the full rental value. The initial return is the percentage return found by dividing the initial net income by the purchase price. Both are sometimes referred to as the investment yield, which is the annual percentage return considered appropriate for a specific investment found by dividing the net income by the capital value. This is the measure of market sentiment about the prospects of an investment. The better the prospects for the investment, the lower the yield or, rather, the higher the capital value relative to the income.

At first sight it might appear paradoxical that the better investments offer the lower yields, but of course higher yields tend to affix themselves to the riskier investments to balance their attractiveness in the market. Millington likens this to the difference between betting on a 100 to 1 outsider compared with the 2 to 1 favourite[6].

Prime yield is the current yield for a fully rented property of the best physical quality, the best location and with the best tenant's covenant. That is, a prime property. This might represent a benchmark against which the yields of non-prime investments can be measured.

Where the initial yield of a property which is not fully let is quoted, this can be fairly meaningless as a means of comparison. In such cases it is usually necessary to have regard to the reversion yield which is discount rate applied to the reversionary income. A slightly different approach is applied in the so-called hard-core method of valuation which divides the income horizontally rather than vertically. In such cases valuers sometimes refer to base or core yields and marginal yields, the latter being the rate at which the top-slice of income is discounted. This type of approach has enjoyed something of a renaissance as one means of dealing with the problem of over-rented property, an animal which has emerged during the current property slump.

Interest rates

Perhaps because interest rates are not the sole province of the valuer, there is a little more coherence in the terminology as distinct from the more esoteric world of property investment valuation. In simple terms an interest rate is the ratio of interest to principle and this is applied from the perspective of both borrower and lender.

Some definitions for specific rates of interest are in general usage, but these are usually clear in that they apply only in very particular circumstances. While these are not directly relevant to property investment valuation they are important in that some set the tone for lending and borrowing generally and will therefore have some influence on the level of investment yields.

The base rate is the underlying rate of interest forming the basis for all other interest rates. This is fixed by the Bank of England and is the rate charged to other borrowing banks, and determines the rate of interest to all borrowers. The base rate used to be known as the bank rate and the minimum lending rate.

The annual percentage rate or APR is a rate determined for certain credit bargains (see MFS May 1993.)

Valuers should also be aware of the accumulative rate, which is the compound interest at which it is known or assumed that a sinking fund will grow.

Discount rates

Discount rates are the rates of interest selected when calculating the present value of a future cost or benefit. This accords with the time value of money principle which determines that holding a sum of money now is preferable to receiving a sum of money in the future. There is a tendency to see this in terms of the obvious depreciatory effect of inflation, but the principle holds true even if there is no inflation. This is because an investor will prefer to hold money rather than wait for it because this enables a free choice over how to utilise that money.

Capitalisation rates are the discount rates at which net income is discounted to ascertain capital value, thus allowing for the time value of money on future income or capital.

Discounting is the process whereby sums due to be received in the future are equated to their current value. It is based upon the supposition that capital could be invested to earn interest rather than being tied up in a specific investment.

Discounted cash flow

Discounted cash flow (DCF) is concerned with those techniques of investment appraisal which discount future cash flows. It should be recognised that even the conventional investment method of property valuation, which discounts future rental flows to arrive at a capital value, is a form of DCF albeit a relatively unsophisticated one.

The discounted cash flow yield is the internal rate of return. This is the rate of interest at which all future cash flows, including the initial investment capital, must be discounted to arrive at a net present value of zero. So, in the case of a property investment, this would be the discount rate which equates the net present value of all future rental incomes to the net present value of the acquisition cost of the investment or its market value. In this context the internal rate of return is usually expressed as either the equated or the equivalent yield – two similar terms with distinct meanings, but terms which have given rise to particular confusion in the past.

The equivalent yield discounts future incomes at current rental values whereas the equated yield takes account of "expected future rental changes due to variations in the value of money"[7]. In other words, the equated yield takes account of growth in rents. The growth rate is the rate at which rents or capital values have increased or decreased in the past or are predicted to change in the future.

The implied growth rate is the rate at which the rental income from a rack rented property will need to increase to match a target gross redemption yield. The implication is that, to be attractive at relatively low yields, property investments, say prime shops at 6%, imply growth at a certain level otherwise they would be unattractive compared with the gross redemption yields on government stock at around 7–8%. This is, of course, the fundamental difference between inflation-prone and inflation-proof investments.

Opportunity cost is the return or benefit foregone in pursuing one particular investment opportunity compared with another. It is often used as the basis of selection for the target or criterion rate as the starting point of DCF analysis to find the net present value of an investment.

Stocks and shares

Time was when property investment valuation was regarded as unique, practised in isolation. It is now widely accepted that property investment takes place in the broader context of investment generally so today's valuer must develop an awareness of other main investment vehicles. Property yields can no longer be seen as isolated from the yields on stocks and shares.

The terms flat yield, running yield and straight yield can all mean the same thing, the present income expressed as a percentage of the current value. In the case of stocks this is distinct from the redemption yield which is the internal rate of return on the stock allowing for income and capital gain and can be expressed either gross or net of tax. The gross redemption yield has the wider significance as the reference point against which many market yields are measured. Still on the subject of stock, the nominal yield is the percentage rate stated on the face of the bond. as distinct from the real rate which is the actual return on capital invested in stocks and shares (see MFS Government Stock, April 17 1993).

Finally, the earnings yield refers to the earnings of a share derived from profits net of corporation tax expressed as a percentage of the share price. It is the reciprocal of the price earnings (P/E) ratio. The dividend yield is the dividend as a percentage of the current share price.

As the valuation profession has tended to borrow its terminology freely, but not always consistently, care should be taken to identify what is meant by a particular term used in a particular context. But there is an increasing need for precision as the world of the property valuer ceases to be independent of other forms of investment.

References

[1]Jones Lang Wootton *Glossary of Property Terms* Estates Gazette 1989 (The definitions for the terms picked out in bold can be referred to in the glossary)

[2] Baum A & Crosby N *Property Investment Appraisal* Routledge 1988

[3] Baum A & Crosby N *Property Investment Appraisal* Routledge 1988

[4] Baum A & Crosby N *Property Investment Appraisal* Routledge 1988

[5] Crosby N *Chartered Surveyor Monthly* October 1991

[6] Millington *An Introduction to Property Valuation* (3rd edition) Estates Gazette 1988

[7] Jones Lang Wootton *Glossary of Property Terms* Estates Gazette 1989

See also:

Calculating the APR "Mainly for Students" *Estates Gazette* 9321:109

Government Stock "Mainly for Students" *Estates Gazette* 9315:139

Contributed by Phil Askham.

CHAPTER 16

Property cycles explained

First published in Estates Gazette November 25, 1995

The slump at present occurring in property values has been described as the low point in the current property cycle. What is meant by the property cycle in this context?

Interest in the concept of a property cycle has been revitalised by the recent boom and collapse in the market. The RICS recently commissioned a study of "Economic Cycles and Property Cycles", undertaken jointly by Investment Property Databank and the University of Aberdeen.

It was interesting that the authors dedicated the report to "all those who saw their jobs destroyed, or their livelihoods blighted, by the property crash of the early 1990s"[1] – clearly highlighting the drastic effect of property cycles on the industry – but it should not be forgotten that the property cycle can have wider implications for the economy as a whole. This most recent downturn has emphasised the relationship between the property cycle and the financial stability of the national economy.

J Coakley, writing on the integration of the property market with the financial sector, concludes that:

the threat posed by the current property crisis to the financial system is relatively more serious than it was in the 1970s, as the main players are the larger banks rather than small secondary banks. This reflects the increased integration of the property and financial markets. One of the worrying aspects of the current crisis is that a recovery in real-estate values seems remote even in mid-1993, and this seems likely to prolong the recession as consumer expenditure remains in a depressed state. The possibility of the property crisis spilling over to the financial system more generally – the so-called contagion effect – is thereby sustained.[2]

And it is not just a phenomenon being seen in the UK. All developed countries have a property cycle. Steven Grenadier, writing in *Journal of Real Estate Finance and Economics*, notes:

the currently distressed state of the US real market is deservedly a matter of great concern. However, the appearance of abnormally high vacancy rates combined with plummeting market values is by no means a new phenomenon.[3]

What may, however, be a more recent development is the emergence of a global cycle. Professor Mervyn Lewis, of the University of Nottingham, [4] shows a very close correlation between changes in nominal rental values for offices in Boston, London, Madrid, Melbourne, Milan, Paris, Stockholm and Zurich.

This suggests that global forces are at work influencing the property cycle, the probability being that this is in some way related to the globalisation of finance in recent years.

Definitions
The discussion so far has concentrated on the importance of property cycles to the property industry, the national economy and the global economy. However, it is clearly necessary to define what is meant by the property cycle and to consider whether there is one cycle or a number of cycles.

However, the RICS brief for the research project on property cycles left the definition of the cycle open; indeed, the report defined the property cycle in a new and unique way.

A useful starting point is to consider the traditional economic cycles, the classic treatment of these being by Schumpeter (1939)[5]. Students may find a more recent review by Sherman (1991)[6] useful.

Essentially a business cycle describes fluctuations in economic activity which, historical analysis will show, proceed in an irregular path with upward spurts followed by pauses and even relapses. The word cycle suggests that there is some regular pattern to these oscillations of good and bad times. Figure 1 shows a simplified version of the traditional business cycle.

- **Depression** . . . A depression is characterised by heavy unemployment, a low level of consumer demand and surplus productive capacity plus low business confidence.
- **Recovery** . . . Employment, income and consumer spending all begin to in crease; investment also increases and business expectations become more favourable.
- **Boom** . . . As the recovery continues, industries become fully

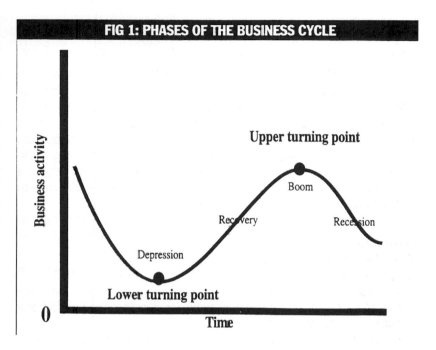

FIG 1: PHASES OF THE BUSINESS CYCLE

utilised and bottlenecks begin to appear – leading to price increases.

- **Recession** . . . Once a recession sets in it tends to gather its own momentum; consumption, employment and investment all begin to fall and business expectations become negative.

More than one cycle?

It is important to appreciate that no two cycles are the same. The extent and depth vary considerably; in some the recession phase is short and therefore the resulting effect on the economy is mild, whereas in others a full-scale period of depression sets in, as in the 1930s. The upturns show a similar range, some having a minimal outcome on inflation, others leading to severe inflation. Students will find it a useful exercise to apply each stage of the business cycle to recent events in the property market.

Richard Barras [7] has taken the four cycles identified in economic literature and linked them to the property cycle.

These are:

- The classical business cycle of four to five years' duration acting on all aspects of economic activity and operating on the property market through occupier demand.
- Long cycles of nine to 10 years' duration which are generated by the exceptionally long production lags involved in property development, creating a tendency for supply to outstrip demand in every other business cycle.
- Long swings with a period of up to 20 years are associated with major building booms; these may occur in every other long cycle of development; they are typically speculative in nature and of a scale sufficient to generate distinctive new phases of urban development.
- Long waves lasting up to 50 years have been proposed to explain alternating phases of high and low growth in the industrialised world economy, with each new wave being initiated by the adoption of a universal new technology such as steam power or electronics.

It should be noted that there is considerable controversy about the existence of longer-period cycles.

To see how the property cycle might operate, it is useful to consider the major building booms of the early 1970s and late 1980s, noting the particular influence that they have had on the property market of the past 25 years.

A conceptual model of how the building cycle may work is proposed by Barras and is illustrated in Figure 2.

The model shows how a building boom is generated by the interaction of the business cycle in the real economy, the credit cycle in the money economy and the long cycle of development in the property market.

A strong business cycle upturn coinciding with a shortage of available property is the starting point. This causes rents and capital values to increase, which in turn encourages new development; if the economy accompanies this upturn a full-blown boom may occur, leading to further speculative developments financed by an expansion of bank credit. A major building boom results. However, because of the nature of the construction industry, supply is, initially, little affected and rents continue to rise. Invariably, when the new buildings come into the market, the business cycle has moved into its downswing, causing a falling demand for property. Thus, just at the point when supply is

Figure 2: How the Building Cycle Works

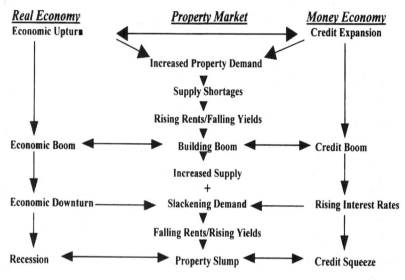

Source: Barras (1994)

increased, demand is falling; consequently there is a dive in rents and hence values. The process tends to feed itself, leading to a property slump characterised by depressed values, high levels of vacancy and widespread bankruptcies in the property sector, a picture all too familiar to members of the property professions.

Barras suggests that the effects of such a slump may well last through the next business cycle; the surplus property means that there is no shortage of space in the next upturn. Furthermore, when the next long cycle of development does pick up, it will tend to be demand-driven with minimal speculative development because the banking system is still grappling with the debt problems of the latest boom. Thus, another long cycle will need to proceed before the necessary conditions will be in place for the onset of another speculative boom. Barras suggests that herein lies the tendency for major property booms to occur in every second long cycle of development, and in every fourth short cycle of business activity.

It is important to appreciate that Barras is suggesting no more than a tendency which could well be disrupted by a wide range of political and economic events.

In its report, the RICS, as already noted above, has developed its own and very specific definition of the property cycle, separating it from the more general business cycle which we have just considered:

Property cycles are recurrent but irregular fluctuations in the rate of all property total returns, which are also apparent in many other indicators of property activity, but with varying leads and lags against the all-property cycle.

The definition adopted follows from the definition of property used – which was commercial investment property with the adoption of the rate of return as the most comprehensive indicator of investment property performance.

Several distinct components of property industry occupier markets make up the cycle – the development industry and the investment markets.

The RICS report concludes:

- The UK property industry shows a recurrent cycle which meets the qualitative definition conventionally applied to economic cycles, but cannot be described definitively by statistical techniques.
- The property cycle is the compounded result of cyclical influences from the wider economy, which are coupled with cyclical tendencies inherent to property markets.
- The critical linkage between property and economic cycles can, in the main, be captured in simple models which are intuitively plausible and statistically sound.

As in economic cycles in general, the property cycle consists of recurrent upswings and downswings which vary in length, scale and composition.

This review of the literature would suggest that there is a range of property cycles depending on the particular aspects of property considered, and activity in the property sector does follow a recurrent pattern of boom and bust. A future article will look at the most recent boom and subsequent collapse in the property market and consider the implications for the industry.

References

[1] Royal Institution of Chartered Surveyors (1994) *Economic*

Cycles and Property Cycles RICS, London.

[2] Coakley J (1994) "The Integration of Property and Financial Markets" *Environment and Planning* 1994 Vol 26.

[3] Grenadier S (1995) "The Persistence of Real Estate Cycles" *Journal of Real Estate Finance and Economics* Vol 10.

[4] Lewis M K (1994) Banking on Real Estate Discussion *Papers in Economics* No 9416, University of Nottingham.

[5] Schumpeter J A (1939) *Business Cycles* McGraw-Hill, New York

[6] Sherman H J (1991) *The Business Cycle* Princeton University Press, Princeton NJ

[7] Barras R (1994) "Property and the Economic Cycle: Building Cycles Revisited" *Journal of Property Research* Vol 11.

Contributed by Dave Egan.

CHAPTER 17

The Loan Arrangements: Mortgages

First published in Estates Gazette January 24, 1998

Many residential mortgages now offer interest rate discounts and other incentives. How do mortgages differ, and what hazards await unwary borrowers?

The prospect of higher interest rates continuing through 1998 underlines the significance of mortgages on the housing market. Although financial advisers usually arrange mortgages, estate agents and general practice surveyors should have a working knowledge of the types of residential mortgage available, and of the factors that determine the best product for each individual borrower.

Mortgage lenders include banks and building societies as well as specialists such as the telephone-based mortgage lenders and insurance companies, which offer products aimed at the self-employed or borrowers with poor credit ratings. Lenders vary their mortgage products in relation to the borrower's financial status, the proportion of the property's value that is being lent or any incentives that are being offered. Mortgages are either "repayment" (also known as "capital and interest") or "interest only".

Repayment mortgages

With repayment mortgages, capital is paid off together with interest over the mortgage term. In the early stages of the term, the bulk of the repayments are applied to cover interest costs. As the debt reduces, more capital is paid off. The mortgage is repaid by equal monthly payments throughout the term, so the longer the term of the mortgage, the lower the monthly repayments but the higher the aggregate sum repaid.

At the end of the term, the repayment mortgage guarantees that the property has been paid for in full, provided all payments have been made. Life assurance cover is not essential for repayment mortgages but is often recommended, especially where the borrower has dependants.

With interest-only mortgages, only the interest element is paid to the lender during the term. Separate contributions are made to an "investment plan" or "savings plan" which is set up to repay the mortgage at the end of the term. The investment plan is usually linked to a life assurance policy.

The investment plan can be an endowment policy, a pension or a personal equity plan (PEP). In some cases, the plan could be a portfolio of investments held by the borrower.

An endowment includes an investment plan and life assurance. A "unit-linked endowment" buys units in an investment fund. The unit price governs the value of the fund. Income from the investments in the fund is reinvested rather than paid to the borrower. A "with-profits endowment" pools the life insurance premiums with those of all others participating in the life fund. The premiums cannot be taken back. The level of profits depends on the performance of the fund, and allows for some of the profits to be allocated to reserves to ensure that bonuses can still be paid in years of poor performance.

When the endowment is due to mature, the lending company may pay a terminal bonus. This is substantially greater than annual bonuses and, with the value of the borrower's units in the fund, aims to pay off the mortgage.

Unit-linked endowments are more common than with-profits endowments, which are being phased out, mainly because they rely too much on the terminal bonus to pay off the mortgage and because of concerns over shortfalls.

The personal equity plan (PEP) invests in equities and enjoys tax-free income and capital growth. Annual contributions to PEPs are limited by law and are subject to changes in legislation. For example, the Chancellor's "Green Budget" of December 1997 proposed the introduction of the Individual Savings Account (ISA), which may weaken the tax status of PEPs.

The proceeds of a pension plan can be used to pay off the mortgage. The tax advantages of pension contributions may mean that the pension plan is more efficient than the endowment. Because the purpose of a pension is to provide retirement income, there is a legal limit to the amount of funds that can be withdrawn. With both pension and PEP investment plans, separate life cover may be required.

Lenders may offer a combination of interest rate discounts, fixed-rate terms, cashbacks and repayment methods within a single loan. A variety of more imaginative products are appearing on the market, for example, overdraft-style mortgages, which provide a cheque book with which to add small amounts of debt to the capital sum; and mortgages that offer lower interest rates in exchange for a share in the capital appreciation of the property when it is sold.

A lender's marketing pitch may be to state discounted headline rates of interest or cashbacks. But further investigation may reveal that they are subject to a 25% deposit requirement, for example, or that the lender's standard variable rate is higher than the rates of lenders who are not offering such incentives.

When arranging mortgages, borrowers – particularly first-time buyers and those at the lower end of the market – can be preoccupied with the initial level of mortgage repayments, and not too concerned about the higher payments that will become due when the discount period or a favourable fixed-rate period ends. If interest rates also move adversely, or personal circumstances change, the borrower's financial position may alter substantially. It may therefore be unwise to borrow the maximum amount allowed. Tax relief such as MIRAS may also be subject to change.

Other costs and restrictions
Some lenders will not charge borrowers any fees, but others may impose a range of additional costs, for example, application fees, valuation fees and legal fees. For fixed-rate mortgages, a reservation fee is usually required because the lender needs to secure the fixed rate from the money markets. With loans that exceed 75% or 80% of the value of the property, lenders will often charge a mortgage indemnity guarantee, which is a one-off payment that effectively insures the lender against loss should the borrower default.

Redemption penalties are imposed by lenders to discourage the repayment of the mortgage, in part or in full, during the early years. Penalties are common with incentive-ridden loans, and are still likely to be imposed after a discount period or a fixed-rate period has ended. Penalties could include repaying the whole or a proportionate part of a cashback, paying a percentage of the amount being repaid, or paying several months' interest on the amount being repaid. Redemption fees for fixed-rate mortgages may not have to be paid if interest rates have moved to the advantage of the lender.

Borrowers should be aware of the lender's policy on crediting payments to the mortgage account. Some lenders will credit the account upon the receipt of funds, whereas others will credit the account only at the end of the financial year. Where the lender operates a policy of crediting the account only at the end of the year, the repayments would be better saved separately to earn interest until being used to pay off part of the mortgage at the end of the year. If the mortgage is paid off in full, or "redeemed", during the year, it will generally be on the basis of an immediate credit. Lenders' policies on this vary and should be checked.

Some lenders insist that borrowers sign up to the lender's own buildings insurance, life assurance or mortgage/income/employment protection insurance. These may not be essential and may not be the most competitively priced products available.

Researching the market

Although lenders may offer similar variable rates, mortgage products can vary greatly in terms of the incentives available, the additional costs and the supplementary products included.

The savings that are possible over the term of the mortgage from competitive interest rates can dwarf the benefits of short-term incentives. Borrowers are advised to research the market to find the best deal to suit their own circumstances, and make historical comparisons of the lending rates of the competing lenders. Unscrupulous lenders prey on the uninformed.

Contributed by Austen Imber.

CHAPTER 18

Stock answers: The UK equity market

First published in Estates Gazette October 4, 1997

Can you please explain how the UK equity market works, what factors influence share prices and the value of the market, and run through the terms used by the financial press?

Investment can be defined as parting with capital, at risk, in return for a future income flow and/or capital growth. Investors may select from a wide range of broad investment opportunities, such as equities, bonds or cash, and will therefore be interested in comparative performance.

Property is often regarded as an equity-type investment, as it shares the characteristics of low initial yields and future capital appreciation. In other respects, property and equities differ, but the general point for students of the property market to appreciate is the way in which the performances of different investment opportunities impinge on each other. Some knowledge of the whole range of investment vehicles is therefore imperative.

Equities

Equities, mainly ordinary shares, are issued by companies to raise money from investors who benefit from dividends and share-price increases. Shareholders include the pension and insurance funds, other companies and private investors. Shares are traded on the Stock Exchange and companies are listed under sectors from Building and Construction, to Leisure and Hotels, and Property. The main index is the FTSE 100 index, or Footsie. This represents the capital value of the 100 largest or "blue chip" companies. The index excludes dividend payments and makes no allowance for inflation. Changes in membership occur as companies grow and decline, or are taken over. Large new issues such as privatisation and the conversion of building societies into banks are other factors. The FTSE Mid 250 index includes the next 250 largest companies.

Trading in shares is via a market-maker. Market-makers make their profit from quoting investors a higher price (the offer price) to buy shares than to sell shares (the bid price). The price range is termed the bid-offer spread. This can be as narrow as 1% for the FTSE 100 companies, but will be wider for smaller companies whose shares are less frequently traded and/or characterised by more volatile price movements. The financial press quote the average of the spread, known as the mid-price, and publish high and low prices that have been reached during the calendar year or during the past 52 weeks, depending on the time of year.

Factors influencing the value of the equity market

Share prices and the value of the equity market are determined by the level of company earnings, the level of dividend payments, future prospects and the returns available from other investments. The most favourable economic climate for equities is low inflation, low interest rates and rising company earnings.

The equity market will be concerned by the prospect of higher interest rates, which will usually result from the need to curb inflationary pressures. The market looks for signs of inflation which include raw material and commodity prices, wage rates, consumer spending and taxation rates. Increased interest rates reduce company earnings because consumer spending is constrained and because the cost of debt financing is higher (possibly also limiting investment expansion and restricting growth).

Companies with high levels of debt will be more exposed to adverse interest rate movements than companies with low levels of debt or cash balances. Certain sectors and industries will be more adversely affected by interest rate movements than others. Furthermore, higher interest rates reduce share prices because future earnings are discounted at a higher rate.

A rise in interest rates will not always cause downward pressure on equity prices. A rise could be a pre-emptive strike to prevent higher rates being required in the future. The market welcomes lower and more stable long-term rates. An interest rate rise may be less than the market had expected, or a decision to increase rates could end the uncertainty and speculation that had, until the announcement, depressed prices.

The exchange rate can also affect companies and sectors in different ways, depending on the overall economic climate. Buoyant consumer spending, for example, may see the UK service sector flourish. Where the UK is at a more advanced stage in the economic cycle than other major trading nations, interest rates may be relatively higher, and still rising, to restrain inflationary pressures. Higher interest rates increase the investment demand for sterling and increase the strength of the pound. A stronger pound makes manufacturers' exports more expensive. Initially, export margins will be squeezed and, in due course, trade volumes may fall.

Combined with the unfavourable conversion of overseas earnings into sterling, and the effects of import penetration, companies' earnings are reduced. Even if the value of the pound subsequently weakens, companies may have lost market share, and recovery will be only progressive. Companies can hedge against adverse exchange rate movements only for so long. Leading shares, such as FTSE 100 manufacturers, which have a strong international earnings exposure, will be particularly hit. Share prices will suffer even though the anti-inflationary consequences of a strong pound can hold interest rates down and benefit the market at large.

The strength of the pound may, at the same time, enable retailers to benefit from cheaper imports and increased consumer spending. The ability for retailers to adopt a profiteering price policy will depend on the underlying competitiveness in the import and domestic retail markets.

Equities will benefit where the economy is controlled by increased taxation rather than higher interest rates. The exchange rate will be more competitive and improved government finances will be more conducive to economic (and possibly political) stability. Economic stability and lower long-term interest rates encourage investment, accelerate economic growth and increase earnings.

Equities are influenced by the returns available from other investments, namely bonds/gilts, cash deposits and, to a far lesser degree, property. The income on gilts is fixed but the price is adjusted to produce the appropriate yield. The Treasury 8% 2013 stock, for example, when issued at £100, yields 8%. If the price rises to £105, it will yield 7.6%. The gilt will be redeemed for £100 in 2013 even though the capital value will vary while the gilt is in issue. Long-dated gilts (over 15 years to maturity) see larger price movements than short-dated gilts (less than five years to maturity) because they are less influenced by the value at redemption.

There is greater risk and uncertainty associated with equities than gilts. Equities always incorporate an equity risk premium. In recent years, gilt yields have been around twice those of equities. It is therefore the prospect of capital gains that makes equity investing worthwhile.

Gilts, like equities, are sensitive to inflation and interest rates. The reaction depends on the level of inflation and the stage in the economic cycle. Signs of economic growth, for example, could cause gilt investors to be concerned about inflation but cause equity investors to anticipate stronger earnings growth. Gilts do best when both inflation and growth are lower than normal in a low interest rate climate.

Gilts will be particularly influenced by the government's finances. If taxation and spending produce a relatively high budget deficit or Public Sector Borrowing Requirement, an additional supply of gilts issued by the government will depress prices and increase yields. Increased gilt yields may make equities less attractive.

Only the income from cash deposits varies, so only higher interest rates will produce higher returns, increasing the attraction of cash holdings compared with equities.

The UK equity market is also affected by world markets. The FTSE 100 index is strongly influenced by Wall Street's Dow Jones Industrial Average in the US, especially where there are large price changes or where prices are falling. The Dow is the equivalent to the FTSE 100 index, although only 30 companies are included. The sterling–dollar exchange rate tends to have a greater impact than other exchange rates on the UK equity market. The sterling–deutchsmark rate tends to have a greater effect on the UK economy as a whole.

Factors influencing share prices

Share prices essentially reflect supply and demand. Market-makers can, however, move prices without trading taking place, sometimes in the absence of price-sensitive information. If prices are expected to fall, for example, market-makers may reduce quote prices in order to avoid big selling orders. The larger stocks will generally have a sufficient number of market-makers to reduce the possibility of unexplainable price movements.

In addition to earnings, dividends, growth potential and the various economic and market factors, share prices will be sensitive to the release of company results, earnings estimates, changes in taxation or other legislation, profit warnings, financial problems, capital reconstructions, asset revaluations, the exposure of creative accounting, brokers' opinion and recommendations, newspaper comment, senior management changes and reports of directors buying or selling shares in their own company.

Takeover bids and merger proposals, or even rumours of them, can cause substantial price increases in the target company. Companies in the same sector are often also affected. The share price of the bidder could fall where it is felt that the company is overpaying, where the benefits of the transaction are questionable, or where surplus funds could be better spent on a special dividend or a share buy-back.

Most investment funds require a greater weighting in the top companies. This is especially true in the case of tracker funds which seek to match the returns from the index as a whole. Promotion into an index, or demotion from an index, will affect prices.

Share prices can be influenced by companies changing sector, by activity in the options market or by speculative trading such as short selling, where investors sell shares which are then bought after the price has hopefully fallen. Share prices will be adjusted downwards where the entitlement to dividends or other rights pass. From time to time prices will be affected by cases of insider trading, market manipulation and share swindles.

Fundamental factors will assert themselves in the long run. In the short term the market will be subject to imperfections and inefficiencies, speculation, sentiment, psychology, herd instinct, fear, greed and mania. These factors cause prices to overshoot or undershoot from their fundamental position, but provide scope for investors to achieve excessive returns.

Even institutional activity can be short term orientated because of the importance of fund managers' quarterly performance figures.

The equity market and price trends
The equity market can be unpredictable and fickle but trends do emerge. When a company reports good results, the market may have already reflected them in the share price. Once it is apparent that the results do not induce a buying of the shares, and a consequent price rise, investors sell to take profits that may have

accrued in anticipation of the results. Better than expected results could see a modest immediate price rise followed by a gradual but significant increase over the following months as the market re-rates the value of future earnings (see price earnings ratio later). Where a company has a good growth record, disappointing results in one year can dramatically reduce a share price which has until then placed a high value on future earnings.

Where profits are falling, or where sentiment has changed, the market often fails to discount the share price as much as it should, causing a progressive decline in the share price. If bad news fails to decrease a share price, it may have reached its lowest point. Similarly, if good news fails to increase a share price, it is unlikely to rise further for the time being.

Where the market retreats, or is expected to retreat after rising progressively, there is a tendency for investors to take profits on the shares that have performed well, such as smaller company growth shares. Investors may then seek the more defensive blue chip stocks. Sharp price falls can occur when investors are confident and overcommitted to equities. An inflow of funds from the public via unit trusts, for example, may have driven the market higher than valuation fundamentals would suggest as being appropriate. Bear trends (falling prices) are sharper than bull runs (rising prices). What was thought to be a market crash at the time can be viewed over the longer term as merely being a correction. The market dislikes uncertainty and will often make a disproportionately large discount to reflect the associated risks.

Financial statistics and price evaluation

A number of performance measures are used in the equity market. The capital value or market capitalisation of a company is the share price multiplied by the number of shares in issue.

The earnings of a company may be expressed as earnings per share (earnings divided by the number of shares in issue) or expressed as the earnings yield (earnings divided by market capitalisation, expressed as a percentage). Earnings per share is considered because the number of shares in issue can vary because of rights issues or mergers, for example.

The dividends paid out by a company will be expressed as dividends per share or the dividend yield (both calculated similarly to earnings). The dividend yield represents the percentage annual return on the current share price, including final and interim dividends. This is expressed either gross of tax or net of tax at the rate of 20%. High yields may seem to indicate good value, but could be due to declining fortunes or higher risk. Investors accept relatively lower dividends where the prospects for capital growth are relatively better.

Dividend coverage is the earnings divided by the dividend. This represents the number of times dividends are covered by earnings and demonstrates the ability to sustain dividend payments.

The price earnings ratio, or the multiple of a share, is the market capitalisation divided by earnings. The P/E ratio is the principal valuation measure for equities and is effectively the discounted present value of future earnings. The ratio is useful for comparing companies, particularly those in the same sector, but is not a good guide for companies with variable earnings. The higher the ratio, the greater the expectation of sustainable growth. The ratio varies between economic and equity market cycles. The ratio can be based on historic or future earnings.

The net asset value of a company is its assets less its liabilities. This is also expressed as net asset value per share. NAV is normally applied to specialist companies such as investment trusts or property companies whose share prices are assessed in terms of the discount or premium to NAV. NAV will also be used when companies are being taken over or folding.

A company's accounts provide more detailed information, enabling attention to be given to factors such as turnover, cost control, profit margins, the composition of earnings, the effects of taxation, liquidity and solvency, funding and debt, and the return on capital. Other useful indicators include the optimism and tone of the chairman's statement or directors' reports, the calibre of senior personnel, unusual or frequent changes of senior personnel, the qualification of an auditor's report, a change of auditors, the share ownership structure and directors' shareholdings. Reports of directors buying and selling shares in their own company can often be a useful guide, especially where trading is by a number of directors.

Finally, for those readers who might be tempted into considering the opportunities that may be available to them as private equity investors, the standard caveats – that the value of shares and other investments can go up as well as down, investors may not get back all or any of the amount originally invested, past performance is not a guide to future performance – should always be borne in mind.

Over the long term, however, equities are expected to yield superior total returns (income and capital growth) to other forms of investment despite seeing periods of volatility and falling value.

Contributed by Austen Imber.

PROFESSIONAL SKILLS

CHAPTER 19

Cross-examination

First published in Estates Gazette June 26, 1993

What are the aims of cross-examination in legal proceedings?

The opportunity for a non-lawyer to cross-examine a witness may arise in many settings. It may be while bringing or defending a "small claim" in the local county court, or while objecting to a decision of some sort before a local government committee, or representing a client at a planning inquiry, or challenging an expert witness at a rent review arbitration, or at any number of other venues (formal or informal) where it has not been possible or necessary or (in some cases) even advisable to use a professional advocate. Just as there are certain negotiating skills of which a beginner can profitably become aware, so there are certain objectives in cross-examination which a non-lawyer can quickly learn. Likewise, there are certain trips and traps which can be the subject of timely early warnings. (See Phil Askham's article on negotiating, [1988] 45 EG 121 reprinted in *The Best of Mainly for Students*, 1993, pp149–153).

Purpose

Cross-examination has three possible purposes, although it would be very undesirable if a non-lawyer found himself in a situation where he had to fulfil all three. These can be summarised as eliciting, undermining and destroying.

- Eliciting evidence (in this context) means the obtaining of information from a witness which he has not previously given, and which there is no reason to suppose he will be reluctant to give if he is asked to do so. He may not have given that information in his "evidence-in-chief" because: he may not have realised its importance; he may have forgotten it; he may not have been asked about it; he may himself be wondering why he has not been asked to mention it. It is the cross-examiner's purpose to bring out all the points which are favourable to his side and, since this may depend upon the co-operation of the witness, it is usually best to do this before turning to any subsequent line of questioning which may cause the witness to become argumentative, resentful or taciturn.

- Undermining the evidence of a witness is, of course, the most obvious purpose of a cross-examination. It is sometimes called "cross-examination as to issue". The purpose of such a cross-examination will show (if possible) that the witness's evidence is irrelevant, mistaken, exaggerated, taken out of context, or otherwise unreliable, even if the witness himself is honest and determined to do his best.

- Destroying evidence (in this context) means seeking to show that the witness is biased, untruthful, self-serving, or otherwise unworthy of belief. It is usually known as "cross-examination as to credit". It is rare outside the criminal courts, and it will often make judges, arbitrators and lay tribunals antagonistic to the party making such allegations if there is no solid basis for this line of questioning. It is almost impossible to combine this approach with eliciting new evidence: it will be very difficult to submit that the witness is reliable in so far as he states things which are helpful to the cross-examiner, but totally incapable of telling the truth in every other regard.

Duties

When a person acts as an advocate his first duty is to the court or arbitrator or other tribunal before whom he is appearing. This takes priority over his duty to his client. He may not make statements or allegations which he knows to be untrue, although he is not under any duty to refer to adverse matters of fact if his opponents have overlooked them. (He will, however, be under a duty to refer to all relevant matters of law, whether these assist the arguments he wishes to put forward or not.) The emphasis here, however, is on what the advocate knows to be true or false, not on what he believes to be true or false. In this respect he is acting in a different capacity from that of an expert witness – which makes it unwise for a professional man to attempt to be both an advocate and a witness in the same case.

It is very important for an advocate not to judge his client because, if he does so, he usurps the function of the court or tribunal which has the responsibility of deciding the issue. This does not excuse an advocate, or any other professional adviser, if he fails to give his client full and fair advice beforehand, but this must stop short of telling him what statements of fact it would be best for him to make when giving his evidence.

Some argue that calling a witness to give his evidence-in-chief is a more difficult task than cross-examining an opponent's witness because it is part of the practice of cross-examination to attempt to put words into the witness's mouth: "Would you agree with me that . . .? What really happened was this, was it not? But the proper thing to do in those circumstances was such and such, was it not?". But in dealing with one's own witnesses care must always be taken not to ask "leading questions", ie questions which are capable of assisting a forgetful, lazy or confused witness by giving, or even hinting at, the answer being looked for. An advocate must therefore content himself with neutral questions.

In addition to duties owed by an advocate to the court or the tribunal before which he is appearing (or, indeed, to the profession to which he belongs) a cross-examiner also owes a duty to the witness he is questioning – known as the duty to "put the case". It sometimes conflicts with the advice usually given to cross-examiners, namely "Don't cross-examine clever witnesses".

"Putting the case"

There is no doubt that it is often wise not to cross-examine a witness at all – if his evidence has not been harmful to the cross-examining party, nothing may be gained, and much may be lost. The questions put to him in cross-examination may remind him of things he previously forgot to say, or give him an opportunity to refer to facts about which his own advocate forgot to question him. Worse than this, the cross-examination will give the first advocate the chance to re-examine the witness, repairing any shortcomings (and clarifying any ambiguities) in the evidence previously given.

Much the same advice is often given in the case of clever, enthusiastic witnesses, who are likely to "score points" in cross-examination. It makes no sense to give them an additional opportunity to harm the cross-examining party, particularly if they have saved up their best answers for the ordeal which they expect to come. Nothing deflates them more than to be dismissed with the comment "I have no questions to ask this witness", as if their evidence had been irrelevant.

Sir Henry Hawkins (1817–1907), who was a very accomplished cross-examiner in land compensation cases (as well as criminal cases), often used to win compensation claims by not cross-examining expert witnesses at all. In his *Reminiscences* (1904) he refers to an amusing example of this technique relating to a claim by the owners of a medical shop in Hungerford Market. This shop, and the whole of the market, had to be cleared away in the 1860s to make room for Charing Cross Station. His opponent in the dispute was a Mr Lloyd and the claim was to be judged by a special jury.

Lloyd had expatiated on the value of the situation, the highroad between Waterloo Station and the Strand, immense traffic and grand frontage. To prove all this he called a multitude of witnesses, who kissed the same book and swore the same thing, almost in the same words. But to his great surprise I did not cross-examine. Lloyd was bewildered, and said that I had admitted the value by not cross-examining, and he should not call any more witnesses. I then addressed the jury, and said: A multitude of witnesses may prove anything they like, but my friend has started with an entirely erroneous view of the situation . . .

Hawkins then went on to argue that a shop selling medical appliances was a very different thing from (for example) a public house selling beer. While farmers arriving for a cattle show in Hungerford Market might buy beer, because of the proximity of a pub, they would not be likely to buy a truss because of the proximity of a medical shop – thus considerably reducing the compensation: "what it lacked in money . . .[it] got in laughter".

The problem with this approach is that most judges and arbitrators and professional decision-makers will strongly object to an advocate who advances an argument, or calls evidence of facts, if those arguments or those facts have not been put to a relevant witness in cross-examination. If, for example, it is an advocate's contention that an expert valuer is valuing the goodwill of a business on the wrong basis, or is using inappropriate comparables, his arguments to this effect (and the evidence of his supporting witnesses) will be devalued and, perhaps, excluded altogether, if the allegations in question were not "put" to the expert valuer in cross-examination.

As an act of natural justice, a witness is entitled to know what allegations are going to be made against him later (or have already been made against him in his absence). This, in short, is the duty to "put the case". It is the reason why the phrase "I put it to you . . ." is often heard in cross-examinations, although there is no need to use such a phrase. Even a question which summarises evidence already given, or to be given, and asks for a response to it, is better than the pedestrian formulation, "I put it to you . . .". Since experts' reports are almost always exchanged in advance nowadays, greater advantage may sometimes be gained from using an impressive report:

Q: Have you received a copy of Dr World-Expert's report? A: Yes.

Q: Would you look at para 6, please. Dr World-Expert says there . . . (reading it out, loudly and sympathetically, but not too extensively). That's the very point you haven't mentioned, I think. Why is that? A: (Explanation given.)

Q: Well that, of course, flatly contradicts what Dr World-Expert says in para 8, doesn't it? (Here some questions about Dr World-Expert's undoubted experience and reputation might be appropriate.) A: (Further explanation.)

Q: I see. Well we should be hearing evidence later on from a Mr Alko. He is going to say that he visited all the public houses in the High Road that day and found them all to be empty. If that is true, would that alter your opinion? A: I can't see how that can possibly be true.

Q: Well, we shall see. Now turning to Professor Mind-Blower's report – would you look at p38 please. Oh, did you not receive a copy?

It should be noted that the obligation to "put" a client's case to opposing witnesses does not require the same ground to be gone over repetitiously with each in turn. The duty may be discharged by cross-examining one witness (perhaps the most vulnerable) and leaving the others alone, unless particular allegations are going to be directed at them individually.

Trips and traps

The biggest trap for the unwary participant in legal proceedings (apart from asking unnecessary questions) is to believe that a cross-examination is an opportunity to make a speech or to argue with a witness. Cross-examination is, of course, about questioning. Short questions are the most effective and so complex points should be broken down. If a document has to be referred to, the witness (and everybody else listening to the questioning) should be referred to the page and paragraph number and/or the date.

(Bundles should always be numbered in advance, and uniformity of numbering should be agreed with all other parties.) The extract should be read out. If it is something which the witness himself wrote, he may be asked (without unfairness) to read it out himself.

There should then follow a short question, such as: "Is that accurate? Why did you write that? Look at the date – that was written two months before the incident you have just told us about . . . Why didn't you mention such and such? That puts a completely different complexion on things, doesn't it?"

Even if a document is not being referred to, short questions are always the most memorable, and portray long and rambling answers in a most unsympathetic way. In this respect, the cross-examination of Dr Crippen by Sir Richard Muir in 1910 is always put forward as a model. (It will be recalled that Dr Crippen denied murdering his wife and claimed that she had left him to go to America.)

Q: On the early morning of the 1st February you were left alone in your house with your wife? A: Yes.
Q: She was alive? A: Yes.
Q: And well. A: Yes.
Q: Do you know any person who has seen her alive since? A: I do not.
Q: Do you know of any person in the world who has had a letter from her since? A: I do not.
Q: Do you know any person who can prove any fact shewing that she ever left your house alive? A: Absolutely not.

Muir then went on (by using similarly short questions) to show that Crippen had not made any timely inquiries and had not even contacted the local cab rank to see whether she had taken a cab to the station. This left Muir free to comment, in his closing address to the jury, that Crippen was acting from the start as a man who knew that his wife was dead.

Just as it may be a mistake to commence a cross-examination when there is no need for one, it may equally be a mistake to continue with a series of question when (perhaps unexpectedly) a favourable answer has been received. The maxim here is, "When you strike gold, stop digging". The continuation of the questioning may cause the effect and significance of the answer to be forgotten. If it constituted a slip of the part of the witness, continuation of the questioning may give him a chance to retrieve the situation.

Sir Edward Marshall Hall (1858–1929) has often been praised for his brilliant cross-examination of a forensic pathologist in the famous case of *R* v *Seddon* (1912) Notable British Trials series. The prosecution had alleged that Seddon poisoned his lodger with one or more large doses of arsenic administered shortly before her death. Marshall Hall first got the scientist (Sir William Willcox) to admit that the arsenic found in each sample taken from organs in the body had to be multiplied by such factors as 200, 60, 50 and so on, in order to reach an estimate of how much arsenic had been found in the body. He then asked Willcox about arsenic found in the hair:

Q: I notice that (in the table which you prepared) you give only an estimation of 0.4 grain in what is called "proximal" hair. That is the hair nearest the scalp? A: Yes.
Q: And the hair which grows at the extremity is called the "distal" end? A: Yes.
Q: . . . What did you find in the distal end of the hair? A: One three-thousandth – about a quarter as much.
Q: You took a length of hair which was about 12 inches long? A: They varied . . . the average would be about 10 inches.

Having then established that human hair grows at a rate of about six inches per year, and referring to a Royal Commission Report on arsenical poisoning, Marshall Hall was then able to return to the fact that arsenic was found in the "distal" end of the hair, 10 ins away from the scalp:

Q: The presence of arsenic in the distal end of the hair is indicative of the taking of arsenic more than 12 months ago? A: Probably.

This answer was a pearl of great price. It showed that, even if the scientific tests were accurate, the deceased lodger must have been taking small quantities of arsenic over a long period of time, perhaps even before she moved into Seddon's house. Some believe that Marshall Hall should have sat down at that point. In fact, he went on to ask many more questions. This gave the witness the opportunity to come up with the explanation as to how the distal end of the hair had been polluted with arsenic from external sources.

Preparation
All cross-examinations are a combination of preparation and flexibility. The cross-examiner should have prepared, in advance, a

check-list of the facts and admissions which he hopes to get the witness to aver or to concede. He can then make these facts the basis of his final submission to the judge, or arbitrator, or other decision-maker. He must know the bundle of documents to perfection, and must have marked every embarrassing part or set of contradictions with which he wishes to confront a witness.

It is sometimes said that a cross-examiner should never ask a question unless he knows the answer. It is more accurate to say, however, that the cross-examiner should be in a position to know what to do even if the answer is not the one for which he hoped. (Ignoring it, as if it were not important, might be one reaction.)

It is good advice to prepare carefully the first and the last questions. However, the first may have to be discarded because another "start point" commends itself. It is often wise to deal with issues which have made an impact, so that a cross-examination may begin with the last document referred to, or with some unforeseen, but unanswerable, point which will make a lasting impression, having regard to the way in which the evidence-in-chief was given.

The first question, therefore, should be a fall-back one, while the last is more likely to be inflexibly adhered to. Few advocates will be able to base their entire cross-examination on last-minute facts, such as those observed by Sir Henry Hawkins while travelling to a compensation court:

On my way I observed in my carriage a gentleman who was very busy in making calculations on slips of paper, and every now and again mentioning figures at which he had arrived – repeating them to himself. When we got to a station he threw away his paper . . . at every stoppage on our journey he increased his amount. After we had travelled 250 miles, the property he was valuing had attained the handsome figure of £100,000 . . . The next day, when he stepped into the witness box he had not the least idea that I had been his fellow-traveller of the previous night.

In the light of this windfall evidence, Hawkins was able to cross-examine as follows:

Q: When did you view this property, Mr Bunce? I understand that you come from London? A: I saw it this morning.
Q: Did you make any calculations before you saw it? A: No.
Q: Not when you were travelling? Did it not pass through your mind when you were in the train, for instance – "I wonder, now, what that property is worth"? A: I dare say it did, sir.

Q: But don't dare say anything unless it's true .A: I did, then, run it over in my mind.

Q: And I dare say you made notes and can produce them . . . You may as well let me have them. A: I tore them up.

Q: Why? What became of the pieces? A: I threw them away.

Q: Do you remember what price you had arrived at when you reached Peterborough, for instance?

At the end of this cross-examination (and list of stations) the upshot was that the arbitrator reduced Mr Bunce's valuation by 90%!

Contributed by Leslie Blake.

CHAPTER 20

Meeting the challenge: the APC interview

First published in Estates Gazette April 19, 1997

Doing your homework is a vital part of the final APC interview. Candidates must present a positive image and be aware of professional concerns.

The last hurdle for the professional associate candidate is the final assessment interview. Held twice a year as part of the Assessment of Professional Competence (APC), the interview serves to satisfy the RICS that candidates are able to express themselves clearly and demonstrate their understanding of the knowledge gained during the training period. It also shows whether they have an acceptable perception of the roles and responsibilities of a chartered surveyor.

Interviews commence with the candidate's presentation of his critical analysis to a panel of assessors, who are selected to reflect his range of experience. The interview covers matters arising from the presentation as well as general training, matters of concern to the profession and professional ethics.

Candidates will be assessed on an overall review of the pre-assessment submission, the presentation and the interview. Unsuccessful candidates will be referred for a further period of training and a further interview. Success means that the candidate is eligible for election as a Professional Associate.

Philip Marshall, who is experienced in APC training, relates a case study of an APC candidate, "George", whose experience serves to illustrate the key points that candidates should grasp before attending the interview section of the final assessment. Some examples of lines of questioning are illustrated here.

For example, a candidate could be asked to name the president of the RICS, and other straightforward questions. Other questions are intended to reveal a candidate's general knowledge in a given subject and may be followed with more leading questions. General reference might be made to the Landlord and Tenant (Covenants)

Act 1995, say, with a follow-up question on matters affecting the assessment of rent at review when a prohibition on assignment is incorporated into the lease.

Candidates should know the fundamentals of all subject areas, but show depth of knowledge in areas that correspond with their experience. George had only commercial agency experience. He realised his lack of knowledge the week before his final assessment when, on a trip to Manchester to view a site with an experienced investor, he was at a loss to contribute to a discussion on the benefits of property securitisation and the differences between valuations on the open-market-value basis and appraisals of worth.

In order to find out exactly where his deficiencies lay, Marshall engaged George in a general conversation on basic subjects. But mention of the Landlord and Tenant legislation methods referred to in the recent RICS Appraisal and Valuations Standards Boards survey of valuation methodology, which uses such terms as "the layer method using equivalent yields" or "short-cut DCF using both equated yields and ARY" left him completely at sea.

After some remedial study, George went to Manchester again with his knowledgeable investor client. He said that he had had a long discussion about a wide range of issues and that his client had now made an offer for the premises they were viewing.

However, a few weeks after his trip to Manchester, George rang to tell Marshall that the RICS had published *APC: Candidate Guide* January 1997, page 13 of which covers the final assessment interview. In a panic, George asked what "current issues of concern to the profession" were likely to be. Would they be about problems created by fee cutting, or difficulties of finding a well-paid job? (George would do well to be informed about this second query.) Marshall's reply was that questions could quite reasonably include everything to do with a general practitioner's work in the landed profession – from, say, difficulties of valuing contaminated land to methods to use when valuing over-rented investment properties. Thus, topics in groups D–E in the table might well come up more often than in the past.

By way of practical advice, some RICS guidance notes from the past give a sketch of an APC candidate arriving late, wearing sandals and dropping his overhead projector notes. His interview did not go well, even though he was a first-class graduate in estate management from a well-known university.

APC Requirements

Qualification as a chartered surveyor requires:

- an accredited academic qualification; and
- completion of a period of structured practical training that concludes with an assessment of your competence to practise.

The APC itself consists of several elements:

- diary
- record of progress
- summary of experience
- critical analysis of a work-based project

Once these have been completed, candidates may submit themselves for final assessment. This involves attendance at an assessment centre for a 60-minute interview that includes a 10-minute presentation on the critical analysis.

Students may wish to refer back to "General Practice Assessment of Competence", *EG* 9231:62.

What you need to know
A: Essential professional practice
Candidates will be examined on their working knowledge of all practice and guidance notes, codes of professional practice, codes of measurement practice, a good working knowledge of the Red Book (1995) especially Practice Statements 1–7.
Degree of importance: 25%

B: Valuation principles and practice
Questions here will cover fundamental valuation issues ranging from growth-implicit and growth-explicit methodology to problems of valuing over-rented property and the analysis of rent-free periods to determine the rent at review.
Degree of importance: 30%

Tip for 1997: Watch out for the February 1997 publication by the ICS/Investment Property Forum (IPF) information paper on Discounted Cash Flow (DCF) techniques and the calculation of the value of commercial property investments.

C: Landlord and tenant matters
Here the questions have ranged from the types of notices which should be served under various Acts to the effects of a Calderbank letter in a rent review dispute.
Degree of importance: 20%

D: Rating matters

Questions here have ranged from the meaning of an antecedent date to contractors' test applications. The 1996 Bayliss Report, for obvious reasons, should also be looked at.

Degree of importance: 5%

E: Other current issues "of concern to the profession"

This ranges from, say, the level of compensation in compulsory purchase cases (and the 1995 RICS Compensation for Compulsory Acquisition report) to VAT and other tax matters of professional concern.

Degree of importance: 20%

Tip for 1997: One could add tax changes in finance leases to the implementation of the Environment Act 1995.

Contributed by Philip Marshall .

CHAPTER 21

Being a wiser witness

First published in Estates Gazette July 26, 1997

How may a surveyor, valuer or other property professional make a good impression when giving evidence in a civil or criminal case?

Expert witnesses, almost by definition, are practitioners of long experience. They are used in cases where the court, or arbitrator, is prepared to hear opinion evidence about scientific, artistic, or technical matters. In disputes about land, they may be valuers, planners, surveyors, architects, builders, or engineers.

The duty of an expert witness is to assist the court, not to act as an advocate for the party who is calling him or her as a witness. But many witnesses tend to either forget this rule or be pressured by their clients into doing so.

This has led to Parliament considering the introduction of a system of court-appointed experts, and excluding the right of parties to call expert witnesses in many civil cases. (This was one of the recommendations of the *Woolf Report on Civil Justice*, commissioned by the last government.)

Perhaps the best enumeration of the principal duties of an expert witness was the list drawn up by Cresswell J in *National Justice Compania Naviera SA* v *Prudential Assurance Co Ltd ("Ikarian Reefer")* [1993] 2 EGLR 183.

Trainees and recently qualified surveyors are not likely to be called as expert witnesses, but they can play vital roles nonetheless. Contractual disputes and allegations of professional negligence often turn upon which party can produce the better set of documents and the more reliable witnesses of fact.

This, in turn, will depend upon which party, and which witnesses, have paid better attention to detail, have a better system for recording information, and a better memory of disputed conversations, phone calls, site meetings, and the like.

Cautionary tales

The law reports contain quantities of stories about statements allegedly made by estate agents, local government officers, and other professional people. In many of these cases, the individuals concerned denied making the statements and were not believed by the court, or could not refresh their memories about what was allegedly said by them many months or years ago.

These hapless individuals often found that their clients or employers were bound by what they were supposed to have said. In some cases, these people were personally sued for damages, either by their outraged clients or by the persons to whom they were speaking.

Perhaps the most famous example of the courts interpreting a thoughtless form of words as a personal promise was the statement made by the Chairman of Brixham Local Board of Health to a builder in *Lakeman* v *Mountstephen* (1874) LR 7 HL 17:

Go on, Mountstephen, and do the work, and I will see you paid.

The chairman, Mr Lakeman, was held to be personally liable to pay the builder once it had become clear that the local board of health had never authorised the work in question.

In *Lever Finance Ltd* v *City of Westminster London Borough Council* [1971] 1 QB 222 a planning officer allegedly told an architect, in a telephone call, that a new planning application was not needed for some changes to the layout of a proposed housing development.

The planning officer allegedly said that the changes to the layout were not material changes and that they would be covered by the existing permission. The Court of Appeal held that the local authority was bound by this statement and could not issue an enforcement notice against the developers of the site.

In *Walsh* v *Griffith-Jones* [1978] 2 All ER 1002 an estate agent reassured some prospective tenants of a house that, notwithstanding the wording of the agreement which they were being asked to sign, the owner would not be exercising her contractual right to put additional persons into the house to share with them.

The circuit judge at Lambeth County Court held that this statement had the effect of turning a "licence agreement" into a protected tenancy under the Rent Act 1977. The circuit judge held that the only remedy available to the owner was for her to sue the agent if, as she maintained, she had never given him authority to make such a statement.

In *Schula* v *Keeble* (an unreported case: Wandsworth County Court, Case No LB603071, January 9 1997) an estate agent allegedly told two prospective tenants of a flat that the landlord had agreed to let them leave after six months, even though the wording of the assured shorthold tenancy agreement was for a term of 12 months.

The landlord denied that he had ever agreed to any such concession, but he did not call the estate agent as a witness or produce any written statement from him. The district judge held the landlord was bound by the estate agent's oral statement, even if he had never authorised the agent to make that statement. Accordingly, the landlord was not entitled to retain the tenants' deposit or to succeed in his counterclaim for lost rent.

The failure of a party to call a witness, if that witness is available is often ground for a court or arbitrator to draw inferences against that party.

In *Slough Estates plc* v *Welwyn Hatfield District Council* [1996] 2 EGLR 219, May J was clearly influenced by the failure of Welwyn Hatfield District Council to call relevant witnesses when he decided that the council had acted in a fraudulent manner towards Slough Estates plc. Near to the beginning of his long judgment he observed, at p220:

It is remarkable that no witness has been called on behalf of Welwyn Hatfield District Council to justify or explain their relevant conduct up to and including the 1987 secret agreement.

Importance of notes

An inexplicably absent witness is always bad news for the party who would normally be expected to call that witness to support his or her case. But worse, even than this, is a witness who attends to give evidence in person, but who is then shown to be unreliable. Such a situation seems to have arisen in *North Cornwall District Council* v *Welton and Welton* (1997) 161 JPN 114. This case was discussed in Legal Notes [1996] 37 *EG* 139 (September 14 1996).

The *North Cornwall* case involved a claim by the owners of a bed and breakfast farmhouse who had been led to spend £34,000 or more on unnecessary improvements to their kitchen because of the oral statements of an environmental health officer.

One of the disputes in this case was a factual one. Had the environmental health officer threatened to use his statutory powers under the Food Safety Act 1990, or had he merely been making recommendations to Mr and Mrs Welton? As to the conflict of evidence on this point, Rose LJ in the Court of Appeal observed:

He [the environmental health officer] was an unsatisfactory witness whose diary and notebook had gone missing and whose evidence, save where it was unchallenged,the judge [in Truro County Court] felt unable to accept.

The Court of Appeal upheld the decision of the county court that North Cornwall Council was responsible for the statements made by its environmental health officer because of the rule in *Hedley Byrne* v *Heller & Partners Ltd* [1964] AC 465 (ie the tort of negligent mis-statement).

The plight of the environmental health officer in the *North Cornwall* case emphasises how important it is for all professional people to keep a contemporaneous note of negotiations, business conversations, phone calls, inspections, and any other incidents which might possibly become a matter of future dispute. Contemporaneous notes are of value for three reasons:

(1) they can be used to prepare a reliable proof of evidence at a later date, if court proceedings (or arbitration proceedings) subsequently take place;
(2) they can be used to refresh the witness's memory when he or she is giving evidence in a civil or criminal court or in arbitration proceedings;
(3) they will be admissible as documentary evidence in civil proceedings or arbitration proceedings.˙

Contemporaneous but not spontaneous

A "contemporaneous" note does not have to be a spontaneous note. It can be compiled at any short time after the event, while the facts of the matter are still fresh in the witness's memory. It may be when he or she gets back to the car or to the office that day, or to his or her home that night.

---

*This last advantage will not necessarily apply to criminal proceedings, where the rules of evidence are more complex.

The note does not have to be in a notebook, or in any particular format at all. (The police and other enforcement agencies are subject to stricter rules about this, to minimise allegations of perjury and fraud.)

A note may be in a tape-recorded form, provided that it has been kept in an unaltered state since it was made. It can then be put into the form of a transcript if the need arises.

If two people are working together, it is permissible for one of them to make a note on behalf of them both. But it will then be necessary for the person who did not write the note to inspect it, and to approve its accuracy, while the facts are still fresh in his or her memory.

In these circumstances, both persons will be able to refresh their memory from the note because it will have the status of a joint note irrespective of the handwriting.

Proofs of evidence

It is important to remember that a proof of evidence does not usually have the same status as a contemporaneous note. (It would only do so if a witness wrote up that proof of evidence while the facts were very fresh in his or her memory.)

This means that civil and criminal courts will not usually allow witnesses to read proofs of evidence in the witness box. If, however, the solicitor or barrister representing the opposing party notices some statement in the oral testimony which contradicts an earlier proof of evidence, this contradiction will be put to the witness in cross-examination.

If, however, the witness's proof of evidence is based upon contemporaneous notes of the facts in dispute, and those notes have been used in the witness box as a memory-refreshing document, such a contradiction will be less likely.

In short, it is always important to remember that "the faintest ink is better than the strongest memory".

Duties of an expert witness

- Expert evidence should be, and should be seen to be, the independent product of the expert, uninfluenced as to form or content by the exigencies of litigation.
- An expert should provide independent assistance to the court by way of objective and unbiased opinions.

- An expert should never assume the role of an advocate.
- An expert should always state the facts or assumptions upon which his or her opinion is based.
- An expert should not omit to mention, and to consider, material facts which could detract from his or her opinion.
- An expert should make it clear when a particular question or issue falls outside his or her expertise.
- If an expert's opinion is not properly researched because not enough data is available, then this must be stated, together with an indication that the opinion is no more than a provisional one.
- In cases where an expert witness has prepared a report but cannot assert that it contains the truth, the whole truth, and nothing but the truth, without some qualification, that qualification should be stated in the report.
- If, after there has been an exchange of experts' reports between the parties, the expert, for any reason, changes his or her view on a material matter, this fact should be communicated to the other side without delay, and – when appropriate – to the court.
- Where the expert's evidence refers to photographs, plans, calculations, analyses, measurements, surveys, etc, these must be provided to the opposite party at the same time as the exchange of reports.

(A summary from the judgment of Cresswell J in The Ikarian Reefer)

Common disputes of fact

- What statements were made to a client (eg during a telephone call?)
- What instructions were received from a client?
- What statements were made to a third party on behalf of a client?
- What admissions were made by a party to a dispute or his or her agent? (even "small talk" may be relevant here)
- What oral statements, if any, were made in order to persuade a prospective tenant to sign a tenancy agreement?
- What oral statements, if any, were made by a surveyor, architect or contractor at a site meeting?
- What were the weather conditions at the time of a site meeting, outdoor inspection, accident or other relevant event?
- What oral descriptions were given of a property by an estate agent?
- What explanation, if any, was given by a person in occupation of land as to his or her rights in that land?
- What, if any, oral statements were made by a planning officer, housing officer,or environmental health officer when inspecting a property or answering a telephone call?
- When did a material change of use take place, or a building operation commence, for the purposes of the Town and Country Planning Acts?

- Was a final agreement ever reached during "subject to contract" negotiations and, if so, what were the terms?
- Did the parties to a dispute reach a final settlement during "without prejudice" negotiations and, if so, what were the terms?

Contributed by Leslie Blake.

CHAPTER 22

Square brackets or round brackets?

First published in Estates Gazette December 11, 1993

What is the correct way to cite law cases when writing an essay, report, or letter containing legal information? What are the principal law reports and their abbreviations?

Until 1865 law reporting in England and Wales was entirely in the hands of private law reporters. Thus, for example, the famous cases of *Hadley* v *Baxendale* (relating to the measure of damages in the law of contract) was reported in a series of reports published by Messrs Welsby, Hurlstone and Gordon between 1847 and 1856. These were known as the "Exchequer Reports" and (of the 11 volumes in that series) *Hadley* v *Baxendale* was reported in vol 9, at p341. The recognised abbreviation for the Exchequer Reports was "Ex" or "Exch", so *Hadley* was (and is) cited with the reference: (1854) 9 Ex 341. The year "1854" is placed in round brackets because it is not necessary to know the year of the case in order to track down the report. The Exchequer Reports were numbered, volume by volume, sequentially, so that any seeker after the report would be able to find the *Hadley* v *Baxendale*, once he knew that it was on p341 of vol 9, and not in any other volume.

Nevertheless, since any person being referred to a decided case would wish to know how old or how modern it was, it was invariably the practice of printers to include the relevant year for the sake of information, invariably in round brackets. Readers of *Estates Gazette* will remember when law reports, articles and other information appearing in the weekly parts could be cited in this way. For example, *Swanbrae Ltd* v *Elliott* (a case on the law of landlord and tenant) appeared in vol 281, on p916, and could therefore be cited as follows: (1986) 281 EG 916. In those days, *EG* was an unbroken sequence of volumes from vol 1 (in 1857), until (by 1986) it was approaching 300 volumes, because it was sizeable enough to form four-bound volumes every year. By this time, however, the publishers were also producing the *Estates Gazette Law Reports*, reprinting in more convenient form all of the cases appearing in the weekly parts, so that *Swanbrae Ltd* v *Elliott* can also be cited as: [1987] 1 EGLR 99. That means that the report commences on p99 of the first volume of the reports for 1987.

Because the volumes are not numbered sequentially from the date when they first appeared (in 1985), the actual year of the report is a vital part of the citation. For this reason the year is placed in square brackets, to distinguish it from those citations which include the year only as a matter of interest. The fact that *Swanbrae Ltd* v *Elliott* appears as "(1986)" in one citation and "[1987]" in another citation reinforces the fact that the year being adverted to is that of the published report, not necessarily the year in which the decision was given.

The *Estates Gazette* no longer uses sequential volume numbers for its weekly parts, but includes the year and the week of publication in a decimal-type notation. This makes it possible to cite cases in a formulation which includes square brackets: [1993] 47 EG 139 being *Tustian* v *Johnston* (a case on agricultural holdings, appearing on p139 of part 47 of the 1993 of weekly parts).

The Council of Law Reporting
The Incorporated Council of Law Reporting (ICLR) was established in 1865. Its purpose was to provide reliable law reporting by a corporate body which (unlike individual law reporters) would never go out of business or become weary with age or die with no one to carry on the work in hand. "The Law Reports", as they were known from the start, appeared some 10 years before the great reform of the courts which was to take place in 1873–75. Accordingly, the first volumes in this series reflect the old courts of common law and equity. The reports were numbered sequentially, volume by volume, and were cited thus (with the year of publication in round brackets):

LRA & E	= Law Reports, Admiralty and Ecclesiastical Cases
LRCCR	= Law Reports, Crown Cases Reserved
LRCP	= Law Reports, Common Pleas
LREq	= Law Reports Equity Cases
LRExch	= Law Reports, Exchequer
LRHL	= Law Reports, House of Lords
LRP & D	= Law Reports, Probate and Divorce
LRPC	= Law Reports, Privy Council

LRQB   = Law Reports, Queen's Bench
LR Sc & Div = Law Reports, Scotch and Divorce Appeals

The legislation of 1873–75 set up the High Court of Justice and the Court of Appeal. The High Court was divided into five divisions and this was reflected in the way in which the law reports were cited after 1875. The new citations no longer used the initials "LR" and the new reports were cited as follows:

App Cas   = Appeal Cases (House of Lords and Privy Council)
ChD   = Chancery Division
CPD   = Common Pleas Division
ExD   = Exchequer Division
PD   = Probate Divorce and Admiralty Division
QBD   = Queen's Bench Division

The volumes were each sequentially numbered, so, once again, there was no need for the year to be cited, except for information purposes (in round brackets).

In 1880 Lord Chief Baron Kelly died and the opportunity was taken to abolish the Exchequer Division (of which he had been the head). Lord Chief Justice Cockburn died in the same year, leaving a vacancy for the head of the Queen's Bench Division. Lord Coleridge (Chief Justice of the Common Pleas Division) was promoted to Lord Chief Justice of England (and head of the Queen's Bench Division). The Common Pleas Division was abolished. Accordingly, the Exchequer Division reports and the Common Pleas Division reports ceased publication in 1880.

In 1891 the ICLR decided to discontinue the sequential numbering of the law reports and to go over to the "annual volumes" method of citation. At the same time, "App Cas" became "AC" and the letter "D" disappeared from the citations, so that (assuming more than one volume per year was needed) a typical citation would be [1981] 1 QB 1.

In 1972 the Probate Divorce and Admiralty Division was abolished. Admiralty work was sent to the Queen's Bench Division and contentious probate work was sent to the Chancery Division. Divorce and proceedings relating to children were dealt with by a new division of the High Court called the "Family Division". Hence the series of reports cited as "P" ceased to exist after 1971. A new series of reports, cited as [1972] Fam appeared in 1971, and has appeared annually ever since.

In 1953 the ICLR decided to bring out a series of reports which would include cases from all divisions of the High Court, as well as from the Court of Appeal, the House of Lords and the Privy Council. Many of these cases would appear later, in the law reports proper. These reports were called the Weekly Law Reports and were cited as follows: [1953] 1 WLR 1. (Traditionally, there have been three volumes in each year.) In a sense, Weekly Law Reports were a belated response to the series of reports brought out by Butterworths in 1936 (All England Law Reports).

Abbreviations

In addition to the official law reports, there are many journals and law reports in print. The following list contains the recognised abbreviations of those most commonly encountered:

ALR	=	Australian Law Reports
All ER	=	All England Law Reports
All ER Rep	=	All England Law Reports Reprint Series (1558–1935)
All ER Ext (1861–1935)	=	All England Law Reports Extension Volumes
AMR	=	All Malaysia Reports
BCLR	=	Butterworths Company Law Cases
BTR	=	British Tax Review
BLR (or Build LR)	=	Building Law Reports
CLR	=	Commonwealth Law Reports (Australia)
CLYB	=	Current Law Year Book
CMLR	=	Common Market Law Reports
Const LJ	=	Construction Law Journal
Cr App Rep	=	Criminal Appeal Reports
Crim LR	=	Criminal Law Review
DLR	=	Dominion Law Reports (Canada)
ECR	=	European Court Reports
EG	=	Estates Gazette
EGCS	=	Estates Gazette Case Summaries
EGD	=	Estates Gazette Digest (until 1984)
EGLR	=	Estates Gazette Law Reports (from 1985)
EHLR	=	European Human Rights Reports
FSR	=	Fleet Street (Patent) Reports
FTLR	=	Financial Times Law Reports
Fam Law	=	Family Law
Fam Law R	=	Family Law Reporter

HLR	=	Housing Law Reports
Hudson's BC	=	Hudson's Building Contracts
ICR	=	Industrial Cases Reports
ILR	=	Insurance Law Reporter
ILT	=	Irish Law Times
ILT Jo	=	Irish Law Times Journal
IR	=	Irish Reports
IRLR	=	Industrial Relations Law Reports
Imm AR	=	Immigration Appeal Reports
JP	=	Justice of the Peace Reports
JPL	=	Journal of Planning and Environment Law
JPN	=	Justice of the Peace Newspaper
Knight's LGR	=	Knight's Local Government Reports
LGR	=	Local Government Review
LRC	=	Law Reports of the Commonwealth
LS Gaz	=	Law Society Gazette
Lloyd's Rep	=	Lloyd's Reports
MLJ	=	Malayan Law Journal
NI	=	Northern Ireland Law Reports
NLJ	=	New Law Journal
NSWLR	=	New South Wales Law Reports
NZLR	=	New Zealand Law Reports
OR	=	Ontario Reports
P&CR	=	Property and Compensation Reports
PLR	=	Planning Law Reports
RPC	=	Reports of Patent Cases
RRC	=	Ryde's Rating Cases
RTR	=	Road Traffic Cases
RVR	=	Rating and Valuation Reporter
SA	=	South African Law Reports
SC	=	Court of Session Cases (Scotland)
SJ or Sol Jo	=	Solicitors' Journal
SLT	=	Scots Law Times
STC	=	Simon's Tax Cases
TC	=	Tax Cases
Tr L	=	Trading Law Reports
VATTR	=	Valued Added Tax Tribunal Reports
VR	=	Victorian Reports (Victoria, Australia)
WAR	=	Western Australia Law Reports

The English Reports

A list of the abbreviations for law reports which existed before 1865 (many of them covering only short periods of legal history) would be a very long list indeed. Fortunately, many of those old reports have been consolidated in the English Reports. For example, *Stilk* v *Myrick* (the famous case of the doctrine of consideration) was reported in three privately published law reports in or about 1809. The references would mean nothing to most readers nowadays: 2 Camp 317 (Campbell's Reports, 1807–1816); 11 RR 717 (Revised Reports); and 6 Esp 129 (Espinasse's Reports, 1793–1810). But most students can find it reported in the English Reports (held in most large law libraries). The reference there is as follows: (1809) 170 ER 1168, ie vol 170 of the English Reports at p1168.

House style

As will be apparent from the way in which this article has been printed, there are certain rules of house style which apply to the citation of cases. The name of a case (but not the citation) is always printed in italics. Most word-processors will have the capability of printing names in this way. But if a letter, report, essay etc is to be typed on a typewriter, or written as a manuscript, the name of the case (but not the citation) should be underlined – this being the common way in which printers are directed to put words or phrases into italics.

No one seems to know why this convention arose. Possibly, it arose by analogy with the practice of putting the titles of books and periodicals into italics, but, if so, it is odd that the same rule does not apply to the names of Acts of Parliament or other forms of legislation, such as the Building Regulations (not *Building Regulations*). Confusingly for beginners, therefore, the use and non-use of italics is just another trap for the unwary, similar to the practice of lawyers when they say "Stilk and Myrick", not "Stilk versus Myrick", however much a case name appears to require the use of the word "versus" when it is read aloud.

Contributed by Leslie Blake.

PLANNING/ENVIRONMENT

CHAPTER 23

The development industry and archaeology

First published in Estates Gazette August 22, 1992

Conflict between the competing interests of the development industry and archaeology has featured heavily in the professional press in recent years. The discovery of the Rose Theatre and the subsequent debate over its future was perhaps the catalyst in bringing this debate into the public eye.

While the Rose issue aroused strong feelings because of its associations with a primary British cultural institution, namely William Shakespeare, it represents in microcosm a situation which is occurring with increasing frequency. The majority of cases, however, receive far less public attention than the *Rose Theatre* case, but the problems created for the developers, planners and archaeologists directly involved may be no less severe.

The increasing public awareness of conservation issues is the underlying cause of the problem. Both central and local government have seen fit to respond to this pressure by instituting various controls and policies to protect the archaeological heritage. The nature of Britain's prehistory and current situation has led to inevitable problems as a result.

The British Isles are richly endowed with archaeological remains. They have been continuously occupied by man ever since the last ice age some 10,000 years ago and there is evidence of even earlier occupation. In terms of the longevity of occupation we are far from unique – much of southern Europe, for example, shows a much longer record of human activity, but the factor which marks out Britain from many other countries is its current high density of occupation.

Ranking among the most densely populated countries in the world, the frequency of development inevitably means that archaeological remains will be more regularly encountered in Britain than elsewhere. This situation is exacerbated by the fact that many towns and cities have been continuously occupied for centuries.

Settlements such as London, Winchester, Chester, York, Lincoln and Exeter were all thriving Roman towns and their substrata reveal evidence from almost every subsequent period of our history.

Industrial cities such as Manchester, Newcastle, Sheffield and Nottingham are all at least medieval in origin and their urban cores overlay potentially fascinating remains from periods which are often less well documented than the Roman. The development pressures are many and varied. New housing, leisure, office and retail developments are common enough in our cities, but rural areas, too, are not exempt from either development pressures or the associated archaeological discoveries. Trunk road improvements and motorway construction are obvious examples, and currently many mineral extraction companies are finding that their activities are under close scrutiny from archaeological interests.

In particular, sand and gravel extraction operations, which tend to concentrate on river valleys, are often finding that these areas were also frequently chosen by neolithic, bronze or iron age people as the best sites for their villages, being on fertile soil and located on a natural river communication network which rendered contact with other settlements more straightforward than risking the perils of a densely forested hinterland.

Value of archaeology

The importance of allowing time for archaeological investigation before development commences and in some cases preserving the archaeological record, either by changing the development proposal or even stopping the project altogether, is, for some, difficult to appreciate. The costs of delay or changed designs can be significant and inevitably tend to colour the developer's view of archaeology.

Nevertheless, archaeology is important for a number of reasons. First, in the case of pre-Roman sites, it is our only source of information about past societies since no written records have survived. Second, every site can yield something which increases our understanding of past societies; the more we investigate and record, the more we will learn. Third, archaeology is valuable both in a cultural sense, providing us with new perspectives on our ancestors, their lifestyles and their interaction with the environment, and in a financial sense, in that the existence of such widespread evidence of the past in the UK attracts tourists and foreign currency.

Another factor which many developers and non-archaeologists fail to appreciate is that the crucial importance of many sites lies not in the possibility of "finds" such as jewellery, swords and burial goods but rather in the much less spectacular evidence of the palaeo-environment, plant and animal species, diet and general economy. What interests many modern archaeologists is not discovering another Tutankhamun but relating ancient humans to their environment and studying their adaptation to it. It is in this area that modern humans, divorced as most of us are from everyday issues of survival by our life in cities and yet faced with mounting environmental problems, may learn much from the evidence left by our ancestors.

Currently, there are some 13,000 scheduled monuments in the UK. Any alteration to these requires scheduled monument consent from the Department of the Environment in addition to normal planning permission. Thus they are effectively inviolate. There are also currently five Areas of Archaeological Importance designated under the Ancient Monuments and Archaeological Areas Act 1979, namely the historic town centres of Canterbury, Chester, Exeter, Hereford and York.

In these areas potential developers must give six weeks' notice to the relevant planning authority of any proposals to disturb the ground, tip on it or flood it and the Secretary of State has the right to delay development by up to four and a half months in order to allow archaeological excavation to take place. But most archaeological sites (known or yet undiscovered) lie outside either of these designations. Currently local authority sites and monuments records (SMRs), which are compiled usually by county authorities, record some 600,000 archaeological sites nationally.

Solutions to the problems
Not every site is of a quality to merit preservation, but all merit investigation, either now or in the future. The discovery of archaeological remains on a site is not, therefore, a disaster for the developer, but it may cause additional costs. Very little money is available via English Heritage to support either investigation or preservation; the emphasis in recent government policy has placed the responsibility for funding firmly with the developer, following the "polluter pays" principle.

Yet the debate continues over whether the discovery of

archaeological remains and their subsequent destruction can really be considered in the same light as, say, destruction of visual amenity or discharge of pollutants into the environment.

In November 1990 the DOE published Planning Policy Guidance Note 16 (PPG 16), Archaeology and Planning in an attempt to clarify this often complex situation. The PPG offers sound advice on the necessity to consult local authorities and English Heritage, and to check the SMR in the feasibility study stage of any development. It also discusses the potential and possible wording of subsequent planning conditions and section 106 agreements (Town and Country Planning Act 1990).

It fails, however, to offer much consolation or assistance in the case of hitherto unsuspected archaeological remains coming to light during the development process. Insurance against such an eventuality is the best suggestion that PPG 16 can make, but it singularly omits any mention of how such risks might be assessed or on what basis premiums might be set.

Overall, PPG 16 is a step in the right direction towards solving a growing problem for the development industry, but the question of who should ultimately pay for archaeology remains to be contested. Is it a clear case of the polluter pays or should society, via taxation, make a contribution to a cause which it has furthered significantly in recent years? Clearly archaeology has reached a level of importance which many of its supporters have striven to attain for a number of years. Many developers would argue that the importance attached to archaeology is excessive, but this misses the point. What must be clarified soon, however, is how we can genuinely reconcile these competing interests in a fashion which achieves the broad aims of both parties without disadvantaging either.

Further reading
Darvill T. *Ancient Monuments in the Countryside*, English Heritage, 1987.
Department of the Environment. PPG 16 Archaeology and Planning, HMSO, 1990.

Contributed by Jon Kellett.

CHAPTER 24

Designated areas as development constraints

First published in Estates Gazette November 14, 1992

There are very many constraints to the development of land in the UK. Among the most obvious are the limitations imposed by Ministry of Defence ownership, by dereliction, by an unwillingness to lose yet more agricultural land of high quality, by the existence of areas of forest and woodland, and by existing buildings and infrastructure. Furthermore, in these days of massive engineering achievements, it is easy to overlook the very real limitations imposed by physical factors such as wetness, altitude, slope and other elements of the natural environment. Other limitations also exist.

It has been estimated, for example, that 11% of England and Wales lies within urban areas, 7% is forest and woodland, and 43% may be included within grades 1, 2 and 3a agricultural land. But, however extensive these areas may be, the limitations which they impose may be compared with the amount of land which is protected by some form of designation under the general heading of "Cherished Land". It is estimated that National Parks cover 9.0% (13,600 km²) of England and Wales, Areas of Outstanding Natural Beauty 12.8% (20,400 km²), green belts 12% (15,500 sq km), and Sites of Special Scientific Interest Interest 6.5% (9,750 km²) (PPG7 1992).

The term "Cherished Land" implies land which is valued in some way, perhaps even cared for, but certainly land which people might want to see being looked after. To understand why people might feel that way it is instructive to read some of the accounts of the pressure groups which developed during the last part of the 19th century, and whose ideas continued well into the 20th. Indeed, their ideas continue to find expression in a vast array of organisations ranging from Government bodies such as English Heritage or English Nature, to groups such as the Ramblers Association or the

Council for the Protection of Rural England. Collectively they represent a very substantial body of opinion, some of it finding expression in some of the political ideas which are associated with the so-called "Greens".

How, then, are these ideas turned into the concept of areas of Cherished Land? The answer lies in the extent to which pressure groups can persuade national and local governments to designate areas for particular purposes. Perhaps it may be to protect a series of plant or animal communities; perhaps to preserve a certain ecological niche; maybe the intention is to conserve a beautiful landscape and to guide its development so that its special characteristics are sustained. Government agencies may themselves be the organisations which promote a particular cause. Whatever the motive, if a political decision-making body can be persuaded to adopt it, then the result may be a new designation with potentially very great implications for the process of development control. In general, developers would find difficulty in obtaining planning permission in any of the areas described below, though it must be stressed that they vary a great deal in the level of control which they represent. In this respect it is worth quoting in full the first paragraph of section 3.1 of PPG7:

In those parts of the countryside where special statutory designations apply, planning policies and development control decisions should take full account of the specific features or qualities which justified designation of the area, and sustain or further the purposes of that designation. In some designated areas additional statutory planning controls or procedures apply, for example through tighter controls over permitted development. Other designations have statutory implications beyond the planning system, but the factors that led to the designation may also be material to planning decisions.

This short article is devoted to a brief description of some designated areas. There is no space here for analysis, but plenty of analyses exist in the literature. Neither is there any attempt to group the areas into types of designation or into a chronological sequence. Instead, a dictionary approach is adopted, with the areas listed alphabetically, an indication of the legislation which created each one and some notes on the implications of designation.

1. Access areas

The National Parks and Access to the Countryside (NPAC) Act 1949 gave National Park Authorities (NPAs) the powers to negotiate access agreements with landowners of areas of open land. A number of access agreements have been signed, principally in the Peak Park, involving a commitment on the part of the NPA to provide a ranger service and compensation to the landowner for reduced farming efficiency.

The 1968 Countryside Act contained powers for all local authorities (LAs) to make access agreements with landowners, and not just in areas of open land but in all areas of rural land. In fact, it appears that remarkably few LAs have taken advantage of this provision. Access to the countryside may also be taken to include the national rights of way network represented by footpaths and other designations. Some long-distance footpaths have been designated by the Countryside Commission. All rights of way are important considerations and should be checked with the county maps.

2. Areas of outstanding natural beauty

Provision for the designation of AONBs was made in the NPAC Act 1949, but they have not received the same attention as National Parks and only in the 1990s are they being more widely acknowledged. AONBs are designated to conserve areas of high landscape value, a function which they share with National Parks. However, although they may be important recreation areas, there is no statutory obligation to promote such activity, although many are engaged in doing so because of the benefits from increased tourism. Planning control inside AONBs rests with local authorities sometimes acting with neighbouring authorities if they share parts of the same AONB. There is a strong presumption against development in these areas, though LPAs do not possess special powers. So far, 39 have been designated.

3. Conservation areas

Until 1967 it was possible to list only individual buildings or monuments. However, by that date it had become clear that this was inadequate, and new measures were introduced in the Civic Amenities Act 1967 allowing whole groups of buildings and their surroundings to be included in designated Conservation Areas (CAs). They are designated in accordance with section 69 of the Listed Buildings and Conservation Areas Act 1990, and as a consequence local planning authorities and the Secretary of State are required to pay particular attention to the character or appearance of the area when exercising their planning control functions. Listings or schedules of buildings and monuments are not affected by CA status and continue to operate in relation to those buildings. Inside conservation areas permitted development rights are restricted and planning applications must be advertised; there are some restrictions concerning trees; and local authorities may pursue enhancement schemes in such areas. Generally, however, their status is very weak, and there is an opinion that so many have been created that their value has been debased. DOE circular 8/87, Historic Buildings and Conservation Areas: Policy and Procedures refers.

4. Country parks and picnic sites

One of the main functions of the Countryside Act 1968 was the abolition of the National Parks Commission and its replacement by the Countryside Commission. It reflected a realisation that the whole countryside, sometimes known as the wider countryside, required conserving – not just those areas within National Parks. It was in this spirit that the Act allowed local authorities to designate country parks: areas often within easy reach of urban areas and sufficiently robust to withstand considerable visitor pressure. The first area to be designated was Wirral Country Park, since followed by several hundred more. They are designated and managed by local authorities, though with support, which may be financial, from the Countryside Commission.

5. Environmentally Sensitive Areas (ESAs)

ESAs are the most recent type of designation. They reflect an aim of conserving the countryside as a whole by encouraging farmers and other users to enter into a partnership with the Government. ESAs are designated with the aim of protecting certain areas of high landscape value, wildlife and archaeological value. Farmers are encouraged to introduce or maintain agricultural practices which are compatible with the overall requirements of countryside protection and receive compensation as a result. Designation may be important in deciding local countryside planning policies and may affect development control decisions. ESAs are recommended to the Government by the Countryside Commission and English or Welsh Nature, and are designated by agriculture departments under the Agriculture Act 1986. So far, 10 have been approved, eight more were recommended in 1992 and a further eight are expected to be approved in 1993.

6. Green belts

Green belts have a PPG Note (No 2) of their own. Conceptually they originated many years ago, but the modern stimulus was Circular 42/55, which allowed local authorities to designate green belts according to three objectives: to prevent the unrestricted sprawl of large built-up areas, to prevent neighbouring built up areas from coalescing, and to preserve the character of historic towns. Since that time the status of green belts has been confirmed by DOE Circular 14/84 and two other objectives have been added: the safeguarding of the surrounding countryside from further encroachment, and assistance in urban regeneration. Their nearness to urban areas also makes them potentially important areas for recreation, and their rights of way networks often receive considerable attention. As with Heritage Coasts, there are no additional development control powers, but there is a general presumption against inappropriate development in them. They are localities which local pressure groups defend resolutely and which many planning authorities have quite a good record of sustaining. In the wider context they provide a context for countryside management and improvement. Since 1981 parts of the urban fringe have been managed through Groundwork projects, some of which were established as independent trusts to coordinate the work of the private, public and voluntary sectors.

7. Heritage Coasts

Heritage Coasts were first proposed in 1970, and since 1973 more than one-third of the coastline of England and Wales has been designated: a total of 1,460 km in 43 stretches. Some are also SSSIs, and about 500 km is owned by the National Trust. The main purpose of Heritage Coast definition is to focus attention on the management needs of such areas, since they are often localities where pressures from landscape and nature conservation interlock with those from recreation, tourism, pollution and water quality. The Countryside Commission has been pressing since 1991 for rigorous control over all forms of development in heritage coasts, but the May 1992 draft PPG on coastal areas indicates that the Government is not prepared to go that far. Countryside Commission, Heritage Coasts, CCP 305, 1991 refers.

8. National Parks

The National Parks and Access to the Countryside Act 1949 created the National Parks Commission with powers to designate areas as national parks. The commission was replaced by the Countryside Commission under the Countryside Act 1968. The Local Government Act 1972 gave National Park Authorities (NPAs) their current powers and responsibilities. There have been two major investigations: the Sandford Report in 1974 and the Edwards Report in 1991. NPAs have two major areas of responsibility: to conserve the landscape; and to promote compatible recreation in the parks. Each NPA produces a National Park Plan indicating how it proposes to achieve those objectives. In addition, the Peak District and Lake District NPAs are the structure plan authorities inside the two parks. All NPAs pursue policies of strict control over development and ensure that appropriate design standards are maintained. Ten national parks were designated between 1951 and 1957. Two other areas have since acquired national park status: the Norfolk Broads in 1989 and the New Forest in 1992.

9. National Trust

Formed in 1895 as a form of protest against the threat to the countryside posed by industrial and urban growth, the National Trust was recognised as a statutory body by the National Trust Act of 1907. Since then it has grown to be one of the most important conservation groups in the country with a membership of over 2m people. Under the 1907 Act the trust was empowered to declare its land and buildings inalienable, which means that they cannot be sold or mortgaged, though the land may be leased. The trust can appeal to Parliament against a compulsory purchase order on its inalienable land. More than 570,000 acres belong to the trust,

140,000 acres in the Lake District alone. It is not a Government agency, but a charity, although it does receive the occasional Government grant.

10. Nature Reserves

National Nature Reserves (NNRs), designated by the nature conservation agencies under the Wildlife and Countryside Act 1981, are reserves of national importance. "Ramsar" sites are wetlands of international importance, designated in accordance with the provisions of the Convention on Wetlands of International Importance, signed at Ramsar, Iran, in 1971. There are 30 sites in Great Britain. Special Protection Areas are areas for the protection of rare and migratory birds under the EC Wild Birds Directive (79/409).

11. Scheduled Ancient Monuments

This category may also be taken to include historic and archaeological sites, although they have not all been scheduled. However, the desirability of preserving an ancient monument and its setting is a material consideration. Designation of archaeological remains or sites of national importance as scheduled monuments is carried out by the Secretary of State under the Ancient Monuments and Archaeological Areas Act 1979, and PPG 16 gives advice on archaeology and planning.

12. Sites of Special Scientific Interest; Sites of Special Biological Interest

A PPG on nature conservation is due to be issued in the near future and will serve a useful purpose of highlighting planning issues in respect of the very complex range of sites which come under that general heading. SSSIs are designated under section 28 of the Wildlife and Countryside Act 1981: so far 4,300 sites have been designated covering 9.750 km^2. Their designation is intended to protect the nature conservation interest of the site. DOE Circulars 27/87 and 1/92 refer.

13. Special Landscape Value

A term applied to areas which, by virtue of their natural beauty, are defined as such in a development plan. Some authorities use the term "Areas of Great Landscape Value".

14. Tree Preservation Orders (TPOs)

An order made by a local authority and confirmed by central Government requiring the preservation of individual or groups of trees.

References

Blunden, J and Curry, N. *A Future for our Countryside*, 1988, Basil Blackwell.

Blunden, J and Curry, N. *A People's Charter?*, HMSO, 1991.

Countryside Commission, *Countryside and nature conservation issues in district local plans*, CCP 317, 1990.

Countryside Commission, *Planning Tools*, CCP 325, 3rd edition, 1990.

DOE, PPG7, The Countryside and the Rural Economy, January 1992.

Contributed by Robert Cumming.

CHAPTER 25

Guiding planning policy

First published in Estates Gazette April 30, 1994

What is the nature and purpose of Planning Policy Guidance Notes (PPGs)?

Consultants in practice increasingly need to be aware of the scope and importance of planning policy guidance notes, as they can seriously affect the outcome of property development decisions. This article offers a guide to PPGs for students on general practice surveying courses. Some definitions are explored initially, followed by some explanation as to why PPGs exist and what status they hold. The coverage of PPGs is also examined, as well as their prospects for the future.

What Are PPGs?

PPGs are expressions of government planning policy. Issued by the Department of the Environment, the first nine were produced en masse in January 1988 and have all since been updated or are in the process of being revised. This gives an indication of the shelf life of a PPG, which is generally assumed to be four to five years from the date of adoption.

PPGs contain national guidance to key land-use planning issues and inform local authority policy of current government thinking on a particular issue. Local-level policy is also informed by Regional Planning Guidances (RPGs) and Strategic Planning Guidances (SPGs), which are area-based, whereas PPGs are topic-based. RPGs tend to contain aspects of more detailed policy, but must be seen in part as area-based applications of the topics addressed in PPGs. These are produced by county councils, but issued by the DOE. In metropolitan areas Strategic Guidance Notes, produced by central government, guide issues such as housing land allocations. The concerns addressed in PPGs, RPGs, and SPGs, are then incorporated into structure plans, local plans and unitary development plans at local level.

Some PPGs deal with fairly broad issues: for instance, PPG1 is entitled "General Policies and Principles", while PPG12 deals with the relationship between regional guidance and local plans. Other PPGs are more detailed, with PPG17, for example, having a whole paragraph devoted to clay pigeon shooting!

Why do PPGs exist?

They exist to provide decision makers in planning with up-to-date guidance on government policy with respect to various planning issues. Previously, government planning policy was contained in a wealth of documents, mainly in the form of circulars, (more than 100 existed at the time of issue of the first PPG), but also in a range of other publications such as Development Control Policy Notes. These old forms of guidance are being updated and incorporated into PPGs as they are produced.

The idea behind PPGs is partly, therefore, to simplify the planning system and to bring all government thinking on a particular topic into one definitive document. In order to bolster this simplification, and make planning issues more accessible to a wider readership, PPGs are written in a non-technical language. This makes them easier to read than central government guidance often has been.

PPGs should be used by planning authorities when drawing up development plans and in making decisions regarding planning applications. However, they also offer general practice surveyors and consultants a useful guide as to possible acceptable courses of action with regard to certain types of property development.

Status of PPGs

When devising development plans, local authorities must pay attention to the content of relevant PPGs. The development plan is a major consideration in the determination of a planning application. To carry significant weight, however, the plan needs to be consistent with relevant national and regional guidance, including PPGs, or be able to justify the difference in the context of local factors. If the plan is not consistent, then the local authority risks losing planning appeals on the grounds that its local policy is not in line with government guidance on the subject. As PPG1 states:

If decision-makers elect not to follow relevant statements of the government's planning policy they must give clear and convincing reasons, (para 21).

Similarly, the advice in a development plan may conflict with that contained in a PPG where the PPG is issued after the adoption of the plan. Where this occurs the policies in the plan may not carry so much weight. In such instances, the decision regarding a planning application may depend more on advice contained in the relevant PPG's. This potential conflict between levels of advice means that developers have a better chance of successfully challenging local authority policy in a given area.

Even draft PPGs carry a certain weight in the consideration of planning applications and the drawing up of policy.

What do PPGs cover?
At the time of writing 18 PPGs are extant. That is to say, they have been issued by the government in their final form and are intended for use by practitioners. Details of these 18 are contained in the table below.

Some PPG numbers are missing – which relate, in the cases of PPGs 9 to 11, to regional guidance that has since been developed into its own series, and, in the case of PPG15, to guidance later subsumed into a revised PPG12.

The draft PPG issued for consultation by the Government relating to matters concerning listed buildings and conservation areas will become the new PPG15.

As indicated in the table, there are three other new guidances in the pipeline which have been issued as drafts. These relate to: planning and noise, (expected April 1994); nature conservation (expected June 1994); and pollution control and waste management, (also expected June 1994).

In addition, PPG2 – "Green Belts" – has recently been issued as a draft, with a final version expected from the DOE later in the year following revision in the light of comments received.

In general terms PPGs have reflected the political mood of the times. Therefore, with the advent of different Secretaries of State at the DOE, and indeed differing government ideologies, PPGs have

Status of Planning Policy Guidance Notes

PPG number	Title	Year of last revision	Draft issued
1	General Policies & Principles	1992	
2	Green Belts	1988	yes
3	Land for Housing	1992	
4	Industrial & Commercial Development & Small Firms	1992	
5	Simplified Planning Zones	1992	
6	Town Centres & Retail Developments	1993	
7	Countryside & the Rural Economy	1992	
8	Telecommunications	1992	
12	Development Plans & Regional Planning Guidance	1992	
13	Highway Considerations in Development Control	1994	
14	Development on Unstable Land	1990	
15	Listed Buildings & Conservation Areas	new	yes
16	Archaeology & Planning	1990	
17	Sport & Recreation	1991	
18	Enforcing Planning Control	1991	
19	Outdoor Advertisement Control	1992	
20	Coastal Planning	1992	
21	Tourism	1992	
22	Renewable Sources of Energy	1992	
x	Planning and Noise	new	yes
x	Nature Conservation	new	yes
x	Pollution Control & Waste Management	new	yes

x = awaiting allocation of number

changed as they have had to do in line with broader government thinking, a good illustration being the recently revised PPG 13, "Highway Considerations in Development Control".

PPGs, like other planning policy documents before them, are primarily concerned with land use. Economic and social issues are not referred to. The ideology of the Government with respect to these issues is reflected in them, but is not explicitly referred to. This can be seen in the first generation of PPGs issued in 1988.

The Thatcher administration had a laissez-faire approach to planning, with aims of freeing the system for business. This manifested itself in advice that was perhaps more pro-development than today. This is illustrated by changes in PPG6. In the original version of 1988, out-of-town developments were encouraged to create competition and improve consumer choice. In the revised version of 1993, the emphasis, although still stressing the need for competition, was more upon maintaining the vitality and viability of town centres. This advice incorporated DOE research which saw the need to reduce the number and distance of car-borne journeys in an attempt to lessen carbon-dioxide emissions. It also recognised the desirability of maintaining activity in town and city centres after dark.

What do PPGs not cover?
Many practitioners in a number of fields have been calling for definitive government guidance in specific areas not presently covered by PPGs. Perhaps the most topical of these areas is that of sustainable development. However, recent research into how planning can be made sustainable has been incorporated into the revised versions of PPG6, PPG12, and PPG13. A definitive statement on planning and sustainability is, however, unlikely to be issued by the DOE in the form of a PPG.

Other issues of direct concern to local authorities, such as local economic development and affordable housing, have also not been covered by PPGs. Indeed, affordable housing was covered by an old-style circular (number 7/91), issued as late as 1991. This guidance has since been subsumed into PPG3.

Prospects for the future
The DOE is on record as maintaining that there will be no more than some 22 PPGs. It is felt that with any more than this the interactions between the PPGs themselves will be too complex, with cross-referrals clouding the issues at stake. However, calls for more PPGs from practitioners, and the likely adoption of three more this year, will bring the number in circulation to 21. It could be that more may be deemed necessary.

Conclusions

PPGs are important in that they set the context for local government decisions. For practitioners and the public they can therefore be a useful tool in attempting to persuade a planning authority to consider a development proposal in a particular way. PPGs can, in some instances, be vague or can be interpreted in different ways. Here we see uncertainty in the system which may have to be resolved at a planning appeal or ultimately by the courts. At whatever level the decision is taken, the content of the relevant PPGs will have a great deal of influence in decisions regarding planning matters.

What can be said for sure is that the property development industry, like local authority officers, will continue to be influenced by the scope and nature of PPGs. They are the lead form of Government planning guidance now that circulars contain mainly detailed advice relating to planning procedures. It is therefore critical that all practitioners: surveyors, planners, and those with an interest in the built environment have an awareness of the scope and content of this important form of Government advice.

Contributed by Karl Dalgleish.

CHAPTER 26

Sustainable development

First published in Estates Gazette June 25, 1994

What is meant by the term "sustainable development" and what are the implications for the surveying profession?

Politicians and planners seem to be using the terms "sustainable development" and "sustainability" in almost every interview, policy document and public pronouncement at the moment. Definitions of these terms, along with reasoned explanations of their implications for urban and rural development and for the surveying profession, are much less common. But there can be little doubt that this very pervasive issue will dominate the environmental agenda in the next few years. It will become one of the main driving forces of planning policy and as a result will have a significant effect on the way in which development is viewed and the way that developers will have to respond in terms of location, design and justification of their schemes in the future. This article seeks to explain some aspects of sustainability, in particular its origins, purpose and some of the mechanisms by which it may be achieved.

The origin of sustainability

The roots of the concept lie in three important reports concerning issues of resource scarcity, pollution and uneven industrial development on a global scale. In the early 1970s, the Club of Rome produced a doomsday scenario of a world which was rapidly running out of fundamental natural resources such as oil, gas, metals and industrial minerals. These dire predictions have been shown to be misconceived as a result of advancing technology, substitution of one resource for another and complex market influences. Nevertheless the debate which resulted from this work prepared the ground for further studies. The *Global 2000* Report in 1980 shifted the emphasis away from resource scarcity to pollution issues and, very crudely speaking, predicted that humankind ran the risk of destroying itself and the environment as a result of insufficient attention to pollution from a wide range of processes such as industry, power generation and vehicle emissions, long before most of the earth's natural resources were exhausted. Finally, in 1987 the *Brundland Report* set the themes of the earlier reports in the context of uneven world development and massive population growth in the third world. It pointed to fundamental disparities such as the fact that the industrialised western economies utilise roughly three-quarters of the global stock of fossil fuels, metals and other valuable minerals, but represent only about a quarter of the world's population. The report's main conclusions were that, in order to reduce soaring birth rates in the third world, its economics must be given a greater share of resources and encouraged to industrialise. Such development would have significant effects on the prosperity and lifestyles of the developed world, while the potential pollution and resource depletion resulting from rapid third world development would have major global implications. As a result a strategy of "sustainable development" would need to be applied world-wide. Brundland defined this strategy as:

Development which meets the needs of the present without compromising the ability of future generations to meet their own needs.

The emphasis is therefore placed on attempting to protect the environment (since this will in turn protect humankind) in the interests not only of today's population but also for generations to come. This definition gives us a broad platform from which to develop other more restricted definitions and from which to develop practical programmes. It should also be recognised that Brundland examined issues which pervade the entire global economy. Loss of rain forest, climate change, desertification, acid rain and third world poverty may seem a long way from the day-to-day business of residential, industrial estate and shopping centre development in the United Kingdom, but the relationship is significant. International expressions of political support for the Brundland concept, such as the Rio Earth Summit (1992) and the various conventions and treaties on ozone layer depletion and acid rain reduction, need to be interpreted and enacted at the national and local scale, and it is here at the grass roots that the implications will become obvious.

Think global, act local

In the United Kingdom we can already see a good deal of attention being paid to the idea of sustainable development. First, we are subject to directives from the European Union. A large number of these are issued every year on environmental topics. The influence of the directive on environmental assessment, for example, has already been discussed in this column (9143 EG). Thus planning regulations and environmental legislation are continually responding to European parliamentary decisions. European Union policy itself is firmly fixed on the concept of sustainable development with the Fifth Action Programme on the Environment, which commenced in 1993, being entitled "Towards Sustainability". The British government is also nearing completion of its revision of Planning Policy Guidance Notes (PPGs) (see 9417 EG) to incorporate the concept of sustainable development into wider planning policy.

PPG12, Development Plans and Regional Guidance, notes that:

The planning system, and the preparation of development plans in particular, can contribute to the objectives of ensuring that development and growth are sustainable. The sum total of decisions in the planning field, as elsewhere should not deny future generations the best of today's environment.

The government has recently published *Sustainable Development: The UK Strategy* (January 1994) in an attempt to give some flesh to the conceptual skeleton of sustainability. This seeks to clarify the interpretation of sustainability in relation to specific activities and land uses. Such advice and legislation inevitably affects development plan policies and development control decisions. Thus developers in their turn must respond both in terms of their input to development plans and in terms of their development proposals. Hence global concerns, treaties and policies finally will affect local issues.

For example, one of the main concerns which has emerged time and time again has been the need to improve energy efficiency. This would necessitate reductions in the rate of oil, gas and coal stock depletion. An associated issue is measures to reduce pollution from power stations and motor vehicles.The latter aim is crucial and has recently been subject to new government policy in the shape of PPG13: Transport. The implications of such considerations for the future pattern of development could be profound. Rather than attempting to differentiate land uses by zoning residential, commercial and industrial areas separately, future planning policy may adopt a more mixed approach in order to reduce commuting levels.

Similarly the recently reissued PPG6, which deals with retailing, has demonstrated a shift of opinion away from out-of-town shopping and back to viable and vital town centres. This policy further demonstrates a means of reducing private car journeys in the interests of the environment. High quantity urban mass transit systems, such as Newcastle's and Manchester's Metros and Sheffield's Supertram, designed to reduce congestion and pollution in the interests of environmental quality are the other side of this coin. The prime locations of the future may well be determined by their accessibility to such systems rather than their relationship to the road network.

If global concerns on energy were to force a rise in fuel prices, either as a result of growing scarcity or market intervention via energy taxes, then novel forms of energy production might become important. Recent wind farm developments in the United Kingdom are an example. Equally, in urban locations, incinerators which serve the dual purpose of burning domestic refuse and thus reducing the need for landfill sites, as well as providing heat and power for local use, are becoming increasingly favoured. The heat grid emanating from such combined heat and power stations could again become a determining factor in the location of mass housing schemes, hospitals, and other large institutions which demand high levels of space heating. An associated issue concerns insulation standards. Energy efficient buildings with consequent low running costs could be placed at a premium. Thus sustainable development factors could be viewed as affecting property values in the future.

Valuing the environment
It emerges from the discussion above that a broader range of environmental factors resulting from development decisions will have to be considered than was the case in the past. Certain environmental factors will need to be costed in to decision-making. Thus the cost of lost recreational opportunities, lost habitat and increased traffic pollution resulting from a suburban housing development may have to be explicitly compared with the environmental costs and benefits of development on recycled

urban land. Such debates will become more explicit and, where possible, subject to quantification. Environmental assessment is a first step in this process, but we are likely to see the development of further techniques and theories of environmental value.

Surveyors will need to appreciate at least the policy background and logic of such changes and many may become involved much more closely in this type of work. It could, for example, become standard practice to set out the contribution of a development proposal to sustainable development, with a quantified statement of environmental costs and benefits included. Such a balance sheet might include detailed information on pollution and waste potential, energy consumption, traffic generation, land take and habitat loss with analyses of the net addition or saving to global carbon dioxide levels, the effect on the diversity of flora and fauna, and resources such as building materials, sand and gravel, wood, metals etc.

In summary it is likely that the global concern to promote sustainable development will affect everyone, since we all in our everyday life exploit and interact with the environment. People involved in decision making about environmental change will be profoundly affected by an ever-growing body of regulation, changing policy directions and the need to develop and exercise new skills. Much of this should be welcomed since it bodes well for our quality of life and that of succeeding generations. It also opens up new and interesting career paths. We should appreciate, however, that there is a huge distance to travel on the path to sustainability. Many of the areas of concern are fraught with contradictions and political difficulties and, in the final analysis, the goal of a sustainable environment and economy for the whole world may be like the crock of gold at the end of the rainbow, a desirable but unattainable dream.

References

Meadows et al (1975) *Limits to Growth*, Pan.

Barney G (1980) *The Global 2000 Report to the President of the US*, Pergamon.

World Commission on Environment and Development (1987) *Our Common Future*, Oxford.

DOE (1992) PPG12: Development Plans and Regional Guidance, HMSO, London.

DOE (1994) *Sustainable Development: The UK Strategy*, HMSO, London.
DOE (1994) *PPG13: Transport*, HMSO, London.
DOE (1993) *PPG6: Town Centres and Retail Development*, HMSO, London.

Contributed by Jon Kellett.

CHAPTER 27

Protecting the countryside

First published in Estates Gazette August 6, 1994

What environmental controls are imposed by English law and by European Community law to protect the environment?

The protection of the environment within the planning law system is twofold. One method is to ensure that environmental issues are considered at the root of planning decisions; this is achieved through a directive of the European Community (Council Directive 85/337/EEC of June 27 1985 on the assessment of the effects on the environment of certain public and private projects), which requires that certain projects are to be assessed prior to their commencement for their effects on the environment (this has been covered in a previous article: see *Mainly for Students* August 5 1989).

The other method is sectoral and works by zoning areas to achieve a special protection for their particular characteristics, whether those are related, for instance, to: their bird populations; the presence of rare flowers; or to the cultural heritage of the nation. The sectoral controls can relate both to the urban and the rural

---

'Since this article was published Directive 85/337 has been amended by Directive 97/11. The amendments increase the coverage of the original Directive – 12 new classes of projects will require environmental assessment and six of the existing classes have been extended. So, for example, intensive pig farms over a certain size are now subject to mandatory assessment. There are also eight new classes of project which will require an environmental assessment if they re likely to have significant environmental effects. These include, for example, wind farms and coastal protection works. The amendments also clarify the way in which decisions are made about whether a project requires environment assessment and, in general, seek to improve the quality and scope of the information provided as part of the process.

These amendments must be implemented by March 14 1999 and are currently the subject of a government consultation process.

environment. This article concentrates on the designation of sites in countryside areas.

In the United Kingdom, sectoral land use planning is a familiar concept, well entrenched in the planning system. Sites of special scientific interest and areas of outstanding natural beauty are both examples of such zoning for environmental purposes. Implementation of the Council Directive 79/409/EEC of April 2 1979 on the conservation of wild birds and Council Directive 92/403/EEC of May 21 1992 on the conservation of natural habitats and of wild fauna and flora is through these existing mechanisms.

Although such zoning is a familiar concept, it is not altogether successful. The designation of special protection areas under the Birds Directive has accounted for only 1% of the territory of the UK. As a group of offshore islands, the UK is an important stopover for migratory birds and for many species represents an important breeding ground. Therefore, 1% is an unacceptably low designation, particularly in comparison with other member states. The European Commission has brought enforcement proceedings against the UK in respect of its failure to designate adequate special protection areas under the birds directive: see *Commission* v *UK* [1992] 6 Land Management and Environmental Law Review 124.˙

Designated areas

Green belts act as a buffer between the urban and the rural environment. They check urban sprawl and restrain development encroaching on the countryside. They are designated by the local planning authority.

Other countryside controls are covered by the Countryside Act 1968 and the Wildlife and Countryside Act 1981. The authorities mainly responsible for them are the Nature Conservancy Council England (called English Nature), Nature Conservancy Council Scotland, the Countryside Council for Wales and local planning authorities. The Countryside Council for Wales was established

---

˙Further issues surrounding the designation of special protection areas have subsequently been heard. See, for example, *R* v *Secretary of State for the Environment, ex p Royal Society for the Protection of Birds* [1996] ECR I–3805 ("the Lappel Bank" case) where it was decided on a reference to the European Court of Justice that economic considerations could not be taken into account when designating a special protection area under the Birds Directive.

under the Environmental Protection Act 1990, section 130.

National parks are one of the earliest forms of control established in 1949 by the National Parks and Countryside Act. They may be designated because of their natural beauty or because of their flora, fauna or particular geographical features. The object of the designation is to preserve and enhance them. Development is strictly controlled and the local planning authority may take positive steps to develop the area for the enhancement of its recreational facilities. They can, for example, build picnic sites or camping sites and can acquire land compulsorily for these purposes.

There are 10 national parks in England and Wales covering in all 9% of the total land there.

Areas of outstanding natural beauty are a separate designation. A national park may also, in ordinary terms, be an area of natural beauty. However, national parks are large tracts of land, whereas an area of outstanding natural beauty is usually a smaller area, such as a hill or an area of downland, which requires some special controls for its preservation or enhancement. The emphasis is not on preservation for the purposes of public enjoyment or recreation, but upon the preservation of natural beauty.

Country parks, on the other hand, are areas specially designated for public enjoyment. They are municipal parks which are set aside purely for recreational purposes. There will be no combined use in a country park. Such a park will not include areas of agriculture, for instance. The emphasis in the modern country park tends to be on activity sports, such as boating, rather than on floral clocks and immaculate flower beds.

Protecting flora and fauna

National nature reserves can be established by the relevant nature conservancy council or the local planning authority where land needs to be managed specially for the study of flora and fauna and the habitats of both, or for the study of the physical characteristics of the land itself. An agreement will usually be entered into with the owner of the land as to the way in which the land should be managed, or the land may be acquired compulsorily. Nature conservancy councils were established by the Environmental Protection Act 1990. There are separate councils for England, Wales and Scotland.

Sites of special scientific interest are designed to protect scientific features as opposed to the conservation of nature of the promotion of recreation. The scientific aspect may be biological (concerned with flora or fauna) or geological (concerned with geological or physiographical matters).

The nature conservancy council informs the owners of the site as to the features which are of special interest and which operations will be potentially damaging: Wildlife and Countryside Act 1990, section 28. Cultivation of the site could be classified as a potentially damaging operation so that a farmer would be restricted from ploughing and sowing a field without notifying the nature conservancy council. The operations which can be notified are quite extensive: see *Sweet* v *Secretary of State for the Environment and the Nature Conservancy Council* [1989] 2 PLR 14. There is then a four-month waiting period, which is designed to promote an opportunity for the owner to enter into a management agreement with the nature conservancy council. If an agreement is not reached, then there is little more that the nature conservancy council can do, as Lord Mustill critically pointed out in *Southern Water Authority* v *Nature Conservancy Council* [1992] 1 WLR 775.

If the site is deemed to be of national importance or the survival of a species is threatened then a nature conservation order under section 29 of the Wildlife and Countryside Act 1981 can be imposed. Such an order imposes more stringent safeguards apply including the power of compulsory purchase where a person gives notice that they intend to carry out a potentially damaging operation.

There are now more than 5,000 sites of special scientific interest in England and Wales, but only about 30 nature conservation orders (imposing a stricter regime) have been made. The efficacy of this method of zoning an area of land where the special interest in it arises because of some scientific feature is clearly in doubt.

The designation of sites of special scientific interest is also the method used in the UK for implementing its obligations under both European Community and international law in respect of the protection of birds.

Under the European wild birds directive of 1979 there is a provision for the establishment of special protection areas to ensure the survival and reproduction of certain species of birds. This, in relation to migratory birds, applies in particular to wetlands. These special areas, once designated, must be notified to the

European Commission and steps must be taken to avoid pollution or deterioration of these habitats so as to affect the birds. In the UK, this directive is implemented through the system of Sites of Special Scientific Interest (SSSI) and through the planning system.

The other European directive which provides for the designation of areas (known as special areas of conservation) for the purposes of the protection of species is the habitats directive. This extends similar protection to that provided under the wild birds directive to other endangered or rare species of animals. It is implemented in the UK by the Conservation (Natural Habitats) Regulations 1994.

There is also an international convention in this field known as the Ramsar Convention which covers the conservation of wetlands and waterfowl by the designation of sites. Contracting parties, of which the UK is one, are under a duty to compile a list of such sites and to promote their conservation. This is undertaken in the UK, as with the wild birds directive, by means of the designation, in the first instance, of SSSI.

The status of SSSIs has been tested in the British courts. In *R v Poole Borough Council, ex parte Beebee* [1991] 2 PLR 27, Poole Borough Council proposed building housing on land which was designated as an SSSI. The land supported a number of protected species, including smooth snakes, sand lizards, the Dartford warbler, the nightjar and the hobby. The nature conservancy council (NCC) objected and asked the Secretary of State to call in the application, which he refused to do. Poole Borough Council went ahead and gave themselves planning permission to build. Applicants representing the Worldwide Fund for Nature and the British Herpetological Society applied for a judicial review of the council's decision.

The judge dismissed the claim to quash the council's decision. This raised the question of the status of SSSIs in the face of a presumption in favour of development. The site had been subject to an outline planning permission for development for residential purposes. There were therefore historical and social reasons to support development. On the other hand, there were also ecological reasons, accepted by all the parties, as to the need to conserve the site. The NCC had stepped into the picture at a late stage in order to protect the area, but, nevertheless, Poole Borough Council accepted that there were sound ecological reasons for conserving the site. The planning committee weighed the competing claims and found in favour of development. This exemplifies the process of planning decision-making in the UK and the manner in which environmental issues are weighed in the balance against all other considerations and may, in the end, be discounted. The judge found that there was nothing in this decision-making process carried out by Poole Borough Council which indicated a failure to take into account any significant matter. He did not, therefore, see fit to interfere with their decision.

Ancient monuments and archaeological areas

Under the Ancient Monuments and Archaeological Areas Act 1979 (as amended) the Secretary of State has a duty to compile and to maintain a list of monuments which are considered to be of national importance. English Heritage must be consulted before a decision on scheduling is taken. Once a monument has been "scheduled", then it is an offence to demolish, destroy or damage it without permission. The offence is absolute, although the level of fine will reflect the degree of negligence on the part of the defendant: see, for example, *R* v *J O Sims Ltd* [1993] Env Law Reports 323, which concerned Winchester Palace, Southwark, London SE1.

Apart from the obligation to consult English Heritage, the Secretary of State is not required to consult the local planning authority or hold an inquiry when considering whether to schedule an ancient monument. As in the example of the discovery of the remains of the Rose Theatre on the south bank of the Thames, he can act on his own initiative.

The Rose Theatre was the playhouse where most of Marlowe's plays were performed and two of Shakespeare's plays staged their first night. When the importance of the site was realised a campaign was launched to preserve it. English Heritage entered into discussions with the developers and an informal agreement was entered into in which the developers promised to revise their plans so as to protect the site and to make access to it possible. As a result the Secretary of State decided not to schedule the site, thus avoiding the payment of compensation and any further delay in development. His decision was upheld in the Queen's Bench Divisional Court: *R* v *Secretary of State for the Environment, ex parte Rose Theatre Trust Co* [1990] 1 PLR 39.

Contributed by Rosalind Malcolm.

CHAPTER 28

Planning in Spain

First published in Estates Gazette November 12, 1994

Previously this column has posed the question "what are the major differences between the town and country planning systems in the United Kingdom and Western Europe?" (*EG* 9221). Subsequently the French planning system was examined (*EG* 9307). The current article examines the Spanish planning system again with this aim of comparison in mind. What emerges is a clear difference in the underlying concepts of the United Kingdom (UK) and Spanish systems. Indeed, taken together, the three articles suggest that the British system is the odd one out and examination of other planning systems in Europe and elsewhere tends to bear out this conclusion. The oft-quoted assertion that the British planning system forms the model for the rest of the world begins to look a little ragged in the face of the evidence.

Knowledge of other countries' planning systems is important to the modern surveyor for two main reasons. First, the market for practitioners' skills is now truly an international one. The European Union (EU) and beyond offer employment opportunities to adventurous graduates, particularly those who possess language skills. Whether this involves full-time commitment or just the occasional visit from a UK base, knowledge is vital. Second, we begin to gain a better appreciation of our own planning system, its strengths and weaknesses and scope for improvement if we have an insight into other systems.

Spain forms an ideal subject for study. Many of us have visited and have at least some, perhaps not entirely, representative mental pictures of her townscapes and countryside. As a nation she is still undergoing a rapid stage of self-renewal. The dictatorship of General Franco from 1936–1975 inhibited and isolated Spain from the rest of Europe. As a result she emerged in the mid-1970s, relatively underdeveloped, poorer, less sophisticated and more sparsely populated than many of her European neighbours. The southern coastal strip had been subjected to intensive and often low-quality tourist development and many of her cities, such as Bilbao, Seville and Barcelona, were run down and badly in need of revitalisation while at the same time attracting a major influx of rural immigrants in search of work. From then until the recent recession Spain's rate of economic growth outstripped most of the rest of Europe. Membership of the European Community in 1986 brought a massive influx of development aid, and events such as Madrid's' year as European city of culture, the Seville Expo and the Barcelona Olympics were all expressions of Spain's intention to rejoin the European mainstream. Urban development has been intense and rapid and the planning system has developed with successive planning acts in 1976, 1990 and 1992 to cope with the pressures which have emerged.

The planning system

The distinction between the theoretical framework of planning and the reality of the current system must be emphasised. In theory a hierarchy of plans exist which parallel the hierarchy of governmental structures. The reforms of the past two decades have produced a significant degree of decentralisation of political power in Spain. Thus there are 17 autonomous regions, such as Andalucia, the Basque country and Catalonia. All these are charged with the ability to produce regional plans on numerous topics. Andalucia, for example, has regional economic, forestry, tourism and water plans in preparation. Theoretically these should provide the framework for urban plans further down in the hierarchy. In reality, conflicts often exist, and in most regions such plans have yet to be produced. Theoretically, too, there is a national plan dealing with large-scale infrastructure and economic development proposals, but this is also more an element of theory than practice.

The reality of planning in Spain is that only at the level of the municipality does comprehensive plan coverage exist. Decision-making on most types of development occurs at this level. Thus the *ayuntamiento*, or town hall, is the seat of real power in the planning field. The most important plan type is the plan general which normally sets out the planning policies and land use zoning for the urban area as a whole. The plan general could loosely be compared with a British Unitary Development Plan (UDP).

However, beneath this level a true hierarchy of plans does exist which deals with much more detailed issues than anything which exists under the British system. In Spanish cities there is a comprehensive system of land use zoning. All land is designated as either urban, that is already developed, urbanisable, that is suitable for development, or non-urbanisable, that is land which is currently undeveloped and should remain so for reasons such as aesthetics, urban containment, ecology or recreation. Urbanisable land is further subdivided into areas programmed for development within the next eight years and areas where development is not expected to take place in the next eight years. For urban and urbanisable land detailed plans covering issues such as road alignments, building and open space siting, building heights and plot ratios are then produced. There are a number of different types of these, for example planes parciales and planes especiales. These are best compared with design briefs in Britain, through they are often more prescriptive and have statutory force which is lacking in the British case.

This concentration on the physical demonstrates the overwhelming importance of architecture and architects in Spanish planning. All Spanish planners are, by training, architects, branching into planning as an extra specialism. To observers steeped in the British system they may often seem to play down or ignore important social and economic factors in order to concentrate on the visual and functional. Second, the existence of such detailed prescriptive plans is a necessary factor because, unlike in Britain, the system is plan-led. Consent is virtually automatic provided the proposed development accords with the relevant plan. Equally, any proposal which departs from the plan can be approved only after a plan modification. There is, therefore, no concept of "material considerations" as in the British system.

The actual process of obtaining consent also contrasts sharply with British practice, in that first, building regulations and planning permission are dealt with jointly and, second, most of the assessment work is carried out by private-sector architects. These must be members of the local professional body or *collegio* and their responsibility is to assure the local authority that the application conforms to all relevant regulations. An acceptable application will be stamped with a *visado* and consequently receive a *licencia de construccion*. The Spanish system thus demonstrates a great deal more certainty than the British, though perhaps at the cost of having less flexibility and ability to respond to changing circumstances. There are further contrasts. In Britain planning permissions normally have a life of five years, while in Spain development must be initiated within six months. Landowners who fail to seek the required planning consents for development may be subject to penalties and developments which have been granted consent and initiated within the six-month period may also be subject to an appropriation of 50% of development value if they do not proceed according to the general schedule. This provision, introduced by the 1992 Act, is controversial since market conditions such as those of the early 1990s may render already consented or initiated developments unprofitable.

Development taxation

A further major area of contrast with the British system is the provision for taxation of development. In Britain several unsuccessful attempts to initiate a system of taxing development gains have led us to abandon the concept. The nearest thing to development tax in Britain is the ad hoc application of planning gain through section 106 agreements. In Spain the system is much more formalised. Landowners are first required to meet the costs of necessary infrastructure provision. Highway upgrading, service modifications and connections are the financial responsibility of the landowner as they would be in Britain. The second point is that, again under the 1992 Act, land equivalent to 15% of development value must be given to the local authority – a provision originally set up to fund the development of social housing. Practice varies as to the final use of such land and whether the appropriation is made on the development site or elsewhere in the urban area. On top of this, particularly when the economy is buoyant, it is not unusual for local authorities to seek to extract yet further planning gain via plan modifications which enhance land values further.

A third concept relating to land values which appears alien to the British observer is the often complex system of reparcelisation of land. Underlying this process is the constitutional requirement that landowners should receive profits based on the scale of their landholding rather than on the nature or intensity of its new use. Thus development for public open space should yield the same profit per hectare to the landowners as development of retail or office space. The operation of this system can be time consuming and contentious, as well as involving valuations of land which apparently bear little relation to actual market values.

Conclusion

Spanish planning presents a fascinating contrast with the British system. On the one hand it demonstrates many of the attributes of other continental European systems in that it is plan led, architect driven and legalistic. It lacks the flexibility and responsiveness to change of the British system, but provides much more certainty and assurance to the developer. It also seeks to promote and encourage development by means of short time-limits and fiscal penalties in a way that the British system does not. Finally, it intervenes powerfully in the development process to ensure that application of development value created by the community is returned to the community and that gains are equalised between landowners regardless of the eventual nature of the development. It may not operate in practice as efficiently as the theory may suggest, but lessons can inevitably be learned from Spain, just as, inevitably, the Spanish can learn from the British system.

Further Reading

Keogh G (1994) "Urban Planning and Development in Spain: an economic perspective" University of Reading, Department of Economics, *Discussion Papers in Urban and Regional Economics* No 92.

Keyes J, Munt I & Riera P (1993), "The Control of Development in Spain" in *Town Planning Review*, Vol. 64, No 1

Marshall T (1990), "Letter from Barcelona" in *Planning Policy and Research*, Vol. 5, No 73

Glossary of Terms

Ayuntamiento	Town hall (local authority)
Comunidad automoma	Region eg Catalonia
Departamento de Urbanismo	Department of Planning
Desarollo	Development
Ley de suelo	Town Planning Act
Licencia de construccion	Planning permission
Plan General	City plan

Plan Parcial/Plan Especial   Both detailed types of local plan
                                  covering a few hectares
Visado   Recognition that a planning
                                  application conforms to the planning
                                  and building regulations

Contributed by Jon Kellett.

CHAPTER 29

Appraisal techniques: environmental cost benefit analysis

First published in Estates Gazette December 10, 1994

What is environmental cost benefit analysis?

Cost benefit analysis is one of a range of project appraisal techniques. It is an attempt by applied welfare economists to evaluate alternative projects (or, more widely, alternative policies). The aim of project appraisal is to identify, from a range of alternatives, the most efficient option. From a social welfare position efficiency is described by the Hicks–Kaldor criterion:

any project should be sanctioned . . . provided those who gained could compensate those who lost and still have some benefit left over.[1]

In simple terms the benefits of a project must be greater than the costs. Notice that the above criterion states only that compensation could take place. The actual imposition of compensation is not envisaged as this would require a whole range of value judgments about the distribution of wealth.

Cost-benefit analysis is separated from other forms of project appraisal by its scope. It aims to evaluate all costs and benefits, social and environmental as well as private. Investment analysis aims only to evaluate private costs, whereas cost effectiveness analysis is concerned merely with identifying the cheapest way of achieving a policy aim. Because of this social context cost-benefit analysis is favoured for assessing public projects such as transport schemes, COBA[2] for roads and, notably, in determining the site of London's third airport.

Cost-benefit analysis, then, is a practical way of assessing a project's desirability where it is vital to take both the long and wide view.

Given the wide nature of different costs and benefits, for them to be comparable a single measuring rod is needed. As in all economic techniques, the measuring rod is money. The technique then endeavours to assess the net benefits of the project by subtracting the total costs from the total benefits:

$$B_1 = \sum^t b_1(t) - c_i(t) - K_i \qquad t - 0 \ldots n$$

$$B_i = \frac{\sum^t b_i(t) - c_i(t) - K_i}{(1 + r)^t}$$

where:

B_i	=	present value of net benefits from project i
$b_i(t)$	=	consumption benefits received from project i in year t
$c_i(t)$	=	costs of project i in year t
n	=	lifetime of the project
K_i	=	initial capital outlay (cost) of project

The long view is needed because the effects of a project do not always occur immediately. The long-term nature of many projects means that the values need to be expressed in real terms at today's prices, ie their present value.

Cost benefit analysis can now be formalised:

Where: $1/(1+r)$ is the discount factor at rate of interest, r.

Having identified the basic numerical framework of cost benefit analysis there are three fundamental issues which need to be investigated, the costs and benefits which are to be included, how these are to be valued and at what interest rate they are to be discounted.

Which costs and benefits are to be included?
The first issue is important in determining the breadth of study which gives cost benefit analysis its status as a social project appraisal technique. The costs and benefits of a project occur both internally and externally. It is the counting of the externalities, especially those affecting the environment, which is particularly problematic. In early examples of cost benefit analysis many of these externalities were classed as intangibles and no value was assigned to them. Before discussing the valuation of these intangibles in more detail, and the recent advances in applied

economics which allow them to be valued, it is necessary to examine the concept of externalities.

Externalities arise in two forms, technological external benefits and costs which are included in the calculations, and pecuniary external benefits and costs which are not included.

Technological externalities affect the levels of production or consumption within the economy. Pecuniary externalities affect prices in the economy, and such changes lead to a redistribution in wealth, not a change in levels of production or consumption.

This can be illustrated by considering the benefits of building a new road. There are direct costs and benefits such as the construction costs, reduced travel times and a reduction in accident costs. However, there is also a set of external costs. The technological external benefits may include benefits to non-users such as pedestrians and property owners who were adversely affected by the traffic before it was diverted on to the new road.

Pecuniary externalities may include increased profits for garages and restaurants on the new road. However, these benefits are not an absolute increase, merely a redistribution, from garages away from the new road to those on it.

Valuing externalities

Once the problem of externalities has been addressed and the relevant effects identified it is necessary to evaluate them by some form of pricing. Since elementary economic theory suggests that markets provide efficient outcomes then market prices should be used to evaluate the value of net benefits. However, a problem arises in cases of market failure, monopolies, unemployed resources or lack of markets (as is usually the case for the environment). In such cases a set of shadow prices (reflecting the opportunity cost of the externality) needs to be assembled.

Given the current situation of high unemployment it is often the employment benefits of projects which are cited. The problem of valuing externalities can be examined in this context. The simplest situation is valuing the services of workers who, before the project, were unemployed. When valuing labour it is necessary to count the social cost of that labour. If the worker is attracted from employment elsewhere there is a cost to society of lost output of that worker. There is no such loss, however, when that person is drawn from the pool of unemployed. But even then there is a social cost in the form of loss of valued leisure time. If reduction in unemployment is to be counted as a benefit then it is this social cost that needs to be counted (the reduction in social costs is the benefit of the project). This social cost can be estimated in the form of a reservation wage – the minimum wage needed to tempt people into the job, not the actual wage that they will be paid. Any reduction in unemployment benefits is not counted since these are redistributions of wealth. However, the reservation wage can be estimated to just above the level of unemployment benefits.

Where markets do not exist, surrogate markets have to be established. During the past 15 or so years four techniques have been established:

1. Hedonic valuation method[3]
2. Travel cost method
3. Contingent valuation method
4. Production function approach

The hedonic method implies a value by considering changes in prices in surrounding markets. The most common use for this is the property market. Changes in the value of an environmental asset are implied by changes in property prices. If, after a change in one area of the environment (eg landscape), house prices fall locally, this decrease in property value reflects the cost of the environmental change. It is important to remember that the change in property prices itself would be a pecuniary change and should not be counted in the cost benefit analysis (the change in price represents a change in the distribution from sellers to buyers and, anyway, including the change would be double counting: once for the environment and again for the property).

The travel cost method attempts to imply a value of the environment by again looking at surrounding markets, in this instance the transport market. It is a method especially useful for valuing recreation sites. Again drawing from basic micro economic analysis, the benefit, or value, of a commodity must be equal to the price paid for that commodity. So, for a recreation site, visiting a park or a trip to the beach, the value gained must be at least equal to the costs incurred in getting there, the travel costs (the method can be adapted to include any entrance fees or parking costs). The total value of the site can then be found by multiplying the average travel costs by the number of visitors.

The contingent valuation method is a "catch all" method which asks consumers directly for their value of a specific commodity. This method sets up a hypothetical market and asks for people's willingness to pay in order to prevent an environmental loss or their willingness to accept the loss (compensation). The use of this method needs to be carefully monitored to prevent "bias" – respondents giving artificial answers to influence an outcome. Such things may include people offering to pay amounts greater then their income to protect the environment. Obviously this is not the effective willingness to pay. This highlights a problem: those on higher incomes can value the environment higher and thus displace environmental damage into poorer regions.

The production function or dose response method can be used where the environmental resource in question has a marketable output. This method is particularly useful for issues of agricultural land degradation. Where soil erosion causes a loss of crop output, that output can be measured and, using market prices for that crop, a value implied for the loss of soil. Alternatively, the cost of fertilisers to maintain output can be used to imply the value of the loss.

It is up to the cost benefit analysis practitioner to choose the method which best fits the externality. In doing this the valuation must, as much as possible, reflect the total economic value of the resource.

$$\text{TEV} = \text{Use value} + \text{Option value} + \text{Existence value}$$

Use value is the value of the resource if it were being used (recreation value of parkland, timber value of wood land etc). Option value is the value placed on a resource to secure its use in the future (this can either be use for the same person or their relatives or, more usually, for future generations). Existence value is the value placed on a resource just because it is there, even though no use may ever be made of it. Thus, most people desire to preserve rain forests even though they are unlikely ever to visit one.

Discounting
Once the valuation problem has been solved and values produced they need to be expressed in present value, involving consideration of the choice of discount rates. There are two broad reasons for discounting:

- the Social Time Preference – because people prefer money now rather then in the future. The preference arises because of inflation, risk of death, uncertainty that the money will arrive;
- the Cost of Capital – to reflect the rate of return available on capital (opportunity cost of capital, the return available on risk-free investments).

Resource allocation should be based on decisions reflecting social returns.

From the earlier equation it can be seen that the higher the discount rate the lower the present value. For example, a benefit of £10,000 occurring in 10 years' time has a present value of £6,139 at a discount rate of 5%, but only £3,855 when the discount rate increases to 10%. The choice of the correct discount rate is critical.

From an environmental perspective discounting is complicated. Both the choice of discount rate and the actual principle create a dilemma. At high discount rates less investment may be undertaken because the present value of future returns appears lower and, hence, fewer natural resources are used.

However, at the same time environmentally benign (or enhancing projects such as growing oak trees) seem less attractive. But resource depletion could also be accelerated as short-term projects appear more desirable. A further problem with high discount rates is that the present value of potential catastrophic events which may appear in the far future (such as accidents involving storing nuclear waste) appear small. Choosing a low discount may allow for more investment to be undertaken and consequently more natural resources depleted.

There is also an ethical issue surrounding discounting. The actual principle of discounting implies a lower value on those circumstances which affect future generations. This is in contradiction to the basic principle of sustainable development which aims to place equal importance on both the future and the present. Economists place little importance on this ethical argument, concentrating more on choosing the correct discount rate. The actual rates used for public-sector projects are determined by the Treasury and are currently 6% and 8%, depending on the nature of the project.[4]

Risk and uncertainty

Finally, any elements of risk or uncertainty need to be addressed. Risk applies to situations where the possible outcomes are known together with the probabilities of that outcome occurring. In cases of risk the value assigned is calculated by the value of the effect multiplied by the probability of that effect occurring. For example, if the outcome of the project is a 30% risk of causing £10,000 of damage and a 70% chance of causing £1,000 of damage the value assigned is

$$0.3 \times 10,000 + 0.7 \times 1,000 = £3,700.$$

It is important to notice that the probabilities must add up to 1, thus ensuring that all possible outcomes have been accounted for.

The treatment of uncertainty is much more difficult. Uncertainty arises when the outcomes or the probabilities of outcomes are not known. In such situations it is almost impossible to provide reliable monetary valuations and it falls to the practitioner to provide a "best guess" estimate.

Because there can be elements of uncertainty involved in a project, it may be necessary to carry out sensitivity analysis. This involves recalculating the net present value using either different monetary values (to reflect the different costs or benefits which may occur) or using a different discount rate.

Conclusion

In summary, cost benefit analysis can be broken down into a number of distinct stages:

- The definition of the project, identifying which resources are to be reallocated along with who gains and loses from this reallocation;
- The identification of influences within the project which will include the creation of extra costs and benefits (additionality) as well as displacements (distribution changes);
- The identification of economically significant factors which implies a normative judgment on what generates welfare;
- Physical quantification of the influences;
- Monetary valuation of relevant effects, the prediction prices over time, correction of market failures and imperfections and the application of relevant valuation techniques;

- Discounting the monetary cost and benefits;
- Application of the net present value test – are the benefits greater than costs; and
- Sensitivity analysis.

Although the formal requirement to submit a cost benefit analysis is mainly limited to public projects and transport schemes it is still a useful tool and is often used to argue against developments (the Forestry Commission has employed environmental valuation extensively in establishing recreation value of the commission's estates, Benson & Willis, 1992) as well as in favour of them (Michael & Pearce, 1989, presented a cost/benefit of reclaiming colliery spoil heaps). The key advantage of environmental cost benefit analysis, over techniques such as environmental assessment, is that it compares different effects against the common measuring rod of money.

References
Benson, J F & Willis K G (1992) "Valuing Informal Recreation on the Forestry Commission Estate" *Forestry Commission Bulletin* 104

Michael, N & Pearce, D (1989) "Cost Benefit Analysis of Land Reclamation: A case study" Paper 89–02 International Institute for Environment and Development

Notes
[1] D W Pearce *Cost-Benefit Analysis* 2nd ed, Macmillan, p16
[2] COBA is the name of the Department of Transport's computer programme for carrying out cost-benefit analysis. It includes elements for time saved and the cost of accidents
[3] Hedonic pricing originates from the 1960s. There are many American studies linking property values with environmental effects.
[4] *Economic Appraisal in Central Government: A Technical Guide*, HMSO 1991.

Contributed by Rob Hetherington.

CHAPTER 30

Explaining contamination issues

First published Estates Gazette August 5 1995

Can you explain the current position concerning contaminated land? Whatever happened to the contaminated land registry?

A legacy of land contaminated by former industrial processes is a feature common to almost all modern economies. In the UK a good deal of this long-standing dereliction and contamination has already been dealt with, though a considerable quantity remains as a challenge to the surveying, engineering and environmental professions. Estimates of the total amount of contaminated land vary between 50,000 and 240,000 ha in the UK.

Solutions to the problem of contamination are needed for a number of reasons. First, environmental quality is an international concern which is high on the political agenda. In particular the EU is committed to raising standards of environmental protection in member states and in those aspiring to become members. Second, public health must be considered. The potential health hazards of heavy metal contamination, for example, cannot be ignored in a modern economy. Third, the positive image needed to attract new investment into a region requires that dereliction and contamination are not simply left to degenerate further. Positive reaction is vital. Fourth, land owners and property professionals are becoming increasingly aware of the potential legal problem of liability attached to contaminated land. While legal systems differ throughout Europe, the fundamental questions regarding the effects of contamination on value, the legal responsibility for contamination and the requirement to provide funds for clean-up are common to all states.

In the UK the Environmental Protection Act (EPA) 1990 was introduced. Section 143 of the Act introduced the concept of a register of contaminated land which was to include all affected sites. The major problem which the property professions recognised was that once a parcel of land was included on the register it could never be removed, even after remedial action had been taken. From the environmentalist standpoint this approach was welcomed, but the potential problem of reduced site values and depressed demand for contaminated sites forced the government to abandon the register. The question of liability was, however, now placed firmly on the agenda. The concept of retrospective liability was tested in the courts. In *Cambridge Water Co* v *Eastern Counties Leather* (1 All ER 53) it was held that a company cannot be held liable for pollution which occurred prior to new legislation being introduced. Furthermore, the RICS has recently issued advice in the form of Land Contamination Guidance for Chartered Surveyors (1995). The table sets out the nature of the problems. The range of hazards is large and the potential targets range from occasional visitors to a site, occupiers, construction workers and those consuming any foodstuffs produced on the site.

The Environment Bill currently before parliament includes 16 new sections relating to contaminated land, including a statutory definition as:

any land which appears to the local authority in whose area it is situated to be in such a condition that by reason of substances in, on or under the land a. significant harm is being caused or there is a significant possibility of harm being caused; b. pollution of controlled water is being or is likely to be caused.

Solutions to the problem
It is the potential solutions, and how they are to be arrived at, which are of particular interest to surveyors. First of all it should be recognised that there are two distinct approaches which can be taken when dealing with contamination. In the United States, Germany and Holland a total clean-up approach has been tried. In these countries the attempt is made to clean the site to a quality where it is capable of any end use. In the UK, however, a different approach, tying the standard and method of clean up to the proposed end use, is advocated. This "suitable for use" approach is mainly justified on cost grounds, although it can also be argued that total clean-up is rarely possible and, as environmental standards increase in the future, further remediation may be necessary even on sites dealt with under the first regime.

Types of contamination and hazards to end users

Contaminations	Hazard	End use
Heavy metals Organic	Ingestion of contaminated soil (children)	Domestic gardens, recreational and amenity
Cadmium lead	Uptake of contaminates by crop plants	Domestic gardens, allotments, agricultural land
Sulphate Copper Nickel Zinc Methane	Toxicity to plants phytotoxicity	Any uses where plants are to be grown
Sulphate Chloride Phenols Oils	Attack on buildings and services	Built development
Methane Sulphur Potentially combustible materials (eg coal dust, oil, rubber)	Fire and explosion	Built development
PAHs Phenols and oils Asbestos Radioactive materials	Contact during construction	Short-term site workers
Phenols Cyanide Sulphate Metals	Contamination of water	Any uses involving run off or leaching

Source: Mallet H. "Strategy, Techniques and the Costs of the Remediation of Contaminated Land" in *Henry Stewart Conference Proceedings, The Property Implications of Contaminated Land*, 1994

For the surveyor who needs to advise on a contaminated site, accurate information is all-important. The latest RICS advice sets out a logical methodology which is designed to produce the required data. The recommended approach involves three stages. First, it is necessary to collect data relating to contamination of the site through examination of the history of the site usage, a walk-over of the site and the tabulation of data regarding the toxicity of substances likely to be present. Second, information regarding the risk attached to the contamination needs to be examined. This process might involve identification of the potential pathways by which contamination may have spread to affect other parts of the site, adjacent land or particular vulnerable targets such as residential areas, schools or hospitals. Gas migration, leaching into water courses or the physical movement of earth or waste are all relevant examples of pathways. It is also necessary at this stage to review the toxicity standards which may be applied. While contamination may exist, its quantity and distribution need to be assessed and set against accepted scientific and legal standards in order to determine the extent of any risk. The third stage in the process involves risk assessment. On the basis of the data gathered in stages one and two the potential for adverse effects on human beings, plants and animals, and other elements of the biosphere such as air, water and climate needs to be assessed, an appropriate margin for error included, and a recommendation made as to the extent of risk that the site presents to particular uses. At this stage proposals as to the preferred method of remediation and its cost should be made.

The remediation methods available fall into four general categories. The choice rests on both cost and on the proposed end use of the site. A site intended for car parking, for example, would not require so rigorous a clean-up programme as would a site intended for residential use. It should be noted that the remediation methods are set out below in order of cost. The further down the list we progress the more expensive is the method.

Siting and design changes

On many sites contamination is not uniformly distributed. It may be possible to change the layout design of a scheme so that vulnerable activities are positioned on safe ground and contaminated areas remain either undeveloped or are subject to less-sensitive uses.

Removal of contamination

The physical removal of contamination is a really feasible alternative only when small pockets or concentrations exist on a site. Where very large quantities of contaminated material exist then this approach simply transfers the problem elsewhere, which does not constitute an environmentally sustainable approach.

Containment of contamination

Containment is the most usually employed remediation method in the UK. The scope can vary according to the nature of the problem and the proposed end use of the site. For example, surface capping, using clay, bentonite, plastic sheeting or some combination of these may prove sufficient to protect surface land users. In other cases, vertical and horizontal boundary layers of clay, sand, polythene, concrete or combinations of these may be needed to completely encapsulate the contamination and inhibit gas migration and leaching of toxins. Such methods can prove very costly because of the need to remove and then replace contaminated material.

Treatment of contaminations

A very high quality of clean-up can be achieved by the use of a variety of remedial treatments of contamination. These include soil washing, chemical detoxification, biological deregulation of toxins using specially introduced microbes, vitrification of contaminated material or high temperature incineration. All these techniques represent both the environmentally most acceptable and most costly options.

Land quality statements

The RICS originally promoted the concept of a Land Quality Statement as a necessary accompaniment to a planning application for development. The most recent guidance has expanded on this idea such that an LQS is seen as a useful tool in any surveyors' report on a site, whether the purpose is a development appraisal, transfer of ownership or a contribution to an environmental management system. The LQS describes the environmental status of the land with associated risk assessment and proposals, where necessary, on how to manage that risk. Again the structure of an LQS can be broken down into three sections or stages of activity. The first stage involves a desk study of the site history, assessment of available contamination data and liaison with other agencies which can provide relevant information. The second stage consists of physical investigation of the site, including sampling, geological/hydrological investigation, interpretation of retrieved data and a risk assessment. The third and final stage is concerned with the choice of remediation method which should be selected in the context of the intended end use of the site. Continuous monitoring of the site and surroundings might be added as a final recommendation. The LQS provides a useful model for surveyors dealing with potentially contaminated sites. In former heavy industrial areas such sites are all too common, so great care should be exercised and it should never be assumed that sites in such areas are free of contamination.

Conclusion

The suitable for use approach advocated in the new Environment Bill, allied to the abandonment of contaminated land registers, is on the face of it a victory for the surveying profession over pressure from the environmental lobby. The net effect will be that contaminated sites will benefit from any kind of remedial treatment only when development is proposed and many sites which represent a real hazard to health will remain untouched. As time progresses, the liabilities attached to such sites will become more difficult to establish and thus the application of the "polluter pays" principle will become more difficult to achieve. Perhaps an opportunity for large-scale environmental improvement has been lost, although the reasons which largely relate to cost are easy to comprehend. Adequate finance to support site remediation is vital. Following the failure of the original scheme proposed under the EPA, perhaps a radical change of approach is required. Taxation of development on greenfield sites is one mechanism which could have the desired effect of both encouraging development on tax-exempt brownfield sites and providing a clean-up fund for site remediation where necessary. For the moment, the professional surveyor needs to be constantly aware of the potential effects on site valuation of contamination and clean-up and remember that, in a situation of rapidly changing environmental legislation, the liability of site owners and their professional advisers should never be overlooked.

References

RICS (1995) *Land Contamination Guidance for Chartered Surveyors.* RICS, London.

RICS (1995) *Environmental Management and the Chartered Surveyor.* RICS, London.

Henry Stewart Conference Studies (1994) *Fourth Annual Conference: The Property Implications of Contaminated Land.* Henry Stewart Conference Studies, Russell House, 28–30 Russell Street, London WC1A 2HN.

Contributed by Jon Kellett.

CHAPTER 31

Statutory Nuisances

First published in Estates Gazette July 6, 1996

What are the powers of a local authority to deal with nuisances occurring on land in its locality?

Parliament's concern with the issue of public health dates back to the cholera epidemics of the 1840s and to the pioneering work of Sir Edwin Chadwick (1800–1890).

The statutory basis of what has since become known as the law of environmental health was the Nuisance and Disease Prevention Act 1848. As was pointed out in the two-part article on condensation (The Curse of the Black Spot,*), this legislation predated any statutory intervention in the law of housing by 20 years. The phrase "unfit for human habitation" was not coined by Parliament until the Artizans and Labourers Dwellings Act 1868.

Environmental Protection Act 1990

The common theme of all public health legislation since 1848 has been a recognition that "the greatest good of the greatest number" cannot be achieved by the exercise of private rights. The tort of nuisance would have been of little use to those who were too poor to afford a lawyer, in the days before law centres and the availability of legal aid.

Moreover, until very recently, children who would be most likely to be badly affected by a health hazard, would not have had any common law right to sue for nuisance because they did not have any freehold or leasehold interests in land. Common law traditionally treated nuisance as a tort against property rights, not a tort against health. There is now a trend away from this view, at

---

*See pages 62–75 of this book.

least in cases where the plaintiff, for example, a child or an elderly relative, occupies a dwelling-house as a home: *Hunter* v *Canary Wharf Ltd* [1995] EGCS 153.*

Because of limited usefulness of private remedies in the law of public health, parliament has identified a number of nuisances where abatement action can be taken by local authorities, whether or not anyone has a private right to claim damages or to seek an injunction against the perpetrator of the nuisance.

Statutory nuisances under section 79 (1). Environmental Protection Act 1990

The list of "statutory nuisances" is as follows:

(a) any premises in such a state as to be prejudicial to health or a nuisance;

(b) smoke emitted from premises so as to be prejudicial to health or a nuisance;

(c) fumes or gases emitted from premises so as to be prejudicial to health or a nuisance;

(d) any dust, steam, smell, or other effluvia arising on industrial, trade or business premises and being prejudicial to health or a nuisance;

(e) any accumulation or deposit which is prejudicial to health or a nuisance

(f) any animal kept in such a place or manner as to be prejudicial to health or a nuisance;

(g) noise emitted from premises so as to be prejudicial to health or a nuisance;

(ga) [This subsection was inserted by section 2 of the Noise and Statutory Nuisance Act 1993]: noise that is prejudicial to health or a nuisance and is emitted from or caused by a vehicle, machinery, or equipment in a street;

(h) any other matter declared by an enactment to be a statutory nuisance.

For example: insanitary cisterns under section 141 of the Public Health Act 1936; fouled or obstructed watercourses under section 259 of that Act; unfit or overcrowded tents, inhabited vehicles, etc, under section 268 of that Act;

---

*But now see the House of Lords' decision in this case: [1997] EGCS 59.

environment by facilitating management control of environmental practices, and assessing compliance with company policies, which would include meeting regulatory requirements and standards applicable.

The crucial points to note are:

- the formal nature of the process
- that it must be repeated periodically
- that environmental audit is a management function
- that it is vital to ensure compliance with various regulations.

A further point not covered by this definition is that, usually, as with a financial audit, external verification by an independent assessor is integral to the process to give it validity.

BS 7750

The background to environmental audit is a familiar one. It developed first in the US as a management technique, practised by companies voluntarily. The European Union, as part of its fourth action programme, proposed measures to encourage industry to integrate environmental considerations into its operating procedures and in 1993 introduced a Regulation on Eco-Management and Audit (EMAS).

A parallel strand was the interest shown in Product Quality Management in the 1980s which in the UK resulted in BS 5750 Quality Management Standard. This standard sought to ensure uniform quality of industrial products in order to move away from, for example, the classic problem of the faulty car produced on a Friday afternoon and was seen as a model for environmental management. Thus BS 7750 Environmental Management Systems (1992) was developed out of BS 5750 and follows a similar approach of data collection, development of policy and standard procedures, documentation and continual monitoring.

While all schemes are at present voluntary, the spur to seek accreditation to the European EMAS standard or to BS 7750 is reflected in the growing body of legislation, particularly the Environmental Protection Act 1990 and the Environment Act 1995 which have toughened the government's stance on emissions to air, discharges to water, ground contamination, waste disposal and public access to environmental information.

Types of environmental audit
Many companies both in the manufacturing and service sectors see positive benefits to be gained from carrying out environmental audits. It is important to recognise that there are circumstances in which an audit may be necessary and these may dictate the scope and form of the audit which is carried out.

Compliance audit
This is probably the most common type and is used to demonstrate that an organisation is not exceeding specified emission levels and environmental targets. Generally such an audit would be carried out site by site. Operation of the procedure at this scale is simpler than dealing with a multi-site company in a single audit. The individual site approach forms the basis of EMAS, under which a company can elect to register individual sites, but does not necessarily have to deal with its entire range of activities.

Health and safety audit
These issues are often closely related to environmental management and, as such, the roles of company personnel and the context of the audit may often overlap. The primary reason for an audit should always be explicit and in this case the health and safety of both workforce, surrounding population and customers forms the basis of the study. Issues such as storage and handling of hazardous substances and emergency procedures are crucial.

Product-quality audit
Links between quality management and environmental audit are made explicit in this type of audit. The quality issue can extend to energy consumption in manufacture and use, process waste minimisation, packaging and eco-labelling. This latter aspect, which stems from another European environmental regulation, seeks to provide objective assurance to consumers about the environmental effects of certain products. Thus a product-quality audit could analyse a product from raw material through manufacture, use and final disposal.

Due diligence audit

Where an organisation is considering purchasing a site or acquiring a competitor company, questions of liabilities such as land contamination, land charges and emission licences are vital in arriving at a valuation. Pressure from regulators to clean up processes, perhaps by installing expensive pollution control technology, can also be important in such an assessment.

Insurance risk audit

Major pollution incidents such as the Seveso dioxin contamination in Northern Italy in 1976, the pollution of the Rhine by Sandoz in Switzerland in 1986 and numerous oil spillages by tankers have alerted the world of insurance to environmental risks. Insurance companies are increasingly likely to demand an environmental audit as part of their risk assessment before issuing cover for a company's activities.

How is an audit carried out?

The basis of an audit is normally a site and concerns the buildings, plant and activities which occur upon it. Environmental auditing can therefore, in some ways, be seen as a natural extension of the preserve of surveyors. The first step in the process is a major data gathering exercise. Typically this might include collecting information on:

- site and building history with particular reference to contaminants, asbestos etc
- evaluation of discharge consents and compliance records
- raw materials purchased and stored
- process materials and activities
- energy use and fuel types
- emissions to air and water
- solid waste creation and disposal
- accident prevention and emergency procedures
- management responsibilities, training and environmental awareness.

It is important to realise that the first time this exercise is attempted it is normal to encounter difficulties. Information is often not available or not held in the format required. An immediate lesson that is usually learned is that systems need implementing to record information on a range of activities so that future audits are more straightforward.

The gathering of such information is often mistakenly regarded as the sum total of the audit process. In fact it is merely the starting point. First, this exercise may point to obvious areas where environmental improvements and/ or efficiency savings may be made. Second, it should contribute to the formulation of an environmental management system.

Organisations embarking on this course of action should be seeking to make continuous improvements in their environmental performance. In order to achieve and measure these improvements, a policy setting out a programme of action needs documenting in a formal environmental management system in just the same way that management accounting or personnel management are formalised within organisations. Thus, after data collection, changes to information recording, environmental monitoring, policy formulation and procedures manuals may all require instituting. The whole process should then be verified by an external independent auditor.

There are, of course, problems with the approach as it currently stands. Because the European EMAS and the UK BS 7750 are voluntary, the credibility of environmental auditing is weakened. Also, because the EMAS scheme is based on individual sites it is possible for a company to reap the public relations benefits of accreditation while still pursuing environmentally damaging operations elsewhere. Finally, accreditation by a formal standard is sometimes criticised as being more concerned with providing the right documentation than actually making real environmental improvements.

There is validity in all these criticisms, but nevertheless the benefits of the concept are irrefutable. Organisations of all types now have an incentive to examine their operations and try to make them less environmentally damaging. Pursuing the holy grail of sustainability, which, although it may never actually be completely attained (EG 9425), still constitutes a worthwhile quest in a world of increasing natural resource exploitation and pollution hazards.

Contributed by Jon Kellett.

CHAPTER 33

When pollution leads to prosecution

First published in Estates Gazette February 22, 1997

An offence of an environmental or environmental health nature is usually dealt with by a prosecution under the relevant statute. Environmental statutes adopt a mixture of administrative notices and criminal prosecutions. Infringements that can be remedied by carrying out works, or by abating a dangerous or offensive state of affairs, are usually dealt with by administrative notices. For example, if a company is making a noise or producing emissions, an abatement notice can be served to stop it. A prosecution will follow only if the abatement notice is ignored.

In cases of water pollution, prosecutions can be brought for causing or knowingly permitting "noxious, poisonous or polluting matter to enter controlled water": section 85 Water Resources Act 1991 – an offence of strict liability. Prosecutions can also be brought under: sections 33 and 34 of the Environmental Protection Act 1990, for the escape of waste and other waste offences; the Health and Safety at Work etc Act 1974, for failures to ensure the health and safety of workers; and the Food Safety Act 1990, for selling food that is not of the quality or substance demanded. Similar liability will arise for conduct that contaminates land or water when the contaminated land provisions come into force.

Such prosecutions by the regulatory bodies will require proof to the criminal standard – beyond reasonable doubt – and are brought in the mainstream criminal courts – normally the magistrates' court, but sometimes the Crown court.

The route taken in such cases is usually to prosecute the company because this is normally considered more effective than prosecuting individuals when dealing with pollution, contamination or risks to health and safety – a primary object of the regulatory bodies.

Prosecuting the company for an environmental offence is not so difficult as prosecuting it for manslaughter. However, there have been mixed results in the past. For instance, in *Tesco v Nattrass* [1972] AC 153, the company was not criminally liable for the acts of a branch manager. But *In re Supply of Ready Mixed Concrete (No 2)* [1994] 3 WLR 1249 a company was held to have breached its undertaking to the court when its executives, in breach of a direct instruction, contravened its terms.

The recent Privy Council decision in *Meridian Global Funds Management Asia Ltd v Securities Commission* [1995] 3 WLR 413 has brought about a welcome clarification. In this case, chief investment officer Mr Koo purchased a substantial stake in a company on behalf of Meridian. He recorded it in the company books, but concealed it from the managing director. It was held that, as he was authorised to buy shares on behalf of the company, his acts were those of the company.

The question of whose acts were to be attributed to the company was to be assessed by looking at the company constitution, by applying the rules of agency and vicarious liability, and by looking at the substantive rule of law in each particular case. It follows that in some cases the knowledge of the board of directors will be necessary; in others, the knowledge of a more junior employee will be sufficient. In *Tesco Stores Ltd v Brent London Borough Council* [1993] 2 All ER 718, the knowledge of a check-out cashier that a buyer of an "18-certificate" video was under 18 was enough to fix the supermarket with knowledge.

So there is flexibility in this area. Given the nature of many of the offences in this context, then such flexibility is to be welcomed. But is the approach of prosecuting the company that the regulatory bodies adopt the correct one?

Director and officer liability

Most environmental statutes impose liability on directors and officers: see, for example, section 157 of Environmental Protection Act 1990:

Where an offence . . . committed by a body corporate is proved to have been committed with the consent or connivance of, or to be attributable to any neglect on the part of any director, manager, secretary or other similar officer of the body corporate . . . he as well as the body corporate shall be guilty of that offence and shall be liable to be proceeded against and punished accordingly.

This clearly covers directors and the company secretary. It includes non-executive directors and shadow directors. A person who takes on a company directorship for prestige, or because they may be in a position to lobby decision-makers, may be acquiring potential liability.

The identification of "manager" may be more difficult. In *Woodhouse* v *Walsall Metropolitan Borough Council* [1994] 1 BCLC 435 Mr Woodhouse was the site manager of a company's main waste disposal site, with responsibility for two other sites within the organisation. The company was convicted of storing waste in a trailer on site without the appropriate consent. Mr Woodhouse was also convicted personally. On appeal, it was held that, although he was a site manager, he was not a "manager" for the purposes of the legislation because he lacked the power and responsibility to decide corporate policy and strategy.

Even if this hurdle has been successfully jumped by the prosecutor, it will then become necessary for him to show "consent or connivance". This must be established beyond reasonable doubt. Consent requires a positive act or state of knowledge; connivance is less precise. Having adequate systems in place may be sufficient to protect a director from an accusation of connivance.

In the Canadian case of *R* v *Bata Industries Ltd* [1993] 6 JEL 107, the chairman of the company was acquitted when he was charged with failing to take all reasonable care to prevent a discharge under the Ontario Water Resources Act. It was held that he was entitled to assume that the on-site manager was addressing environmental concerns; and he was also entitled to rely on the systems that had been put in place, provided he was not aware that they might have become defective. He was not saved because he did not know, but because he had instituted an adequate system.

Attorney-General's Reference (No 1 of 1995) [1996] 1 WLR 970 considered the question of the personal liability of directors. The defendant argued that he had never heard of the relevant statutory provision and therefore could not have consented. The Court of Appeal held that, where the director consented to the relevant activities, the fact that he did not know that it was an offence to undertake them without a licence was simply ignorance of the law and no defence.

Penalties

A director or officer may suffer a fine – many offences may warrant a fine of the £20,000 maximum in the magistrates' court or an unlimited fine in the Crown court – or may be sent to jail – six months maximum in the magistrates' court or two years in the Crown court. In special cases such as special waste offences, the maximum is five years.

Imprisonment is rare, but there have been two recent cases. The first immediate custodial sentence was announced by the Health and Safety Executive on January 23 1996 (HSE Release E13: 96). In the past, custodial sentences have always been "suspended".

The defendant, Ron Hill of Ridings Farm, near Bristol, was charged with offences under the Control of Asbestos at Work Regulations 1987 and the Asbestos (Licensing) Regulations 1983. Mr Hill had demolished a former Lucas building in Bath Road, Brislington, Bristol, in December 1994. An excavator was used for the demolition, without any precautions being taken to prevent the spread of asbestos contained in roofing sheets and pipework lagging. Mr Hill was sentenced to an immediate custodial sentence of three months' imprisonment, and ordered to pay £4,000 costs.

At York Crown Court in February 1995, the director of a waste company in North Yorkshire was found guilty of charges relating to the unlicensed disposal of waste. He was sentenced to three terms of six months' imprisonment to run concurrently. His three sentences represented the fact that he was charged as an individual, as a director of the waste company and as a director of the landowning company.

Why prosecute the director?

When a director has been convicted of an indictable offence, then he can be disqualified from acting as a director or being concerned in the promotion or formation or management of the company, according to the Company Directors Disqualification Act 1986. The maximum period of disqualification is five years in the magistrates' court and 15 years in the Crown court. In 1992, Mr Chapman was the first director to be disqualified from holding company directorships for health and safety offences which involved unsafe working practices at a chalk quarry. He was fined £5,000 and disqualified for two years. The disqualification prevents an individual from setting up a new company or running his own.

Much protection for a director comes from having environmental management systems in place and being sure they are working properly. This may mean that a "due diligence" defence is available. Many environmental offences are not absolute – a defence is available. These offences can be found in statutes where phrases such as "reasonably practicable", "all due diligence and reasonable precautions" and "best practicable means" are used.

Contributed by Rosalind Malcolm.

CHAPTER 34

Regeneration game

First published in Estates Gazette September 6, 1997

Funding for regeneration projects has been handled in a variety of ways since the 1970s, and the emphasis now is on assisting private-public partnerships in local areas

In the four years since this column last considered regeneration policy and funding ("Grants for early 1990s inner-city regeneration"), a great deal has changed: a new government; the return of confidence to the economy in general and the property market in particular and a major shift in the funding of urban regeneration initiatives. Yet, despite all this, urban deprivation remains. However, it was 1994 that saw one of greatest policy changes in the allocation of resources for regeneration, with the creation of the single regeneration budget or SRB.

This article will consider how policy has changed and how funding is organised under the SRB. It will examine some of its components and the issues that are now emerging.

The principal policy drive behind regeneration funding is the need to encourage inner-city redevelopment by injecting public-sector money into areas where development would not otherwise be viable owing to low rents, lack of occupier demand, high development costs and poor infrastructure. For some time it has been accepted that public funding is inadequate to solve all the problems of inner-city areas.

Hence the attempts to target specific groups and areas in order to achieve a degree of success. Current policy recognises the need to give priority to economic projects, to certain areas (referred to as spatial targeting), and to disadvantaged communities. The overall objective is to ensure the economic and effective use of funds.

Introduction of the SRB

In 1989 the Audit Commission Report Urban Regeneration and Economic Development, drew attention to the unfocused nature of the urban programme and referred to the "patchwork quilt of funding regimes". Specific government responses to the report included the establishment of Government Offices for the Regions, the launch of English Partnerships and the single regeneration budget, which combined 20 separate programmes previously operated by five different government departments (see Table 1).

GOALS OF THE SRB

The single regeneration budget has two main aims:

- to fill gaps in the main existing programmes that are concerned with regeneration;
- to provide flexible, locally responsive support for initiatives to improve local areas and enhance the quality of local people's lives, by tackling need, stimulating wealth creation and improving competitiveness.

Its specific objectives are to:

- enhance the employment prospects, education and skills of local people;
- encourage sustainable economic growth and wealth creation;
- improve housing;
- promote initiatives to benefit ethnic minorities;
- tackle crime and improve community safety;
- protect and improve the environment and infrastructure;
- enhance local people's quality of life.

REGENERATION FUNDING VEHICLES

A: Programmes brought under the SRB

Urban Development Corporations
English Partnerships
Housing Action Trusts
Estate Action

City Challenge
Urban Programme
TEC Challenge
Programme Development Fund

B: Other initiatives outside the SRB

City Pride
Manchester Regeneration
Coalfield Areas Fund
European Regional Development Fund
Special Grants Programme
Local Investment Fund
New Towns
Letchworth Garden City Corporation

A: Programmes brought under the SRB	B: Other initiatives outside the SRB
Regional Enterprise Grants Ethnic Minority Grants Inner Ethnic Minorities Business Initiative Grants for Education Support and Training City Action Teams	Enterprise Zones Cities Religious Council

The new Regional Government Offices brought together the regional offices for the departments of Environment, Trade and Industry and Transport as single points of contact, each with its own regional director, responsible for its own budget, the SRB. Regional offices advise on the development of bids and are responsible for monitoring and evaluation. English Partnerships was set up in November 1993 under the Leasehold Reform, Housing and Urban Area Act 1993. Operational from April 1994, its brief was to reclaim derelict land and bring together all urban regeneration initiatives except urban development corporations. They took over the administration of both City Grant and Derelict Land Grant from the DOE.

Outline of pre-SRB initiatives
The Urban Programme, developed by the Home Office in 1968, was a response to the growing perception of multiple deprivation in the inner cities. The concept was to supplement existing central and local government spending by providing additional grants for schemes to meet social needs in urban areas.

The *White Paper Policy for the Inner Cities* (HMSO 1977), confirmed the view that these needs were the consequence of structural change in national and international economies rather than inherent social problems. The White Paper was followed by the 1978 Inner Urban Areas Act, providing the Secretary of State with powers to designate areas with special needs. The Urban Programme was criticised for not clearly articulating its objectives and consequently making meaningful evaluation of the effectiveness of the policy all but impossible. Despite this targeted funding, many of the areas designated were still suffering deprivation.

During the 1980s there were attempts to shift the balance

towards private investment through the introduction of urban development corporations, enterprise zones and simplified planning systems. There are 13 UDCs in the UK. The first two were set up in 1981 under the Local Government Planning and Land Act to regenerate designated areas. These are all due to be wound up by mid-1998. In 1988 the government set up urban priority areas under its Action for Cities initiative. In all, 57 inner-city local authorities were designated. This was essentially property led, "the concept being that property development would attract new companies into the area, which would provide new jobs, which would in turn benefit the wider community" (Cadman and Topping, 1996).

In 1991, City Challenge was launched to target run-down inner-city areas in Urban Priority Areas. This introduced a number of changes in emphasis. Funding is directed towards public/private partnerships on a competitive basis. It is concerned more with social provision through close links with the local community. Under City Challenge, teams were invited to bid for five-year grants, and the first two bidding rounds resulted in 31 partnerships, each receiving £7.5m per year for five years.

The principle aim of City Challenge is to provide support strategies to assist defined areas through the attraction of outside investment to stimulate wealth creation and widen social provision. Its intention is to create a climate of environmental quality and enterprise culture likely to attract people to live and work in the area. Funding is intended to support the development and implementation of locally devised and time-limited plans for the regeneration of disadvantaged areas within cities for the significant benefit of the residents of those areas, providing added value to current public and private initiatives.

This requires the promotion of effective mechanisms for the delivery of plans, including effective co-ordination of the resources available. The development of successful partnerships is also important for the development and delivery of the plans between local authorities and all those having a stake in the area, including the public, private and voluntary sectors and local communities. This was intended to develop the capacity within the areas selected for self-sustaining regeneration which would continue after the period of funding.

SRB funding

The single regeneration budget was established to provide some consistency across the various existing grant regimes and a single point of contact for applicants. At present the greater proportion of funding is directed towards English Partnerships, the urban development corporations, City Challenge and housing action trusts (HATs are non-departmental government bodies dedicated to the regeneration of housing and the improvement of social, economic and environmental conditions in areas of run-down former council housing). UDCs, City Challenge and HATs are existing funding schemes which have been taken over by the SRB and will "expire" at the end of their current term.

The remainder, the Challenge Fund, is an increasing proportion and will become the key to SRB funding in the future. This is allocated on a competitive basis to locally based public/private partnerships with funding going to schemes showing an integrated approach to social issues (see Table 2). Partnerships can encompass a wide range of interests including employers, the Employment Service, the police and probation services, schools, TECs, health authorities and the local community.

EXPENDITURE WITHIN THE SRB (£m)

	1993–4	1994–5	1995–6	1996–7	1997–8 (est)
UDC's	343.1	258.0	217.9	193.8	168.0
Docklands Light Rlwy	28.1	29.1	37.1	20.7	33.9
EP	164.9	191.7	211.1	229.6	209.6
HATs	78.1	92.0	92.5	87.7	88.7
Challenge Fund	–	–	136.4	264.9	481.6
Estate Action	357.4	372.6	315.9	256.7	169.9
City Challenge	240.0	233.6	226.8	230.1	143.0
Other	425.1	281.3	117.9	65.5	21.2
Total SRB*	1.636.7	1.458.3	1,355.5	1,349.0	1,370.0

Source: DOE ANNUAL REPORTS

In 1995–96 the total SRB sum was £1.3bn pa, of which £1bn was allocated to support existing programmes including UDCs, HATs (six in severely run-down estates), Estate Action (500 schemes to improve local authority estates) and City Challenge (31 winners). A total of £800m over three years was made available for new projects via the Challenge Fund.

In the two bidding rounds to 1996, 400 schemes have benefited to the tune of £2bn Challenge funding plus £5bn private-sector investment. In round 1, 48% of bids were approved with a median bid of £2.29m. The average ratio of public to private resources was 1:2.5.

Issues

Like City Challenge, the SRB is notable for introducing the principles of partnership and competition. It has been argued that the policies of the 1970s and 1980s failed in some measure, based as they were on a "trickle down" effect which had not worked for local communities. Previous approaches concentrated too much on central initiatives rather than the local. The emphasis now is on policy which is supported from the grass roots, this has been referred to as "bubble up". Hence the local community and also the local authority are seen to have an important role as distinct from the previous emphasis on central government and non-governmental bodies.

The essential characteristic of policy in the 1990s is the concept of partnership and joint approaches to projects in certain specified areas via an overtly competitive approach between them.

Arguments in favour of this approach point to the development of genuine partnerships, locally led. Against this it is argued that competition takes funding from non City Challenge areas, benefiting those places with the best submissions, not necessarily those in most need.

Challenge Funding, it is argued, has engendered new working relationships and (at least in winning areas) has proved highly successful. Challenge Funding has some similarities with the policies of the 1980s (development corporations, enterprise zones) since it is area-based and time-limited (5 years). But it differs in so far as the leading role as enabler or provider is taken by local authorities, so the community benefit is direct, not the result of trickle down.

Challenge Funding fosters genuine partnerships through a multi-agency approach. It is concerned with people as well as capital and its comprehensive strategy engages government departments other than the DOE.

Despite these apparent successes, some recent commentaries do point to issues of accountability and equity. Documents published are not available to the public, and competition necessarily means that money is not going to the most deprived areas. There are also suggestions of regional inequity. Of the £125m allocated to new bids in 1995–96, £36.25m went to London. Above all, SRB can be seen as inefficient: in Round 1 there were 256 losing partnerships and, with bids costing in the region of £100,000, this is a huge resource issue. Overall, total funding for urban policy is being reduced. The SRB masks an overall reduction in urban expenditure by the government of some £300m between 1993–94 and 1997–98.

Conclusions

Key principles of urban regeneration policy in the 1990s, such as co-ordination, partnership and competition, now seem to be firmly established. This concentrates the declining resources and encourages leverage of additional funding from the private sector.

The community is now a major partner, and human as well as physical capital is targeted with greater emphasis on social rather than economic needs. The evaluation of initiatives is oriented towards specified outputs, and overall strategy is arguably more comprehensive and the partnerships more genuine.

It is not yet clear what the new government's attitude to the SRB is. It has approved round three of the Challenge Fund (bids to be submitted in September 1997), but beyond that it could make changes.

The government seems to be committed to the fundamental principles of the single regeneration budget but might be expected to place even more emphasis on the community aspect, albeit with a shift away from competition, and towards need, but it is likely that partnerships will remain as the primary regeneration vehicle.

Contributed by Steve Crocker.

CHAPTER 35

Clean-up Acts

First published in Estates Gazette February 7, 1998

Pollution is covered by UK legislation, with local authorities and civil cases playing a large role. But EU actions could mount.

Most acts of pollution are small scale and local. They may sometimes result from a single incident, but more usually result because of a continuing process. A local factory, building site, or waste incinerator might be the most likely culprit, both for one-off acts of pollution and for the continuous emission of chemicals into the air or water or for depositing waste on land.

Local authorities

The first port of call for controlling localised pollution is the environmental health department (or the planning department) of the local authority. The powers available to local authorities include:

- The service of enforcement notices (and stop notices) under the Town and Country Planning Act 1990;
- The service of abatement notices under the Environmental Protection Act 1990;
- The licensing of facilities under the Environmental Protection Act 1990;
- The imposing of conditions (when planning permission is granted);
- The revocation of permission (subject to a duty to pay compensation);
- The prosecution of offenders; and
- The seeking of an injunction under section 222 of the Local Government Act 1972, eg for the suppression of a public nuisance.

If pollution is caused by a factory which has been using complex processes, highly contaminating substances, or pre-existing waste materials, the relevant statutory controls may be those which Parliament has given to the Environment Agency.

Whether the Environment Agency or a local authority brings a prosecution depends upon many factors, including local and national politics, the political presumption in favour of economic development and the Code of Practice which has been issued for the guidance of the Crown Prosecution Service in ordinary criminal cases.

Private proceedings

In addition to the pollution controls recognised or created by English public law, private individuals (and this includes companies) may bring proceedings to protect their interests. The threat of civil proceedings followed by an injunction and/or large damages (not to mention legal costs) can work as an effective deterrent to developers, industrialists, and plant managers.

Apart from actions at common law (eg for nuisance), certain Acts of parliament sometimes entitle private plaintiffs to bring an action for "breach of statutory duty". A recent example is provided by *Blue Circle Industries plc* v *Ministry of Defence* [1998] EGCS 93. In that case the High Court awarded Blue Circle Industries plc damages in excess of £5m because radioactive pollution frustrated the sale of some land to a willing purchaser. (This claim was based upon section 12 of the Nuclear Installations Act 1965.)

Damages awarded by a civil court for a tort such as nuisance or breach of statutory duty may well result in a higher financial cost to the developer or property owner than a fine in the criminal courts. This is particularly likely if the criminal prosecution takes place in the lowest (and, therefore, the least powerful) of the criminal courts – the magistrates' courts.

Historically in the UK the use of private law proceedings has been a powerful force in the control of pollution. Angling associations have, in the past, been active campaigners against the pollution of rivers. Until the organisation of the laws against water pollution, private actions brought by angling associations were a most powerful force for the quality of river water: see, for example, *Pride of Derby and Derbyshire Angling Association Ltd* v *British Celanese Ltd* [1953] Ch 149.

The availability of remedies in private law does not necessarily mean that private individuals will be able to take advantage of them. This depends upon whether those who have the right to sue have the financial resources (and the degree of knowledge) which empowers them to do so.

In the case of the poorest of litigants, legal aid may be available, but there are many formidable obstacles to be overcome before legal aid is obtained. The UK does not yet have the tradition of enabling environmentalists and other activists to bring private law "class actions" for damages against manufacturers and large businesses. Quite reasonably, therefore, the victims of pollution tend to look to public law remedies to resolve their plight.

International law
The number of international treaties which now address the problem of environmental degradation is evidence of a changed attitude among governments throughout the world. The significant date which marks the beginning of this change is 1972 – the date of a United Nations conference in Stockholm.

International law is sometimes described as "soft law", in contrast to national law, which is sometimes described as "hard law". This describes the difference in their enforceability. The enforceability of a treaty may sometimes amount only to moral pressure (brought to bear upon a defaulting state by the co-signatories). This may be aided by a well-structured agreement which relies on regular meetings and reporting requirements on compliance and the existence of a secretariat designed to monitor compliance.

Where such pressure fails then international arbitration, or an application to the International Court of Justice, may be the next step. This, in turn, depends upon the willingness of the parties to attend such an arbitration and to submit to its decisions (or to submit to the decisions of the International Court of Justice).

Another difficulty is the extent of the treaty itself. The more parties that can be committed to signing it, the more likely it is to be watered down and to become bland in its wording. The less specific it is in its requirements, the less likely it is to achieve compliance.

An example which can be cited here is the Wetlands Convention. This contains vague expressions, such as the obligation to "promote the conservation of listed sites", but it hardly imposes any legally binding duties to protect such sites. The true test of the acceptability of any international agreement is the extent to which it imposes clear commitments which the signatories are willing to implement by way of national legislation.

Some countries (outside the common law tradition) give legal effect to international treaties in their own courts and tribunals without any need for legislation to ratify or to incorporate those treaty obligations into national law. This is not the case in the UK or in most other English-speaking countries. The common law of England categorises a treaty as an "act of state" – an executive act of foreign policy. It is not categorised as a legislative act and it cannot be enforced or relied on in the English, Scottish or Northern Irish courts unless Parliament has stipulated otherwise (in an "Act of Parliament").

Once the UK Parliament has implemented an international treaty, the enforceability of those international obligations depends upon what powers have been given to enforcement agencies and to the courts and upon the willingness of the UK courts to attach due weight to the treaty and any "preparatory works" which led to the wording of that treaty.

In reality, it is often non-governmental organisations which police the implementation of international environmental treaties and protocols. Yet such organisations (for example, Greenpeace, Friends of the Earth, and the Royal Society for the Protection of Birds) can usually act only as a thorn in the side of the government, depending for their powers upon the political support which they may receive.

In certain cases they may be accepted to have sufficient locus standi to make an application for judicial review, if they have a strong case that there has been an error of law or a significant failure to follow the correct procedures: see, for example, *R v Hammersmith and Fulham London Borough Council, ex parte People Before Profit Ltd* (1981) 80 LGR 322; but see also *R v Secretary of State for the Environment, ex parte Rose Theatre Trust Co* [1990] 1 PLR 39.

European Union

The European Union is a supra-national organisation with all the paraphernalia of institutions for the democratic control of its business, the execution of its policies, and the judicial determination of its disputes. It has a Commission, which acts as its civil service, a Council and a Parliament, which represents the interests of the citizens of Europe, and a Court of Justice, which determines disputes, and which (since the Maastricht Treaty) has the power to fine defaulting states.

Directives and Regulations relating to environmental issues are passed by the council and by the European Parliament. "Framework Directives" provide controls on every aspect of the environment, including water quality, waste disposal, and atmospheric pollution. Further directives (known as "daughter directives") provide detailed controls on emissions, water quality and so on.

The range of laws passed at European level are comprehensive, detailed, and compulsory. Each of the member states has no option but to implement those laws into their national legal systems unless they have applied for, and have been granted, a derogation for special reasons.

The implementation of European Community law is relatively easily checked. Many of the Directives require a report to be made to the commission indicating the timing and manner of implementation in the member state. A more complex question is how effectively (or otherwise) those laws are enforced, once they have been incorporated into the legal system of each member state.

Where a member state has failed to implement a directive properly, enforcement becomes a complex matter. The first port of call would be the national courts. But who is to bring such an action? The regulatory body would itself be an emanation of the defaulting state. It would therefore fall to a private individual to apply for judicial review of the decision or inactivity of the regulator or minister.

For example, Friends of the Earth has challenged the defective implementation of the water directives (in the UK) and Twyford Down Parish Council and the Twyford Down Association have challenged the failure of the UK government to conduct an environmental assessment in accordance with an EC directive in the case of the M3 motorway construction project. Such proceedings are slow, expensive and not certain to succeed. British judges may adopt a traditional common law approach which does not include environmental protection as a fundamental tenet.

An alternative procedure is to approach the European Commission and to report the failure of the member state to implement the directive. The commission has power to bring enforcement action against the defaulting state in the European Court of Justice. But the number of cases which have been brought before the court is only a small percentage of those cases where a breach has in fact occurred.

European Environment Agency

The newly formed European Environment Agency represents one of the best examples of multi-state co-operation and enforcement, but is not intended to act as a policeman. Its function is of a database and a forum for the collation of information regarding implementation. It will also develop a scientific expertise, but it is unlikely to disprove the criticism that the EU has adopted a hit and miss approach to the implementation of environmental laws.

Contributed by Rosalind Malcolm and Leslie Blake.

SURVEYING

1 sq ft	= 0.0929 m^2
1 m^2	= 10.7639 sq ft
1 acre	= 0.404686 hectares
1 hectare	= 2.471 acres

References

[1] *Estates Gazette*, "Correspondence", p47, November 21 1992.
[2] *Estates Gazette*, "Correspondence", p59, September 19 1992.
[3] *Estates Gazette*, "Correspondence", p39, January 16 1993.

Contributed by Phil Askham.

CHAPTER 37

Ordnance Survey

First published in Estates Gazette July 10, 1993

Surveyors in all branches of the profession make extensive use of maps and plans. Ordnance Survey plans are so familiar to us that we almost certainly take them completely for granted. Perhaps we need to be reminded that Ordnance Survey, as a mapping service, is unique to this country, producing large-scale maps and plans of the highest quality.

As with so many areas of professional relevance, map and plan use is being influenced by technological developments and it is worth reviewing the range of maps and plans produced by the OS, both in familiar paper form as well as digital products which are becoming increasing available.

History

Ordnance Survey takes it name from the Board of Ordnance which, in the 18th century, was responsible for the defence of the realm.

The earliest advocate of a national system of maps was Major-General William Roy who had been responsible for producing a military map of Scotland following the Jacobite revolution of 1745. He was later commissioned by the Royal Society to measure a baseline on Hounslow Heath and to link up the Royal Observatories of Greenwich and Paris by triangulation.

Ordnance Survey was set up in 1791, a year after Roy's death, and the Hounslow Heath baseline was used to extend the triangulation over the whole of Britain. This became the foundation of the control framework upon which subsequent surveys were based.

At that time the threat of invasion from France concentrated efforts on mapping the south coast of England and the first 1in map, of Kent, was published in 1801.

The 6in scale was introduced in 1825 during the mapping of Ireland, owing to the overriding need for a map which would show sufficient detail of features such as boundaries and acreages required for the purposes of local taxation.

For some time thereafter there was considerable debate over the most appropriate scale for national mapping – 1in maps were not suitable for the detail required by Tithe surveys or for engineering works required by the railways, whereas the 6in map was not suitable for the implementation of sanitary reform, land registration and poor law legislation.

By 1848 in London this work was carried out to a scale of 60in to the mile. By 1863 however, the 1in scale was established as a general topographical map with the 25in map for cultivated areas, the 6in map for mountainous and moorland areas and a scale of 10ft to the mile for built-up areas. By 1938 three basic scales were established 1:1,250 (50in), 1:2,500 (25in) and 1:10,650 (the 6in scale).

Relief representation in the form of contours, bench marks and spot heights were the result of the first geodetic levelling which began in 1841 with a datum, establishing mean sea level, fixed to a tide pole in Liverpool's Victoria Dock. Greater precision demanded the subsequent establishment of further datum points in Newlyn in Cornwall, Dunbar near Edinburgh and Felixstowe in Suffolk. From these a network of fundamental bench marks was set up.

Once again, at the time of the first world war, the military function of Ordnance Survey became uppermost, but in the post-war period new legislation on land registration, town planning, land drainage, slum clearance and land valuation required further work on detailed mapping.

In 1936 it was decided to retriangulate Great Britain in order to resurvey the country on a metric national grid. Two bases were measured on the Ridgeway in Wiltshire and at Lossiemouth in the Moray Firth. Almost 20,000 triangulation stations were established and more than 6,500 of these were marked by the familiar, but now mainly redundant, concrete triangulation pillars.

The first 1:25,000 scale maps were produced in 1945. These were to become the Pathfinder and Outdoor Leisure series which now cover the whole of the country. The first National Grid 1:10,650 scale maps were produced in 1946 and the first 1:1,250 scale map in 1947. These new maps were the first to utilise the National Grid.

The National Grid

The necessity to locate points on a map with precision requires that a reference framework be established. One of the major changes recommended by the Davidson Committee, reporting in 1938, was the introduction of the National Grid. Prior to that the mapping of Great Britain had proceeded on a county by county basis, so far as projection and sheet lines were concerned. As a consequence, discontinuity between counties could be considerable and the matching together of different sheets was virtually impossible.

The National Grid is based on the intersection of arbitrary lines of latitude and longitude using the Transverse Mercator Map Projection System. This reduces the spherical surface of the earth to a two-dimensional plane. The projection maintains ground shape, although distance and direction can be in error, the amount of error increasing with the distance from the origin of the production. Even on large-scale maps these errors are negligible for most purposes, but corrections can be calculated when required for very large-scale surveys.

The true origin of the National Grid is 2 degrees west of longitude and 49 degrees north of latitude, although in practice a "false" origin, which occurs a little to the SW of the Scillies, 7'33" W and 49'46" N, is adopted to avoid negative coordinates.

From this point the grid divides the country up into 100km squares. It provides a national system of reference by which a point can be located on any map irrespective of scale, by its unique reference number.

The 100km squares are subdivided into 10km and then 1km squares, both of which are shown on the 1:25,000 and 1in maps. Thus, small-scale maps form the index to the largerscale maps, producing a national series of maps based on a common system.

Maps

Ordnance Survey is still most familiar in terms of its traditional map products.

Maps are defined as "a representation to scale of the features of the surface of the earth" including tangible and visible features. The main current series are produced to the following scales: 1:1,250, 1:2500, 1:10,000, 1:25,000, 1:50,000, 1:250,000 and 1:625,000. These are often still referred to in terms of their imperial scales: 50in, 25in, 6in, 2in and 1in etc to the mile, but the OS has been producing maps using metric scales since the 1930s.

Scale is of course the relationship between distance measured on the map and true distance on the ground. It is normally expressed as a ratio or the representative fraction. Thus the representative fraction for the one inch series was 1:63,360, the latter figure being the number of inches in a mile.

The largest-scale maps, and those which are probably most familiar to practising surveyors, are the 1:1250 maps (50in to the mile). More than 57,000 sheets are available covering most urban areas. Each sheet covers an area of 500m × 500m.

The 1:2,500 maps cover virtually the whole of Great Britain with the exception of certain remote mountain and moorland areas. These are the old 25in maps, sometimes referred to as the County Series.

The 6in to the mile maps, now 1:10,000, cover the whole of Great Britain with each sheet covering an area of 5km^2. This is the largest scale of mapping available for those remote areas not covered at the 1:2,500 scale.

The Pathfinder series at 1:25,000 (2 inches to the mile) are maps covering an area usually 20km × 10km. These are notable for showing rights of way and a high level of detail including field boundaries. As a consequence these are in popular use for walking.

Landranger maps at 1:50,000 (1in to the mile) remain the all-purpose leisure and tourist maps, each covering an area of 40km^2 with the whole of the British Isles covered in just over 200 sheets. The second series 1:50,000 Landranger coverage was completed in 1989.

The smallest-scale Travelmaster maps are 1:625,000 (10 miles to the inch), covering the whole country in two sheets and, at 1:250,000, national coverage in a further eight sheets.

The largest-scale maps show all permanent details including buildings, walls, hedges, kerb lines, street names, spot heights and bench marks. The 1:2,500 maps include some field parcel numbers and areas and administrative and parliamentary boundaries. Contours are shown on the 1:10,000 which, for mountain and moorland areas, is the largest scale of map available. In urban and rural areas the 1:10,000 maps are produced by deriving information from the maps at the two larger scales.

Modern developments

From the earliest stages of modern map-making to the first quarter of the 20th century, map-making techniques changed little. Before the introduction of modern photographic, electronic and global systems, all maps were based on a traditional topographical survey using the chain and theodolite.

This required the determination of mean sea level as a point of reference for altitudes, the selection of suitable points for triangulation and the determination of latitude, longitude and azimuth to tie the map to the earth's surface.

The topographical survey commenced with the chain measurement of a baseline followed by triangulation using a theodolite to determine horizontal angles from the base and triangulation points and measurement of vertical angles to determine altitude. This provided the basic framework to which detail such as contours, rivers, woods, settlements, routes and names would be added.

Modern developments began with aerial photography which was first used experimentally in 1925. This enabled the addition of more accurate detailing.

By 1954 the tacheometer, a combined theodolite and optical distance-measuring instrument, was introduced rendering the chain virtually redundant. This was followed by the electromagnetic distance measuring device (EDM).

Modern surveys are carried out using the Global Positioning System. This utilises signals from orbiting satellites to provide the survey control network.

Digital mapping

Since 1970 a digital database of map information at 1:1,250 and 1:2,500 has been built up. In simple terms this is a map in computer readable form where map details are represented by strings of coordinates which are recorded on magnetic media. At the present time the digital database covers the main urban areas, but it is expected to provide complete national coverage by 1995.

This makes regular updating possible and forms the basis of Geographical Information Systems (GIS) which are increasingly being utilised as a property-management tool. GIS enables the digitised map information to be linked to all manner of data including tenancy information, financial data, floor areas, census information and even pictorial images. GIS is being used by the emergency services for route finding, by public utilities as records of location of apparatus and for system maintenance and planning, by land surveyors for three-dimensional terrain modelling and by local authorities for estate terriers.

Digital mapping also forms the basis for "Superplan" marketed by the OS through a network of local agents in most major cities. National Superplan coverage will be completed by December 1995. This makes large-scale mapping available at any scale between 1:200 and 1:5,000 on a flexible basis.

Maps can be printed out from digital data using plotters, on standard National Grid format or on a site-centred basis. Plans can even be specifically customised to suit particular needs, omitting or emphasising particular detail as required. That well-known version of Murphy's Law which determines that the plot you want is normally located at the junction of four OS sheets, may soon become a thing of the past!

The technological developments in map production are taking place so rapidly that it is impossible to predict what future changes will take place. Portable ground-positioning systems are already available, vehicle route guidance systems are fact rather than fiction and the applications of GIS are becoming rapidly appreciated in an ever-widening range of surveying fields.

Further reading
Readers interested in the historical development of the Ordnance Survey can refer to the excellent and detailed history:
Seymour W A (Ed), *A History of the Ordnance Survey*, Dawson (1980).

For GIS applications see:
Thirlby P, "Geographic Information Systems in Commercial Property", *Property Management* Vol 11 no 10;
Clegg P, "Geographic Information Systems: Property Management Applications", *Property Management* Vol 10 no 2.

Further information on OS products is available from:
Ordnance Survey, Information Branch, Romsey Road, Maybush, Southampton SO9 4DR

Contributed by Phil Askham.

CHAPTER 38

Satisfying buyers and lenders

First published in Estates Gazette February 5, 1994

What is the difference between the new Home Buyers' Survey and Valuation and the original House Buyers' Report?

During the past decade, the need for a detailed report and valuation, falling somewhere between a mortgage valuation and a full structural survey, has been satisfied by the standard House Buyers' Report and Valuation (see "Mainly for Students", November 1988). This has now been replaced by the new RICS/ISVA Home Buyers' Survey and Valuation, drawn up jointly by the two bodies. Published towards the end of 1993, this is now the only style of report available and, since the first of January this year, is the only form of report which should be used by practitioners.

The original format provided multiple copies of a standard pro forma utilising headings covering a range of structural and other elements. This ran to four editions, reflecting minor changes such as the that of domestic rates becoming the community charge and then the council tax. Surveyors should be aware that the new Home Buyers' Survey and Valuation (HBSV) is more than just the latest edition of the House Buyers' Report and Valuation, combining the previously separate House and Flat Buyers' Reports. It is, in fact, something quite new with a different format and rationale.

As with the old HBRV, the new report is intended for the homebuyer, and is a survey and valuation. The latter is on the same terms as a mortgage valuation (as set out in the White Book) in the hope that it will prove more acceptable to the building societies. The valuation definition in the old-style report differed in some respects from the definition of value for mortgage purposes so that it could be used only as a mortgage valuation with the addition of a further page.

It is a fact that the function of the old House Buyers' Report was not well understood. Its use was limited to about 10% of all purchasers, the majority, presumably, relying solely on the more limited mortgage valuation. The attempts of the main surveying bodies to encourage wider use of the extended report format, with its additional mortgage valuation, appear thus far to have been relatively unsuccessful. With the introduction of the new-style report, and its attendant marketing package, the professional bodies hope that the take-up will increase.

There are a number of very important reasons underlying the introduction of the new format, representing increased co-operation between the RICS and ISVA, which, up until now, each published their own similar but separate pro forma.

One of the major differences between the old and new reports is reflected in the Conditions of Engagement, which have been considerably extended in order to help avoid misunderstandings between the client and the surveyor with regard to the extent and nature of the inspection and report. At the same time, an attempt was made to satisfy the needs of outside bodies. This effort has been partially successful, to the extent that the Consumers Association has responded positively to the new report, although the Council of Mortgage Lenders, consulted during the development of the HBSV, do not see it as an alternative to the mortgage valuation, even though this was one of the objectives of the joint committee. So, despite the adoption of a valuation which fits the definition of the mortgage valuation, it seems likely that purchasers will, in many cases, still be faced with the need to obtain both their own survey and valuation in addition to a further mortgage valuation required by the lender.

Main changes
In order to fit in with current thinking, the format has been updated. It also addresses the concerns of professional indemnity insurers in response to issues which have arisen in litigation.

The formerly separate house- and flat-buyers' reports are now combined. The RICS/ISVA offer a combined package of documentation, including the conditions of engagement, and a response form for completion by the client. A written response to the conditions of engagement must be returned by the client before inspection. This identifies the property to be inspected and the extent of the inspection if this needs to be specified in addition to the standard conditions. The client confirms that he has read the conditions and agrees that they should apply. This is an absolute necessity because it is estimated that a high proportion of the problems which do occur on this type of survey arise simply because the parties are not clear about the nature and extent of the survey. Confirmation of acceptance of the conditions of engagement makes clear the contract with the client as well as establishing and limiting the surveyor's liability.

Within the conditions of engagement the extent and nature of the inspection is clearly defined The extent of the inspection is thought to be the same as for a full building survey, but with a more concise report. In the case of flats and maisonettes, the client will actually determine the extent of the inspection with regard to common parts as well as other elements of the structure outside the subject property. The conditions make it clear that there is an absolute avoidance of parts of the structure which are covered and there is a total veto on the testing or assumptions about services, although tests can, of course, be agreed in addition if required.

Unlike the House Buyers' Report, there is no indication as to the range of properties for which the new HBSV is thought to be appropriate; the conditions leave the question of suitability entirely to the surveyor's judgment. The conditions do, however, make it clear that the surveyor retains the right not to proceed with a survey if, on arrival, the property is found to be unsuitable: reasons could include size, age or nature of construction. Clearly, suitability is better determined in advance, and the surveyor should have a reasonable idea of what to expect, but clients can be remarkably vague on these issues.

Both the conditions of engagement and the report itself place emphasis on the role of the legal adviser in highlighting matters which need to be confirmed before exchange of contracts. The new report also includes an insurance valuation.

RICS Books are in the process of producing a Report Writer package which, when published, will include site note format, guidance notes, glossary, checklist and guidance manual. This will be produced in loose format with an updating service. The glossary of terms, building diagram and maintenance notes can be appended to individual reports to provide the client with further and better information. The site note format will include an inspection check list and a concise means of recording information gathered on site. (The recording of site notes is, of course, crucial and will be dealt with in a subsequent article.)

The report

This is in the same format, with side headings and marginal notes. It is recognised, however, that many practices are now taking advantage of the licensing scheme – which provides greater flexibility, less waste and, some would argue, a more readable and attractive report. Existing licence users will be able to use the new format in exactly the same way.

The report, which runs to nine pages, is in six separate sections, as follows:

A: Information

This includes general information, the name and address of the clients and the property inspected, council tax banding, date of inspection, weather, tenure and tenancies. "Limits to Inspection" provides the surveyor with the opportunity to specify at the outset the extent to which floor coverings and furniture limited the inspection. Other factors to be stressed here would include snow falls, lack of access to underfloor areas and lofts, locked or inaccessible outbuildings, inspection chambers which could not be lifted and so on.

B: General description of property

Section B's general description is intended as the only descriptive part of the report and represents one of the major changes. This enables the writer to distinguish between descriptive comment and condition, the latter being dealt with in sections C to E. As before, this section includes comment on the overall construction, age and accommodation but, in addition, now covers parking, orientation, location and amenities. These are matters which most surveyors and clients would consider important but which were not specifically included in the previous versions of the House Buyers' Report.

Amenities will include location, transport, education, town centre facilities, shops, recreation and sport, as well as disadvantages and environmental factors which may affect the value of the property.

C: External and D: Internal condition

Sections C and D are concerned only with condition. Where appropriate, cross reference can be made to the descriptive comment in section B, but it is felt that this arrangement avoids the repetition which tended to occur with the old-style report. This includes all the usual elements from chimneys and roofs to services and fittings.

As the surveyor considers each element of the structure in these sections, there are a limited number of possible comments that he can make with regard to condition. Either the element is acceptable, requires further investigation, needs immediate repair or renewal, or may be satisfactory but is likely to require future repair. So here the surveyor will consider each element in turn in these terms, specifying where necessary the precise nature of the need for further investigation or immediate or future repair.

E: Common parts and services

This deals with common parts and services including lifts, security and fire escapes. Obviously this will normally (though not exclusively) apply to flats and maisonettes and so can be left out of house reports in most cases, especially where the licence arrangement is being used.

F: Further advice and valuation

Section F deals with further advice. It is probably this section which includes much additional material, some of which may have been included under the old summary section. This is now separated out and specified in terms of different elements. Under the old format, the summary was, among other things, a restatement of major defects or problems referred to elsewhere in the report. This often meant that the client was presented with two differently worded statements dealing with the same matter. To avoid this potential difficulty, subsections in the "Further Advice" section of the new report will simply cross reference back to original statements rather than reiterating them in summary form. As a result, it is hoped that the client will be provided with much clearer advice.

The section includes comment on roads and footpaths and any matters which need to be checked by legal advisers, drawing attention to any liabilities, easements and planning proposals. This is followed by a series of sections covering matters which might affect the value of the property and matters requiring immediate attention.

Finally, there are three valuations. The first is the reinstatement

likely to be the only evidence that the surveyor has exercised the proper level of skill and care. Good field notes can demonstrate that the surveyor's process has been sound, even though the wrong conclusions may have been reached. Such evidence will not be indicated by the report alone.

The surveyor, therefore, must make and retain good site notes which must be legible and well ordered, and which can be referred to at a later date. The form of the notes should ensure that all the relevant information is obtained on site and, ideally, in an order which facilitates report writing.

What options are available to satisfy these requirements?

Methods of recording

The practice of individual surveyors will, of course, vary. Dictation of notes may be acceptable, provided these are transcribed immediately and retained. This is not always practicable and may be totally inappropriate in certain circumstances; consider the nervous vendor who insists upon following the surveyor's every move!

Blank note books or A4 pads are a possibility, but these offer no support as a check list. A check list of all matters that need to be taken into account can be useful but unwieldy, and in any event will tend to vary from property to property. Some surveyors actually use blank House Buyers' survey forms to record their notes. This has the advantage of ensuring that all matters to be reported are covered, but these are in an order which will not necessarily coincide with the order of inspection, which in any event will differ from property to property and from surveyor to surveyor.

A viable alternative is to use field sheets devised to reflect the content of the report, cross referenced to its numbered sections, but in an order which is a better reflection of the normal order of inspection. This acts both as a check list and a logical record. The format needs to be flexible enough to be adapted to different types of property, but, by use of continuation sheets to cover differences in accommodation, it is possible to cover the common items, in approximate inspection order.

It would be wrong to prescribe a "correct" inspection order as this is a matter for each surveyor to determine, but most approach the task in broadly the same way whatever the property.

The example shown is one way of solving the problem. It covers all the elements of the HBSV in a logical inspection order. It also includes space for valuations, plans and other matters, representing not only the record of inspection but also a record of the valuations. The use of A4 sheets printed on one side provides the flexibility to use the reverse for additional notes and sketches where necessary.

The field notes illustrated do appear to be rather long, but, if properly ordered, too much shuffling of paper can be avoided on site and the elements which are likely to vary with different types of property, such as accommodation and elevations, appear on different sheets so that these can be excluded where not required, thus reducing the bulk of paper taken on site. Usually the surveyor will have a good idea of the type and size of property, even before arriving on site, so the sheets can, to a large extent, be arranged beforehand.

The following fictitious example is based on the inspection of a three-bedroomed semi-detached house built in the 1920s. It is stressed that this is not an actual record of inspection and is merely intended to illustrate how such a field note format can be used.

As the surveyor's hand writing is illegible, the notes taken on site have been transcribed. This will not always be necessary, although in all cases the original notes taken should be retained.

Order of inspection

The following process is assumed:

Before going on site the surveyor checks the OS sheet and sketches out a plan showing the orientation which can be checked on site for detail. Preliminary information such as client and vendor's name and council tax banding can be inserted at this stage, along with possible comparables from office records which can be checked on site.

On site, the surveyor commences by looking at the property overall, describing construction details, the site and locality. Further comparable properties in the immediate locality which have been sold or are on the market are noted. Factors limiting the inspection, details of location and amenities should be recorded at this preliminary stage.

External and site measurements are taken and noted on the site sketch along with the location of inspection chambers and trees.

Looking at the property itself, each elevation is inspected in turn, noting construction details and defects.

Having completed the external inspection, the inside of the property is considered, commencing with a brief walk around the accommodation to draw up the internal floor plans. This is followed by the survey of the accommodation room by room, making notes on all the elements as required. A final check to fill in comments on overall matters such as services will complete the inspection.

Inevitably there is some compromise between the ordering of the report and the order of inspection, but with care this can be kept to a minimum. So far as possible the field notes should reflect the order of the inspection rather than the report.

The sections on the field note sheets are cross referenced to the paragraph numbers in the standard HBSV report form. Continuation sheets are used for further elevations and for the accommodation. It will almost certainly be unnecessary to fill in all sections on each of these sheets where they have been covered adequately in previous sections; thus full details for each element in each room can be covered by "as above", further detailed comment being necessary only when a feature is particular to a given room. In the example, notes on the rear elevation and other accommodation are omitted, as these merely repeat what has already been covered.

Surveyors should be encouraged to develop their own format, reflecting the nature of the inspection, the type of property and their own inspection approach. The notes can be tested on site and continuously improved until the best and most concise format is achieved.

TYPICAL FIELD NOTES

Present: Vendor: Mr Jones	Others: None
A7 Tenure: F/H	A5 Weather: Dry & Sunny
B4 Age: 1925/1963	B1 Description: Bk/slate SD house, 2 floors
Unusual factors: None	

B2 Accom: K, 2R, Hall; 3B, Bath, WC

B3 Outs: Bk Gar single attached   Parking: One Space on drive

B7 Summary of Construction: 11" Cavity bk walls, FF cement rendered, under slate hipped and gabled roof on a timber frame, garage and ss extension under a flat felt roof

B6 Location & Amenities: located close to town centre with all usu amenities. Main bus route, schools nearby. F&C shop, bottom Acacia Ave – 150 m

A6 Limits to Inspection: Most floors with ftd cpts, some c. concealed by PS tile finish, rendered FF all elevations

INTERNAL ROOM: Kitchen
Floors: Solid concrete

Walls & Partitions: Part solid masonry, part timber stud, all plastered

Ceilings: Presume orig. lath and plaster, concealed by PS tiles.

Dampness: Some condensation mould around window opening on rear wall. ? inadequate ventilation.

Timber: Softwood ext and internal doors and skirtings.

Services: Gas cooker. Sink has plastic waste and copper dist. pipes.

Fittings: Well fitted with mod. oak units, adequate storage. SSSU with DD.

Fireplaces: None

D12: Services:

D12.2 Gas: Main supply serving CH boiler, lounge fire and cooker. Dist. pipework appears to be copper. Meter under stairs.

D12.1 Electricity: Mains. Consumer unit etc. under stairs. Visible wiring in PVC except lighting circuit in loft space – DIY appearance! test required. Adequate pp's on GF but only FF landing

D12.3 Hot Water: Cooper HW cylinder in bath. Lagged. Elec IH. HW also from CH boiler. Ec. 7 fitted.

A: PRELIMINARY:
A2 Address: 25 Acacia Ave, Anytown
A1. Client: Mr J Smith, 27 Acacia Ave
A4 Date 1.4.94 A6 Tax Band: C Ask. Price: £59950 (Agreed)

VALUATION NOTES:
Comparables:

39 Acacia Ave: 4B SD Gar CH	Ask £65,000
29 Acacia Ave: 3B SD	Sld £52,500 May '93

CMV

3 B Gar and CH Good cond say	£57,000
Allow for immediate repairs	3,500
	£53,000
F6 Existing Slate £53,500	F6.2 After Works £57,000

INSURANCE: BCIS Guide 1920s Ave size SD Good Q, Jan '93 = £575/m²

Dimensions:		108.7m² " 575	62,502
(8.6 × 6.1) × 2	104.92	Plus:	
2.1 × 1.8	3.78	Gar single bk	5,000
		Allow 1.5% inflation	1,012
F5.2 Floor area M²	108.7		

F5.1 Reinstatement Figure £68,500

ELEVATIONS: FRONT:

C2 Roof: Welsh slate appears sound, occasional loose and missing slate. Ridge tiles need repointing esp. on hips.

C4 Walls: Areas of loose render between bays, other areas may need attention. Some hairline cracking around window openings but otherwise sound.

C8 SITE:
Front: Shallow front garden with dwarf bk wall. Tarmac drive to gar.
Side: Garden area with flagged pathway. 1.8m close boarded fence in poor cond.
Rear: Lawned gardens, close boarded fending. Not closely overlooked.

C7 Garage & Outs: Bk/felt attached with light and power. Concrete floor

F1 Roads & FP's: All made up and adopted

F2.1 Rights of Way etc: None evident

EXTERNAL CONDITION GENERAL:

C9 Drainage: mains assumed, combined system. 1 IC lifted no evidence of blockage. Falls appear to be adequate

C1 Chimney stacks and Boiler Flues: Single bk stack needs some repointing. Flashings in lead appear to be original. Balanced flue in utility room.

C4 DPC: Two course blue engineering brick throughout. Some evidence of injection in front bay.

C5 Windows, Doors & Joinery: Recent hardwood framed d/g casement windows. H/w front door, softwood rear rotting needs replacement. Metal U/O gar. door. Softwood soffits and bargeboards.

C6 Decorations: Fair, the whole of the external, inc render requires redecoration

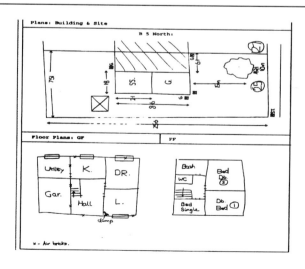

INTERNAL, GENERAL:

D5 Floors: Suspended timber in main receps with T&G finish. Solid conc. elsewhere hardwood block finish in hall. Adequate air bricks on all 3 elevations. No evident deflection. Note extensive fitted carpets.

D3 Walls & Partitions: Masonry and timber stud. All plastered. Areas of hollow plaster on some parts of external walls.

D2 Ceilings: Lath and plaster and plasterboard

D6 Dampness: Condensation in K & Bath. Some rising damp in front F. Staining on DR c from leaking cylinder 2 yrs. ago (vendor)

D7 Timber Defects: Evidence of past WW attack in floor of front bed single. Treated 5 yrs ago, guarantee available.

D8 Internal Joinery: Modern softwood throughout.

D11 Insulation: D/G windows throughout. Plumbing in loft adequate lagged. Further insulation needed to rising main entering garage.

D9 Internal Decs: Generally good

D8 Staircases: Conventional timber, note loose handrail.

D1 Loft Space: Conventional timber. Construction appears adequate. Not underlined, orig. torching falling away. Quilt insulation laid between joists 4" thick.

Contributed by Phil Askham.

VALUATION

CHAPTER 40

Agricultural Valuation – I

First published in Estates Gazette October 2, 1993

What are the main factors to be taken into account in valuing agricultural property?

The valuation of agricultural property is a specialised activity not to be undertaken lightly by those without a detailed and intimate knowledge of farming practices. Even so, the market for agricultural land is interesting in that the factors influencing values, whether they be vacant possession values, investment values or rents, are wide ranging, giving rise to greater fluctuations in value than those experienced in other property sectors.

Whilst agricultural valuation is a specialised operation, many general practice surveyors, may, from time to time encounter the need to value some types of agricultural property so that an understanding of the main principles underlying valuation should not be overlooked. Most general practice surveying courses exhibit an almost total urban bias and yet many of the surveyors trained in this way will find themselves working in areas which include agricultural properties.

As with any other property type, the main factors determining value will of course be the physical attributes of the property itself and the balance between supply and demand for property in the market. These factors tend to be unique and, although agricultural values do, to some extent, reflect changes in property values generally, there are a great many others to be considered. Unlike residential and commercial property values which, though cyclical, have tended to demonstrate an overall trend of increase over the long term, average farm values are lower currently than they were 10 years ago. So, along with the physical factors, it is also necessary to consider elements such as the legislative background, the state of the economy, the political climate and the level of farm incomes, the latter being dominated by the European Community and its notorious Common Agricultural Policy (CAP), as well as developments in world trade such as the current GATT (General Agreement on Tariffs and Trade) negotiations.

Physical factors affecting value:
Soil

A farm is unique in the sense that the property itself, the land, is a factor of production rather than just the context within which economic activity is undertaken, as is the case with most other property types. The principle physical factor influencing agricultural value will then be the quality of the soil. This will determine the productivity of the land and therefore its profitability. Logically one would expect the amount of profit to be extracted from the land to be the principle concern of the owner and tenant, determining how much should be paid either in terms of rent or capital value.

Soil is a highly complex material consisting of mineral particles, decayed organic material, water and living organisms. The texture of the soil depends to a large extent on the size of individual particles. Sandy soils have large particles whereas, at the other extreme, clay soils are composed of a high proportion of very fine particles. Between these two extremes are a wide range of silts and loams which are intermediate in character containing a mixture of particles of different sizes.

Light sandy soils, although easy to work, tend to dry out quickly and require greater inputs of soluble plant foods to maintain fertility, as the mineral constituents tend to leach away more quickly. Heavier clay soils are naturally richer and more productive, but can be difficult to work when wet and tend to be colder, cropping later. Good drainage, both natural and artificial, is an important factor on heavier soils. The silts and loams might be seen as an ideal compromise, sharing the positive characteristics of both extremes being both naturally fertile and workable.

Whatever its make-up, an ideal soil will be one which is suited to a variety of crops to allow flexibility of enterprise. It should have a reasonable depth because shallow soils will be suitable for grass or, at best, cereal crops, but will not support the high-value cash crops such as potato and sugar beet.

Topography and climate

Lower elevations usually experience longer growing seasons and are also capable of producing earlier in the year. South- and west-facing aspects get more sun and also tend to produce earlier and longer. Contours should not be so steep as to prevent the land being worked by normal machinery. The land should not be too exposed.

Such topographical factors, along with the quality of the soil, will combine to determine the nature of the farming operation. A high, hilly farm with a shallow limestone soil, for example, is not conducive to arable farming. Again, the ideal will be a location which is capable of supporting a wide range of farming enterprises and crops.

Climate and rainfall are also important factors in determining the type of crops which can be grown. In general terms, in this country, climate improves southwards with a longer and earlier season, while rainfall decreases eastwards. Within this general picture there are many variations which may be determined by specific local conditions so that other considerations include the influence of the gulf stream, producing a more promising micro-climate in otherwise exposed western locations, and, at the other extreme, the damaging exposure sometimes experienced on farms in the flat plains of the generally favourable eastern half of the country.

Factors such as soil type, exposure and contours and climate and rainfall are reflected in the MAFF Agricultural Land Classification, which divides land into five grades, grade 1 being the best, typically Fenland silt and grade 5, land subject to the most severe constraints, normally with high altitude and poor soils. The classification is rather generalised, but does offer an initial guide as to the overall quality of agricultural land to be expected in a given locality.

Other physical factors

As with all property, location is a key factor. In the case of agricultural property the ideal is probably reasonably close to towns for markets and other facilities, with isolated farms proving generally unattractive commercially. Proximity to urban areas can, of course, present its own problems in terms of trespass and general interference.

Generally, it is necessary to consider the depreciatory effect of any wayleaves or easements and public footpaths which might intrude upon agricultural operations.

The land should be accessible and ideally within a ring fence with no areas severed by major roads, the necessity to move stock and slow-moving machinery across busy roads being an undesirable hazard. All of the farm should be accessible by machinery all year.

Size also seems to be a factor with, generally speaking, smaller farms attracting higher rents and capital values per hectare because of greater demand for smaller units, which require less capital investment and lower levels of labour. However, it tends to be only the larger units which attract institutional interest as investments.

These, then, are the main physical factors pertaining to the land itself. But of course a farm is more than just a block of productive, well-situated land, and one of the main additional features will be the character and quality of the farmstead. The house itself should be modern in terms of its facilities. Rising residential values have had a marked effect on the values of smaller agricultural units where a good-quality house may have a significant influence. Farm buildings should be modern and flexible. Specialised buildings such as pig and poultry units are not well regarded because they cannot easily be converted to other uses. Buildings should ideally have sufficient capacity to house stock, machinery and produce. On larger holdings good cottages will be a factor in attracting farm labour. All buildings, houses and cottages should be well maintained and in good repair.

Mains services should be available to the house and buildings and there should also be water supply to fields used for stock. Often it is an advantage to have a private water supply – ponds and streams, for example – for stock and irrigation which can be costly if supplied from the mains. However, these must be of good quality and free from pollution if used to supply stock, especially for dairy herds. Another service factor is the potentially high cost of effluent disposal.

Other fixed equipment will include hedges, fences, gates, ditches and drains. Stockproof hedges are essential for keeping animals in place, but also provide shade and protection. Other items should be well maintained, for, while gates and hedges might seem to be marginal elements, in cases of severe neglect they can absorb substantial expenditure.

Finally, there is the standard of farming itself. A well-farmed, neat and tidy, productive unit which has been well improved will always command a premium value.

Other physical factors which have a bearing on value include commercial woodlands and sporting potential: woods for shooting cover; lakes, ponds and rivers for fishing. Many farms, especially those close to urban areas, have potential development value, not forgetting mineral exploitation and including conversion of derelict buildings, all of which can vastly enhance value.

Because of the tendency for smaller units to command a premium in the market, larger units which can be lotted will often produce higher total values.

In the modern context of production restraint, quotas are increasingly important. Although these can be purchased (with the exception of sugar beet), a farm which does not already have adequate quotas appropriate to its productive capacity will clearly be less valuable than one which has.

At times of restriction on production and falling producer prices diversification is another significant factor. Bed and breakfast, camping and caravanning and farm gate sales will all help to supplement the farm income.

It is often said that land prices bear no relation to the profitability of farming operations. Other factors to be considered include the residential element and the attractions of agricultural land as a means of avoiding inheritance tax liability.

Vacant possession value
The only real approach to the valuation of agricultural property with vacant possession is the comparative method based on knowledge of the farm itself and the local market because, generally, apart from large or specialised units, markets tend to be fairly localised.

Farmland Market, published quarterly by *Farmers Weekly* in association with the RICS, gives full details of transactions county by county, as well as providing national data. It is probably the most useful source of market evidence.

Average prices can be misleading in the extreme as there are great variations in this market sector, but vacant possession prices of equipped farms appear currently in the range of £4,000 to £4,500 per hectare (£1,600 to £1,800 per acre).

Average prices have shown significant fluctuations during the

CHAPTER 41

Agricultural valuation – II

First published in Estates Gazette October 30, 1993

What are the main factors to be taken into account in valuing agricultural property?

A previous article outlined the principal factors to be considered in undertaking a valuation of vacant possession agricultural property. This article continues by looking at the additional considerations necessary for the valuation of investment farms and the assessment of farm rents.

Investment farms

Until the mid-19th century the relationship between landlord and tenant was governed by local custom. This had developed variously over time to create a patchwork of arrangements which varied across the country, influenced by the traditional farming enterprises undertaken in different localities. By 1875 much of this was incorporated into the Agricultural Holdings Act 1875. Since then there have been a number of further statutes which were eventually consolidated into the Agricultural Holdings Act 1948 which, until recently, formed the body of law governing the landlord-tenant relationship.

During the late 1970s concern was expressed as to the amount of agricultural land in institutional hands. The Northfield Committee, which reported in 1977, was set up by the Government to investigate this and other issues.

The Northfield Report found that, whereas in 1908 88% of agricultural land was held on tenancies, by 1977 this proportion had fallen to 35%. With more or less absolute security of tenure provided by the 1948 Act, it was felt that the proportion would continue to fall and that this was undesirable as very few farms would be available to new tenants. Many of the Northfield proposals were embraced in the Agricultural Holdings Act 1984. All legislation subsequent to and including the 1948 Act has since been consolidated in the Agricultural Holdings Act 1986.

Broadly speaking, legislation perpetuates the contractual relationship between the landlord and tenant, but makes special provisions in relation to:

- security of tenure
- succession on death
- compensation on quitting
- repair obligations
- rent on review

This article will not consider succession or compensation on quitting, both rather specialised areas, but will concentrate on the main elements determining rental and investment value.

Rental value

Capital values of investment farms are normally assessed by adopting the traditional investment method of valuation and the main variable is therefore the rental value of the holding.

There is no statutory restriction on the amount of rent payable and the parties are free to reach a negotiated agreement. However, either party may demand a reference to arbitration on the question of rent payable from the next day on which the tenancy could have been terminated by notice to quit, any alteration in rent to take effect not less than three years after either the commencement of the tenancy or the date of a previous variation. This means, in effect, that most agricultural tenancies are reviewed every three years.

In such cases the review rent is defined in section 2 of and Schedule 12 to the 1986 Act:

the rental properly payable in respect of the holding shall be the rent at which the holding might reasonably be expected to let by a prudent and willing landlord to a prudent and willing tenant

The schedule further refers to relevant factors to be taken into account which include:

- the terms of the tenancy;
- the character and situation and locality of the holding;

- the productive capacity of the holding and its related earning capacity;
- the current level of rents for comparable lettings.

A number of different approaches to rental valuation are available, the most common being a comparative approach which simply applies a spot figure per hectare to include land, houses, cottages and buildings. This is obviously based on a detailed knowledge of the locality and of comparable rental evidence.

Types of rental evidence

This evidence can take a number of different forms. Actual rents are primary evidence, but require a detailed knowledge of the comparable farm which should be in close proximity, similar in terms of type of farming, with comparable fixed equipment and letting terms. It is necessary to disregard any scarcity value in the rents of comparable holdings as well as marriage value, premiums, tenant's improvements and dilapidation and comparable rents may require further adjustment on account of these additional factors.

Comparable rents may include open market rents, but if these have been fixed by tender, care must be taken to allow for any premium arising due to shortage. Prospective tenants are often willing to pay a high premium to get established in a holding, in the knowledge that the rent can always be renegotiated downwards in three years time, at the next review. Currently, tender rents are well in excess of negotiated review rents. In 1991, for example, tender rents in the East Midlands reached almost £220 per hectare (£90 per acre) compared with sitting tenant rents at £120 (£50 per acre).

Sitting tenant rents are not, of course, market rents. These might be low, reflecting the particular relationship between landlord and longstanding tenant. A landlord will be anxious to retain a tenant of ability whose very presence will do much to maintain the long-term value of the holding. Such tenants are often prepared to spend their own capital improving the farm and may well cover repairs well in excess of the actual liability under the tenancy agreement.

Arbitration rents are those fixed by an arbitrator on review. These will accord with the statutory definition of market rent. It is interesting that very few rent review negotiations reach this stage and most are settled by negotiation.

There is also a body of secondary evidence from statistical

sources usually derived nationally to give the average of rents on the open market at lettings and reviews, as well as the percentage increase in rents over a given period. This type of evidence is published in the Farmland Market.

Other approaches to rental valuation

The field-to-field method is similar to the basic comparative approach but requires a detailed analysis of land and buildings, with rental values being applied individually to each different element of the farm.

A further approach, the profit or gross margin method, can be distinguished in that it looks at the profitability of the holding itself, rather than market evidence. This is somewhat akin to the profits method of valuation as applied to certain types of commercial property. As a method of determining agricultural rents, it has arguably become more relevant now that the statutory definition of rent refers to both the productive and related earning capacities of the holding.

Rent is a function of profit and no two farms will have the same profit potentiality. Equally, tenants will demonstrate different farming abilities. In theory, at least, a competent farmer farming a productive and well-equipped holding will generate higher profits and so can afford to pay a higher rent. However, maximisation should not be pursued in isolation if this is at the cost of damaging the long-term value of the farm.

The gross margin method relies on the preparation of a detailed budget on the basis of the farm's enterprises to give the gross output. Fixed and variable costs are deducted to give net income or profit. This profit can then be split three ways:

- return on tenant's working capital
- tenant's remuneration
- rent.

The tenant will normally take 45%–60% of the residue as remuneration after deduction of return on capital. The remainder is available to the landlord as rent.

This approach needs to be applied with caution. There are so many variables to be taken into account in determining profitability that the method depends on a great deal of knowledge of the actual farm and its enterprises. Such an approach is thus well beyond the capabilities of the average general practice surveyor and is best regarded as the province of the specialist. In any event, it is probably wise to check the results against market evidence, where available, to highlight any anomalies.

The method does at least highlight the relationship between profit and rent and the increasing importance of farm incomes. Between 1982 and 1992 real farm incomes have actually fallen, while over the same period rents have increased by 14.9% from an average of £96 per hectare (£39 per acre) in 1982 to an average of £110 (£44 per acre) 10 years later, the diverging trends placing an ever-increasing burden on profitability. At the present time both farm incomes and rents appear to be static.

Investment valuations

Generally, any tenant of an agricultural holding, subject to an agricultural tenancy, enjoys absolute security of tenure, subject only to limited grounds for possession. Thus, in valuing an investment farm it is usual to assume that the full rental income will be available in perpetuity. Because of the dearth of farms to let contrasted with a seemingly inexhaustible demand, existing tenants are unlikely to default and so the rental income is normally regarded as tenant secure.

In valuing an investment farm, all the physical factors outlined in the first article will, of course, be relevant, but it is further necessary to consider the quality of the tenant and his farming abilities, as this will influence both the rent and the long-term capital value of the holding.

It is normal to adopt the traditional investment method of valuation, capitalising the net income at the appropriate yield. Traditionally yields for agricultural investment have always been low. During the 1970s, the period of greatest institutional involvement, they fell to around 2% and even lower during a period of rapid rental growth where rents could be expected to double between triennial rent reviews. In more recent years yields have risen to between 5% and 7%, still low by comparison with most other forms of property investment.

The conventional justification for low investment yields is normally explained in terms of security of income and capital as well as the potential for windfall gains resulting from development or vacant possession.

Low yields can be further explained in that the supply of land is at best fixed, even declining, while there has been a permanently increasing demand for agricultural produce. In the post-war years, the nation's desire to become self-sufficient in food production led to Government support for farming in terms of grants, subsidies and tax concessions. Other, less tangible, but nevertheless important, attractions seem to be based on the tradition that in some way, owning land was an indication of wealth, status and power.

To a significant extent all these appeals are now questionable. Controls on production introduced by the EC to curb oversupply have seriously affected farm incomes, and, for a variety of reasons, the political climate, which has encouraged successive governments to support agriculture by a wide range of tax and other concessions, has been reversed in recent years and farmers find themselves generally out of favour. Intensive methods of cultivation, which have done so much to increase productivity, are now being blamed for the pollution of rivers and watercourses and for the destruction of wildlife habitats, all this at a time when the problem of surplus and over production results in the absurdity of spending taxpayers' money to pay farmers to take land out of production.

Outgoings to be deducted from the rent to find the net income, include repairs which can be as high as 12%–15% of the rent. A tenant faced with an increase in rent on review is likely to be more demanding in terms of repairs. Generally, unless otherwise stated in a written tenancy agreement, repair liability will be determined in accordance with the "model clauses" contained within the Agriculture (Maintenance, Repair and Insurance of Fixed Equipment) Regulations 1973 (SI 1973 No 1473, as amended by SI 1988 No 281).

Management might be as high as 20% and will cover land agents' fees as well as legal and accountancy fees. It is not unusual for the total deduction for outgoings to exceed 30% of the rental income.

The capitalisation of net income at the going discount rate currently appears to produce investment values of around 45%–50% of current vacant possession values. In view of the dearth of investment purchasers it is often the case that a farm can be offered to the sitting tenant who may well be prepared to pay a premium over and above the investment value, although in practice this is unlikely to exceed more than a margin above the investment value.

Investment values have tended to follow capital values, and appear generally to be around 50% of the full vacant possession value. Again, averages are misleading but from a high in the early 80s of around £3500 per hectare (£1410 per acre), investment values are now down to about half this figure.

Farm rents are clearly more closely tied to the productive capacity of the holding, more so now that these are factors to be taken into account at a rent review. The future prospects for rental values would therefore seem to be bleak in the long term if there is no confidence in any prospect of farm incomes increasing, although some commentators have suggested that, with yields at around 6% and more, some institutions are again beginning to show an interest in agricultural investments.

Notes

Examples of the gross margin approach to rental valuation can be found in:

Williams R G, *Agricultural Valuations*, Estates Gazette 1991 (Chapter 20).

Rees W H, (Ed), *Valuation: Principles into Practice*, Estates Gazette 1992 (Chapter 1). This also contains examples of the investment method applied to agricultural property.

Readers interested in aspects of Agricultural Holdings legislation should refer to Scammell and Densham's *Law of Agricultural Holdings*.

Prices and rents are quoted in hectares, although many analysts still seem to be using acres. Approximate per acre figures are given in parentheses based on the conversion factor, 1 acre = 2.47 hectares.

Contributed by Phil Askham.

CHAPTER 42

Valuing overrented property

First published in Estates Gazette May 28, 1994

"I am somewhat confused by the variety and complexity of valuation methods which have appeared recently, dealing with the problem of overrented property."

As a consequence of the worst commercial property recession in most living memories, overrented property has become commonplace, especially in the retail and office sectors, and in particular in those locations which enjoyed high levels of growth during the boom years of the late 1980s. Overrenting occurs when the rent payable under a lease with upwards-only reviews exceeds the full open market rental value, so that the occupier is, in fact, "enjoying" a negative profit rent. With rents now at best static it may be some time before growth of any sort returns to the property market – and even when it does the margin between current rental values and high rents fixed at the top of the market suggests that valuers will continue to encounter the overrented phenomenon for some years to come.

Such market circumstances have, of course, existed in the past, but were relatively short lived. Commercial rent indices covering the past 30 years clearly show periods of static rental growth in the late 1960s, the mid-1970s and the early 1980s – but nothing to compare with the steep decline from the last peak in 1989–90. The Jones Lang Wootton index of commercial rents, for example, shows a fall of 100 points between 1990 and 1993.

The depth and length of this present recession has resulted in some rethinking of conventional valuation approaches. A number of writers have addressed the problem, providing a range of solutions varying in mathematical complexity, many of which are quite difficult to follow. Some solutions, while undoubtedly mathematically correct, are so complex that it is unlikely that the simple valuer would be tempted to adopt them in practice. Articles describing a range of solutions are referred to for those readers who wish to research them up in more detail.

This article will deal with one of the more simple responses by considering a not untypical example, looking first at the conventional approach to valuation and then comparing this with a "real" value alternative which will serve to underline the deficiencies of the conventional approach.

Example

A valuation is required of the freehold interest in a prime office which was let three years ago on a 20-year lease with five-year upward-only rent reviews. The rent was agreed at £200,000 pa on full repairing and insuring terms. Since then, rental values in the locality have fallen and it is estimated that the current full rental value on the same terms is only £125,000 pa.

There is enough market evidence to suggest that a fully let freehold property on sale would reflect a capitalisation rate of 8%.

Conventional hard-core approach

At the valuation date the income of £200,000 contains an overrented element amounting initially to £75,000 pa. This could continue until the end of the lease in 17 years' time because the upwards-only reviews will maintain the rent payable at the current level. It is, of course, possible that during this time, if rental growth is sufficient, the market rent will at some point again exceed the rent passing. Equally, faced with the prospect of a continuing negative profit rent, the tenant may just decide to pack his bags, leaving the freehold investor with the prospect of reletting at the lower full rental value (FRV), thus losing the whole of the excess income. At least this lower figure represents an attainable core income receivable in perpetuity which, given present market circumstances, does underwrite his investment to the tune of £1,562,500, assuming, of course, that the property would relet.

The real question, then, is to what extent can the investor count on any further value in respect of the temporary overage or froth income resulting from the excess above FRV?

In conventional terms it would seem that the two slices of income, the full rental value and the overrented portion, need to be valued separately so as to distinguish the different qualities of the core and overage. Many have concluded that the hard-core method is the most appropriate means of achieving such a distinction.

Valuation 1: Hard-core approach
Valuation

1. Core income

FRV	125,000	
YP perp @8%	12.5	1,562,500

2. Overage

Rent passing	200,000	
ERV	125,000	
Top slice	75,000	
YP 17 years @13%	6.7291	504,682
Value		£2,067,182

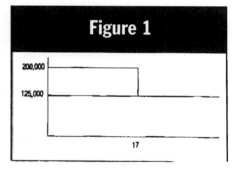

Figure 1

Income flows for the hard-core valuation are illustrated in Figure 1. The core income or bottom slice is capitalised in perpetuity at the all-risk yield for similar rack-rented property derived from market evidence. The income will be available in perpetuity and, once things return to normal, will presumably reflect future growth. The top-slice or overrented portion of income must be valued at a higher discount rate to reflect:

(a) that this is a fixed income which is unlikely to enjoy the benefits of growth in the foreseeable future; and
(b) the tenant risk attached to the receipt of a temporary additional income in excess of the full rental value.

Core income yield is determined by market evidence (8%), but the higher top-slice yield is difficult to determine – except by intuition. It clearly needs to be higher, but how much higher?

It should at least equate with medium-term fixed interest securities (currently, say, 7%) adding for normal property risks such as management costs, lack of liquidity, marketability etc. Arguably the question of additional covenant risk should be ignored altogether as, in the absence of a sound tenant covenant, it would be wrong to take account of any excess income. If the tenant is going to default this is likely to happen sooner rather than later, leaving the freeholder not only short of income but also facing dilapidations and a possible void before reletting can be achieved.

Apart from the difficulty of selecting the yield differential, the hard-core method does contain fundamental flaws. The all-risk yield adopted to discount the core income reflects future growth potential and results in a double counting of the part of the overage shown as the shaded area in Figure 2.

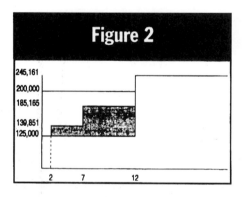

Growth-explicit valuation

This all-risk yield which reflects investor perception of the future growth expectations recognises that a return to more typical rental progression is not far away. Assuming a target rate of return for fixed-income investments plus a margin reflecting the normal risk characteristics of property, the valuer might arrive at a target yield of, say, 13%, which just happens to be the top-slice discount rate adopted in valuation 1. A combination of the all-risk yield on fully let freeholds on conventional lease and review terms and a target yield of 13% implies an average growth in the rental value of 5.7739% pa. This rate can be found by using one of the implied growth rate formulae (see Crosby or Donaldsons investment tables).

Assuming that the full rental value experiences this rate of growth, it will have the effect of increasing the bottom slice income over time, as reflected in the growth-implicit yield of 8%. The freeholder will benefit from this growth only on the occasions of the rent reviews and these changes in the core income can be taken into account explicitly. However, this growth will also result in a corresponding progressive reduction in the top-slice income.

First, it is necessary to consider what happens at each of the rent reviews/renewal which will occur in 2, 7 and 12 years' time, assuming the implied growth rate:

Uplift calculations

ERV	125,000	
× Amt of £1 in 2 yrs @ 5.7739%	1.1188	139,851
ERV	125,000	
× Amt of £1 in 7 yrs @ 5.7739%	1.4813	185,165
ERV	125,000	
× Amt of £1 in 12 yrs @ 5.7739%	1.9613	245,161

It can be seen that by the third review, 15 years into the original lease term, that the rent will actually exceed the current market rental value. The actual point at which this occurs has been referred to as the "breakthrough".

This new core income profile is illustrated in Figure 3.

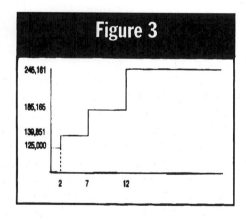

Figure 3

Valuation 2: Growth-explicit approach
Core income

1. Term	FRV	£125,000	
YP 2 yrs @ 13%		<u>1.6681</u>	208,512

2. Reversion	EFRV	£139,851	
YP perp @ 8%	12.5		
x PV in 2 yrs @ 13%	<u>.783</u>	<u>9.7893</u>	<u>1,369,053</u>
Core value			1,577,565

Overage

3. 1st 2 Years

	Rent passing	200,000	
	ERV	<u>125,000</u>	
		75,000	
YP 2 yrs @ 13%		<u>1.668</u>	125,108

4. Years 3–7

	Rent passing	200,000	
	ERV	<u>139,851</u>	
		60,149	
YP 5 yrs @ 13%		3.517	
PV in 2 yrs @ 13%	<u>.783</u>	<u>2.7538</u>	165,680

5. Years 8–12

	Rent passing	200,000	
	ERV	<u>185,165</u>	
		14,835	
YP 5 yrs @ 13%		3.517	
PV in 7 yrs @ 13%	<u>.425</u>	<u>1.4947</u>	<u>22,179</u>
			<u>£1,890,531</u>

The two approaches can now be compared:

	Hard-core	*Growth explicit*
Core	1,562,500	1,577,565
Top-slice	<u>504,682</u>	<u>312,967</u>
Total value	<u>2,067,182</u>	<u>1,890,532</u>

Although the core values are very close, they differ because the 8% yield, adopted in the hard-core calculation, is the fully rack-rented yield which reflects a full five years to the next review. In fact, though the core element is a full rack rent, the next rent review is somewhat closer, being only two years away.

The difference between the total values is in excess of 9% and this occurs mostly in the top-slice valuation and results from double counting the part of the overage (shaded) in the hard-core method (Figure 2).

In effect, valuation 2 is a "real" value DCF method of valuation using a short-cut approach, although a full-blown DCF would, of course, provide the same answer:

Full DCF: core incomes

Year	Income	PV @ 13%	DCF
1	125,000	0.8850	110,620
2	125,000	0.7831	97,893
3	139,851	0.6931	96,924
4	139,851	0.6133	85,774
5	139,851	0.5428	75,906
6	139,851	0.4803	67,173
7	139,851	0.4251	59,445
8	185,165	0.3762	69,652
9	185,165	0.3329	61,639
10	185,165	0.2946	54,548
11	185,165	0.2607	48,272
12	185,165	0.2307	42,719
12	3,064,516*	0.2307	707,002
Total			£1,577,565

* Rent on renewal £245,161 x YP perp @ 8%

Using growth-explicit valuation methods does not provide a solution to the problem of target discount-rate selection, but this is no more, and probably less, intuitive than the selection of the top-slice rate required for the conventional hard-core valuation. Using short-cut DCF methods does at least overcome the danger of double counting inherent in the conventional approach while adhering to a recognisable valuation format.

Note on rounding

Calculations have been carried out to six decimal places, but these are shown shortened to four places in the illustrations.

Further reading

Goodchild R, "Valuation issues for the 1990s", *Estates Gazette*, February 29 1992, p85.

Lyon J D S, "Top-slice valuation, a pure mathematics approach", *Estates Gazette*, June 13 1992, p82.

Martin D, "Valuation of overrented property", *Estates Gazette*, December 7 1991, p52.

Tyser B, "Valuation analysis: cutting out froth to get better estimates", *Estates Times*, February 26 1993.

Epstein D, "Modern valuations (2) Overrented investments", *Estates Gazette*, April 17 1993, p120.

Crosby N, "Valuing commercial investment property" *Chartered Surveyor Monthly*, October 1991, p9.

Contributed by Phil Askham.

CHAPTER 43

The Mallinson Report

First published in Estates Gazette February 18, 1995

"What are the implications of the Mallinson Report and what is being done to implement its recommendations?"

The Mallinson Report(1), published in March 1994, is the report of the RICS chairman's Working Party on Commercial Property Valuations. Given the breadth of its brief to "investigate, comment upon and produce recommendations on any aspect of commercial property valuation which (they) thought appropriate", the number and extent of its recommendations (43 in all) came as no surprise and the report itself represents a thorough, though not definitive, review of the whole process and practice of valuation. As such Mallinson and subsequent fall-out represent essential reading for students and practitioners alike. Given the comprehensive nature of the report, it is not possible to consider the material in detail. This article seeks merely to draw attention to some of the main issues.

The periodic necessity for professional navel contemplation seems to arise following spells of property market recession. The rising market provides immunity by masking errors. In such circumstances it is extremely difficult to prove an overvaluation; indeed, in such circumstances the market seems to ensure that such problems do not arise. Not so in a falling or even static market, as a glance at the significant number of recent valuation negligence cases will confirm. This is perhaps a timely blow to the arrogance of a profession which thought it knew best, a profession once rudely awoken by the noise of the market crash in 1974 which seemed to have dropped off to sleep again during the boom years of the late 1980s.

One of the consequences of the 1970s collapse was the introduction of the Red Book, itself a key area of debate contained within the Mallinson Report. At that time concern surrounded the effect of valuations of assets as the basis for secured lending in a falling market. The RICS responded by establishing the Asset Valuation Standards Committee which produced its first manual in 1976 with the current version, the third edition, Statements of Asset Valuation and Guidance Notes in 1990, concerned with valuations of commercial property in the public domain. (see "Mainly for Students", March 23 1991 and May 18 1991).

The 1970s also gave rise to the other principal source of guidance for practitioners, the White Book. Broader in coverage than the Red Book, though not mandatory, these guidance notes were published in 1980 and incorporated into the *Manual of Valuation Standards*, providing the valuer with guidance on procedures for valuations other than those covered by the Red Book.

If the Red and White Books represent the response of the profession to the problems following the 1970s collapse, Mallinson is the rejoinder to the difficulties of the 1990s. A key recommendation was the preparation and publication by the RICS of:

a comprehensive and user-friendly manual of valuation standards and guidance which draws on elements of the Red and White Books and other suitable material

Scope
Mallinson identified faults and areas of contention concerning the services of commercial property valuers in terms of reliability, credibility and clarity. Credibility would be achieved only by valuers operating within an effectively regulated framework. Reliability depends upon the use of valuation bases which are appropriate, with supporting evidence and accurate and consistent results. Finally, to ensure clarity it is essential that the client and valuer understand one another.

The value of Mallinson as an agenda lies in its breadth. Even a glance at its contents reveal coverage which encompasses the whole scope of the valuation process:

- knowledge of the client and establishment of clear instructions understood by both parties
- definitions of price, worth and value;
- valuation methodology;
- use of data;

- communication of results to the client.

In his foreword, Michael Mallinson identifies four key requirements:

- The need to demonstrate that all valuers work within "a common body of knowledge, application and expression";
- The need to demonstrate that the profession is regulated and subject to discipline;
- The clearer expression of what valuers do and do not do;
- The improvement of the technical elements of the valuer's skill in terms of mathematical models and access to, and use of, data.

The report concludes by identifying four fundamental steps:

- The appointment of a valuation overseer to direct and manage all subsequent action;
- The organisation of the Red and White Books, with the additional material we suggest into a coherent, user-friendly and enforceable manual.
- Any necessary expansion of the regulatory powers of the RICS.
- The commissioning of the necessary research and preparatory work for new valuation bases and methodologies.

The debate

Leaving aside the debate about the colour of the new Red Book (suggestions include pink and candy striped), the key issues seem to be centred on what is understood by "worth" and "value" and the meanings of the two main bases of value.

The need for a common Open Market Value definition is recognised as is the desirability to keep to a minimum the number of different valuation bases to avoid confusing both client and valuer. While Mallinson firmly approved of the retention of OMV, the tendency for misinterpretation of the details of the definition was highlighted. In broader terms the definition had been criticised as being backward looking and difficult to apply with accuracy in markets with few or no comparables.

These concerns resulted in the recommendation for a further new (at least in Red Book terms) definition, the Estimated Realisation Price or ERP.

For an Open Market Valuation the valuer has to identify the price at which the property would sell at the valuation date, assuming that a suitable marketing period had already taken place. The valuation and completion date are taken to be the same and the market is assumed to be as it is at this date. It is likely that such a valuation will be based on comparable transactions which are inevitably an historic reflection of the market.

The ERP definition arises out of the need for an estimate of the price at which the property might actually be bought and sold. This is the requirement of many clients, especially lending institutions, who will wish to know how much they will raise if they decide to sell. This can be distinguished not only as a forward-looking approach which takes account of current prices but as one which also seeks to reflect market changes likely to occur during the marketing period which takes place after the valuation date.

Mallinson rightly comments that there is a need for valuers to provide estimates of worth as well as price. Once the need is identified it is important that valuers are equipped to provide the service lest others, such as accountants, do it for them. However, the report recognises difficulties associated with the concept of "worth" and the need to develop a definition as well as a means of assessing and expressing it. In this context it is also noted that the report comments on the inability of the profession to provide appraisal advice which recognises the broader context of property investment appraisal.

The need for improved communication between client and valuer is addressed in a number of ways. The valuer should understand the particular needs of the client, something akin to the Financial Services Act "know your client" provisions, but also in the simple expedient of written instructions. It is often quoted that something like 50% of all negligence claims arise from the failure of one or other party fully to specify, understand and agree instructions. Finally, the report refers to the need for clarification of assumptions, data and methodology which should be addressed specifically in the valuation report.

The emphasis on appraisal as well as the need to communicate gives rise to concerns about methodology. The conventional all-risks yield approach is not dismissed, for it remains a valuable market measure, but it should be recognised as a unit of comparison important in market valuations if not expressions of worth. However, it is not widely understood outside the property profession and serves often to conceal important information.

Appraisal implies wider advice and the valuer needs knowledge and experience of a broader financial environment as well as techniques which reflect this.

DCF or real value methods are more explicit and may also provide a better measure of subjective worth. But in turn these are often derived from the all-risk yield and are not necessarily valid and reliable in their own right in the context of market valuation. The broad recommendation for further guidance, and the development of common standards as well as further investigation into new methodologies and information bases, arises from these concerns.

The profession's response

The response to the report was encouragingly swift, a reflection no doubt of just how seriously the problems addressed were regarded by the profession at large.

In August 1994, under the chairmanship of George Grover, the Valuation Integration Group published the *Consultation Draft Manual*(2), which sought to implement the Mallinson recommendations, in particular the amalgamation of the Red and White Books making the White Book Guidance Notes mandatory.

The Consultation Draft of Statements of Valuation and Appraisal Practice and Guidance Notes were produced by the Valuation Integration Group under George Grover with the remit:

- to merge the contents of the Red and White Books;
- to incorporate those recommendations from Mallinson as considered appropriate and desirable;
- to remit other recommendations for further attention.

The document considers all the Mallinson recommendations and while it would be inappropriate to consider each in turn it does also identify a number of important issues.

Within the definition of Open Market Value it suggests that the concept of repeatability (what is meant by the "best" price, the highest bid or one which several purchasers would be prepared to pay?) would be difficult to apply and that the present definition should be retained. To change the name of the definition to Estimated Realisation Price would, the group felt, lead to further confusion, although it was conceded that there is a need for "greater education" as to the definition and that whatever definition is adopted by the valuer should appear in reports.

The manual contains Practice Statements, which are mandatory, and further guidance and information on good valuation practice and methodology.

The Consultation Draft Manual does not apply to:

- evidence and pre-hearing statements;
- RICS/ISVA Home Buyers' Survey and Valuation Scheme;
- compensation claims, rating and council tax;
- asking, offer and guide prices provided in the course of estate agency work.

The consultation period closed in November 1994 and one of the main areas of contention arising from comments received concerns the introduction of the new basis of valuation, the Estimated Realisation Price, as an addition to the established basis of Open Market Value. The attention of the reader is drawn to recent correspondence in *Estates Gazette* as well as articles such as that by John Rich (3).

The definition of ERP appears at paragraph 4.6 of the Consultation Draft:

The amount of cash consideration before any deduction of costs of sale, and taking no account of any additional bid of a prospective purchaser with a special interest, which at the reporting date, the Valuer considers could reasonably be expected to be obtained by a willing seller for the interest in the subject property on completion of an unconditional sale on a date assumed and stated by the Valuer, such date to be one following the period and method of marketing considered by the Valuer to be necessary to achieve that amount.

The merged Red and White Book Appraisal and Valuation Manual is due to be published in September 1995.

Mallinson has undoubtedly proved to be an important review of the whole process of valuation. It has stimulated a valuable debate which itself has resulted in greater awareness of those issues and problems which the profession and its members ignore at their peril. That debate is as yet unresolved and practitioners are far from agreement on many of the key issues – but at least the issues are being addressed.

References

1. Michael Mallinson, *The Mallinson Report*, Report of the President's Working Party on Commercial Property Valuations, RICS, March 1994
2. Consultation Draft of Statements of Valuation and Appraisal Practice and Guidance Notes, RICS, 1994
3. John Rich, The Wonderland of OMVs, ERPs and DAVs, *Estates Gazette*, November 26 1994, 9447.

Contributed by Phil Askham.

CHAPTER 44

Rent free periods

First published in Estates Gazette May 13, 1995

I would be grateful if you would consider the topic of rent-free periods and their application in rating valuation . . . some surveyors insist on allowance being made for rent-free periods during negotiations.

In the present market, incentives such as rent-free periods are becoming increasingly common to encourage tenants to enter into a long-term commitment. It might reasonably be assumed in such cases that the effect of the rent-free period is to reduce the effective liability below the level of rent actually paid. This is simple enough in principle, but how should it be applied in practice?

I asked some colleagues for their views on how they would deal with the following deceptively simple question.

A tenant takes a new lease on a building for a 10-year term with a single upwards-only review after five years. The first year is rent-free and is fixed thereafter at £50,000 per annum. What is the true effective rental value?

I received a bewildering range of potential solutions. In each case these are summarised briefly, providing a basis for broader discussion of the issues. The solutions are proffered in ascending order of complexity. For the sake of clarity, the definitions of headline rent and equivalent rent are taken from the RICS Consultation Document, *Rental Valuation of Commercial Lease Inducements – Valuation Guidance Notes*:

Headline Rent: the rent payable after inducements, etc, have expired.

Equivalent Rent: the rent adjusted to take inducements into account. It is sometimes also referred to as the core rent.

Solution 1
£50,000 may well.be the true full rental value
is merely an incentive to attract a tenant off
who might otherwise have been reluctant to enter
commitment.

Solution 2
Calculate the total rent paid over the first five years and divide this
by the number of years to the first review. The present value is then
discounted over the period to review to find its annual equivalent
value.

Rent	50,000	
× 4 years	4	200,000
Divide by years to first review		
Equivalent rent		**£40,000**

Solution 3
Adopts a similar approach to solution 2 above, but this time the
rental payments are discounted to find their present value.

Rent	50,000	
× YP 4 yr @ 8%	3.31	
× PV 1 yr @ 8%	.925	153,253
Divided by YP 5 yr @ 8%		3,993
Equivalent rent		**£38,400**

Solution 4
Similar to solution 3 above, but recognises that the combination of
an upwards-only review and relatively low rates of rental growth
ensure that the headline rent may predominate over the market rent
at the first review, so that the equivalent rent must be discounted
over a longer period – in this case the whole term of the lease. For
the rent to exceed £50,000 at the first review the average annual
growth would need to be in excess of 5%.

Rent	50,000	
x YP 9 yr @ 8%	6.25	
x PV 1 yr @ 8%	.926	289,375
Divided by YP 10 yr @ 8%	6.71	
Equivalent rent		**£43,125**

...tions 3 and 4 are arithmetically identical to two of the approaches adopted in the RICS consultation paper, which calculates annual equivalent of the present capital value of the incentive, which is then deducted from the headline rent to find the core rent.

It is submitted that these do not represent all the possible solutions, but these different treatments do illustrate the issues which require careful examination and which can be summarised as follows:

- What is the nature of the inducement?
- Should the rental payments be discounted?
- If so, at what interest rate and over what period?
- Is it necessary to take account of growth?
- What benefits and costs might accrue to both the landlord and the tenant?

The nature of the inducement
If the rent-free period is simply to provide time for the tenant to fit out and prepare for occupation, the tenant is not actually benefiting from occupation during the rent-free period and this would have no bearing on the equivalent rent. In these circumstances solution 1 would appear to be correct. However, where the rent-free period is an incentive to pay higher levels of rent in later years, it is a different matter, and the effect of such incentives must be taken into account.

The object must be to determine the financial effect of the rent-free period of occupation by adding together the present values of the rental flow to establish the total capital cost and then spreading this cost as an annual equivalent to compare with the normal position of a straightforward letting at the full market value with no incentives (Epstein).

Should the rental payments be discounted and, if so, at what rate and over what time period?
Arguably, solutions 2–4 all satisfy the need to determine the financial effect of the rent-free period. However, method 2 does not allow for discounting the costs and benefits. Although this solution was offered on the grounds that it reflects the robust approach of the actual players in the market and has the obvious attraction of simplicity, it is hard to support on theoretical grounds.

So far as the discount rate is concerned, both solutions 3 and 4 offered 8% on the grounds that this is the rate adopted in rating analysis for the discounting of premiums and improvements. This may or may not be the case, but the theoretical basis of the discount rate adopted requires further examination.

There are a number of possibilities: the statutory discount rate (5.5% for the 1995 rating list), the appropriate property risk yield, prevailing investment/borrowing rates or the opportunity cost.

If the tenant is enjoying the benefit of a saving on rent in the early period of the lease, this saving could be set aside to accumulate interest at a suitable investment rate. However, if the benefit is regarded as a form of loan from landlord to tenant, it might be more logical to adopt a higher rate to reflect the cost of borrowing.

This point is discussed in detail in Epstein, who uses 11% in examples, arguing that a rent-free period is effectively unsecured borrowing. The actual rate could be much higher if the tenant's circumstances are such that he is unable to borrow from any other source, or if he has short-term liquidity problems.

The worked examples contained in the RICS document appear to utilise the all-risks property yield. The rationale behind this choice is not explained beyond the statement that the valuer must make subjective judgment as to the appropriate discount rate.

Both Epstein and Baum agree that discount rates are subjective and will vary between landlord and tenant. Clearly, the higher the discount rate, the lower the equivalent rent.

Adopting a discount rate of 12% in solution 3 reduces the equivalent rent to £37,614. Applying the same rate in solution 4 produces an equivalent rent of £42,105. In both cases the equivalent rent is decreased by just over 2%, and it might be concluded that the choice of discount rate is of relatively minor significance.

The period over which the incentive is to be annualised, however, is of far greater consequence. Normally, if the reviews are to open market value, the rents should be equated only to the first review. However, in the case of upwards-only reviews, it could be that the open market rent on review is actually lower than the headline rent already agreed. The latter, higher figure will prevail, and the effect of settling for the rent-free period will result in an additional cost to the tenant in the later years of the lease. This situation is partially recognised in solution 4, which spreads the value of the incentive over the full term of the lease, but accurate analysis requires a further explicit assumption about future growth rates.

The discounting process should also reflect the actual terms for payment of rent – quarterly in advance – and it is evident that a true DCF approach is more accurate in comparing all costs and benefits of the position both with and without incentive to arrive at the net present value of all the costs and benefits. Such an approach, while it may be theoretically accurate, again requires assumptions about future growth, and does not appear to attract popular support among practitioners.

What benefits might accrue to the landlord and the tenant?
In all cases the valuer must attempt to place him- or herself in the shoes of the parties to the bargain, to view the transaction in its true light. It is reasonable to assume that any such bargain has been arrived at because it offers benefits to both landlord and tenant.

In the simple case used in this illustration, there are some fairly tangible costs and benefits. From the tenant's perspective, these can be identified as the saving of the full headline rent of £50,000 in the first year at the cost of a higher rent for years two to five and the possibility of further excess rents during the period after the review, the latter cost being dependent on the actual rental growth.

The benefit to the landlord may include underpinning the capital value of the investment – a good covenant tied into a long lease has its own attraction – but the ultimate payment of rent above market value could result in additional risk which might reduce the capital value. It has been argued (and refuted by Epstein) that benefit to the landlord also includes avoidance of empty rates and other outgoings.

The benefit to the tenant is a short-term cash bonus at the expense of higher subsequent rent, which could be regarded as effectively unsecured borrowing from the landlord. There may be the additional risk where future reviews are upwards only, but the rent-free period may still be an attraction for the tenant with short-term liquidity problems. For both parties there is the added complexity of taxation considerations.

It is clear from the foregoing that there can be no single solution to the problem of analysing rents to take account of incentives, and that each case must be considered on its merits. For the valuer there is the additional problem that, unless he or she is acting for one or other party to the actual transaction, the true nature of the incentives is unlikely to be known – a situation exacerbated by the widespread existence of confidentiality clauses and side letters. Nor is it likely that the valuer will be fully aware of the relative financial circumstances of both, if any, of the parties involved in the transaction.

As far as the question of using such evidence in a rating context is concerned, the simple answer might be to ignore such rents altogether, but the problem is far more widespread owing to the wider context of the effect of incentives on market rental values and, of course, capital values. For the valuer reliant on comparison as a means of arriving at market values for any purpose, the presence of incentives has created yet another major challenge to the accuracy of valuations.

Further reading

For more detailed discussion of these issues the reader should refer to the following:

Epstein D, Modern Valuations (3) Effective Rental Value. *EG* 9361:86

Epstein D, Effective Rents: a postscript. *EG* 9345:113

Andrew Baum, The vexed issue of inducements. *CSW* 21.1.93

RICS Consultation Document, *Rental Valuation of Commercial Lease Inducements – Valuation* Guidance Notes.

Contributed by Phil Askham.

CHAPTER 45

Rental adjustments for rating use

First published in Estates Gazette April 29, 1995

Last month's article (March 18) reviewed some of the changes relating to the 1995 revaluation. It was suggested that for the first time in recent memory the revaluation had taken place against the unfamiliar background of a tenant's market, with the consequence that the list had been compiled on a paucity of rental evidence. Furthermore, in the present market (and indeed, in 1993, the Antecedent Valuation Date (AVD)) it is not unusual for landlords to offer a range of incentives to encourage occupation so that current rental evidence, such as is available, may well require adjustment to arrive at rateable value. This article will consider the principles involved in making these adjustments in some of the commoner circumstances which are likely to arise.

In fact, the question of incentives is becoming a highly contentious matter for valuers operating in many areas of the market, with implications reaching far beyond the sphere of the rating valuer. All rental valuations which rely on the use of comparable market evidence will be rendered more complex if the particular market is subject to widespread incentives, whatever form they take. Furthermore, if the rent is affected by incentives, this will undoubtedly influence both investment yields and capital values.

These wider implications, especially those relating to rent-free periods, have proved especially contentious and this particular issue will be considered in a later article.

Returning then to the more mundane, if hypothetically challenging, world of rating, it is important as a first principle not to lose sight of what the valuer is trying to achieve. In simple terms this is governed by the definition of rateable value as set out in para 2 Schedule 6 of the Local Government Finance Act 1988:

the rent at which it is estimated the hereditament might reasonably be expected to let from year to year if the tenant undertook to pay all usual tenant's rates and taxes and to bear the cost of repairs and insurance and the other expenses (if any) necessary to maintain the hereditament in a state to command that rent

It is well established that the best evidence of value is the rent being paid for the property where this is one which will reflect all the advantages and disadvantages of the property concerned as perceived by the market. Unfortunately, in many cases this will not accord with the definition outlined so that such a rent is likely to require some adjustment. This much is clear from the body of long-standing rating case law[1].

Common adjustments to the rent paid will include:

- the date at which the rent is fixed where this does not accord with the AVD;
- the relationship between the landlord and tenant;
- improvements made by the tenant;
- and the circumstances surrounding the fixing of the rent – whether settled in the open market at the commencement of a lease, at renewal, on review; by agreement, arbitration or fixed by an independent expert, or on renewal.

Each of these circumstances, being influenced by different constraints and requirements, has the potential to produce a different answer. Capital payments such as premiums and improvements must also be taken into account as well as the presence of any incentives such as rent-free periods.

Rent from year to year

Most modern commercial leases will be fixed for a term of years with regular periodic reviews to open market value. However, the definition of rateable value refers to a letting "from year to year". Is there a difference?

A tenant may, of course, be prepared to pay a higher rent at the beginning of a long lease if it is envisaged that market rents are likely to increase over the period between reviews. Conversely, a landlord desiring security of income may be encouraged to accept a lower rent from a good covenant who is prepared to enter into a long-term commitment. Such a desire cannot be over-stressed given its effect on both the capital value of the investment and the owner's ability to secure borrowing. There is also an increasing tendency for a preference among tenants for shorter leases which maximise their ability to respond to change in an increasingly uncertain economic climate.

It has been argued that the interim rent determined for tenants holding over under the Landlord and Tenant Act, being an annual rent, is the closest thing to the tenancy from year to year. However, constrained as it is by statute, even this does not equate to the definition of rateable value.

It should be noted that the tenant from year to year is envisaged "as a tenant capable of enjoying the property for an indefinite time"[2]. It is fairly well established by case law that rents paid on the normal longer commercial terms (25 years with five-yearly reviews) do not require adjustment, but this would certainly be necessary in the case of leases with unusually long periods between review.

Premiums and improvements

Premiums paid at the outset of a lease in return for a reduced rent clearly do need to be taken into account in arriving at the full rental value. In such cases it would be normal to spread the premium over the term of the lease or the period to the first review where the latter is to be to the full open market rental value.

Improvements carried out by a tenant or expenditure required to put the premises into a state of repair will have a similar effect, the expenditure being in the nature of a capital sum which will increase the virtual rent. However, careful consideration needs to be given to whether the improvements are rateable and whether they do, in fact, add to the open market letting value. Thus, improvements which are personal to the occupier, such as multiple house style shop fittings, are unlikely to enhance the market rent payable by any other occupier, who would be inclined to strip them out and start again.

While it is true that the actual tenant must be considered as one of the hypothetical tenants, the rental bid of the actual tenant will be influenced by the hypothetical bids of other tenants in the market.

Assuming that improvements undertaken do indeed add to the rental value, the question of whether such costs are discounted over the whole lease term or a longer or shorter period will depend upon specific circumstances, and each case needs to be considered on its merits. Rent review clauses will typically exclude from consideration the value of authorised improvements carried out by the tenant and, here, the term of the lease is appropriate rather than the period to review. It may be necessary to extend this beyond the term of the lease, having regard to the possibility of renewal under the Landlord and Tenant Acts or the alternative payment of compensation for improvements upon termination. Short-term improvements will, of course, be discounted over a much shorter period.

In all cases the process of analysis is to annualise any capital payments over the appropriate period and add this annual equivalent to the rent passing. It has been the practice for some years to apply a dual rate year's purchase reflecting the cost of capital and the fact that such expenditure is a wasting asset.[3] However, both the discount rate adopted and the application of the dual rate principle are themselves contentious issues.

Rates

Few commercial properties are let on inclusive terms these days, so the need for direct adjustment is rare. However, the long-running debate about the rent-rates equation is still very much alive. In the definition of RV, the tenant is assumed to pay all rents and taxes, if business rates represent a significant part of the total cost of occupation then the higher the rate liability the lower amount the tenant can afford to pay in rent. It can be assumed that tenants will enter a commitment to pay rent with some knowledge of the other outgoings which will arise from occupation. However, sudden changes in liability may well distort the equation. Alterations in rate liability during the currency of the list are more certain now that the annual increase in the UBR is tied to the Retail Price Index, but more dramatic modifications are likely at revaluation. Transition is designed to smooth out these changes, but will also create significant distortions.

Consider the case of offices in central London. Valuations under the 1995 list may well be some 50% lower than in 1990, but, where such assessments are subject to downward transition, the immediate benefit is limited and an artificially high liability will occur in 1995/96. If, however, downward transition is abandoned at some point during the list, this could give rise to a significant reduction in liability, effectively increasing the amount of rent that such a tenant would be prepared to pay. It has been argued that such circumstances are likely to exert significant upward pressure on market rents.

Other adjustments
Rents which do not accord closely with the antecedent date must be adjusted to take account of any change over time. Rental indexes can provide a useful general guide to the movement of rents over time, but care should be exercised in their use. Obviously, the further away in time from April 1 1993 and the greater the change over the time, the less reliable will be such a rent.

Where the rental bargain has been struck between a landlord and tenant who are related in some way, such as associated companies, or where the rent payable is part of a larger financial transaction, for example sale and leaseback, such evidence as these bargains provide should all be treated with suspicion.

Hierarchy of rental evidence
To conclude, all evidence of value needs to be considered, but there is a body of case law[4] which gives a clear indication as to the weight which needs to be attached to different sources of evidence. The appropriate weighting of evidence will be critical in such a thin market where untainted rental evidence may well be hard to find.

The first consideration will be the rent passing where the property is let. The closer this is to the definition of RV, the more reliable it will be. The greater the number of adjustments which need to be made, the more suspect.

The valuer should then look at the rents of comparable properties to check the consistency of the rent passing with prevailing levels of value, always having regard to the circumstances in which these rents were negotiated and agreed. An open market rent freely negotiated between an unconnected landlord and tenant at the commencement of the lease will be the best evidence.

Review rents may be suspect because upward-only review clauses may not, in present circumstances, reflect the true market rent but instead reflect a situation where agreement has to be reached and where the parties cannot walk away from a poor bargain. There must, similarly, be doubts even when the rents are determined by arbitrators or independent experts. Likewise, renewal rents may not be helpful, reflecting, as they do, Landlord and Tenant Act provisions. These latter circumstances are somewhat removed from the concept of "the tenant coming fresh to the scene".

The final, and, in present market circumstances, perhaps the most important, source of evidence will be the assessments of comparable properties. In *Howarth* v *Price*[5], it was concluded:

with the passage of time the volume of established assessments acquires weight as evidence of accepted values.

Even this will be far from conclusive, reflecting acceptance of liability, which may now be influenced by transition, rather than acceptance of value.

The vexed issue of rent-free periods will be considered in a later article.

Cases

[1] *Robinson Brothers (Brewers) Ltd* v *Durham County AC* (1938) 158 LT 498 and *Poplar AC* v *Roberts* (1922) 2 AC 93.
[2] *R* v *South Staffordshire Water Works Co* (1885) 16 QBD 359.
[3] See *Trevail* v *C A Modes Ltd* (1967) RA 124.
[4] See *Lotus and Delta Ltd* v *Culverwell (VO) and Leicester City Council* (1976) RA 141.
[5] *Howarth* v *Price* (VO) (1965) RRC 196.

Contributed by Phil Askham.

CHAPTER 46

New-build residential valuations

First published in Estates Gazette September 30, 1995

As a valuation surveyor undertaking mortgage valuations, I have encountered problems with assessing the worth of new houses where there appears to be a significant premium over and above the prices of comparable secondhand properties. Valuation problems are further complicated by the range of incentives offered by many builders to obtain sales. Should such incentives be taken into account?

In the present residential property market recession, the sale of new houses represents an increasing proportion of the total market, currently estimated at some 24% of all transactions. It is now clear that buyers are paying premium prices for newly built houses. There is evidence of some conflict between mortgage valuers and builders inasmuch as builders naturally fix their prices by reference to cost, which does not, of course, necessarily relate to the market value definition which is the concern of the valuer.

The position is further clouded by the wide range of commonly available incentives now offered by most builders. While the RICS White Book offers some guidance to valuers, and while it is clear that incentives to purchase need to be disregarded, it is not always easy to identify the effect of these incentives on value. This article will examine the reasons for the existence of the new-build premium and consider the resultant valuation problems.

It is evident that new-build prices are significantly above secondhand prices and a new-build premium does exist. Halifax Building Society statistics from the second quarter of 1995, for example, quote a national average price for new detached houses of £98,801, compared with that of secondhand ones built post-1960 of £92,060. Newly constructed terraced houses average £54,746, compared with secondhand post-1960 houses at £47,530 and those built between 1946 and 1960 at £43,587.

Such averages always need to be treated with caution, but the statistical evidence points to a differential of the order of 10% to 15%. This premium could simply be a reflection of the added value of new houses, resulting from higher standards of construction and materials. It has been suggested that the cost of bringing a 30-year-old house up to modern standards may be as much as £17,000(1), a figure which might appear to explain the apparent difference in average prices.

However, the issue would appear to be more complex. The new-build premium arises in part from the differences in standard and quality, but is also partly a consequence of the presence of incentives.

Housebuilders need to continue to construct and sell houses to stay in business, and they cannot easily reduce their activity at times of recession. Hence the use of incentives to try to encourage sales. However difficult market conditions might be, sales must take place at prices which produce a profit and, while builders have undoubtedly been forced to trim their margins, pricing policy will be determined by reference to cost, plus a profit margin. This is a perfectly logical approach to the pricing of a commodity and most valuers would accept the validity of the residual approach to arriving at the value of building land.

This is not to suggest, however, that houses should be valued by reference to cost. It is clear that some valuers are trying to side-step the issue by taking a cost-based approach by valuing new houses on a price per square metre basis, but there is no reliable correlation between cost and value. The problem with the cost/metre approach is that size is not the only factor influencing the value of residential property. Even if differences between sites and locations could be accounted for, questions such as design, accommodation and specification are likely to be far more important than mere size. It is equally misleading to try to quantify the new-build premium by a percentage addition to secondhand values, and it should be concluded that the complexity of residential valuation cannot be reflected in such simplistic analysis.

Valuation guidance

Some guidance on the question of valuation for mortgage purposes is offered by the White Book. The mortgage valuer is instructed by the lender who, if a building society, is required by law to obtain a valuation. The valuation is for security purposes, the lending institution needing the assurance that, in the event of default, the amount of the loan can be recovered on resale.

Paragraph 4.3 of Valuation Guidance Note 2A, "Valuation of Residential Properties for Mortgage Purposes", identifies the role of the valuer in advising the lender of the open market value and specifies that:

the valuer will not include any element of value attributable to furnishings, removable fittings and sales incentives of any description when arriving at an opinion of the value. Portable and temporary structures are to be excluded also.

Paragraph 6.8 of the same guidance note outlines the approach to be taken to new-build valuations and suggests that these should be no different from any other valuation.

Comparable evidence should be drawn from sales and resales on the development if sufficient evidence of such transactions is available. If not, new property on other developments and comparables from the secondhand market in the locality should be used as evidence, making appropriate adjustments for: improvements in design and layout; ease of maintenance; amenities which the property enjoys; environmental and other factors materially affecting the value; and any other factors which influence the decisions of purchasers but excluding those matters mentioned in paragraph 4.3 – that is, any furnishings, removable fittings and sales incentives.

Quantifying the new-build premium and distinguishing between the factors properly to be taken into account from mere incentives is the valuer's problem. To assess this it is worth considering what influences purchasers to pay more for a newly built house than a comparable secondhand property.

Added value of new houses
Research in the early 1990s undertaken for the New Homes Marketing Board, which undertook a survey of the attitudes of potential new housebuyers, identifies a whole series of advantages which clearly influenced potential and actual purchasers of new homes, the main ones being:

- the 10-year NHBC guarantee;
- absence of a chain;
- improved security fittings;

- energy efficiency;
- low maintenance and the lack of major repair and renewal liability such as rewiring and replacement windows, all of which will tend to reduce the capital burden on the purchaser;
- design factors. This will include modern layout. There is, for example, a preference for separate dining rooms and en suite bathrooms and a reduction of redundant circulation space. The standardisation of the 600mm kitchen fitment module provides greater flexibility in the location of appliances. Modern features such as French windows and balconies are also perceived as important benefits;
- modern lighting and wiring and better quality insulation, ventilation and heating systems which offer more effective control, producing savings in energy costs;
- prestige;
- higher specification and extra and better- quality fittings;
- more space;
- larger gardens; and
- good-quality finishes.

This impressive list of advantages could easily explain the premium, even though these should be set against a range of perceived disadvantages also revealed in the surveys which included: smaller floor areas, higher densities, lack of garden privacy, poor finishes and lack of character and maturity on new developments. Any valuer would recognise the elements on these lists as being precisely those factors to be weighed in undertaking an open market valuation.

Incentives
However, in the same surveys, potential and actual purchasers also identified a range of incentives offered by builders which need to be considered separately. These include:

- choice of colours and fitting;
- selection of location of power points;
- finance deals;
- the ability to move straight in;
- free holidays;
- mortgage subsidies;
- payment of stamp duty and solicitors' fees;

- cash-back payments and discounts;
- part-exchange to those stuck in the present market;
- kitchen fitments, carpets and appliances;
- redundancy protection;
- fixed interest rates; and
- a car on the drive(2).

Such incentives have become widespread. A check in the new homes section of a recent local property guide revealed: fitted carpets to the value of £1,250; provision of built-in cookers and hobs; fridge freezers; fitted curtains; provision of a deposit up to £2,900; £1,250 towards legal fees including stamp duty and survey fees; sponsored sale plans covering agents' fees on the sale of existing property up to £1,000; and part-exchange deals.

All the above may also help to explain the new-build premium, but can, and should, be distinguished from the pure advantages. A builder providing any of the above incentives does so at a cost. It seems reasonable to assume that this cost has to be recouped and that recoupment will be in the form of an increase in the basic price. In some cases the incentives are being provided by the building societies, anxious to maintain market share in an increasingly troubled market. They can afford to do this at a time when the differential between lending and borrowing rates makes lending profitable. Building society incentives will not influence pricing policy, as the costs will be recouped from the profits of the mortgage business and not the sale price of the home.

In all cases though, if on resale, when such incentives are not available, a lower price would be achieved, then such incentives must be discounted in the open market valuation as defined in paragraph 4.3 of the guidance note.

The distinction is not always clear cut. The guidance notes require the exclusion of furnishings and removable fittings, but in a recent case(3) it was decided that fitted carpets, curtains and blinds, although removable, should be regarded as fixtures, as they are clearly intended to remain in place until worn out. The same logic applies to certain white goods which are physically fitted, wired or plumbed in. The effect of such a decision is lessened by the express desire of the Council of Mortgage Lenders that it does not wish to see the RICS guidance changed.(4)

Notwithstanding such blurring of the boundaries between the definition of fixtures, fittings and furnishings, the valuer's position is, in principle at least, quite simple: the valuer should consider all the advantages of buying a new home, but reflect in the value only those factors which would continue to enhance the open market value on a subsequent resale. The best evidence of value will therefore be resale transactions on the same or similar developments. In the absence of such evidence new-build prices must be treated with some suspicion and must always be supported by comparable secondhand market evidence. There can be no support for cost-based valuations, pro rata values or percentage adjustments.

A recent article in the *Sunday Times*(5) claimed that building societies and their valuers were jeopardising the housing market recovery by undervaluing new homes, referring to a culture of caution in an uncertain market. While it is true that valuers will not make themselves popular if the market value approach results in valuations significantly below the purchase price fixed by the builder, equally they would be subjected to worse criticism in the longer term if lenders find that they are unable to recoup a significant proportion of loans advanced on excessive valuations.

Surely the only response is to continue to base market valuations on appropriate and reliable evidence and to discount pure incentives in accordance with advice contained in the White Book.

References

1. Figures recently released by the New Homes Board.
2. See comment by Mary Wilson (*Estates Gazette*, August 12, p58).
3. *TSB Bank plc* v *Botham* [1995] EGCS 3 (subject to appeal).
4. As reported in *Chartered Surveyor Monthly* July/August 1995, p22.
5. *Sunday Times*, June 30, p1.

Contributed by Ian Brookes.

CHAPTER 47

The new Red Book

First published in Estates Gazette January 6, 1996

Now that the various amendments have been incorporated into the new "Red Book", how does its application affect the practitioner?

Readers are referred to articles in the "Mainly for Students" series on asset valuation and on the Mallinson Report (Asset Valuation, *EG* 9111:123 and 9119:137, The Mallinson Report, *EG* 9507:119) which considered the application of the old Red Book and the debate surrounding the changes which have now come into effect. One of the main outcomes of the Mallinson report was the merger of the old Red and White books. After months of speculation about its colour, the new combined version turns out to be exactly the same shade of red as its predecessor. It is, however, decidedly bigger and certainly enlarged in scope, so perhaps this new version should be celebrated as the Big Red Book.

The RICS *Appraisal and Valuation Manual* was published in September 1995 by combining *Guidance Notes on the Valuation of Assets* (*Statements of Asset Valuation Practice and Guidance Notes* (1990) and the *Manual of Valuation Guidance Notes* (1992). The original Red Book in its three editions covered valuations for specific purposes where information contained in valuation reports was likely to be relied upon by third parties. Its rules, which became mandatory in 1991, covered the bases of valuation to be adopted in given circumstances and identified who can provide such services. The White Book was more general in its application and was concerned with the mechanics of practice. Mallinson concluded that the existence of two books was confusing, led to duplication and a potential lack of consistency.

Identified in the new Red Book are the minimum standards required. A substantial part is mandatory and this now covers a wider range of valuation services which is likely to affect all professionals giving advice rather than just the specialist asset valuer. While any valuer ignored the old Red Book at his or her peril (even for those not engaged in asset valuation it provided much valuable practice advice) the new version demands the attention of all valuers and should be required reading.

The aim is to better understand and satisfy the needs of the client, to provide valuations on consistent bases and assumptions, to provide a high standard of competence and comprehensible reports based on clear, accurate and sufficient information.

It is concerned with the mechanics of practice and not valuation theory or methods, although the latter was covered by the Mallinson recommendations concerning valuation methodology. As a result, a working party chaired by Nick French of the University of Reading is to consider valuation methods and the outcome of their deliberations will the subject of information papers to be issued during 1996.

The old Red Book was withdrawn on December 31 1995 and from January 1 1996 the Practice Statements in the new book became mandatory for members of the RICS, the ISVA and the Institute of Revenues Rating and Valuation. RICS Bye-law 19(7) and Conduct Regulation 23 require all members to comply with the statements, their annexes and appendices with effect from January 1 1996. Departure is possible in special circumstances, but the valuer must always be prepared to justify this and must make a clear declaration in the valuation report that the Practice Statements have not been followed.

What follows is an outline of the contents of the *Appraisal and Valuation Manual*. For reasons of space, full definitions are not given and readers are strongly advised to refer to the Red Book itself for specific detail.

The book consists of two parts, Practice Statements and Guidance Notes. Practice Statements 1–7 apply to all valuations. The appendices to the Practice Statements are also mandatory. The Guidance Notes are not mandatory, but provide further information on good valuation practice. It is likely that any valuer departing from these Guidance Notes would need to have clear reasons for doing so in the event of defending any claim for negligence.

Practice Statements 1–7
The book begins with a section on definitions which distinguish appraisal, valuation and estimation of worth (see Figure 1).

Figure 1. Definitions

Appraisal	The written provision of a valuation, combined with professional opinion or advice on the suitability of the subject property for a defined purpose
Estimation of Worth	The provision of a written estimate of the net monetary worth of the subject property to the client
Valuation	The provision of a written opinion as to the price or value of the subject property on any given basis. It is specifically not a forecast, which is defined as the prediction of the likely value on a stated basis at a future specified date

Practice Statement 1 is concerned with the application of the manual which is extensive and covers "appraisals, valuations, revaluations, valuation reviews and calculations of worth . . . for all purposes" subject to a series of exceptions which include the provision of evidence in connection with legal proceedings for property-related disputes, decisions and reports of arbitrators, independent experts or mediators, internal valuations which will not be relied upon by third parties, tax and compensation valuations, valuations quoted during negotiations, estate agency advice (although sale and purchase reports are not excluded), valuations for development schemes and forecasts. Most are common sense but others are excluded, not because regulation is thought to be unnecessary, but because these are already covered adequately by statute or elsewhere.

Many of the exclusions are familiar from the old asset valuation regulations, but coverage is clearly much more extensive. The new regulations, for example, will cover mortgage valuations and Home Buyers' Reports which were previously excluded.

Practice Statement 2 concerns the requirement to understand the needs of the client. The purpose of the valuation must be clear and the service must be recorded. To this end, standard conditions of engagement are recommended for use where possible. Practice Statement 2 also identifies the minimum requirements of what needs to be defined by the valuer at the outset:

- The purpose of the valuation
- The subject property
- The valuation bases
- Any assumptions to be made
- The valuation date

- The currency in which the valuation is to be expressed
- Any restrictions
- The requirement to seek the valuer's consent prior to publication
- Third party limitations
- Information to be provided by the client.

Once the level of service to be provided has been agreed, this must be recorded in writing in a way which will facilitate use at some later stage in the event of any dispute. The recording of comparables and the analysis of transactions is covered in Practice Statement 6.

Where there is conflict between the specific guidance contained in practice statements 8–22 and the general guidance contained in statements 1–7 then the specific guidance (8–22) takes precedence.

Valuation bases

The valuation base must be agreed at the outset and should be suitable for the client's purpose. In no circumstances may this override statutory definitions. When Estimated Realisation Price is requested there is also a necessary requirement to provide Market Value or Open Market Value. It is necessary to distinguish a calculation of worth from the Market Value or Open Market Value.

The practice statement defines categories of asset and the valuation bases appropriate. These are summarised in Figure 2.

It would appear that there are now some 14 valuation bases (one of Mallinson's recommendations was to avoid too many) although in some cases these are only subtle variations of the basic starting point, which is open market value. This is developed from its previous incarnation by the addition of assumption (e) "that both parties to the transaction had acted knowledgeably, prudently and without compulsion". Market Value is actually the same as Open Market Value but appears as the definition used by the International Valuation Standards Committee.

It is inappropriate here to go into the detailed definitions of all the valuations bases and there can be no substitute for direct reference to the Practice Statement. However, the following points indicate some of the highlights:

- Open Market Rental Value (OMRV) is added for the first time. Here, the valuer must make the assumption of a new lease as distinct from a renewal.

Figure 2. Application of valuation bases

Base definition	Rental value	Plant and machinery	Other
Market value (**MV**)			
Open market value (**OMV**)	Open market rental value	Open market value plant and machinery	
Existing use value (**EUV**)		Value of plant and machinery to the business (**VPMB**)	Existing use value for registered housing associations (**EUV RHA**)
Estimated Realisation Price (ERP)	Estimated future rental value (**ERFV**)	Estimated realisation price plant and machinery (**ERP P&M**)	
Estimated restricted realisation price (ERRP)		Estimated restricted realisation price plant and machinery (**ERRP P&M**)	Estimated restricted realisation price for the existing use as an operational entity valued having regard to trading potential (**ERPPEU**)
Depreciated replacement cost (**DRC**)			

- Also new is Estimated Future Rental Value (EFRV) and, like Estimated Realisation Price (ERP), is the determination of a future value. Estimated Future Rental Value is the rent on the completion of a new letting at some time in the future. The future date is to be specified by the valuer, which allows a sufficient time for the proper marketing of the property having regard to its characteristics.
- In the case of ERP it is necessary to consider what changes are likely to occur in the market for the property during the marketing period, including external factors such as the quality of the location etc.
- Existing Use Value (EUV) is, as before, Open Market Value subject to additional assumptions as to use.
- Estimated Realisation Price (ERP) is, in effect, Open Market Value but with completion assumed after the date of valuation and where the valuer is required to specify the appropriate marketing period.
- Estimated Restricted Realisation Price (ERRP) is not forced sale (which should not be used in any circumstances), but is where

the estimate is subject to a marketing period defined by the client which does not allow for proper marketing.

- And Value of Plant and Machinery to the Business (VPMB) broadly corresponds to Open Market Value for Existing Use (OMVEU).

Practice Statement 5 covers qualification requirements in relation to specific areas of legislation as well as conflicts of interest. It is worth noting here that where the old red book referred to relevant experience, the new book points to knowledge, understanding and skills as well as knowledge of the particular market.

Practice Statement 6 covers inspections and investigations. Practice Statement 7 identifies minimum requirements for reports. The aim of the report is to provide information which does not mislead the client or any third party. Where there is an intention to publish a reference to a report the valuer must provide a statement for inclusion in the published reference. The valuer cannot give consent to publication before seeing drafts of the material. This is to ensure that any reference to the valuation, in company accounts for example, is not misleading.

Practice Statements 8–22 relate to specific types of valuation including Residential Mortgage Valuations and Home Buyers' Reports and Valuations.

Appendices to the Practice Statements include material on the plant and machinery typically included in a valuation of land and buildings, model conditions of engagement, standard valuation report paragraphs, schedules and summaries, and model report forms.

Finally, the Guidance Notes which form section 2 of the manual provide further advice on good valuation practice. The general guidance in Guidance Note 1 covers knowing the client, conditions of engagement, records, referencing, physical factors, planning etc. Guidance Notes 2–18 refer to, among other things, environmental factors, residential mortgage valuations, lease inducements, depreciation, plant and machinery, goodwill, petrol-filling stations, restaurants, surgeries, local authority assets, forestry and woodland, current cost accounting and development land appraisals.

This article has not touched on the controversy over the introduction of Estimated Realisation Price and whether this will resolve or compound the problems of credibility which gave rise to

Mallinson in the first place. These issues have been thoroughly debated. There is a view that the need to look forward in providing valuation advice has been imposed on the profession by the lending institutions and could actually result in more rather than less claims for negligence against the valuation profession. No doubt this one will, as they say, run and run. However, whatever view is taken, it is clear that, because of its wider application, the new Red Book is essential reading. It offers significant general advice and support with respect to all elements of the valuation process and is no longer limited to those more specialised areas which might be encountered by most valuers only in exceptional circumstances. It is undoubtedly a very important document.

Contributed by Phil Askham.

CHAPTER 48

Rule (5) compensation

First published in Estates Gazette June 22, 1996

Can you explain the application of Rule (5) of the Land Compensation Act?

Rule (5) of Section 5 of the Land Compensation Act 1961 allows compensation to be based on the cost of equivalent reinstatement. It is the exception to r(2), where compensation is based upon open market value. It states:

Where land is, and but for the compulsory acquisition would continue to be, devoted to a purpose of such a nature that there is no general demand or market for land for that purpose, the compensation may, if the Lands Tribunal is satisfied that reinstatement in some other place is bona fide intended, be assessed on the basis of the reasonable cost of equivalent reinstatement.

The rule is borne of a principle established by cases under the Lands Clauses Consolidation Act 1845, that value is value to the owner not the acquiring authority. Application of the rule has been interpreted as having four essentials to be satisfied by the claimants on whom the burden of proof rests (*Sparks (Trustees of East Hunslet Liberal Club) v Leeds City Council*):

- That the subject land is devoted to the purpose, and but for the compulsory acquisition would continue to be so devoted;
- That the purpose is one for which there is no general demand or market for the land;
- There is a bona fide intention to reinstate on another site;
- These conditions being satisfied, that the tribunal's reasonable discretion should be exercised in their favour.

Only if the first three practical essentials are satisfied will the tribunal consider exercising its discretion. The interpretation and application of the four essentials are considered in turn.

Devoted to a purpose

Devoted has been held to mean intention and is not limited to *de facto* use (Aston Charities).

The date upon which premises are required to be devoted is not statutorily determined. In *Runcorn FC* v *Warrington* it was held to be the date of the notice to treat. However, it must also be shown that but for the compulsory acquisition there would be continuance of the devotion. Evidence of continuance has been presented in varying ways. In Sparks the club put into evidence six years' accounts and the argument that such clubs seldom went out of business was accepted by the Lands Tribunal.

Perhaps the most extreme interpretation is to be found in *Trustees of Zoar Independent Church* v *Rochester City Council*. A purchase notice was served in 1964 when there was a congregation of 12. In 1966, when the roof of the building fell in, the congregation of three or four people "scattered". New premises were bought in 1967 and at the date of the Lands Tribunal hearing in 1970 the new church had a congregation of 30, only one of whom was from the original church.

The tribunal refused r(5) on grounds that "Zoar was dying". However, reversing the tribunal decision in 1973, the Court of Appeal commented that the question was whether the purpose was reinstated. The new place of worship answered the description of a meeting house having the characteristics of *Zoar* and would constitute reinstatement.

Likewise in *Nonentities* v *Kidderminster* the Lands Tribunal held that r(5) would apply even though the theatre could continue only with local authority financial support.

No demand or market

In *Sparks* it was submitted that a market existed evidenced by 34 planning applications for extensions to other clubs in one year together with 23 increases in rating assessments. The Lands Tribunal said there was no evidence that any would have been in the market.

Likewise, in *Nonentities* v *Kidderminster*, evidence was submitted that over a 10 years there had been 22 sales and eight long leases granted for theatres, the majority in London. The tribunal viewed this as evidence of negligible proportions and allowed r(5).

In the above cases the purposes for which the lands were used were non-profit making. However, in *Wilkinson* v *Middlesbrough*, where the occupier was a private veterinary practice, evidence showed that in a 20-year period there had not been a single sale in the area. The tribunal considered vets multi-practices, evolved through partnerships, sold by the owner to the incoming principal after a period of working in dual harness and as such pointed to a market. R(5) was rejected.

Intention to reinstate

In determining whether this essential is satisfied it is necessary to consider the real intentions of the parties. Thus, in *Edge Hill Light Railway* v *SOS for War* no bona fide intention was demonstrated because the claimants had not drawn up any plans and, therefore, failed to show directness of purpose.

The ability to reinstate may be argued to be linked with the claimant's financial ability. In *Zoar* the Court of Appeal commented that bona fide intention was not in question and the fact that realisation of the intention is dependent upon the receipt of compensation assessed under r(5) does not deprive the intention of any necessary quality. That the necessity of receiving compensation to reinstate does not bar a r(5) claim was also confirmed in *Nonentities* and *Sparks*.

The tribunal's discretion

Where the tests are satisfied the question remains whether the tribunal will exercise its discretion in the claimant's favour.

A narrow interpretation of the principle was argued for in *Festiniog*: it was suggested that "may" expressed in r(5) means "must", provided that the other conditions had been met. This the tribunal rejected and commented that the legislature intended r(5) to be permissive.

The wide nature of the discretionary application of the rule has included reference to the amount of compensation required to reinstate. In *Nonentities* the member expressed some difficulty in the sheer amount of compensation (£167,000 compared with the r(2) figure, under £36,000), but said "if that is necessary to secure equivalence it is necessary". However, a totally opposite view was expressed by the Court of Appeal in *Festiniog*:

Reinstatement usually resorted to . . . where the displaced undertaking was some non-productive enterprise such as a church or hospital . . . not intended to make a profit but perform some public service which could not be equally well performed in another situation . . . . Reinstatement may be applied to a commercial concern.

The court concluded: that as £3,000 was paid for a controlling interest in the railway in 1954, the cost of the proposed deviation (£180,000) was larger than the total value of the whole business. R(5) was refused.

Clearly, the first three criteria laid down in r(5) do not directly express the exclusion of commercial undertakings. However, the decisions referred to above indicate that this is generally the case.

It was clearly the view of both the tribunal and the Court of Appeal in *Harrison & Hetherington* v *Cumbria CC* that the criterion of a market was satisfied when there was a latent demand even though this may not become apparent until the chance to make a bid arose by a property being offered for sale. The House of Lords, however, took a contrary view and accepted that the few transactions known (18 during 1957 to 1985) were not sufficient to prove that a general demand or market existed. More important, Lord Fraser opined that "a latent demand . . . is not a general demand in the sense of r(5)".

The review of r(5) cases above demonstrates the difficulty in isolating the determinants of the rule's application. It could be argued that it is applied generally to a narrow group of charitable, non-profit-making and religious bodies.

However, application of r(5) has widened: the Land Compensation Act 1973 (section 45) applies the rule where a dwelling is substantially adapted or constructed to meet the special needs of a disabled person; and in *Harrison & Hetherington* v *Cumbria* the House of Lords allowed r(5) in the case of a commercial livestock market.

Whether the application of r(5) is now wider than before will be shown in time.

Valuation aspects

As in all cases where valuation has to be carried out within a legal framework, a prime matter to be determined is the date of valuation. The difficulties of linking the valuation date with the date of the notice to treat were superficially removed by *West Midlands Baptist (Trust) Association (Incorporated)* v *Birmingham Corporation*. In r(5) cases the date of valuation is the earlier of the dates at which reinstatement becomes reasonably practicable or the date of physical possession. This award provided a significant increase in the available compensation to the trust from a cost base of £50,025 as at 1947 (the date of the notice to treat) and a cost of £89,575 as at 1961 when the chapel was to be reinstated. Indeed, it was the demonstrable shortfall of compensation in relation to costs of transfer amounting to £39,550 and the disequity so caused which led to the revision of a valuation date rule that had stood for 100 years.

The meaning of reinstatement is not defined by the rule. Whether it is the building or the purpose which is to be reinstated is left open. Of necessity, either the building is to be replaced elsewhere or the use reinstated in some other existing building. As the original building is not replaced it is the use which is reinstated. It is submitted, therefore, that the correct view is that it is the purpose which is reinstated and not the building (see also *Zoar*).

Reinstatement of purpose immediately raises questions as to what is being valued. The new premises required to continue the purpose are to be of a size and type with related site needs which must both satisfy planning requirements and match market availability.

Leaving such issues aside, the approved form of valuation is generally accepted as that shown right.

Replacement site
Clearly, the new location, and the distance (or radius) within which this can be accomplished, must allow the original purpose to be continued. In *Aston Charities Trust* v *Stepney BC* it was accepted that a dancing club could be reinstated 4 miles away. Likewise it was held that a redundant church hall could not be reinstated by a new building located elsewhere and serving the needs of a different locality (*Trustees of St James Parish Hall Charity, Dover* v *Dover Corporation*).

The size of the new site is rarely questioned although where the opportunity to expand is taken the claimant is likely to be compensated on a pro rata basis. Thus in *Sparks* the value of the nearby existing site was approved since the new land was by choice substantially larger to allow for premises almost twice the size.

Since a leasehold interest can be the subject of an r(5) award (*Runcorn*) the issue becomes significant since it is unlikely that the terms of the new tenancy will precisely match those of the old. The rental payable in regard to the new tenancy is liable to be full rental value. Any profit rent attaching to the old premises is therefore lost.

Replacement building

The size of the replacement building will be determined by continuation of the original purpose. In *Trustees of Zetland Lodge of Freemasons* v *Tamar Bridge Joint Committee* it was held that it was for the claimants to decide the size of building required. Similarly, in *Sparks*, compensation met the cost of replacing an equivalent size building although the claimants chose to double the area of their original premises.

When site works are required, such as the provision of a car park, their cost will be met even though they were not available at the original premises provided they are required as a planning condition of the new premises (*Sparks*).

Where an older building is reinstated, benefit may be gained from a new improved building, better location and layout. None of these factors is however, taken into account in the award of compensation (*St Johns Wood Working Mens Club* v *London CC*). Compensation is not, therefore, reduced on grounds that the claimant is left with premises of better design and layout than before.

Repairs to original building

As in all approved cases, the *Sparks* valuation (outlined) shows a deduction made for repairs required to the old building and the costs to bring them up to a bylaw standard. This is made despite repairs being required because of neglect following knowledge of the impending acquisition.

Disturbance matters

As compensation of the basis of equivalent reinstatement is to leave the claimant in a position which is "substantially unaltered and undiminished" (*A & B Taxis Ltd* v *Secretary of State for Air*) a normal claim for disturbance under r(6) (referred to as "Crawley Costs" above) is available. If the r(6) claim were not allowed, clearly the claimant would be left with a shortfall of compensation.

In *RC Diocese of Hexham & Newcastle* v *Sunderland CBC* a claim was made for temporary loss of income during the period of reconstruction, but this was disallowed on the grounds that it was insufficiently substantiated.

Conclusion

Overall, there appears, from the brief review of decided cases, to be a difficulty in determining when r(5) is to be allowed. But, once the rule's application is accepted the quantum of compensation appears to be more or less calculated in a common way. A matter requiring consideration concerns whether compensation should be paid only as and when reinstatement takes place and not on the prospect of reinstatement. This would prevent a claimant from receiving compensation and then failing to carry out the planned reinstatement. Furthermore, if this were adopted and compensation were paid out to meet costs, perhaps as stage payments, increased costs or savings would no longer need to be "guessed" at the date of valuation.

Cases

Aston Charities Trust v *Stepney Borough Council* (1952) 3 P&CR 82

RC Diocese of Hexham and Newcastle Trustees v *Sunderland County Borough Council* (1962) 14 P&CR 208

St James Parish Hall Charity, Dover Trustees v *Dover Corporation* (1962) 184 EG 291

A & B Taxis Ltd v *Secretary of State for Air* [1922] 2 KB 328; 91 LJKB 779;127 LT 478; TLR 671; 66 SJ 633

Edge Hill Light Railway v *Secretary of State for War* (1956) 6 P&CR 211

Festiniog Railway Co Ltd v *Central Electricity Generating Board* (1962) 13 P&CR 248

Harrison & Hetherington Ltd v *Cumbria County Council* [1985] 2 EGLR 37; (1985) 275 EG 457, HL

Nonentities Society (Trustees) v *Kidderminster Borough Council* (1970) 22 P&CR 224

Runcorn Association Football Club Ltd v *Warrington & Runcorn Development Corporation* [1982] 2 EGLR 216, LT

Sparks v *Leeds City Council* [1977] 2 EGLR 163

St Johns Wood Working Mens Club v *London CC* (1947) 150 EG 213

Zetland Lodge of Freemasons v *Tamar Bridge Joint Committee* (1961) 12 P&CR 326

Zoar Independent Church Trustees v *Rochester Corporation* [1974] 3 All ER 5

West Midlands Baptist (Trust) Association (Inc) v *Birmingham Corporation* [1970] AC 874

Wilkinson v *Middlesbrough Borough Council* (1979) 250 EG 867.

Contributed by John Storr.

CHAPTER 49

Valuation and Compensation: Compensation under the Landlord &Tenant Acts

First published in Estates Gazette 14 September 1996

Can you provide some indication of how future receipts and liabilities arising from compensation under the Landlord and Tenant Acts should be reflected in valuation?

This is a complex question which obviously requires some appreciation of the combined provisions of the Landlord and Tenant Acts of 1927 and 1954 and the Law of Property Act 1969, concerning compensation for improvements, for loss of security of tenure and the renewal of leases. Beyond that, an understanding of the treatment of future receipts and liabilities is necessary.

These issues are probably best addressed by reference to a typical examination question:

A freehold factory is held on a 21-year lease with five years to run. The tenant carried out proper improvements four years ago, with the consent of the landlord, increasing the full open market rental value by £1,000 pa. These improvements, if carried out today, would cost £7,500. The rent payable under the lease is £5,000 pa and the full rental value, including the value of the improvements is £10,000 pa. The rateable value is £12,000.

Value the freehold interest on each of the following assumptions:

a) the tenant vacates on termination;
b) a new lease is granted on the expiry of the existing lease;
c) the landlord repossesses at the end of the existing lease for his own occupation;
d) the landlord repossesses for redevelopment at the end of the existing lease.

Preliminaries

Before embarking on any of the valuations, it is necessary to calculate the rents payable at the various review/renewal dates; these in turn will depend on assumptions as to what might happen at the end of the existing lease.

Aside from the different assumptions set out in the question, it is necessary for part (b) to make further assumptions about the precise nature of the new lease. The parties could establish the length of the new term and its review patterns by negotiation. In the absence of agreement, the courts would be obliged to offer a new lease for a maximum of 14 years, which may incorporate a single review. In determining the nature of the new lease, the courts will normally have regard to the pattern of the existing lease and, taking this into account, an alternative possibility might be a new 10-year lease with a review after five years. The latter is assumed to be the case.

Also influencing the pattern of income flows is the value of the improvements. The improvements have been carried out with the landlord's consent, they are proper improvements (section 1(1) 1927 Act) and the main consequence of this is that they must be disregarded until after the expiry of the 21-year period (1969 Act). Thus the improvements cannot be included before 2013 at the earliest, 21 years after they were carried out in 1992. In practice, this will be the first review or renewal date after the expiry of 21 years, which will be 2016 on the assumptions set out above. The projected income flow is shown in Figure 1.

Figure 1: Income flows

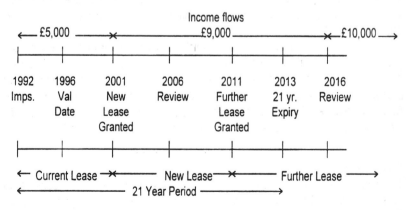

Rents
1. To end of current lease
From the valuation date to the end of the current lease in 2001, the current rent payable under the current lease, £5,000 pa, will, of course, prevail.

2. From beginning of new lease to first review
Assuming that a new lease was granted by the courts or agreed in negotiation (10 years with a review after five years), the new lease will be at the full rental value but disregarding the value of the improvements which were carried out during the current lease, that is, £10,000 − £1,000 = £9,000 pa.

3. New lease review to end of lease
At the first review in the new/renewed lease, the rent might increase to the full rental value of £10,000. However, if the review clause in the new lease contains the normal section 34 disregards, the rent will still exclude the value of improvements carried out within the last 21 years and would thus remain at £9,000 pa. This is assumed to be the case.

4. End of new lease
At the end of the new lease the courts could grant a further lease or the parties could agree by negotiation to a further renewal. In either case the value of improvements will still be excluded by virtue of the 21-year rule, but will be included by the time of the next review in 2016.

Having thus established the rental flows, reflecting reasonable assumptions which take account of the 1954 and 1969 Acts' provisions on renewal and the treatment of improvements, it is possible to construct the various valuations. But these will have to take compensation for both improvements and loss of security into account as appropriate, and these will be dealt with next.

Compensation
Disturbance compensation will be payable where the tenant is denied the opportunity to renew the lease. The amount of compensation is based on the rateable value and the multiplier set

out in the Landlord and Tenant Act 1954 (Appropriate Multiplier) Order 1990. Where the tenant has been in occupation for less than 14 years the multiplier is 1, and for 14 years or more it is 2.

Improvement compensation will be the lesser of the cost of carrying out the improvements or the net increase in value of the landlord's interest as a result of the improvements. Both parameters are determined at the time of the payment of compensation, that is, the end of the lease. The basic compensation calculations are shown in Figure 2.

Figure 2: Compensation

Disturbance
1954 Act compensation
2 × RV (£12,000)   £24,000

The tenant has been in occupation for more than 14 years and so the higher multiplier will apply.

Improvements
Cost today		£7,500
Value		
Inc. in FRV	£1,000	
YP per @ 8%	<u>12.5</u>	£12,500

The cost of carrying out the improvements today is given at £7,500. The value to the landlord of the improvements is simply the increase in rental income which will occur, capitalised at the property discount rate. Because this is significantly higher than the cost today, the former figure – £7,500 – will prevail in this case.

Treatment of compensation payments
In carrying out the valuations required by the question it might simply be the case that the compensation payments are deducted from the capital value of the freehold interest (and added to the value of the leasehold interest).

Life, though, is never that simple and some further adjustments are necessary to account for any change in the amounts which might be foreseen.

Furthermore, from the landlord's perspective, because these are certain future liabilities which will arise under a lease, some recognition needs to be made of the way such liabilities might be provided for in practice.

Both compensation payments are future liabilities on the landlord. They are not immediate outgoings. As such it would be possible to set aside a lower capital sum now which could then accumulate, at the appropriate rate of interest, to cover the whole sum when it becomes due at the end of the lease.

The valuer then needs to consider:

(a) any change in the amount of compensation;
(b) the interest rate used to discount these sums.

Each payment is considered in turn.

The actual disturbance payment at the end of the lease is a function of the rateable value (RV) and the statutory multiplier. While the RV might change at the next revaluation (antecedent date presumed to be 1998), the multiplier will change only as a consequence of the introduction of a new Order. The RV will change only if rents generally change by the next antecedent date and, in present market circumstances, the valuer might be justified in assuming that such a change will not be significant. This will not always be the case and judgment needs to be exercised especially in cases where the rateable value is high and the consequent compensation payment therefore very significant. The multiplier is likely to change only as a result of significant changes in value (the last time following the 1990 revaluation). In the present case, then, the original calculation of £24,000 seems to be appropriate.

Improvement compensation payment, however, must be regarded slightly differently. The cost today of carrying out the improvements might be £7,500, but it seems reasonable to suppose that these costs will tend to increase, at least in line with inflation.

Therefore the valuer must make some sort of projection over the period between the valuation date and the time when compensation becomes due, by inflating the today's cost. In the example this has been taken at the current rate of 3% pa, being a reasonable projection of the effect of inflation over the period to the end of the lease.

Discount rate

The selection of discount rate can be narrowed to a choice between three alternatives:

1) the all-risks or property yield;
2) the sinking fund rate; or
3) the opportunity cost or money market rate.

The property yield can be rejected quite easily. In this case the property yield is taken to be 8%, which is the all-risks yield for this particular property investment which reflects all its positive and negative features including, of course, its growth potential. However, as we have seen, any change in either of the compensation elements will not be influenced by future growth in rents or any other property-related feature.

Arguably, the second alternative is more logical. The landlord could calculate the annual sinking fund to replace the expected liabilities at the end of the lease and deduct this from the income received, discounting at the risk-free yield which could be as low as 3%. However, similar objections can be raised to those applied to the valuation of leasehold interests; using unrealistically low risk-free discount rates is inappropriate at a time when investors are likely to benefit from higher returns. It is submitted that this should be at least equal to the average return on medium-dated government stock (five years), currently about 7%.

It is now possible to proceed with the different valuations. For the sake of simplicity in all cases a conventional approach is adopted using the all-risks yield of 8% in the reversion, with the lower 7% reflecting the greater security in the term. (Such an approach has been criticised as illogical and, arguably, one of the short-cut discounted cash flow (DCF) methods might be more appropriate, but the treatment of the compensation payments would be the same.)

Valuations
a) The tenant vacates on termination:

Term

Rent	5,000	
YP 5 yrs @ 7%	4.1	20,500

Reversion

FRV	10,000	
YP per def 5 yrs @ 8%	8.51	85,073
		105,573

Deduct
1927 Act compensation for improvements

Cost today		7,500	
Value			
Inc. in FRV	1,000		
YP perp @ 8%	12.5	12,500	
Comp lesser		7,500	
add inflation			
5 yrs @ 3%		1,159	
		8,694	
PV 5 yrs @ 7%		.713	6,199
Net value			**£99,374**

b) A new lease is granted on the expiry of the existing lease:

First 5 years	as (a) above		20,500
Next 15 years			
Rent		9,000	
YP 15 years @ 8%	8.559		
PV 5 years @ 8%	.68	5.82	52,384
Final reversion			
FRV		10,000	
YP perp def 20 yrs @ 8%		2.68	26,818
Total value			**£99,502**

c) The landlord repossesses at the end of the existing lease for his own occupation:

Value	as (a) above		99,375
Less:			
1927 Act compensation	as (b) above	6,199	
1954 Act compensation			
2 × RV (£12,000)		24,000	
× PV 5 yrs @ 7%	.713	17,112	23,311
Net value			**£76,191**

In valuation (a) it is assumed that, at the end of the lease, the property would be relet to a new tenant paying the current full market rent but that the landlord will be obliged to compensate the outgoing tenant for improvement, although there will be no

Figure 3: Cash flow appraisal

Qtr	1	2	3	4	5	6	7	8	9	Totals
Sale units										40
S curve	5%	5%	10%	15%	15%	20%	15%	10%	5%	100%
			4	6	6	6	6	6	6	40
Sale proceeds			440,000	660,000	660,000	660,000	660,000	660,000	660,000	4,400,000
Construction costs	−95,000	−95,000	−190,000	−285,000	−285,000	−380,000	−285,000	−190,000	−95,000	−1,900,000
Professional fees	−14,250	−14,250	−28,500	−42,750	−42,750	−57,000	−42,750	−28,500	−14,250	−285,000
Sale fees			−11,000	−16,500	−16,500	−16,500	−16,500	−16,500	−16,500	−110,000
Land cost			−154,000	−231,000	−231,000	−231,000	−231,000	−231,000	−231,000	−1,540,000
Quarterly cash flow	−109,250	−109,250	56,500	84,750	84,750	−24,500	84,750	194,000	303,250	
B/Forward		−112,418	−228,097	−176,573	−94,486	−10,018	−35,519	50,659	251,754	
Sub total		−221,668	−171,597	−91,823	−9,736	−34,518	49,231	244,659	555,004	
Interest @ 2.9%	−3,168	−6,428	−4,976	−2,663	−282	−1,001	1,428	7,095	16,095	6,099
C/Forward	−112,418	−228,097	−176,573	−94,486	−10,018	−35,519	50,659	251,754	571,099	6,099
Profit										571,099

Figure 4. Traditional residual

Completed development value			4,400,000
Less			
Construction costs	1,900,000		
Fees	285,000		
	2,185,000	2,185,000	
Finance*		277,932	
Profits		437,000	
Sales and marketing		110,000	
		3,009,932	3,009,932
Residual			1,390,068
Site finance			
PV 2 yr @ 12%			0.77
			1,077,198

*Finance can be calculated according to the rule of thumb approaches either adopting the full cost over half the construction period or, alternatively, half the costs over the full period. Here the former approach is adopted:

Cost + Fees	2,185,000	
Half cost + fees	1,092,500	
× (Amount of £1 over 2 yrs @ 12%)−1		
$((1 + .12)^2) -1$	0.254	**277,932**

cash flow for each period, which amounts to the difference between the costs incurred during the period and any income from sales which will offset the costs and effectively reduce borrowing.

It can be seen from the cash flow totals that sale proceeds, construction costs, professional fees and sale fees are precisely as calculated for the traditional residual. The only difference is the assumptions about the timing of payments and receipts. As a consequence, the amount of finance is dramatically reduced and this results in significant increases in both the profit and the amount paid to the landowner.

Sale fees are assumed to occur at the time of each sale. The land cost is spread over the development period, based on 35% of the total value of units sold. The net quarterly cash flow is the sale proceeds for the quarter less the sum of construction costs, professional fees, sale fees and land cost.

Quarterly cash flow

The quarterly cash flows start as negative sums but soon become positive as units are completed and sold. To each quarterly cash flow is added the cash flow from the previous quarter to provide the current accumulated balance for the period in question. Again, this balance may be positive or negative.

If it is negative, finance charges will be accrued. If positive, the developer will be able to reinvest the balance and will (in theory at least) be in receipt of interest, providing additional income.

Interest is accumulated using the amount of £1 formula at the quarterly rate calculated as follows:

$$(1 + 0.12)^{0.25} = 1.029$$

Arguably, interest on costs and receipts will not accrue at the same rate.

The risks involved in development are such that short-term finance charges are likely to exceed the interest which could be earned by the developer on short-term deposit. This distinction could easily be built into the cash flow model but, in the examination room, is probably an unnecessary complication.

The rolled up interest is calculated through to the end of the development period and, in this case, the final total is positive. The cash flow allows the profit to be calculated by totalling all the costs in the final column and deducting these from the completed development value. The site value is, of course, reflected in the periodic payments to the owner.

It is interesting in this case that the cash flow approach demonstrates a higher payment to the landowner as well as a substantially higher developer's profit.

This is a very long calculation to carry out manually but note that it carries 15 of the 25 marks. In such circumstances it may be necessary to provide a skeleton calculation, perhaps working fully through the first two periods or so and providing a detailed commentary on how the rest of the calculation would be undertaken. This should provide sufficient evidence that the candidate has a full understanding of the method.

Note: The calculations in this article were carried out using Excel spreadsheets, generally rounding to the nearest whole £.

References

Darlow C (Ed) (1982) *Valuation and Development Appraisal*, Estates Gazette

Cadman D and Topping R (1995) *Property Development*, 4th edition, E & F N Spon

Summary of good examination technique

From the above investigation of the sample question a number of points emerge.

- Read the rubric carefully and make sure you comply with it.
- Read each question carefully before making your choice.
- Plan your answer before you start.
- Make sure the framework of your answer is logical and consistent with assumptions made.
- Allocate your time in relation to the marks available.
- Use conventional valuation layouts.
- Show workings separately.
- State all yields and reasons for their choice and any departure from them.
- Often a question requires some interpretation of the law and this should be provided at the outset in your commentary.
- Do not use advanced valuation techniques unless they are specifically asked for in the question.
- Get the valuation down in outline at least and return to it if time permits.

Contributed by Phil Askham.

Secondary market trends

Investors in secondary property may not be discouraged by a poor investment profile, provided that the price enables them to secure value.

The prices paid for some secondary investments, particularly smaller lots, can be substantially determined by whether the tenant is willing and able to buy; whether the tenant requires funding; or by the extent to which the tenant recognises the reduced worth to investors. Prices can also be influenced by the degree of enthusiasm or desperation the tenant demonstrates for buying, and by whether the tenant has access to professional advice.

Prices can reflect the method of disposal. At auction, subject to exceeding the reserve, the highest-worth individual, such as a tenant, needs only to outbid the highest-worth investor. Under a tender, the highest-worth bidder is unaware of the extent of other bids, and may offer far more than the eventual auction price might have been.

Owners may be indifferent about selling and leave a property on the market at an unrealistically high asking price in the hope of capturing a high-worth purchaser. Where transactions are infrequent, this can distort the perception of values. This is because asking prices, however unrealistic, can have a psychological effect on valuations, and on prices achieved. Conversely, an owner's financial predicament can enable a cash purchaser to pay a price below market value because of the substantial worth to the owner of securing immediate funds.

Evidence of rentals and yields may be thin, diverse and inconsistent, and may represent a range of factors that cannot be assimilated and adjusted to produce a reasoned and reliable valuation. Valuations may not be confined to a "comparison approach" by considering other transactions, and may have to be based on an "investment approach" that considers rates of return which reflect wider financial investment criteria.

Investment valuation

Where a property is rented at market value, or is "rack rented", the rental can be capitalised at the "all risks yield" (ARY) or the "market yield" by "year's purchase (YP) in perpetuity". The ARY derives from comparison with other transactions. The YP is the "multiplier" of the income which accounts for income being received periodically rather than immediately, and represents the present value of future cash flows. The valuation is shown in Figure 1. Because the ARY incorporates the potential for rental growth, it is a "growth-implicit" yield, with the assumed rate of growth not actually being quantified.

Figure 1. Rack-rented valuation

Adopting an ARY of 9%:

Rent	£10,000
YP perpetuity at 9%	<u>11.11</u>
Capital value	£111,000

Where a property is not fully rented and/or has some additional potential, there is a term and reversion (and is therefore a "reversionary" investment). The term, or terms, could be the period until market rental value can be established on rent review or lease renewal, the point at which the value of improvements could be rentalised or, particularly for secondary properties, the lease expiry, or a break date, when redevelopment potential could be realised. Where a property is over-rented, the reversion could be to a lower rent at lease expiry or at a downward review.

The rent for the term, or the "rent passing", is capitalised by YP for the given number of years. The market/reversionary rental value is capitalised by YP in perpetuity (or alternatively, the reversion could be a redevelopment/capital value).

The value of the reversion (or any second or further terms) is discounted to present value by "present value (PV) of £1". This is necessary because the value of the reversion is being purchased now but cannot be realised until the end of the term. As with YP, the higher the yield, the lower the resultant capital value.

Discounting is at the ARY to account implicitly for the growth in the value of the reversion which accrues over the term. Figure 2 shows a valuation by the term and reversion method which adopts a yield of 9% for each stage of the valuation (so the ARY is effectively the "equivalent yield").

Valuers should also be familiar with variations to the term and reversion method, such as the layer/hard-core method which would separately capitalise the £5,000 term income and the £3,000 top-slice element of the reversionary income into perpetuity, with the reversionary top-slice being discounted. For most secondary

Figure 2. Growth-implicit term and reversion valuation

Rent passing	£5,000
YP three years at 9%	<u>2,531</u>
Value of term	£12,655
Market/rack rent	£8,000
YP perpetuity 9%	<u>11.11</u>
	£88,800
PV 3 years at 9%	<u>0.772</u>
Value of reversion	£68,554
Capital value	£81,209
say	£81,000

investment valuations, however, choosing the appropriate yields tends to be more important than considering such variations in valuation methodology.

The growth in the value of the reversion that accrues over the term could be explicitly accounted for by adopting discounted cash flow (DCF) techniques and applying a growth rate to estimate what the value of the reversion would be at the end of the term.

The growth rate is determined from the ARY and the "target rate of return", also having regard to the frequency of rent reviews as growth is actually realised at the time of each review and not annually. The target rate of return, or the "equated yield", is the return over the life of the investment, including any capital gain realised on disposal. It is, therefore, a fixed rate of return.

The equated yield can be derived from a comparison with returns from long-dated gilts. The addition, or "risk premium", to gilts reflects the increased risk, illiquidity and management costs associated with property generally, together with factors related to the specific property. The risk premium for prime property could be 1–2% (depending on the level of gilt yields at the time). The risk premium for secondary property would be significantly higher than for prime property.

Because gilts are a not generally a realistic alternative investment for investors in the poorer secondary properties, the choice of yield can be subjective and relatively wide ranging.

The growth rate is used to uplift the value of the reversion by using "Amount of £1" tables – the amount to which £1 would accumulate at compound interest. Because the inflated value of the reversion is fixed, it is discounted to present value at the equated yield. The equated yield is also used to value the term income on the basis that it is a fixed income.

The short-cut DCF valuation of a reversionary investment is shown in Figure 3.

Figure 3. Initial calculation for short-cut DCF growth-explicit reversionary revaluation

Adopting an ARY ("a") of 9% and an equated yield ("e") of 15%, but first establishing the implied annual growth rate ("g"). Rent reviews ("n") within the ARY are five-yearly.

$$(1+g)^{n(5)} = \frac{\text{YP perp a (9\%)(11.11)} - \text{YP n(5) years e(15\%)(3.352)} = 7.758}{\text{YP perp a (9\%)(11.11) x PV n(5) years e(15\%)(0.497)} \quad 5.522} = 1.405$$

$(1+g)^{n(5)} = 1.405 - (^2\sqrt{1.405}) - 1 = 1.07$
growth rate = 7% pa.

Short-cut DCF (growth-explicit) reversionary valuation

Rent passing	£5,000	
YP three years at 15%	2,283	
Value of term		£11,415
Market/rack rent	£8,000	
Am. £1 three years at 7%	1.225	
Inflated rent	£9,800	
YP perpetuity 9%	11.11	
PV three years at 15%	0.657	
Value of reversion		£71,533
Capital value		£82,948
say		£83,000

A rack-rented investment could also be valued by the growth-explicit short-cut DCF method by, for example, adopting the period until the next review as a term of fixed, rack-rented income, and uplifting the reversionary value and discounting in the normal way, such as: rent passing £10,000 × YP five years at 15%; rack rent £10,000 × Am. £1 five years at 7% × YP perpetuity at 9% × PV five years at 15%.

With the full DCF, the rent is uplifted as in the short-cut DCF, and each period of income – such as the term income and the income expected over following review periods – is separately capitalised and discounted at the target rate of return.

The final stage is to capitalise the uplifted rack rent into perpetuity and, again, discount at the target rate. Figure 4 shows a full DCF where the rent is inflated by 7% pa and capitalised into perpetuity at 9% at year 14 (and effectively assumes that the property is sold at that time and at that yield).

Figure 4. Full DCF valuation

Year	Rent	YP 15%	PV 15%	
1–3	£5,000	2.283		£11,415
4–8	£9,800	3.352	0.657	£21,582
9–13	£13,745	3.352	0.327	£15,066
14–perp.	£19,278	11.11 (9%)	0.163	£34,911
Capital Value				£82,974
say				£83,000

DCF is not necessarily a solution to producing a more accurate market valuation, but has the advantage of accounting explicitly for growth for each period of contracted and expected income. The method could use different growth rates for each year, and could provide for rental voids (provided that market-derived yields do not already allow for voids).

For some secondary properties, simple growth-implicit valuation methods may be preferable, but although the intricacies of DCF valuation methods may be unnecessary for some secondary property investments, they are still required as a framework for calculations of worth. It should be noted that any valuation which determines the present value of a cash flow is effectively a DCF, but the use of the term DCF is often confined to a situation where growth is accounted for explicitly.

Investment approach and worth
The short-cut or full DCF is defined as an investment approach because it utilises rates of return. Only an investment approach can undertake calculations of worth. Growth-implicit valuations are not calculations of worth.

The investment approach assesses market value where the valuer formulates rates of return having regard to the characteristics of the property – particularly covenant strength and the unexpired lease term for secondary property – returns from similar risk property investments and returns from other financial investments such as gilts.

It should be noted that all-risks yields (which are not rates of return) should not be assessed in relation to gilt yields (or equated yields), as growth potential is reflected in all-risks yields, but not in gilt yields. The investment approach should not be used exclusively to establish market value, but does act as a check on comparison methods.

The investment approach assesses worth where target rates of return and other requirements of specific investors are adopted. The assessment could reflect the investor's unique ability to secure specific rentals and levels of growth, the investor's view on growth, or it could reflect the investor's tax position.

The assessment could also have regard to deposit account rates or borrowing rates to reflect the investor's financial circumstances and the investor's opportunity cost of capital. The investor's time horizon (the period the investment is held for) and required exit yield (the yield on ultimate disposal) can be reflected in the point at which the rent is capitalised into perpetuity. More detailed assessments could reflect specific assumptions regarding obsolescence, rental voids or specific costs such as empty rates charges.

Quarterly, rather than yearly, time periods could be provided for, and the assessment could be adapted to calculate internal rates of return. Calculations of worth can be undertaken by incorporating such factors into the DCF models set out above. The investment approach makes it easier to ensure, for example, that values are not becoming unsustainably high in an overheated market and the approach can more easily identify the prospect of a market downturn.

Conclusion

The valuer should understand the characteristics of secondary investment markets, assimilate the thought processes of potential investors, appreciate the distinction between market value and worth, consider comparable evidence with caution, be able to employ both the comparison and investment approaches to valuation, appreciate the wider financial context of property investment, and be able to make instinctive judgments and apply appropriate yields.

Valuations should be constructed in accordance with the New Red Book, and in accordance with sound valuation principles. Valuations should inevitably be cautious, but clients should be advised of the potential range of prices that could be achieved, including specific consideration of potentially high-worth bidders, such as tenants, and how best maximum worth could be captured.

Yields and discount rates

The following commentary outlines some of the key factors influencing yield selection.

Rack rentals can be capitalised at the ARY/market yield into perpetuity. For reversionary investments, the valuer also needs to choose yields to capitalise the rent passing and discount the reversion. Where there is a relatively long-term and/or a substantial reversion, there is a greater need to account adequately for growth in the value of the reversion.

For some secondary properties, investors may just capitalise the rent passing into perpetuity to encapsulate all the relevant factors, such as unlet parts of the property, profit rent situations, over-renting or hope value for alternative uses, including redevelopment.

In certain situations, surveyors may consider that they can reflect market sentiment and establish market value by adopting a similar approach.

For secondary investments, the choice of yield is particularly influenced by covenant strength and the fortunes of the tenant's business. This can also make the valuation of over-rented situations problematic. Generally, the less secure the rental, the greater the difference between term and reversion yields.

Where the rent is below market value during the term and the tenant enjoys a profit rent, the rent is more secure, and investors may accept a relatively lower yield. Where the rent is fixed, investors may require a relatively higher yield to account for the lack of growth potential.

The choice of yield would reflect the level of growth that could otherwise have been available in order to judge how disadvantageous the fixed nature of the term income actually is.

Traditional valuation

The valuation of fixed income is also dependant on the nature of the term. Where the term is within a modern rent review cycle, say three years to the next five-yearly review, the traditional valuation approach could be adopted.

Here, the term income is valued at say 7% compared with an ARY of 9% to reflect the additional security of income which results from the tenant enjoying a profit rent. The traditional approach emanates from the time that inflation was insignificant and investors placed less emphasis on rental growth.

The fixed income for the three-year term is effectively viewed as being no more fixed than an open-market rental similarly having to wait until the next review to secure further growth. This contrasts with the valuation of the term in the growth-explicit method at the equated yield of 15% (although for secondary property, the valuer may be at liberty to adopt say 13% to reflect the additional security of the tenant enjoying a profit rent).

On balance, the valuer may consider it appropriate to adopt the traditional adjustment for terms within a modern rent review cycle, and have regard to equated yields for longer terms. The traditional approach may also be preferable where only low levels of growth could otherwise have been available had the income not been fixed.

Valuing the term unrealistically at the equated yield undervalues the property. Proponents of the equated yield/DCF approach point out, however, that for most valuations, the undervaluation of the term can be counter-balanced by the relatively higher value of the reversion.

Furthermore, the actual choice of the equated yield is often insensitive to the value of the reversion, especially for terms of less than 10 years. This is because, for example, the higher the equated yield, the greater the growth rate and the uplifted rent, but the greater the discounting.

An undervaluation of the term and overvaluation of the reversion is a particular danger for secondary property because of the premium placed on covenant strength and security of income during the term, and the uncertainty in securing anticipated levels of growth, or even in being able to relet the property at reversion.

It may be an overelaboration to extract a growth rate from the ARY and the equated yield where there is a potentially wide valuation range, where evidence of yields is imprecise and possibly unreliable, and where the choice of yields is particularly subjective.

Furthermore, these yields establish a long-term growth rate which may be adequate for the more distant reversions, but unrealistic for short terms, and particularly problematic in variable markets and/or over-rented situations.

A growth rate could be intuitively determined. Technically, the growth rate should reflect market evidence, market expectations and market sentiment, as forecasts of growth rates could render the valuation a calculation of worth.

An intuitively determined growth rate may also be preferable where the reversion is a development/capital value, as the rise in development values may not be commensurate with rental growth rates.

Similarly, in the growth-implicit method, it may not be appropriate to discount a development value at the ARY.

Where the value of the reversion is not expected to grow, the growth-explicit/DCF method would not uplift the value of the reversion. The growth-implicit method would discount the reversion at a higher yield than the ARY.

Factors affecting the sustainability of the term income may be substantially different from factors affecting the ability to secure the reversionary income, especially where the reversion is to a lease expiry rather than to a rent review.

Comparable evidence

The ARY used to capitalise a contracted rack rent may be lower than an ARY used to capitalise a reversionary rack rent because there may be uncertainty as to the ability to secure the reversionary rack rent. This is particularly so where comparable evidence is weak.

Landlords will not always be able to impose hypothetical rent review provisions with artificial assumptions designed to uphold market value, nor will they always be able to secure third-party determination by an expert (where evidence may not be required) rather than by an arbitrator (who can consider evidence only).

Investors may require a higher yield where they find it unattractive to earn a relatively lower return on their total investment during the period of the term.

Reversionary investments having a relatively imminent opportunity to review the rental (where terms are less than the normal review pattern), are generally perceived to have greater growth potential than rack-rented investments and, accordingly, may command a lower yield.

The valuer must have regard to the prospects for reletting the property, which for secondary properties may be poor, as they can often be characterised by substantial void periods. For some secondary properties, however, vacant possession can secure higher prices from owner/occupiers than investors would have been prepared to pay had the property been let.

Traditional investment tables assume that income is received annually in arrears. Tables are now available which assume that income is received quarterly in advance (and produce a higher capital value for the same yield). Investors will not necessarily begin to pay different prices for property because new investment tables are available, but rates of return may be perceived to be different than otherwise thought. Clarification should be sought when obtaining comparable evidence.

Contributed by Austen Imber.

CHAPTER 52

Value and worth

First published in Estates Gazette May 16, 1998

It is one thing to assess a property's market price but its worth can be quite different, as this depends on this benefit to the owner.

The identification of market price is important, but increasingly clients need to know the worth of a particular property. What is worth, however, and how can it be calculated? The meanings of price, worth and value are not clear. Dictionaries seem to regard them as synonyms, one for another, so that normal definitions are unhelpful.

Distinction between price and worth

The RICS manual contains two different definitions relating to price. These are Open Market Value (OMV) and Market Value (MV). The definition of Market Value is that outlined by the International Valuation Standards Committee (IVSC). The wording of the definition is different from Open Market Value, but the institution considers that its application results in the same valuation figure.

These definitions refer to the word "value", which to many implies worth rather than price. The Mallinson report addressed this problem by making the suggestion that the definition of Open Market Value should be renamed Open Market Price. The general consensus is, however, that the name of the definition will remain the same.2

Both definitions have perhaps added to the confusion which clients, and in some instances, valuers have about the precise meaning of the words price and worth.

It is argued that an asset can only be worth what you can get for it. However, this view could arise because valuers tend to be transaction-driven. What should be borne in mind is that an interest in a property will be used for some purpose, and the use to which it is put can attach a value to the owner which may differ from its price.

Price may be the figure which has to be paid to secure the benefits of ownership, or will be the price which can be achieved on disposal, but the value of ownership will be the property's worth.

Thus price and worth are by no means synonymous and only coincidentally will they be equal. Any suggestion that worth must be the same as price fails to recognise the underlying motivation of a particular investor.3

A rational investor will only purchase an asset if the price in the market is below his/her assessment of worth. Likewise, it will only sell where the market price is at least equal to or greater than his/her assessment of worth.

The RICS has attempted to address the problem by defining price, value and worth. Price means the actual figure that an owner would have achieved if his/her property or investment was sold today. Value means the estimated figure that the owner would achieve if he/she decided to sell the property or investment. Worth is the value to the owner.

The distinction between a valuation, an appraisal and a calculation of worth

In addition to understanding the difference between the meaning of the words worth, value and price, valuers and clients need to be fully aware of the difference between a valuation, an appraisal and a calculation of worth.

The RICS manual defines valuation, appraisal and calculation of worth. According to these definitions, it can be concluded that a valuation is a prediction of the most likely selling price; a calculation of worth is an estimate of what an investment is worth to a particular buyer or seller; and an appraisal is a combination of the two.

Price

Price is a market function determined by the balance between supply and demand. The greater the demand – assuming that supply remains fixed – the greater will be the price. Alternatively, the greater the supply – assuming demand remains fixed – the lower will be the price. Thus, in order to determine the price of a particular property or investment the valuer must assess the forces of supply and demand.

The crucial difference between a valuation to determine the price of an asset and a calculation to determine the worth of an asset is that, in determining price, the valuer relies on indications from the market to determine factors, such as the discount rates and growth rates.

The valuation does not attempt to mirror explicitly the underlying thinking of investors within the market. In forming a calculation of worth, the discount and growth rates are determined by the client and the only factor which is determined by the market is the capitalisation rate or exit yield.

A valuation to determine price is, therefore, not subjective but purely a market matter.

Worth

In addition to assessing the market value or price of an investment, the client could also require the valuer to determine the worth of a particular investment so that the client can be properly advised on when to buy or sell it. Thus investment worth is the value to a specific investor, reflecting unique circumstances, perceptions, objectives, financial and tax status, the ability to secure funding , alternative investment opportunities and required rates of return.[4]

The client should also note that there are two separate aspects to investment worth. Firstly, there is individual worth, which is the maximum price an individual will pay taking into account all the available information in an efficient manner.[5]

Secondly, there is market worth, which is the price at which an investment would trade on a market where buyers and sellers were using all the information available in the most efficient way.[6]

A calculation of worth must mirror explicitly the underlying thinking of the investors within the market, and the method used must reflect the increased level of data and information required for such a valuation. The RICS, therefore, suggests that worth is best calculated by the use of explicit DCF techniques.[7]

Nick French, Robert Petro and Gillian Bowman, in their practice paper on price and worth,[8] argue that this technique is the only acceptable method for calculating worth. This is basically to ensure that the assumptions upon which the calculation is based are exposed to the client.

With the conventional all risks yield method of calculation, it is difficult to explain what the implicit assumptions are as they are all encapsulated within the one yield. Explicit methods are more appropriate for a calculation of worth as they are transparent and highlight, to the client, all the assumptions made within the calculation.

The RICS refers to the Net Present Value method (NPV) and the Internal Rate of Return method (IRR). The RICS adopts what it terms a Gross Present Value approach to calculating worth which involves discounting the current value of future cash flows at an appropriate rate, excluding an initial purchase price.

It adopts such an approach because, it argues, when conducting a calculation of worth the price may not be known and, if price is not known, then an NPV or IRR calculation would not be possible.

If the market price of the property investment is known, then the NPV method can be used to determine investment worth. This would simply involve the valuer building into the calculation factors such as the client's perceptions of growth and his/her individual discount rate, tax liabilities, voids and fees etc.

Once the projected income flows are discounted and the price and other outgoings are deducted, the resulting NPV figure, if positive, would be added to the market value to give the true worth of the investment to the client or, if negative, would be deducted from the price to illustrate the true underlying worth.

A negative NPV would clearly show that the investment property would be worth less to the client than the current price. The client would not, therefore, bid for the investment.

Conclusion

Worth and price are by no means synonymous. Any suggestion that worth must be the same as price fails to recognise the underlying motivation of an investment decision.

The RICS, within its *Information Paper on Calculations of Worth*,9 has addressed the problem of confusion between the meaning of the words price and worth by giving succinct definitions.

The inputs to pricing and worth valuation models are based upon different criteria. The pricing model is objective and does not attempt to mirror explicitly the underlying thinking of investors within the market. Price is market driven and based upon market discount, growth and capitalisation rates. The worth model is not market driven, it is a subjective concept and based upon the client's particular circumstances.

An explicit method needs to be adopted so that the assumptions upon which the calculation is based are exposed to the client. It is not possible to state the precise form which such a calculation will take as the factors taken into account will vary between one individual and another. The calculation will need to reflect factors, such as the client's particular circumstances, perceptions of growth, objectives, finance and tax status, his/her ability to secure funding, opportunity cost and required rates of return.

Certain factors which are important to one individual may not be important to another and, therefore, no calculation of worth will be the same as another.

In order to produce a valid and useful calculation of worth, the valuer needs to be in close liaison with the client in respect of his/her individual requirements and judgments in order to agree on the matters that should be taken into account.

Market value is defined in the Appraisal and Valuation Manual as the estimated amount for which an asset should exchange on the date of valuation between a willing buyer and a willing seller in an arms-length transaction after proper marketing, wherein the parties had each acted knowledgeably, prudently and without compulsion (Practice Statement 4.1.1)

Open market value is defined in the Appraisal and Valuation Manual as an opinion of the best price at which the sale of an interest in property would have been completed unconditionally for cash consideration on the date of valuation, assuming:

a) a willing seller;
b) that, prior to the date of valuation, there had been a reasonable period (having regard to the nature of the property and the state of the market) for the proper marketing of the interest, for the agreement of the price and terms and for completion of the sale;
c) that the state of the market, level of values and other circumstances were, on any earlier assumed date of exchange of contracts, the same as on the date of valuation;
d) that no account is taken of any additional bid by a prospective purchaser with a special interest; and
e) that both parties to the transaction had acted knowledgeably, prudently and without compulsion. (Practice Statement 4.2.1)

Price: the actual observable exchange price in the open market (p13, *Calculation of Worth: An Information Paper*, RICS Business Services, 1997).

Value: an estimate of the price that would be achieved if the property were to be sold in the market (p13, as above).

Worth: specific investor's perception of the capital sum which he would be prepared to pay (or accept) for the benefits which he expects to be produced by the investment (p13, as above).

Appraisal: the written provision of a valuation, combined with professional opinion, advice and/or analysis relating to the suitability or profitability, or otherwise, of the subject property for defined purposes, or to the effects of specified circumstances thereon, as judged by the valuer following the relevant investigation. The appraisal may incorporate a Calculation of Worth (see below) as requirements dictate (*The RICS Appraisal and Valuation Manual*, Definitions, p1).

Calculation of Worth: the provision of a written estimate of the net monetary worth at a stated date of the benefits and costs of ownership of a specified interest in property to the instructing party reflecting the purpose(s) specified by that part (as above, p3).

Valuation: the provision of a written opinion as to capital price or value, or rental price or value, on any given basis in respect of an interest in property, with or without associated information, assumptions or qualifications. However, a valuation does not include a forecast of value (as above, p6).

References and further reading

1 RICS (1996), *RICS Appraisal and Valuation Manual*, RICS Books.
2 Petro, R, French, N and Bowman, G (1996). Price and Worth: Developments in Valuation Methodology. *Journal of Property Valuation and Investment*, Vol 14 No 4. pp79–100.
3 French, N (1996), Investment Valuation: Developments from the Mallinson Report, *Journal of Property Valuation and Investment*, Vol 14 No 5.
4 Value of Theory & Practice, *Estates Gazette*, November 1, 1997, issue 9744.
5 Baum, AE, Crosby, N and MacGregor, B (1996). Price Formation, Mispricing and Investment Analysis in the Property Market, *Journal of Property Valuation and Investment*, Vol 14 No 1. pp36–49.
6 Baum, N Crosby and B MacGregor (1996), *ibid*, p37.
7 RICS (1997) *Calculation of Worth An Information Paper*, Investment Property Forum, RICS Books.

8 Petro, R, French, N and Bowman, G (1996). Price and Worth: Developments in Valuation Methodology. *Journal of Property Valuation and Investment*, Vol 14 No 4. pp79–100.
9 RICS (1997) *Calculation of Worth, An Information Paper*, Investment Property Forum, RICS Books.

Contributed by Chris Gaskell.

COMMERCIAL LAW

CHAPTER 53

Partnership or company

First published in Estates Gazette February 19, 1994

Is it better for a small business to be a partnership or as a limited company?

Businessmen are faced with a very basic choice as to which trading medium they should use. They may (two or more together) set up in partnership or as a limited company. It is proposed here to consider some distinguishing features.

The partnership or firm (a company should never be referred to as a "firm") is governed by the legislative framework set out in the Partnership Act 1890. The Act is not a comprehensive code, but generally only "fills in the gaps" which exist in any agreement that has been drawn up. Herein lies one of the very basic distinctions between a partnership and a company. A company is subject to detailed rules contained in Acts of Parliament such as the Companies Act 1985 and the Insolvency Act 1986. Generally the provisions of these Acts apply notwithstanding any agreement between those setting up the business.

An important factor for those establishing a business is bound to be the tax position. Wherever there is a partnership the profits of the firm are allocated to individual partners, who pay ordinary schedular income tax on those profits at the usual income tax rates. By contrast, a company has a separate identity and is liable to corporation tax on its profits. Corporation tax is levied at rates of 21% and 31%. The rates will be reduced by 1% in 1999/2000 tax year. Where a company pays out dividends to its members, it pays advance Corporation Tax (ACT) on those profits at 20%. The recipient receives a tax credit for this when paying tax. It is not possible to say, in general terms, where the balance of advantage lies. Much will depend upon the nature of the business and the circumstances of those setting it up. However, the tax question is certainly a crucial factor.

Access to limited liability is one reason why people often incorporate. In a firm the partners will have unlimited liability, whereas in a company the extent of a member's liability will usually be the member's liability on his shares. The possibility of setting up a "limited partnership" (governed by the Limited Partnership Act 1907) is not usually a viable option. At least one partner in a "limited partnership" has to have unlimited liability and, furthermore, a limited partner will sacrifice his limited liability if he participates in the running of the business. It is useful for sleeping partners only. In practice it must be said that the limited liability "tag" may be a chimera. For example, if a budding corporate business wishes to borrow money from a bank, it is unlikely that the manager will wish merely to rely on the company's assets as security. He will almost certainly ask for collateral security from the company's directors.

An important advantage possessed by the company is its perpetual nature. Companies such as Hudson's Bay Trading Co have been in existence for hundreds of years. In a partnership (which does not have a separate legal personality) there can be no such longevity. Generally the death or bankruptcy of a partner will mean that the partnership has to be reformed. This can be inconvenient.

Where people have set up a company limited by shares, those shares are transferable to others. This is attractive to those who may wish to realise their investment. There may be some restrictions on transferring shares in a private company, but in a public company quoted on the Stock Exchange shares will be freely transferable (there is a market mechanism which indicates what the shares will fetch).

In a partnership (unless it is a limited one) all the partners are agents of the firm. In a company it is possible to separate ownership from control. Those who hold shares cannot bind the company, only the company's management (its directors) may do that. In a private company often the shareholders and directors are one and the same (this may be literally true as a private company may now be set up with only one member). But they may be quite different.

It is usually said in comparing a firm with a company that it is easier for the company to raise money. This is certainly true of a public company, which may offer its shares and debentures to the public. In the case of the private company, the ability to raise money with ease is not so apparent, but a private company, like a public one, may mortgage all its undertaking to secure a loan by way of a "floating charge". A partnership cannot do this.

Lest it is thought that all the advantages are with the company, some drawbacks should be mentioned. Chief of these is undoubtedly the welter of legislation that applies to the company. Most lawyers do not understand the nuances and complexities of much of the legislation, so the layman has little chance of doing so. There are numerous cumbersome formalities for the limited company, such as filing an annual return and annual accounts. Firms are happily free of these requirements. Coupled with these formalities is the need to make public certain of the company's affairs via the registrar of companies – its financial position, its directors etc. Once again, the partnership does not have to make anything public.

By and large, the advantages of incorporation are purchased cheaply. The certificate of incorporation setting up the company costs £20. Filing the annual return at Companies House is £15. However, the legal costs of setting up the company may be considerable, while drawing up a partnership agreement should not be costly. More significant is the annual audit. This may be crippling for a small business.

Outlined is a checklist of the chief advantages and disadvantages of setting up as a company or as a partnership. It is not intended to come down decisively pro or contra either form of business as different factors are given different weight according to circumstances.

Comparison of partnerships and limited companies

Partnership	Limited company
Governed by Partnership Act 1890	Governed by Companies Act 1985 and Insolvency Act 1986
No comprehensive statutory rules	Complex rules, which need interpreting by a lawyer
Partnership profits allocated to partners and taxed at normal rates	Company profits liable for corporation tax at 21% and 31% Shareholder given tax credit for amount paid by company on any dividend paid

The Court of Appeal considered that the position would have been the same if the "money in lieu of notice" clause was construed as a "liquidated damages" one, ie a genuine estimate of the executive's probable loss as a result of summary termination.

Where *Abrahams* applies the executive has a right (which would be enforceable by summary judgment) to money in lieu of notice as a contractual debt. The executive would then be under no duty to mitigate his loss or to give any credit for actual or imputed earnings during the notice period; the employer would have no right to apply any discount for accelerated receipt. Where the executive has a long period of contractual notice the financial consequences of *Abrahams* can be very severe to an employer and very favourable to an employee.

In most cases termination without giving the notice stipulated in a service contract is "wrongful" or "unlawful" dismissal (unless, of course, the termination is for good cause). Even if money in lieu of notice is immediately paid to the departing executive, it is still a breach of contract to terminate his employment without notice. Many service contracts provide one method only of lawfully terminating the executive's employment (without good cause), ie by giving the full period of contractual notice. Non-competition covenants in the service contract become unenforceable if the employer terminates the contract unlawfully.

The only purpose of a "money in lieu of notice" clause in a service contract is to provide an alternative method of lawfully terminating the executive's employment, summarily and without cause, while preserving for the employer the benefit of any "non-competition" covenants (sometimes known as "restraint of trade clauses" or "restrictive covenants"). Such covenants may restrain the executive from working for named competitors for a given period after termination, from soliciting the employer's customers for their business, or from poaching the employer's key employees.

Although covenants of this kind are prima facie void as being in restraint of trade, and so contrary to public policy, they may be enforceable if they are considered by the court to be necessary to protect legitimate proprietary interests of the employer and to go no further in space or time than is necessary to protect those interests.

It follows that a "money in lieu of notice" clause will benefit the employer when (and only when) the service contract contains a non-competition covenant. A non-competition covenant should be used only where the employer has genuine "protectable interests" (trade secrets, confidential information, customer connections, or the stability of the workforce), and where a so-called "gardening leave" clause (see below) cannot provide adequate protection.

Since *Abrahams*, it is essential to realise (at the drafting stage) that there is a trade-off between the enforceability of the non-competition covenants on the one hand, and the freedom to negotiate about compensation on the other. In some contracts, the inclusion of a "money in lieu of notice clause" will be unnecessary and it may turn out to be very expensive for the employer. And yet the omission of a "money in lieu of notice clause" may render the non-competition covenants unenforceable, with disastrous results for the profits of the business.

Company law considerations

Where the executive is a managing director or an executive director, the service contract must satisfy all relevant provisions of the Companies Act 1985, including:

- section 322A: the directors who are granting the contract must be acting within their powers;
- section 319: any service contract for more than five years must have the approval of the shareholders;
- section 312: any payment to a director by way of compensation for loss of office (as director, not as employee) will be unlawful unless it has shareholder approval (but this approval will not be required for any bona fide payment of damages for breach of contract – section 316(3));
- section 315 – it is the duty of a director of a company who is directly or indirectly interested in any contract (or proposed contract) with the company to declare the nature of this interest at a meeting of the directors of the company.

The directors also have a duty to consider the best interests of the company when approving the terms of a service contract and this is particularly relevant when considering the length of a notice period. An unusually long period of notice will be void if it is not genuinely required in the interests of the company.

The directors should also check the company's articles of association to see whether the approval of the shareholders is required for the appointment.

After *Abrahams*

Two important consequences flow from the lawful termination of a service contract in accordance with a "money in lieu of notice" clause:

- the employer will not have terminated the employment in breach of contract and the benefit of any non-competition covenants will be preserved;
- "money in lieu of notice" will be payable by the employer, without any deduction, immediately upon termination of the employment, as a contractual debt.

Debt versus damages

There is a distinction between a "contractual debt" and "damages for wrongful dismissal".

The court will award damages for wrongful dismissal based on the executive's salary (net of tax and national insurance) and the financial equivalent of all his contractual benefits for the period of notice. This is the ultimate sanction which lies behind the negotiating positions of the parties. The aim is to put the executive in the same financial position as he would have been in if proper notice had been given. The court will apply an appropriate discount for accelerated receipt and the executive's duty to mitigate his loss. The employer is required to compensate the executive only for his actual loss suffered as a result of the "wrongful" dismissal. The first £30,000 is tax-free (Income and Corporation Taxes Act 1988, sections 148 and 188), but the balance (being taxable in the executive's hands) must be grossed up at the appropriate tax rate (normally 40%).

Where the service contract provides for lawful termination with money in lieu of notice, the employer is not able to negotiate a discount for mitigation of loss and/or accelerated receipt or any other discount. There is no question of compensating the executive for any loss he may have suffered and so there is no requirement for the executive to give credit for his earnings (or potential earnings) from any alternative employment, even if he finds another job at a higher salary the next day. The full amount of the money in lieu of notice is payable, at once, as an enforceable contractual debt.

However, the payment of money in lieu of notice will be fully taxable under PAYE (with no tax-free £30,000). The amount payable will be treated as contractual profit from the employment for income tax purposes.

Wrongful dismissal and unfair dismissal

"Wrongful dismissal" merely means that the dismissal was carried out in breach of the contract of employment, giving rise to a claim for damages at common law. "Unfair dismissal" is a statutory concept under the Employment Protection (Consolidation) Act 1978, giving rise to a claim in the industrial tribunal, either for "reinstatement" or "compensation" for the loss suffered as a result of the unfair dismissal. To avoid a finding of unfair dismissal, the employer must not only have an acceptable reason for the dismissal (which may be capacity, conduct, redundancy or "some other substantial reason" such as a business reorganisation), but must also have followed a fair procedure. The current maximum compensatory award for unfair dismissal is £11,300 (there is also a basic award equivalent to the statutory redundancy entitlement). This maximum does not apply in cases of sex discrimination or race discrimination.

In Scotland, the employment appeal tribunal ruled in *Finnie* v *Top Hat Frozen Food* [1985] IRLR 365 that pay in lieu of notice was an independent payment to which the executive had a separate contractual right and which was not to be set off against the compensation awarded by an industrial tribunal for unfair dismissal. However, in England the Court of Appeal held in *Addison* v *Babcock FATA Ltd* [1987] ICR 805 ("*Babcock*") that any damages already received for "wrongful" dismissal (apart from money in lieu of notice for the statutory minimum notice period) must be set off against the compensatory award because the executive cannot recover twice for the same loss. (*Babcock* does not apply in Scotland, where the Court of Session hears appeals from the employment appeal tribunal.) It seems probable that English industrial tribunals and courts will continue to credit the employer with a payment of money in lieu of notice even when made under a provision of the service contract when deciding the compensatory award.

Industrial tribunals are required to compensate for loss actually suffered as a result of unfair dismissal. Receipt of payment in lieu of notice as a contractual debt still wipes out the loss of pay during the notice period.

Drafting considerations

A "money in lieu of notice clause" can be drafted to give the employer the right to choose whether to terminate the contract with notice or to pay money in lieu of notice. This might (although such a clause has not yet been tested in the courts) distinguish a service contract of this nature from the contractual arrangement in *Abrahams*. In that case, the executive had the right to two years' money in lieu of notice if the employer terminated without notice.

According to *Abrahams*, provision in the service contract for payment of money in lieu of notice does not give rise to a claim for liquidated damages but for contractual debt. Nevertheless, such a provision is intended to be an estimate of the probable loss to the executive on summary termination without good cause.

The "money in lieu of notice clause" could therefore include a contractual percentage discount for mitigation of loss and accelerated receipt. It might also be advisable to specify that only basic salary will be payable (with the financial equivalent of contractual benefits, such as a company car) if the employer elects to terminate summarily and pay money in lieu of notice. Items such as the payment of a bonus or commission often give rise to disputes about quantum.

Gardening leave

A "gardening leave" clause is an alternative to a post-employment "non-competition covenant". This may satisfy the employer's need for protection and remove the need for a "money in lieu of notice" clause. This provision allows the employer to send the executive home, with full pay and all contractual benefits, for a reasonable period, probably not exceeding six months. The court will enforce "gardening leave" only if the employer genuinely needs this protection and it will make its own estimate of the period for which it would be right to protect the employer.

It will be important to include any "gardening leave" provision in the express terms of the service contract. If such a clause is not included, the employer's refusal to allow the executive to work could, in itself, be a breach of contract and this would immediately release the executive from all his duties of loyalty and fidelity to the employer.

Contributed by Martin Moyes.

Company directors and criminal charges

First published in Estates Gazette February 8, 1997

In what circumstances may a company, its directors, and/or its managers be guilty of a criminal offence if a fatal accident occurs or the environment is polluted by the business activities of that company?

When a watercourse is polluted and the fish die, or a worker is killed through some careless act, or a foreign body contaminates food and a child is injured, who is liable? Who should be liable? What should be the extent of their liability? Is a fine sufficient or should a jail sentence follow? It might be possible to identify an individual who committed the criminal conduct, but it may be that a company is responsible instead of, or with, that individual. A company is a legal person but, in the criminal context, a company conviction may be unsatisfactory.

As one judge said:

If there is evidence against the company, there must be evidence against the directors, mustn't there? I can't send the company to prison, can I? The trouble is, a great number of construction workers meet their deaths in this country because the employer doesn't provide a safe place to work . . . It must be made clearer to employers they will face prison.

The Times, March 15, 1996

The criminal law provides two possible approaches to liability. One, through the mainstream criminal system, is to prosecute for manslaughter. Such an investigation and prosecution would be handled by the police and the Crown Prosecution Service (CPS), and would be subject to the same common law principles as any offence of manslaughter. The other route is to prosecute for an environmental or environmental health offence which are all created by statute. The investigation and prosecution would be conducted by the relevant enforcement bodies:

- Health and safety offences: Health and Safety Executive or local authority;
- Food safety offences: the local authority;
- Water pollution: Environment Agency;
- Atmospheric pollution: Environment Agency or local authority;
- Statutory nuisance: the local authority;
- Contaminated land:* Environment Agency or local authority;
- Waste offences: Environment Agency.

These enforcement bodies have powers to bring prosecutions in the criminal courts and they are, by and large, subject to the same investigative procedures as the police when they are investigating criminal offences. In particular, they are subject to the provisions of the Police and Criminal Evidence Act 1984 and the codes of practice produced under that Act. They must therefore administer the same caution as the police when interviewing suspects. This means that any answers thereby obtained may be used in the court, but the suspect will not be obliged to answer those questions.

One exception to this important principle relates to health and safety offences. The Health and Safety at Work etc Act 1974 provides that a person (whether a suspect or not) may be required to answer the questions of the investigation officer.

The *quid pro quo* to this is that the answers obtained under these powers may not be used in evidence against the person interviewed or against their spouse.

If there has been a fatality arising unexpectedly or as a result of an accident, then there will be a coroner's inquest. The purpose of the inquest is to determine the cause of death, not civil or criminal liability. Thus, the verdict may be accidental death, unlawful killing, misadventure, suicide or, where the position is not clear, an open verdict.

Following proceedings in the coroner's court, there may be a CPS decision to bring a prosecution for manslaughter. This does not prevent the environmental enforcement body from bringing criminal proceedings against the company and/or director for an environmental offence. In fact, the latter course of action is much more likely to follow than a prosecution for manslaughter by the CPS. There are many difficulties in bringing a prosecution for manslaughter.

---

*These provisions are not yet in force.

Manslaughter prosecutions

The CPS must first decide whom to prosecute: the company, director (or senior officers of the company) or both. The appropriate form of manslaughter is known as "involuntary manslaughter" and is available where death results from a criminal act which any reasonable person would recognise to be likely to expose another person to the risk of injury, or where death is caused by a grossly negligent act or omission.

In bringing an action for manslaughter against a company, it is often difficult to prove that the "mind" of the company was affected. That is, in showing that directors or other senior officers of the company were involved in the course of events which led to the death. The decisions which they made (or failed to make) must have caused the fatality.

This presents a difficulty where the company is very large and a number of people may have been involved in the development of policy or in the taking of managerial decisions.

This is illustrated by the case involving the disaster at Zeebrugge when a ferry, *The Herald of Free Enterprise*, sank with considerable loss of life. In *P&O European Ferries (Dover) Ltd* (1991) 93 Cr App R 72, it was held that a company could be indicted for the crime of manslaughter through the controlling mind of one of its agents who committed an act which fulfils the prerequisites of the crime of manslaughter. Two directors and a senior manager were prosecuted for manslaughter, but the case was withdrawn from the jury on the ground that there was no evidence that the people who represented the controlling mind of the company had formed the necessary criminal intent or had acted in a grossly negligent way.

This undoubtedly makes it easier for a small company to be successfully prosecuted than a large one. Where the company is a "one-man firm" then it will be easier to establish that the one man who is the director/manager has been responsible for the events which led to the accident and this can be imputed to the company.

In 1994 OLL Ltd and its managing director, Peter Kite, were both convicted of manslaughter in respect of the deaths of four young people on a canoe exercise at an outdoor pursuits training centre run by the company in Lyme Bay. It was relatively easy to establish liability, given that the managing director had personal knowledge of the inadequacy of his safety precautions, in particular because he had received letters of complaint from previous instructors. It is always possible to prosecute the individual who has committed manslaughter. In this case both the company and the managing director were convicted of manslaughter.

The point is, that in making a company liable for manslaughter, the liability is personal to the company, not vicarious. The company is made liable for its own acts, not for those of an employee. A company cannot think or feel pain so a fiction has to be enacted to identify the acts and thoughts of a human person with those of the company. This is explained by Lord Reid in *Tesco Supermarkets Ltd* v *Nattrass* [1972] AC 153 at p170:

A living person has a mind which can have knowledge or intention to be negligent and he has hands to carry out his intentions. A corporation has none of these: it must act through living persons, though not always one or the same person. Then the person who acts is not speaking or acting for the company. He is acting as the company and his mind which directs his acts is the mind of the company.

A further limitation on liability is that a company cannot be prosecuted where the only available penalty is physical in nature. The penalty for murder is life imprisonment and because a company cannot be sent to jail, it follows that a prosecution for murder can never be brought against the company. Manslaughter is possible because the penalty can be a fine.

Law Commission proposals

On March 5 1996 the Law Commission proposed a new offence of "corporate killing". Under this new offence a company would be liable if a management failure resulted in death and that failure constituted conduct far below what could reasonably have been expected. The convicted company would be liable to an unlimited fine and would be liable to remedy the fault which led to the accident. The Law Commission did not recommend prison sentences for directors, but it would seem that the courts are prepared to move in that direction. Jail sentences of two and three years have been recently imposed on managing directors.

In turn, the difficulties involved in bringing manslaughter prosecutions are great. Despite much public concern, as expressed in recent poisoning cases where landlords have failed to maintain gas installations, such prosecutions are rarely successfully brought.

Contributed by Rosalind Malcolm.

CHAPTER 56

The law of fraudulent statements

First published in Estates Gazette May 31, 1997

A series of famous cases has established the difference in law between "negligence", "recklessness" and "fraud" – and the rulings apply to false statements as well.

In 1889, the House of Lords had to consider a case where the directors of a tramway company issued a misleading prospectus to the public. The prospectus claimed that the company had obtained statutory powers from Parliament to run steam trams. In fact, this type of power could only be used with the consent of the Board of Trade, without which the company was limited to the use of "animal power". The first electric trams did not run in Great Britain until 1891 (in Leeds*).

Panel 1: FALSE PROSPECTUS

One great feature of this undertaking, to which considerable importance should be attached, is, that by the special Act of Parliament obtained, the company has the right to use steam or mechanical motive power, instead of horses, and it is fully expected that by means of this a considerable saving will result . . .

From the Prospectus of the Plymouth, Devonport, and District Tramways Company, February 1883.

Case of the false prospectus

The directors of the company had taken the view that the consent of the Board of Trade would be a mere formality and had therefore made no mention of this requirement in the prospectus. The

---

*This is a city which seems to have learned from its mistake in abolishing trams: see the Leeds Supertram Act 1993

prospectus was therefore a false prospectus as it contained an important misrepresentation. The maxim of the law is suppressio veri, suggestio falsi: "a suppression of truth is a suggestionof falsehood".

The Board of Trade subsequently refused its consent to the use of steam power and the company went into liquidation. A claim was brought by a disappointed shareholder who had relied upon the prospectus and had bought his shares in the belief that steam trams would be the thing of the future.

The shareholder's claim for misrepresentation against the company was valueless. It was irrelevant whether the misrepresentation had been an innocent or a fraudulent one. The company was insolvent and could not refund the price of the shares. Instead, therefore, the shareholder decided to sue the directors personally.

This claim had to be brought in the law of tort because the shareholder had no contractual relationship with the directors. The only conceivable claim against the directors was for fraud (known as the tort of "deceit") – the tort of "negligent mis-statement" (in cases of pure economic loss) being unknown in the 19th century. Indeed, such a cause of action was not accepted by the House of Lords until 1964 – in the famous case of *Hedley Byrne & Co Ltd* v *Heller & Partners Ltd* [1964] AC 465.

Lord Herschell's definition

The House of Lords held that the conduct of the directors of the tramway company, although negligent and unbusinesslike, had not amounted to fraud. Lord Herschell (1837–1899) gave a very narrow definition to the concept of "fraudulent" statements (see panel 2).

All this happened in the case of *Derry* v *Peek* (1889) 14 App Cas 337. In company law, this decision led to strict statutory obligations being imposed on persons who issue prospectuses to potential shareholders and investors. In the general case of liability for false statements, it eventually led to the creation of the separate tort of"negligent mis-statement". The decision of the House of Lords drew a dividing line between fraud and negligence for all time.

Fraud is akin to criminality and wickedness. It is to be found in the mind of the maker of the statement, false to his own beliefs about the facts of the case. It is a "subjective" concept. The more astonishing the belief, the more likely it is that the maker of the

Panel 2: LORD HERSCHELL'S DEFINITION OF FRAUD

. . . fraud is proved when it is shewn that a false representation has been made (1) knowingly, or (2) without belief in its truth, or (3) recklessly, careless whether it be true or false. Although I have treated the second and third as distinct cases, I think that the third is but an instance of the second, for one who makes a statement under such circumstances can have no real belief in the truth of what he states. To prevent a false statement being fraudulent, there must, I think, always be an honest belief in its truth . . .

per Lord Herschell in *Derry* v *Peek* (1889) 14 App Cas 337

statement is lying when he claims to hold such a belief. But, as the facts of *Derry* v *Peek* have shown, even experienced men of business can sometimes delude themselves with false beliefs (and certainly with false hopes).

Negligence is a human failing. It consists of failure to exercise reasonable care, or to have exhibited reasonable skill, and this failure may be momentary, not necessarily persistent. It is an "objective" concept, and the standard which is applied is always that of the "reasonable" person (in appropriate cases, this will be the reasonable workman or the reasonable professional person).

Obviously, on this test, the directors of the tramway company were negligent (one could even say, "grossly negligent"), but they had not been fraudulent.

Recklessness

If fraud is wickedness and negligence is a blameworthy lapse which even honest people can sometimes commit, where does this leave "recklessness"?

Traditionally, recklessness has been treated as "the blood brother of intention": per Lord Edmund Davies in his dissenting judgment in *R* v *Caldwell* [1982] AC 341. Together with the concept of a criminal intention, it is one of the two states of mind which can make a person "malicious" in the eyes of the law. For the most famous illustration of this principle, we have to turn, once more, to Leeds.

On April 30 1881 a man named Martin left the gallery of the Theatre Royal, Leeds, just before the performance was due to end. He turned out two gas lamps on the staircase and bolted one of the two exit doors. Many people were seriously injured in the panic and crush which ensued.

Martin was charged with "maliciously inflicting grievous bodily harm" on two of these victims. These charges were, of course, specimen charges. The statutory provision which the prosecution relied upon was section 20 of the Offences Against the Person Act 1861.

Martin argued that he could not be guilty of this statutory offence (usually known as "malicious wounding") because he had not acted out of malice towards anyone. He had only intended a practical joke.

The jury convicted Martin and this decision was unanimously upheld by the Court for Crown Cases Reserved. Stephen J observed that a man acts "maliciously" when he wilfully and without lawful excuse "does that which he knows will injure another": see *R v Martin* [1881] 8 QBD 54.

R v Martin was uppermost in the mind of Professor CS Kenny (1847–1930) when, in 1902, he wrote the first edition of his textbook *Outlines of Criminal Law*. His definition of "malice" became famous and is used today (see panel 3).

Panel 3: PROFESSOR KENNY'S DEFINITION OF RECKLESSNESS

. . . in any statutory definition of a crime "malice" must be taken not in the old vague sense of "wickedness" in general, but as requiring either (i) an actual intention to do the particular kind of harm that in fact was done, or (ii) recklessness as to whether such harm should occur or not (ie the accused has foreseen that the particular kind of harm might be done, and yet has gone on to take the risk of it).

"Advertent recklessness"

Professor Kenny's definition of "malice" provided, almost by accident, an authoritative definition of "recklessness" also. It was not a synonym for "negligence" (or even for "gross negligence"); it was a subjective concept, akin to purposeful wrongdoing. It only arose if the person in question had actually foreseen all or some of the consequences of what he was doing.

This definition of "recklessness" was subsequently upheld by the Court of Criminal Appeal in *R v Cunningham* [1957] 2 QB 396. This was a case where a thief seeking to steal coins failed to realise that poisonous gas would escape if he wrenched a pre-payment meter away from a gas pipe. The court held that he had been wrongly convicted of (non-fatal) poisoning because he had not intentionally poisoned the victim, nor had he been "reckless" within Professor Kenny's meaning of that word.

The type of recklessness defined by Kenny has subsequently become known as "advertent recklessness" – the recklessness that flows from knowingly taking an unjustified risk.

"Inadvertent recklessness"?

In ordinary English dictionaries, the word "reckless" does not have the special meaning which Professor Kenny gave to it. It simply means "acting without reck or heed".

This dictionary definition has led some judges to use the word "recklessness" in a way which is almost indistinguishable from the concept of "gross negligence". This most notoriously happened in *R* v *Caldwell* [1982] AC 341, a case involving the conviction of a drunken chef for reckless arson.

In those rare cases where this definition of "recklessness" is used, the concept thus created is called "inadvertent recklessness". It is usually summarised as a "failure to think about obvious risks". However, it is quite clear that this type of "recklessness" has no relevance to the law of fraud.

In *Large* v *Mainprize* [1989] Crim LR 213, a deep-sea fisherman was charged with recklessly submitting a false statistical return about the quantity of fish that he had caught; this was a statutory offence created in order to enforce EC directives about fish-quotas. The defendant had understated the weight of his catch by about 50%. His defence was, in effect: "I must have pushed the wrong button on my calculator". The prosecutor alleged that the defendant's failure to double-check his calculations, and his handing in of a wildly wrong statistical return, was a form of recklessness in itself – even if his original mistake had been an honest one.

The Divisional Court held that this definition of "recklessness" was not acceptable in the law relating to false statements. Only advertent recklessness would do – the sort of wilful blindness described by Lord Herschell in *Derry* v *Peek*. Accordingly, it was held that the defendant was entitled to be acquitted of the statutory offence if, when he handed in the statistical return, he had honestly believed it to be true.

"Representations are continuing"

In *With* v *O'Flanagan* [1936] Ch 575 the vendor of a business informed the prospective purchaser that the income of the business was £2,000 pa. After making that statement the vendor became ill, and in the next four months the income of the business dropped away considerably. The vendor allowed the purchaser to sign the contract to buy the business without telling him about the loss of income.

The Court of Appeal held that the vendor had no right to keep silent about the facts which had invalidated his earlier statement. The relevant maxim was "representations are continuing".

Thus the purchaser was entitled to claim that he had entered into the contract under the influence of a misrepresentation, newly made, so to speak, immediately before he signed the document. It was no defence for the vendor to argue that the statement had been true when he made it in the early stages of the pre-contract negotiations (four months earlier).

Welwyn Hatfield case

With v *O'Flanagan* is usually discussed in the context of the law of contract. The purchaser was entitled to set aside the contract to buy the business because of the vendor's misrepresentation: nowadays he would have relied upon the Misrepresentation Act 1967.

A misrepresentation will give significant remedies to the other contracting party even if the statement in question was made innocently (let alone, if it was made negligently). There is no need to allege fraud in a claim for misrepresentation.

In *Slough Estates* v *Welwyn Hatfield District Council* [1996] 2 EGLR 219, the plaintiff could not rely on the law of misrepresentation. There was no contractual relationship between the two parties. The plaintiffs were a property development company and the defendants were the local planning authority for Welwyn Garden City.

Most of the site, called the Howard Centre, which the plaintiffs wished to develop as a shopping centre, was owned by British Railways, and it included Welwyn Garden City railway station.

By coincidence, Welwyn Hatfield District Council was the long leaseholder of a site over the A1(M) motorway, about three miles from the Howard Centre which in due course became known as the A1 Galleria. This motorway site was the subject of a planning application by a company in the Carroll Group and included 18,580m² (200,000 sq ft) of lettable space, although the planning application principally referred to a leisure centre, ice-rink, gymnasium, and exhibition area.

When in 1984 the plaintiffs heard about the proposed redevelopment of the motorway site they sought reassurances from the council that this would not become a rival attraction to the centre they proposed. The council assured Slough Estates that there would be a tenant-mix agreement which, for a period of five years, would confine the tenants of the motorway site to those retail outlets appropriate to a leisure complex.

The plaintiffs thereupon continued their negotiations with British Railways and, in 1988, they started to build the Howard Centre. They seem to have been continuously reassured that the shopping public would be attracted to the Howard Centre for their regular needs of food, drink, kitchenware, clothing, household goods, and so on, but that they would only be attracted to the A1 Galleria for their regular needs of ice-skates, tracksuits, dumb-bells, ski boots, toboggans, organic yoghurts, and similar lifestyle accessories.

In fact, in 1987 the council had secretly decided to relax the tenant-mix agreement and allow the motorway site to become a more significant rival to the Howard Centre. The plaintiffs did not discover the existence of this decision until 1990. They then made an application for judicial review which was successful. Kennedy J quashed the council's decision to relax the tenant-mix agreement and adjourned the case so that the plaintiffs could continue with the proceedings as a claim for damages.

The plaintiffs argued that they would not have gone ahead with the redevelopment of the Howard Centre if they had known that a secret decision had already been made to relax the tenant-mix agreement at the rival site.

May J awarded the plaintiffs £48.5m as damages for the tort of deceit. He held that the original reassurances to the plaintiffs had become false because of the secret agreement in 1987. He therefore calculated the plaintiffs' losses from that date. He had no difficulty in interpreting the council's conduct as fraudulent within Lord Herschell's definition in *Derry* v *Peek*.

He observed:

From July 1987 onwards Welwyn and Hatfield District Council were nursing a lie and they had set themselves a timebomb. . . The lies were watered down wherever possible, but they were conscious lies. The principal agent who peddled lies was [the then chief planning officer] . . . but I think that it would be unfair to pile the whole responsibility on to him when he was acting out the consequences of a decision taken by the full council on the recommendation of three of their senior officers (of whom he was one). . .

This leaves open the interesting question of what will happen if a local authority, or a landlord, or a professional person makes a statement which induces another person to act upon it, perhaps over a period of many years.

Will the maker of the statement be held liable for the tort of "negligent mis-statement" if the statement becomes untrue, and he absentmindedly fails to notify his previous listener or reader of the change?

Contributed by Leslie Blake.

CHAPTER 57

The law of negligent statements

First published in Estates Gazette June 28, 1997

The difference between a "misrepresentation" and a "misstatement" is important to lawyers (and sometimes to litigants) but probably not to anybody else. Indeed, outside the artificial matrix of the law, it must be confessed that there is no linguistic difference between the two words.

A "misrepresentation" merely means the presentation of something (to the mind of another person) which is not true; a "misstatement" merely means the stating of something which is not true. The linguistic difference between the two words becomes even more obviously untenable once it is accepted that a "statement" does not have to be spoken, or even written. Even a nod or a wink can be a statement, and every estate agent knows the dangers of using a misleading photograph.

In *Chandrasekera* v *R* [1937] AC 220 the Privy Council even went so far as to describe the accusatory gestures of a woman who was dying from serious throat wounds as a "verbal statement".

So far as the legal difference between the two words is concerned, we may start with the obvious fact that students will encounter the law of "misrepresentation" when they are studying the law of contract, whereas they will encounter the law of "misstatement" when they are studying the law of tort. In other words, the law of misrepresentation will be of no use to a person who does not enter into a contract with the maker of that misrepresentation. (The law of agency may be relevant here, in order to discover who, in law, is the true "maker" of the misrepresentation.)

An example of a person who could not successfully rely on the law of misrepresentation was the plaintiff in *Derry* v *Peek* (1889) 14 App Cas 337. As readers of Mainly for Students* may recall, the plaintiff in that case (Mr Peek) found himself in an unfortunate situation.

---

*See p394 of this book.

Innocent misrepresentation

Prior to the Misrepresentation Act 1967 an "innocent misrepresentation" meant one which had not been made fraudulently. Given the narrow definition of "fraud" adopted by the House of Lords in *Derry* v *Peek* (it even excluded cases of gross negligence), the definition of "innocent misrepresentation" was very wide indeed.

Nevertheless, equity gave remedies for innocent misrepresentation. These remedies were rescission of the contract (with restitution of the purchase price, rent etc) and, in suitable cases, the payment of an "indemnity".

An "indemnity" is not the same thing as "damages". An indemnity is merely a penny-for-penny reimbursement of sums necessarily and unavoidably paid under the contract while it was in force. It does not include such heads of claim as loss of profits or sums of money paid foreseeably (but not unavoidably) under the contract.

Indemnities are not damages

A useful illustration of the limitations of an "indemnity" as a remedy is provided by *Whittington* v *Seale Hayne* (1900) 82 LT 49.

The plaintiff in that case was a breeder of prize poultry. He signed a lease of certain premises after he had been assured by the landlord that they were in a "thoroughly sanitary condition". In fact the water supply was poisoned by defective drains and the plaintiff's manager became seriously ill. Much of the poultry died and the remainder became valueless. To add insult to injury, the tenant (who had the repairing obligations under the lease) was ordered by the local authority to renew the drains.

The plaintiff claimed rescission of the lease and an indemnity for (among other things) medical expenses, loss of stock, loss of profits, loss of the breeding season, rent, rates, and the cost of repairs.

In the High Court, Farwell J granted rescission of the lease and an indemnity to cover the sums paid by the tenant as to rent, rates, and repair costs. But he refused to include any of the other heads of claim. These losses did not arise from the tenant's compliance with the covenants in the lease. He was not under any obligation to be a poultry breeder or to make any use of the water supply on the premises.

Negligent misrepresentation

Of course, if the poultry farmer in *Whittington* v *Seale Hayne* had been able to prove that the landlord's misrepresentation had been made fraudulently, he would have been entitled to damages at common law for the tort of deceit, as well as to rescission and an indemnity in equity. The award of damages would have included all the foreseeable losses suffered by him, including all the heads of claim which Farwell J had excluded from the definition of an "indemnity".

The poultry farmer's problem arose out of the fact that innocent misrepresentation was a concept invented by equity, not by the common law. This meant that Farwell J could grant rescission and an indemnity (these being equitable remedies). He also had the power to award damages instead of rescission (this power had been given to the courts by Parliament in 1858), but he could not grant both equitable remedies and award damages at common law for something which was not contrary to the common law at all (namely, innocent misrepresentation).

The fact that equity did not distinguish between an entirely innocent misrepresentation and a negligent misrepresentation was a glory of the system, not a shortcoming. Equity looked upon all misrepresentations as a species of equitable fraud. Even if a misrepresentation had not been made fraudulently, it would become an act of fraud on the part of the maker of that representation to keep contractual benefits once it had been transparently proved that the other party had been deceived. This is why misrepresentations are always studied in the context of the law of contract, and why great importance is placed on the question: did the misrepresentation cause the making of the contract?

Nevertheless, the availability of damages (at common law) for fraudulent misrepresentation, but not for negligent misrepresentation, came to look increasingly untenable after the decision of the House of Lords in *Hedley Byrne & Co Ltd* v *Heller & Partners Ltd* [1964] AC 465.

In that case, as is widely known, the House of Lords held that D (the maker of a statement) might owe a duty of care to P (the recipient of that statement), even if they did not have any contractual relationship with each other, and even if P's losses (caused by relying on the statement) were purely economic.

After *Hedley Byrne* it could wisely be asked: if a non-contracting party can sometimes claim damages for "negligent mis-statement", why cannot a contracting party claim damages for "negligent misrepresentation"? Surely a contracting party should have more rights than a non-contracting party? The denial of damages to such plaintiffs as the shareholder in *Derry* v *Peek* and the poultry farmer in *Whittington* v *Seale Hayne* was looking increasingly out of kilter with the times.

Misrepresentation Act 1967

It was in this context that Parliament passed the Misrepresentation Act 1967. This Act allows the victim of a negligent misrepresentation to claim damages, as well as rescission and an indemnity. (In practice, the damages will supersede the indemnity.) If, for any reason, rescission is not appropriate, the court has the power to award additional damages for loss of this right.

The Act goes further than *Hedley Byrne*. Once a representation is proved to be false, and is proved to have caused the making of the contract, the burden of proof will move to the other party (the maker of the statement). It will be for him to prove that he was not negligent. He will have to show that he had reasonable cause to believe the statement to be true, not only when he made it but also at all subsequent times until the contract was signed or otherwise agreed. (The maxim "representations are continuing" will apply here.)

If negligence is disproved, the maker of the misrepresentation will be in the same situation as the landlord in *Whittington* v *Seale Hayne*. He may be ordered to pay damages, or to grant rescission of the contract (with an indemnity), but he will not be ordered to do both. But, in practice, a landlord who nowadays inaccurately states that his premises are in a "thoroughly sanitary condition" (or that they are otherwise free from defects) will be able to rebut the presumption of negligence only if he was relying on an expert's report, or a guarantee from an appropriate contractor, or some other credible evidence.

After the Misrepresentation Act 1967, the phrase "innocent misrepresentation" is a confusing one. It is no longer helpful to use this phrase in the context of a "non-fraudulent" misrepresentation. The modern practice is to divide misrepresentations into three subcategories: fraudulent, negligent, and (entirely) innocent.

Fraudulent misrepresentation

Fraudulent misrepresentation is just one aspect of the tort of deceit. In cases in which a fraudulent statement causes the victim of the fraud to enter into a contract with the maker of that statement, the cause of action may be described as misrepresentation because the victim will certainly be seeking rescission of the contract as well as damages for deceit. Nevertheless, an allegation of fraud in such circumstances has several disadvantages. Allegations of fraud must be precisely pleaded and clearly proved. The person accused of fraud will also have the right to apply for the case to be tried by jury, this being one of the few situations in which juries are still used in the civil courts.

Most victims of fraudulent misrepresentation will prefer to bring a claim for negligent misrepresentation under the 1967 Act. The remedies will be just as wide-ranging and the burden of disproving negligence will lie upon the defendant to that claim.

Nevertheless, fraud (the tort of deceit) has one advantage over the Misrepresentation Act 1967. It can be used as a cause of action against persons who have never entered into a contract with the deceived person. For example, in *Slough Estates* v *Welwyn Hatfield District Council* [1996] 2 EGLR 219 the plaintiffs sued a local planning authority for fraud. The plaintiffs had not entered into a contract with the planning authority, but they had been misled by its statements. This led them to proceed with a redevelopment which they would have abandoned had they known the truth.

Fraud also has one advantage over negligent mis-statement as a tort. A duty of care to prevent another person incurring loss of profits or any form of "pure economic loss" is exceptional in the tort of negligence and, although negligent mis-statement is one of these exceptions, the relationship between the maker of that statement and the recipient of that statement has to be very close, if not special.

If, however, fraud can be proved, the relationship does not have to be close or special and it will not matter that the loss inflicted on the victim may have been purely economic. Indeed, fraud is usually intended to cause economic loss to the victim, and to bestow economic gain on the fraudsman.

Negligent mis-statement

Whereas the word "misrepresentation" can (and is) used by

lawyers on its own, without any accompanying adjective, the word "mis-statement" is used by lawyers only as part of the phrase "negligent mis-statement".

If a statement is made fraudulently, it will usually be dealt with as part of the tort of deceit and (in contractual cases) it may be described as a "fraudulent misrepresentation".

If a mis-statement is made entirely innocently (without negligence or fraud), there will be no remedy at all outside the law of misrepresentation and the law of contract. The concept of an "innocent mis-statement" therefore has no relevance to lawyers.

Negligent mis-statements, however, now form a distinct branch of the law of tort, partly because (as the *Hedley Byrne* line of cases shows) the courts have had to compensate for the lack of third-party rights in the English law of contract.

Something in common?

Misrepresentation and (negligent) mis-statements will be actionable only if they are statements of past or present facts. The proper place to tie a person down to a promise or a prediction is in a contract, supported by consideration or executed as a deed. Thus if, for example, a landlord promises some benefit to a prospective tenant if he (the tenant) signs the lease, this promise should be treated as a "collateral contract" and evidenced by a side letter or (better still) contained in a deed. An oral promise will be binding, if it can be proved, because – as in the case of a side letter – the tenant will be able to argue that his signature on the lease was good consideration for the landlord's additional promise: see *City & Westminster Properties (1934) Ltd* v *Mudd* [1959] Ch 129.

If D makes a promise to P which he has no intention of keeping, or expresses an opinion which in truth he does not hold, P will be able to sue D in the tort of deceit. This is because, as Bowen LJ once remarked, "the state of a man's mind is as much a fact as the state of his digestion": *Edgington* v *Fitzmaurice* (1885) 29 ChD 459 at p483.

If D expresses an opinion (or makes a prediction or gives a valuation) which he honestly believes to be valid, but he also states, expressly or impliedly, that he has made use of competent, professional, methods in reaching his conclusions, this will be a negligent misrepresentation and/or a negligent mis-statement if these methods have not been complied with: *Esso Petroleum Co*

Ltd v *Mardon* [1976] QB 801; *Smith* v *Eric S Bush* [1989] 1 EGLR 169.

If D makes a false statement of fact to P (whether fraudulently or otherwise) and P does not believe this statement to be true, or would have proceeded with the transaction even if he had known the truth, P will not be able to prove any causative link between D's statement and his own financial or other losses. Accordingly, P will not be able to succeed against D in the law of misrepresentation or in the law of tort: *JEB Fasteners Ltd* v *Marks, Bloom & Co* [1981] 3 A11 ER 289.

Example

- Mr Peek had bought shares in the Plymouth, Devonport & District Tramways Co after reading a prospectus issued by that company;
- that prospectus contained a negligent misrepresentation (in those days known as an "innocent misrepresentation" because of the absence of fraud)
- he could not successfully sue the company for misrepresentation because the company was insolvent;
- he could not sue the directors of the company for "innocent misrepresentation" (however wealthy they were) because he had not bought the shares from them personally;
- he could not sue the directors for "negligent mis-statement" because that tort did not exist in the 1880s;
- he could not sue the directors for fraud (known as the tort of "deceit" because they had not acted dishonestly.

Contributed by Leslie Blake.

CHAPTER 58

The measure of damages for fraudulent and negligent statements

First published in Estates Gazette August 23, 1997

The penalties for misrepresentation caused by deception differ from those caused by negligence. We look at the court decisions that support current legal practice.

Fraud is almost always a crime as well as a civil wrong. It may amount to the offence of obtaining property by deception, contrary to section 15 of the Theft Act 1968, or to more particular types of fraud under that Act or under other Acts of Parliament. If two or more people are involved in the fraudulent enterprise, it may also amount to conspiracy to defraud, which is in breach of common law.

In *R* v *Scott* [1975] AC 819 the principal defendant and nine other persons were charged with conspiracy to defraud when they agreed to make "pirate" copies of cinema films. The particulars of the charge were that they "conspired together and with other persons to defraud such companies and persons as might be caused loss by the unlawful copying and distribution of films . . . and by diverse other subtle, crafty and fraudulent means and devices".

The defendants argued that they had not committed (or agreed to commit) any act of fraud because their conduct did not involve the making of any false statements. All that was agreed to be done was for a cinema projectionist to borrow a film in secret, and to allow copies to be made from it. The film would then be returned, undamaged and, they presumed, without anyone knowing that it had ever left the cinema.

The House of Lords held that the common law offence of conspiracy to defraud did not depend upon any agreement to tell lies or to forge documents or to make any other false statements. It would be enough if the parties agreed, by dishonesty, to deprive another person of something which was his, or of something to which he was, or would be, or might be entitled, or in any dishonest way to injure some proprietary right of his. Accordingly, the House of Lords upheld the conviction of the defendants for conspiracy, even though they had intended to perpetrate a secret breach of copyright, not any form of deceptive conduct.

Yet, even though the definition of fraud is very wide, it is still possible for fraudulent conduct to be a tort without it also being a crime. This seems to have been the state of affairs in *Slough Estates plc* v *Welwyn Hatfield District Council* [1996] 2 EGLR 219. In that case, councillors and senior officers of a local authority fraudulently deceived a developer into thinking that a rival shopping centre in the same town, Welwyn Garden City, would not be allowed to sell similar goods or to attract trade competitors as anchor tenants.

Civil rather than criminal

Although this fraudulent conduct amounted to the tort of "deceit", it is difficult to see what, if any, criminal offence was committed by the individuals concerned. Certainly a criminal prosecution was never contemplated by the police or by the victims of the fraud.

The damages awarded against Welwyn Hatfield district council came to a total of £48,500,000. This was because the judge accepted that the developers would not have proceeded with their redevelopment of the site if they had known that the rival shopping centre was going to be given its head, so to speak, to act as a trade competitor by the local authority acting as its landlord.

Put at its simplest, the judge had applied the test of causation known to generations of law students as the "but-for" test: "But for the defendant's wrongdoing, would the plaintiff have suffered this loss or damage?"

The problem with the "but-for" test is that it is good for identifying red herrings (things which did not play any part at all in causing the plaintiff's misfortune), but it is not good for distinguishing important causes from unimportant causes. "It is infinite to know the cause of causes and the consequences of consequences" as Lord Wright observed in *Liesbosch Dredger* v *Edison* [1933] AC 449.

Let us suppose that D's misconduct causes P to buy something that he would not otherwise have bought. Is D then to be held liable for the full amount of P's loss if the market value of the property falls because of an economic recession or some other factor that is outside the control of both parties?

The answer to this question, so far as the tort of negligence is concerned, was authoritatively given by the House of Lords in *South Australia Asset Management Corporation* v *York Montague Ltd* [1996] 2 EGLR 93. Lord Hoffmann illustrated his answer with the following example:

A mountaineer, about to undertake a difficult climb, is concerned about the fitness of his knee. He goes to a doctor who negligently makes a superficial examination and pronounces the knee fit. The climber goes on the expedition, which he would not have undertaken if the doctor had told him the true state of his knee. He suffers an injury which is an entirely foreseeable consequence of mountaineering, but has nothing to do with his knee.

Lord Hoffmann's answer was that the doctor was not to be held liable for the injury (notwithstanding the outcome of the "but-for" test) because the mountaineer would have been similarly injured even if his knee had not been defective. The doctor's negligence may have caused the mountaineer's accident in the sense that it put him in the wrong place at the wrong time, but it might equally well have put him in the path of a Swiss trolley-bus. Would the doctor have been liable for a street accident or a hotel fire or a violent robbery on the way to Heathrow Airport?

Given that the answer to these questions must be that the "cause of causes" and the "consequences of consequences" cannot go on being reckoned for ever, and that the doctor is not to be held liable for the mountaineer's ultimate misfortune, then the equivalent answer must be that a negligent valuer is not liable for a subsequent fall in market values, even if this valuation was a principal cause of the purchaser buying the defective or otherwise over-valued property. It is self-evident that the property would have suffered a devaluation, even if it had been properly surveyed and valued in the first place.

The remaining law lords in the *South Australia* case agreed with Lord Hoffmann's judgment and did not give separate judgments of their own. But that case was not about a fraudulent valuation or a fraudulent misstatement. It was about a negligent valuation. There is a strong argument that defendants who commit fraud should not be cosseted in the same way as those defendants who, although honest, lapse into negligence, as all human beings are destined to do from time to time.

In *Doyle* v *Olby (Ironmongers) Ltd* [1969] 2 QB 158, Lord Denning MR put the matter this way:

The fraudulent defendant is bound to make reparation for all the actual damages directly flowing from the fraudulent inducement. The person who has been defrauded is entitled to say: "I would not have entered into this bargain at all but for your misrepresentation".

Lord Hoffmann conceded that this approach had two advantages: (1) it was a deterrent to fraud; and (2) it allowed damages for fraud to be a restitutionary remedy. He noted that there was one unreported judgment that had a confining effect on damages for fraud, similar to the approach in the *South Australia* case, but he did not express any final opinion on the validity of that judgment. It was the judgment of Hobhouse LJ in *Downs* v *Chappell* [1996] 3 All ER 344.

Hobhouse LJ had taken the view that the damages for fraudulent misrepresentation should not be greater than the loss which the innocent party would have suffered had the represented state of affairs actually existed. Lord Hoffmann interpreted this to mean that a fraudulent defendant would not then be liable for any loss which would have been a consequence of the transaction, even if the representation had been true.

The case of *Whittington* v *Seale-Hayne* (1900) 82 LT 49 can be used as a focus for discussion here. In that case, a poultry farmer signed a lease of certain premises after he had been assured that they were in a "thoroughly sanitary condition". The conduct of the defendant in that case was not fraudulent (although, by today's standards, it might well have been negligent). Assuming, however, that such a statement was made fraudulently by an independent consultant, or building surveyor, or local government officer, would that defendant be liable for the loss of the farmer's poultry if they died because of an outbreak of fowl pest spreading from a neighbouring farm?

In such a case, the defendant would argue that the unsanitary nature of the farm, eg defective drains, had nothing to do with the death of the poultry. He could have quoted Macbeth: they "should have died hereafter". (Macbeth, of course, was using the Scottish idiom, "should", meaning "would" to southern British ears.)

In reply, the poultry farmer would have argued that "but for" the false statement he would not have signed the lease. He would also have to show that he would have taken his stock of poultry to another place, out of the reach of the contagion that afterwards afflicted the locality.

In short, the defendant would argue: "Your poultry would have died, even if I had told the truth." The plaintiff would reply: "But for your lies, my poultry would have lived".

If Hobhouse LJ is correct, the poultry farmer would not be entitled to damages for the loss of his poultry, even if the misrepresentation about the sanitation of the premises had been made fraudulently.

Reserved judgment

Lord Hoffmann expressly reserved his judgment on this point, as if, with a prophet's eye, he knew that the measure of damages in fraud might come before the appellate courts before long. Nevertheless, he made the observation that "liability for fraud or under section 2(1) of the Misrepresentation Act 1967 for a negligent misrepresentation inducing a contract with the representor, has usually been thought to extend to all loss suffered in consequence of having entered into the transaction".

Lord Hoffmann's reference to section 2(1) of the 1967 Act, where negligence and fraud are put on the same footing, is the reason why our hypothetical example of the poultry farmer has to be a dispute with a surveyor or other third party, not with the landlord of the property. If the landlord, or his agent, had made the statement about the premises being in a "thoroughly sanitary condition", the poultry farmer's claim would have been for negligent misrepresentation, under section 2(1), where since 1967 the damages for that statutory tort would be the same as for fraud. It is therefore first necessary to discover the correct measure of damages for fraud.

Slough Estates plc v *Welwyn Hatfield District Council* was heard by May J in the Queen's Bench Division and the judgment was given in the month following the decision of the House of Lords in the *South Australia* case.

May J described his dilemma as follows: "I therefore have to decide whether I am bound by *Downs* v *Chappell* to apply Hobhouse LJ's qualification" or whether Lord Hoffmann's reservations in the *South Australia* case meant that *Downs* v *Chappell* was "out of line with the usual understanding, that liability for fraud extends without qualification to all losses suffered in consequence of having entered into the transaction": see [1996] 2 EGLR 219 at p245.

May J referred to the famous decision that relates to the law of precedent in the Court of Appeal: *Young* v *Bristol Aeroplane Co Ltd* [1944] KB 718. That decision allows the Court of Appeal to depart from the rule that it is bound by its own previous precedents if, by mischance, two of those precedents are in conflict. In such a case, the Court of Appeal is entitled to choose which of those two precedents to follow. Self-evidently, therefore, a High Court judge has the same right in a similar predicament.

May J decided that the House of Lords in the *South Australia* case had noted that *Downs* v *Chappell* was in conflict with the previous decision of the Court of Appeal in *Doyle* v *Olby (Ironmongers) Ltd*, the case in which Lord Denning MR had made his statement about "all the actual damages directly flowing" from a fraudulent inducement. May J further decided that Lord Hoffmann's judgment in the *South Australia* case clearly indicated that he should follow the *Doyle* case "without the *Downs* v *Chappell* qualification". Applying, therefore, the "but-for" test, May J awarded Slough Estates damages, which included the subsequent devaluation of their shopping centre because of a fall in market values.

The measure of these damages (not the finding of fraud) was to be the subject of an appeal by Welwyn Hatfield district council. It has subsequently been reported in the *Sunday Telegraph* on July 6 1997 that the parties have reached a settlement figure of £29,750,000.

Out-of-court settlements, of course, do not have any value as precedents, particularly as Welwyn Hatfield district council probably could not have found the original damages of nearly £49m in any event. Assuming the judgment of May J to have been correct, the only two restrictions on damages for fraud (or for negligent misrepresentation under the 1967 Act) would appear to be those mentioned by Lord Hoffmann in the *South Australia* case: (1) a victim of fraud cannot claim damages for those losses that he would have suffered even if he had not entered into the transaction; (2) a subsequent cause may "negative the causal effect" of the misrepresentation.

The first of these caveats is a simple restatement of the "but-for" test. Fraud is irrelevant if the "victim" of that fraud would have suffered his losses in any event, even if he had walked away from the transaction.*

---

* *Barnett* v *Chelsea and Kensington Management Committee Hospital* [1969] 1 QB 428 is the classic example in the law of personal injuries. It involves the death of a patient who would have died in any event, from poisoning, even if he had not been denied admission to the hospital.

The second of these caveats seems to be a reference to the concept usually known by the name *novus actus interveniens* (a new act intervening). This raises larger issues than can be discussed in this article, but an escaped lion from a menagerie (eating all the poultry farmer's chickens) will suffice as an example for present purposes.*

Contributed by Leslie Blake.

---

*But what would the answer be were the chickens to be eaten by foxes?

PROCEDURE & EVIDENCE

CHAPTER 59

Famous cases: *Marbury* v *Madison*: The birth of judicial review

First published in Estates Gazette February 4, 1995

The judgment of the US Supreme Court in *Marbury* v *Madison* (1803) 1 Cranch (5 US) 137 was a pivotal decision in American constitutional law. It completed the system of checks and balances between the legislative, executive and judicial powers of the federal government. It established the doctrine of judicial review and gave the courts the power to declare an Act of Congress to be void if it conflicted with the constitution.

The seeds of the dispute were sown in 1801 when President John Adams (a federalist) lost the presidential election to Thomas Jefferson (a republican). Adams tried to retain as much power as possible for his party by appointing as many federalist judges around Washington DC as he could. In some cases, he even created new judicial posts for the federalists.

"Midnight judges"

All in all, the outgoing president appointed 16 circuit judges and 42 justices of the peace. During Adams' last night in office, all but four of these commissions had been delivered. The judges who received their commissions that night became known as the "midnight judges".

When James Madison, the new Secretary of State, entered his office the next day, he found the four commissions on his desk, but was told by the new president, Thomas Jefferson, not to deliver them. William Marbury, one of the four appointed justices of the peace whose commissions had yet to be delivered, sued Madison. He applied to the US Supreme Court for a writ of *mandamus*, ordering Madison to carry out his official duty.

When the Chief Justice of the Supreme Court, John Marshall, said he would consider Marbury's case, the predominantly republican congress changed the date of the Supreme Court terms, effectively suspending the court for over a year. But when the Supreme Court reconvened in 1803, Marshall reaffirmed his decision to hear the case.

John Marshall's dilemma

Marbury relied on section 13 of the Judiciary Act of 1789, which purported to give the Supreme Court jurisdiction to issue the writ of mandamus against a government official who had ignored the law of the land. Congress had passed this law to give additional powers to the Supreme Court (beyond those expressly set out in the constitution). In reality, John Marshall knew that if he acted upon this power and ruled in Marbury's favour, Madison would probably ignore the writ of mandamus. This would take away what little power the Supreme Court already had and would deprive it of its growing prestige.

In deciding *Marbury* v *Madison*, Marshall asked himself (and the Court) questions:

(1) Has the applicant a right to the commission he demands?
(2) If he has a right, and that right has been violated, do the laws of the United States afford him a remedy?
(3) If they do afford him a remedy, is it the writ of *mandamus* issuing from the Supreme Court?

As to the first question, Marshall agreed that Marbury had the right to the commission. John Adams had signed the appointment during his term as president and it had been sealed and completed by the former Secretary of State, who happened to be John Marshall himself. (He was, therefore, one of the "midnight judges" created by President Adams.) Marbury had the right to be a justice of the peace for five years and it was therefore the duty of the Secretary of State to deliver the commission.

As to the second question (the availability of a remedy), Marshall said that one of the first duties of the government is to afford protection from injury. He also said that the government of the United States was a "government of laws, not men" and should therefore supply a remedy for the violation of a legal right. The Judiciary Act of 1789 had expressly authorised the Supreme Court to "issue writs of mandamus in cases warranted by the principles and usages of law to any person holding office under the authority of the United States".

There now seemed little to prevent Marbury from receiving his commission.

Judicial self-restraint

Marshall's answer to the third and final question was stunning – a shrewd legal masterpiece. Writing the judgment on behalf of himself and the four other judges sitting with him, Marshall ruled that mandamus was not the proper remedy, notwithstanding the clear provisions of the Judiciary Act of 1789.

He explained his decision in the following logical way. First, the constitution was a supreme law and could not be changed by a mere Act of Congress. Therefore any law which conflicted with the constitution was void. There would have been no need for article III of the constitution (setting out the jurisdiction of the Supreme Court) if the court's powers could be added to, reduced, or otherwise varied by ordinary legislation.

Second, Marshall pointed out that the power to issue writs of *mandamus* was not part of the original jurisdiction of the court as defined by the constitution. (Marbury was not appealing to the Supreme Court from any other court within the United States; he was asking the court to make use of its "original jurisdiction".) Therefore, in order to issue a writ of *mandamus*, the court would have to be exercising its appellate jurisdiction, which in this case it clearly was not.

Third, Marshall stated that, because section 13 of the Judiciary Act of 1789 purported to alter the constitution (by bestowing an addition "original jurisdiction" on the court), that section was in conflict with the constitution and therefore void. Because that provision was void, writs of mandamus could not be issued by the court and, therefore, Marbury could not receive one.

In effect, Marbury received a declaratory judgment in this favour, but no imperative remedy. Seeing that he had no way of getting his commission, he gave up. But the Supreme Court had laid claim to its exclusive right to interpret the constitution and to pronounce upon the validity of Acts of Congress. This claim was a controversial one at the time and for many decades afterwards. (Thomas Jefferson, Andrew Jackson and Abraham Lincoln were three famous presidents to dispute the all-pervasive power of the Supreme Court to resolve constitutional questions, not to mention President Nixon in our own time.)

Before and after
Did Chief Justice Marshall invent "judicial review"? He certainly did not coin an idea that had never been formulated before. American lawyers well remember that Sir Edward Coke had argued, in *Dr Bonham*'s case (1610) that the common law would prevail over an Act of Parliament if it was contrary to custom and common reason. And, whatever pretensions to supremacy the British Parliament claimed for itself, lawyers in pre-revolutionary America and in the West Indian colonies would have been very familiar with the jurisdiction of the Privy Council to overrule colonial legislatures.

Yet, whatever debt the US Supreme Court owed to its common law antecedents, it repaid many times over to the English-speaking world with its decision in *Marbury*. It has been the inspiration for judicial review in many Commonwealth countries with written constitutions and has encouraged English (and European) judges to be more robust in reviewing the conduct of governmental bodies. In the United States, the decision made the judicial branch of the government an equal partner with the legislative and executive branches. Without that equality the system of checks and balances in the US constitution could not have worked and the USA could not have made its famous claim to be a "nation of laws".

Alexander Hamilton (1757–1804) wrote that the judiciary would always be the "least dangerous branch" of the state, because it would have "no influence over either the sword or the purse" and "no force nor will, but merely judgment". It is interesting to wonder whether he would have revised his opinion had he foreseen the words of Chief Justice Marshall:

It is emphatically the province and duty of the judicial department, and nobody else, to say what the law is.

Contributed by Anthony Lau.

CHAPTER 60

"Brandeis briefs"

First published in Estates Gazette August 19, 1995

What is meant by a "Brandeis brief"? How far (if at all) are Brandeis briefs used in English legal proceedings?

Louis Brandeis (pronounced "Brandize") was an associate justice of the United States Supreme Court from 1916 to 1939. He was born in Louisville, Kentucky, in 1856 and he died in Washington DC in 1941, aged 84. He made successful use of a document (more than 100 pages long), subsequently known as a "Brandeis brief", when acting as an attorney (and advocate) in *Muller* v *Oregon* 208 US 412 – a case heard by the US Supreme Court in 1908. On the first face of things, therefore, such a document belongs solely to US legal procedure and must be understood in that context. Nevertheless, two perceptible changes have been taking place in the procedures of the English civil courts in recent years, namely: (1) an increased use of written submissions to the courts (particularly the appellate courts); and (2) an increased use, by litigants, of the "trump card" (European Community Law) when challenging, or seeking to interpret, British legislation. These two factors make *Muller* v *Oregon* a case which it is well worth English (and Scottish and Irish) lawyers looking at, even if it is only to avoid the emphasis on written submissions which is such an obvious feature of US and continental European court procedure.

Muller v *Oregon*

Muller v *Oregon* was a challenge, brought by the owner of a laundry, against a law passed (in 1903) by the state of Oregon to limit the working hours of women employed in factories and laundries to 10 hours per day.

Muller had been fined $10 by a court in Portland, Oregon, because his foreman had required an employee, Mrs Gotcher, to work more than 10 hours on September 4 1905. This conviction was upheld by the Supreme Court of Oregon, and Muller then appealed to the US Supreme Court, claiming that the "10-hour law" violated the 14th Amendment to the US Constitution. This amendment contains the phrase: "nor shall any State deprive any person of life, liberty, or property, without due process of law". By 1908, this phrase in the 14th Amendment had already become a strong basis for discovering new constitutional rights which needed to be protected by "due process", as well as a safe stronghold for defending "life, liberty, and property" in the narrowest meaning of those words. (This approach was, and still is, known as the law of "substantive due process".)

In *Muller* v *Oregon*, the owner of the laundry argued that the "10-hour law" infringed his common law (and therefore his constitutional) right of "freedom of contract". In arguing this point, he had a previous decision of the US Supreme Court in his favour: *Lochner* v *New York* (1905) 198 US 45. In that case, the US Supreme Court had decided (by five votes to four) that a law passed by the state of New York infringed "liberty of contract" because it limited the working hours of men and women in bakeries to 10 hours per day and to 60 hours per week.

In *Muller* v *Oregon*, Louis Brandeis was allowed (by the Attorney-General of Oregon) to appear on behalf of the National Consumers' League and to file a brief in support of the "10-hour law".

A "brief" in the American sense of that word is addressed to the court, not to the lawyer who is about to argue a case before that court. It is a detailed legal argument, in writing, filed well in advance, so that the judge (or judges) can read this document before the case is heard. This undoubtedly creates much work, and no doubt causes many lawyers to work more than a 10-hour day, before the "day in court" arrives. Much time, however, is saved during the court hearing because the American courts impose a strict time-limit on advocates when they are presenting their arguments orally. The US Supreme Court, for example, imposes a 30-minute time-limit on each advocate and will cut him (or her) off in mid sentence once that time-limit has expired. It has been said that oral argument cannot win a case before the US Supreme Court, but it can undoubtedly lose a case. This is because American judges, like their British counterparts, are adept at exposing the weaknesses in a case by questioning the lawyers, in argument, when they appear before them and seek to bring, or to defend, an appeal.

In *Muller* v *Oregon*, Louis Brandeis (and his colleagues) filed a brief in the following form:

- Pages 1 and 2: legal precedents (including, of course, Lochner v New York).
- Pages 3 to 17: Excerpts from the statutes of other US states and from foreign nations, showing that Oregon was in good company when limiting the working hours of women.
- Pages 18 to 112: quotations from American and European factory and medical reports, showing that long hours had an adverse effect on the health of workers, especially female workers.

The unique feature of this "Brandeis brief" was the mountain of socioeconomic and medical information contained in the last 95 pages. Brandeis reasoned (and, in his short oral argument before the US Supreme Court, he emphasised) that the laws of a state legislature would be valid, and would be defensible, in the light of the US Constitution if there was at that time sufficient evidence to show a legitimate interest on the part of that state to legislate to suppress a mischief or to promote a public benefit (such as the benefit of health and safety at work). This argument was successful. In a unanimous decision, the nine judges of the US Supreme Court upheld the validity of the Oregon "10-hour law", noting that the evidence showed that "healthy mothers are essential to vigorous offspring" and that the physical well-being of women was an "object of public interest and care".

English civil procedures

The nature of "pleadings" in the English courts have been discussed in the "Mainly for Students" series on a previous occasion: see March 3 1990, p83, reprinted in *The Best of Mainly for Students*, (1993), pp433–440. A "statement of claim" in the High Court, and the "particulars of claim" in county courts, do not concern themselves with arguments of law. They are allegations of fact, supported (where necessary) by reference to statutory provisions and naming (but not discussing) the causes of action on which the plaintiff proposes to rely. Except in cases of the utmost complexity, eg a building contract dispute, the pleadings are likely to be less than 20 pages long, even when the defendant's defence and counter-claim is included in this bundle. Quite clearly, the notion of a "Brandeis brief" is alien to traditional English court procedure. There are three main reasons:

(1) Until the UK joined the European Community there was nothing in the nature of a written constitution which could be used to challenge the validity of British Acts of Parliament. Even the basis for challenging byelaws and other forms of delegated legislation was a narrow and almost exclusively legal exercise, not a factual one.

(2) English, Scottish, and Irish legal procedure has traditionally given paramount importance to the presentation of oral evidence in court, together with the cross-examination of witnesses, including expert witnesses. There is considerable difficulty in presenting statistical or other factual information to an English, Scottish, or Irish court otherwise than as part of the evidence of relevant witnesses who can be cross-examined about the reliability of that evidence.

(3) English and Irish barristers, and Scottish advocates, are expected to make their submissions to the court in the form of an oral argument, not in the form of a written thesis.

European influence

British membership of the European Community (now known as the European Union) has not made, nor is it intended to make, any direct changes to English civil or criminal procedures. Nevertheless, the Treaty of the European Union (previously called the Treaty of Rome) and the regulations made under that treaty, and (in some cases) the directives from Brussels, now provide a superior source of law against which the validity of British legislation can (and must) be judged. For example, article 119 of the Treaty of the European Union requires equal pay for equal work and the "Equal Treatment Directive" requires member states to move towards equal treatment for male and female employees in all areas of work not already covered by the requirement to give them equal pay for equal work.

The relevance of socioeconomic and statistical information to a court or tribunal considering these matters is now abundantly clear. For example, in *R* v *Secretary of State for Employment, ex parte*

Equal Opportunities Commission [1994] IRLR 176 the House of Lords held that the statutory restrictions on the employment rights of part-time workers was, in substance, a discriminatory measure which adversely affected female workers. Part-time working is more common among female employees than among male employees.

This judgment has now been followed by a very recent decision of the Court of Appeal: *R v Secretary of State for Employment, ex parte Seymour-Smith and Perez The Times*, August 1 1995 (news report p1), August 2 (news report p2) and August 3 (law report). In this case, the Court of Appeal has held that the "two years' continuous employment" rule is a discriminatory measure against female workers. (This statutory rule was introduced in 1985. With very few exceptions, it does not allow an employee to seek a remedy for unfair dismissal unless and until he or she has worked, continuously, for two years with the same employer, or with one employer and that employer's predecessors in the same business.) The Court of Appeal has held that this statutory provision is contrary to the European Union's "Equal Treatment Directive" because female workers have a greater tendency to move in and out of employment than male workers, thus accumulating shorter lengths of continuous service than their male counterparts are likely to enjoy.*

Neill LJ is reported as having said, in his judgment, that the statistics showed that a higher percentage of men than women were in the "advantaged group" (enjoying two years' continuous employment or more). He also observed that, although the two-year threshold had been introduced with the objective of maximising employment opportunities, there was not, in fact, any evidence that this objective had been achieved. He concluded:

On that evidence, the threshold of two years is neither suitable nor requisite for attaining the aim of increased employment. It follows that this discriminatory measure has not been justified.

The similarity between this line of reasoning and the statistical

---

*The Judicial Committee of the House of Lords has now referred a number of questions arising out of this case to the European Court of Justice: see *R v Secretary of State for Employment, ex parte Seymour-Smith* [1997] ICR 371. The Government has also published a White Paper *Fairness at Work* (Cm 3968) (May 1998) in which it is proposed to reduce the qualifying period for unfair dismissal claims from two years to one year.

arguments employed by Louis Brandeis in *Muller* v *Oregon* is a very striking thing to note.

Skeleton arguments

The increasing relevance of socioeconomic data to arguments about the validity (or otherwise) of British legislation has coincided with an increasing use of "skeleton arguments" in the English courts.

The Court of Appeal (Civil Division) has recently issued a Practice Statement and a Practice Direction in an effort to curtail the length of oral arguments in civil appeals: see *The Times*, July 27 1995. It is anticipated that applications for leave to appeal (in those cases where that leave is needed) will limit oral submissions to 20 minutes each in ordinary cases, and 30 minutes each, in judicial review cases. Other suitable time-limits will be imposed before full appeals are heard.

It has been suggested that, if "Brandeis briefs" are to become a feature of English civil litigation, this will be through the medium of enlarged "skeleton arguments". However, it must be noted that a "skeleton argument" is not supposed to be a self-contained legal submission, defended like a doctoral thesis before a body of erudite questioners. It is intended that oral argument should remain the principal method of making submissions to a court, albeit without the need (any longer) to prepare the ground with the judges, as if they do not know anything of the documentation already placed before them.

The Practice Statement expressly goes out of its way to state that skeleton arguments should not normally exceed 10 pages (in disputes of law) or 15 pages (in disputes of fact). Given these limitations, it appears that lengthy statistical data and other information (so obviously typical of a "Brandeis brief") will have to be adduced as evidence in the normal way, even if that information comes from public documents. Perhaps, therefore, English and Irish barristers, and Scottish advocates, will increasingly have to give the same attention to the documentation which goes before a court that expert valuers already have to give when deciding whether they can rely upon evidence of "comparables" in a rent review arbitration.

Contributed by Leslie Blake.

CHAPTER 61

Famous cases: *R* v *Müller*: The nature of circumstantial evidence

First published in Estates Gazette October 14, 1995

It is the first principle of all civil and criminal trials that evidence must be relevant. Relevant evidence may be either "direct" or "circumstantial".

No case has inspired lawyers, writers and broadcasters to think more about the nature of "relevance", and about the nature of "circumstantial evidence" in particular, than the "first railway murder": the trial of Franz Müller in October 1864.

It was the most sensational trial of its day. The victim of the murder, Mr Thomas Briggs, had been the chief clerk of a bank in Lombard Street, London EC3. He had been travelling home in the first-class carriage of a train on the North London Railway, when (probably asleep) he had been savagely attacked, robbed and thrown out of his carriage between the stations of Bow and Hackney Wick. He had been cut off from any chance of escape or assistance (and from the railway company's inspection of his co-traveller's ticket) by the absence of a corridor on the train.

There is something for everyone in the trial of Franz Müller. Railway historians may find in this case the reason why communication cords were installed in railway carriages.

Students of the changing character of neighbourhoods will marvel at the fact that a leading banker would (and could) travel from his niece's house in Peckham by horse-bus, then in a first-class railway carriage from Fenchurch Street, EC3, to Hackney, and then (hoping to follow his daily practice) to walk to his large town house at 5 Clapton Square, London E5.

Architects may repine – they certainly ought to do so – the destruction of the wonderful Italianate stations of the North London Railway, purpose-built to make the people of north London feel that they had walked into the banking hall of a Lombard Street bank.

But lawyers will always refer to *R* v *Müller* as the classic case for proving facts by circumstantial evidence. For no one ever saw Franz Müller on that train or anywhere near that railway on the night when Mr Briggs was killed.

What is relevance?

If evidence must be relevant, the question arises: what is relevance? How does an advocate answer the question from the bench (or from the chairman of a tribunal), "where is this evidence taking us?".

The American jurist James Bradley Thayer (1831–1902) put it this way in *A Preliminary Treatise on Evidence at the Common Law* (1898), chapter VI:

There is a principle – not so much a rule of evidence as a presupposition involved in the very conception of a rational system of evidence, as contrasted with the old formal and mechanical systems – which forbids receiving anything irrelevant, not logically probative. How are we to know what those forbidden things are? Not by any rule of law. The law furnishes no test of relevancy. For this it turns to logic and to general experience – assuming that the principles of reasoning are known to its judges and ministers, just as a vast multitude of other things are assumed as already sufficiently known to them.

The English jurist Sir James Fitzjames Stephen (1829–1894) had earlier attempted a codified definition of "relevancy" in the first edition of his book *A Digest of the Law of Evidence* (1876). It included the following "general definition" (Article 9):

Facts, whether in issue or not, are relevant to each other when one is, or probably may be, or probably may have been

- the cause of the other;
- the effect of the other;
- an effect of the same cause;
- a cause of the same effect:
- or when the one shows that the other must or cannot have occurred, or probably does or did exist, or not;
- or that any fact does or did exist, or not, which in the common course of events would either have caused or have been caused by the other . . .

Thayer dismissed this mechanistic definition as an attempt to "take the Kingdom of Heaven by force". Indeed, even Stephen seems to have had second thoughts about it. In the fourth edition of his book

(1881) he adopted a simpler approach (while still defending his original definition in a footnote). His new definition read as follows:

The word "relevant" means that any two facts to which it is applied are so related to each other that, according to the common course of events, one either taken by itself or in connection with other facts proves or renders probable the past, present, or future existence or non-existence of the other.

Stephen had drafted the Indian Evidence Act in 1872. Then and afterwards he had been moved to think that "relevance" could be codified because of the logical perfection of proof by circumstantial evidence. He and other writers had been inspired to take this view because of the trial of Franz Müller.

Proof by circumstantial evidence

Circumstantial evidence may be defined as any evidence which allows a court to infer the existence or non-existence of a fact in issue. As there was no direct evidence of Müller's guilt the jury had to consider the strength of the circumstantial evidence brought against him by the prosecution. The proximity of the railway to Müller's place of residence and work was not a very strong item of circumstantial evidence in 1864.

So exclusive was railway travel in the 1860s that even the Solicitor-General (when prosecuting Müller) had to make the following concession: "I cannot suppose Müller was in the habit of resorting to the railway."

Franz Müller was an apparently harmless and inoffensive man, aged 24. He had come to England from Germany in 1862 and was probably a deserter from the German army. He worked as a tailor in Threadneedle Street, London EC2 – a street which was evidently still being true to its name in those days. He lodged with a family in Victoria Park, Hackney Wick, London E9. He was known to be very poor and probably could not have afforded a railway ticket, even though the North London Railway was an easy route between Victoria Park and the City of London.

The Solicitor-General, lacking any eye-witness identification of Müller at or near the railway, could do his job only by pointing out that this route was not out of Müller's way home and by extolling the virtues of circumstantial evidence over direct evidence. He reminded the jury that: "Müller is not committed in the presence of witnesses, and to require direct evidence of murder would be to establish an impunity for the crime and to endanger human life."

Two years after Müller's trial, the presiding judge, Lord Chief Baron Pollock (1783–1870), undoubtedly remembering the intricacies of Müller's case, put forward a description of circumstantial evidence which has subsequently become famous.

In *R* v *Exall* (1866) 4 F&F 922 he likened circumstantial evidence to a "rope of several cords":

It has been said that circumstantial evidence is to be considered as a chain, and each piece of evidence as a link in that chain, but that is not so, for then, if any one link breaks, the chain would fall. It is more like the case of a rope comprised of several cords. One strand of the cord might be insufficient to sustain the weight, but three stranded together may be of sufficient strength. Thus it may be in circumstantial evidence – there may be a combination of circumstances, no one of which would raise a reasonable conviction or more than a mere suspicion; but the three taken together may create a conclusion of guilt with as much certainty as human affairs can admit of.

The rope of several cords

What, then, was the evidence against Müller? The prosecution was able to construct a rope of many cords:

(1) The motive of the murder was robbery. Mr Briggs had been robbed of a gold watch and chain. It was known that, for several months prior to the murder, Müller had been short of money and had been trying to raise the money to go to America (the fare was £4). Müller therefore had a motive to commit the murder, but so did half the population of London.

(2) Mr Briggs had not been robbed of the money in his pockets or of other valuables and this indicated that he had probably been attacked not by two or more assailants but by a single assailant (who had time only to take his watch and to push Mr Briggs out of the carriage as the train got nearer to Hackney Wick Station).

(3) Hackney Wick Station was near where Müller lived. In those days it was sometimes known as "Victoria Park Station".

(4) Müller had been so poor that, about the month before the murder, he had pawned his own watch and chain. They were still in the pawnshop at the date of the murder. But there could have been very little of evidential value in this. The lines of the nursery

rhyme ("Pop goes the weasel") refers to tailors pawning the tools of their trade, let alone their watches, so it must have been a very common occurrence.

(5) Two days after Mr Briggs' murder (he had been murdered on a Saturday, so this was the Monday), Müller took a watch-chain to a jeweller in Cheapside and exchanged it for a different chain and a ring. He subsequently gave a false explanation to some friends about where he had obtained the new chain, saying that he had bought it from a man at the London docks.

(6) Müller pawned the chain with another pawnbroker and then went through a series of transactions with pawnbrokers and friends. He was eventually able to redeem his old watch from a pawnbroker and to buy a ticket for the United States of America. He bought this ticket on the Wednesday (four days after the murder).

(7) A hat, identified as being Müller's hat (or one very similar to it), was found in the carriage where Mr Briggs had been attacked. Mr Briggs' own hat could not be found on the train or anywhere on the railway track.

(8) When Müller was arrested in New York (the police had overtaken him on a faster ship) he was found to be in possession of Mr Briggs' watch and a hat, which was not his usual hat. He was unable to produce his usual hat and said that he had thrown it away.

(9) The hat which Müller had with him when he arrived in New York was a hat such as Mr Briggs had worn, but it had been cut down in size, to alter its appearance and perhaps to remove the maker's name. The work had been done by someone who was not a hatter, but who was, nevertheless, very skilled with a needle.

The trial

The strongest evidence against Müller was his possession of Mr Briggs' watch and the apparent loss and gaining of a hat. But possession of the watch did not prove murder in itself. Müller might have bought the watch from the murderer or from a handler of stolen goods. But then, if he did buy that watch from another person, where did he get the money to purchase it? Müller's silence on this point would not, in those days, have been any evidence against him. It was not until 1898 that defendants were allowed to give evidence on their own behalf in a criminal trial. (Indeed, even the fact that the parties to a civil action could give evidence in a common law court was new in 1864; Parliament had not permitted it until 1851.)

Müller would never had been arrested, and Mr Briggs' watch would never have been traced, had it not been for the hat which was found in the blood-stained carriage when Mr Briggs had been attacked. It was a poster depicting this hat and offering a reward which had brought forward a cabman who recognised it as Müller's hat.

At Müller's trial the cabman (Matthews) was cross-examined about his motives for coming forward to give evidence for the prosecution. Müller's counsel asked him: "Have you told your creditors that you will settle with them when you receive your share of the reward?" Matthews denied this and his answer was final.

His denial fell within the scope of a rule known as the rule in *Attorney-General* v *Hitchcock* (1847) 1 Exch 91. This rule states that evidence cannot normally be adduced to refute a witness' answers to questions put to them in "cross-examination as to credit".

There are many exceptions to this rule. For example, if a witness in a civil or criminal trial denies (or does not distinctly admit) that he or she has previous criminal convictions, evidence can be adduced to prove the existence of these convictions. Another exception relates to allegations that the witness has been bribed. But in *Attorney-General* v *Hitchcock* the defendant did not have any evidence that the witness had been bribed. The defendant's counsel merely put it to a prosecution witness, in cross-examination, that he had told a third party that he had been offered £20 to give false evidence. The witness denied saying any such thing. It was held that the judge had been right to exclude any evidence which would pursue such a "collateral issue". One of the judges in the Court of Exchequer Chamber (Rolfe B) observed:

If we lived for a thousand years instead of about sixty or seventy, and every case were of sufficient importance, it might be possible, and perhaps proper, to throw light on matters in which every possible question might be suggested . . . But I do not see how they could be; in fact, mankind finds it to be impossible.

In his closing address to the jury the Solicitor-General dealt with this issue quite simply: "Why offer rewards, if not to induce persons to come forward and to give evidence?"

The verdict

In his summing-up Lord Chief Baron Pollock was concise and matter of fact by today's standards. The prosecution had objected to tailors and bootmakers serving on the jury. The defence had objected to publicans and butchers. But whoever served on that jury, they would (in those days) have been men of business and property; the judge clearly thought that their time was too valuable to detain them for very long. He refused to condemn the pre-trial press publicity, which had been universally hostile to Müller; he even went so far as to say that it was an advantage if the jury came to court with some previous knowledge of the case.

He referred to the evidence relating to the hats in these terms:

There is no direct evidence that the cut-down hat was Mr Briggs (and a hat said to be Müller's is found in the carriage), but these are not separate links in a chain. They are distinct circumstances, and stand on separate and distinct grounds, and if any one of them is made out to your satisfaction, it is sufficient.

The jury returned after retiring for 15 minutes. They brought in a verdict of "Guilty". Müller was sentenced to death and there was no Court of Appeal for criminal cases in those days. (This was not established until 1907.) Only the most recondite points of law could be reviewed by a large assemblage of judges sitting in a court known as the "Court for Crown Cases Reserved". Müller's case did not raise any points of law of this nature.

While awaiting execution (the condemned man was always allowed three clear Sundays) the Reverend James Hamilton, of Campden Church, published a sermon about Müller's crime and using as his text 2 Kings ch8 v13: "But what! is thy servant a dog, that he should do this great thing?"

But there was at least one lone voice that thought he might be innocent. A barrister, Dr James Walter Smith, published a penny pamphlet entitled: *Has Müller been tried? What appeared and What did not appear and What was laughed out of Court.*

Müller was hanged and it was reported that, just as the trap fell, he said "I did it" to his Lutheran pastor. But even if he had never said this, could his guilt be doubted?

A man might innocently (or even dishonestly) buy a watch which he afterwards finds out to have been stolen during a murder.

He might lose his hat, or some other item of property, which afterwards finds its way into the hands of a murderer or is left coincidentally at a place where a murder subsequently gets done.

He might acquire (and alter) a hat, or some other item of property, which strikingly resembles the likewise thing which was worn or carried by a murder victim until his murderer took it away from him or caused him to lose it.

Each strand in this cord might, in itself, be just a little too weak to prove a criminal case beyond reasonable doubt. But how could one innocent person be the subject of all these three misfortunes? As Lord Chief Baron Pollock subsequently put it: "the three [cords] taken together may create a conclusion of guilt with as much certainty as human affairs can admit of".

Dr James Walter Smith's pamphlet on the trial ended with a plea to his readers:

Do not suffer yourselves to be asked, as jurymen, to condemn a man whose evidence cannot be received, though he is all the time anxious to satisfy every inquiry, and solve every doubt. Urge upon our legislature to remove those irritating obstacles to the admission of testimony which have an almost equal tendency to convict the innocent, and to set free the guilty man. This should be a national work.

Such a reform in the laws of criminal evidence did not take place for another 34 years. Yet it is difficult to see how Franz Müller could have benefited from the right to give evidence at his trial. He had called some alibi witnesses in his defence, but they had been discredited in cross-examination. How could Müller have survived cross-examination at the hands of a skilled prosecutor who had already woven around him a rope of such strong cords?

Contributed by Leslie Blake.

CHAPTER 62

Civil proceedings – legal terminology

First published in Estates Gazette February 17, 1996

Students and litigants often misuse legal terminology – for example, the verbs "to prosecute" and "to sue".

The following list does not claim to be exhaustive, but it is likely to be useful not only to students and litigants but also to expert witnesses, translators, and other professional people who come into occasional contact with the law.

Initiating proceedings

Leaving aside special proceedings (such as applications for judicial review), we can say that a civil action is commenced in the High Court by a writ and in the County Court by a summons. There is also a procedure (in the High Court) which is commenced by means of an originating summons. This is used where the parties are not disputing any significant questions of fact but wish to obtain no more than the court's determination of a disputed question of law, such as the proper interpretation of a legal document, eg a will, trust deed, contract, or lease.

If either party to civil litigation (whether that litigation has been commenced or not) wishes to offer a compromise, by way of settlement, to the other party, this can be done by means of a "without prejudice" letter or in a without prejudice conversation. Such letters are usually headed "without prejudice" and such conversations are usually expressly opened on the understanding that they are to be "without prejudice". Nevertheless, it will be the nature of the occasion, and the evident intention of the party making (or responding to) the communication, which will give the attempted compromise the protection of the without prejudice rule, not the precise form of words which he uses.

If a "without prejudice" offer is rejected, the other party will be prevented from referring this offer in the court proceedings. Any such letter (or memory or record of a conversation) will be subject to a rule of evidence known as private interest privilege. Letters between the parties (or their lawyers acting on their behalf) which are not subject to the "without prejudice" rule are known as open letters (or as open correspondence). It is not uncommon for a "letter before action" (which is invariably an open letter) to be accompanied by a "without prejudice" letter which sets out a proposed compromise that is acceptable to the plaintiff.

The "without prejudice" rule also applies to arbitration proceedings and to proceedings before tribunals, such as the Lands Tribunal.

If a party to civil proceedings wants to make an offer to settle the case, but wishes to reserve the right to bring this offer to the attention of the court (or tribunal or arbitrator) if and when the issue of legal costs is being considered, the offer is usually made in the form of a letter which expressly reserves this right. The popular name for such a letter is a "Calderbank letter": after *Calderbank* v *Calderbank* [1975] 3 All ER 333. The person making the offer will usually head the letter with the words: "without prejudice except as to costs".

A "Calderbank letter" is generally used where the claim is not a claim for damages but involves some other issue between the parties, for instance, a claim for an injunction or a dispute about matrimonial property, or a boundary dispute or a rent review arbitration.*

If the claim is one for damages or some other capital sum, the party against whom the claim is made can protect his position somewhat by making a payment into court or – in the case of arbitration proceedings or a claim before the Lands Tribunal – a sealed offer. The other party will be notified of the amount of the offer but, if he does not accept it, the judge or arbitrator or member of the Lands Tribunal will not be told about the amount of the offer, nor (if this is possible) about the existence of any offer at all.

If, at the end of the proceedings, the judge or arbitrator or member of the Lands Tribunal awards less, or at least no more, than was paid into court (or set out in the sealed offer) then he will invariably penalise the overconfident party in costs. A "Calderbank

---

*See the article on "Calderbank Letters", pp442–448 of this book.

letter" will have the same effect if it shows that the recipient unreasonably refused a sensible settlement of the dispute prior to the final judgment of the court or the final award of the arbitrator.

The plaintiff to an action is said to be suing the defendant. The verb "prosecute" is reserved for criminal proceedings, except when that word is used in the more general context of "prosecuting an action". In arbitration proceedings, the person initiating those proceedings is called the claimant and the person defending them is called the respondent. The verb "sue" is not used. The claimant is said to be referring the dispute to arbitration or (more generally) making a claim in arbitration proceedings.

Procedure

If an action is commenced in the High Court by means of a writ, it must be accompanied or followed by a statement of claim. In the county court the equivalent document is known as particulars of claim. In arbitration proceedings a similar document is used and it is called the points of claim.

The defendant or respondent is required to enter an appearance to the proceedings and to file a defence. He may also make a counterclaim against the plaintiff or claimant and that party will then have to file a defence to counterclaim. In the High Court and the county court, the defendant is sometimes described as being "plaintiff to the counterclaim" and the plaintiff is sometimes described as being "defendant to the counterclaim".

If a defence (or a defence to counterclaim) raises a new allegation of fact, eg an allegation of misrepresentation, the opposing party will then be entitled to file a reply to defence (or a reply to defence to counterclaim).

If any of these documents (known as pleadings) are imprecise, ambiguous, Delphic or vague, they are said to be "embarrassing" to the other party. This word has a technical meaning. It does not mean that the pleading in question is insulting, over clever, indecent, or ungallantly revealing of facts which the other side would like to keep to himself. It means that the allegation or explanation in question is too vague or too terse to be meaningfully answered or understood. In such a case the recipient is entitled to serve on the other party a pleading known as a "request for further and better particulars". (An example might be a request for further and better particulars of an allegation of negligence.)

If a "request for further and better particulars" is justified, the party in default must file an answer to that request. He will risk having his pleading struck out if he fails to comply. Any disputes about the reasonableness of the request or the adequacy of the answer can be dealt with in the interlocutory proceedings. ("Interlocutory proceedings" are any proceedings which have to be dealt with by the court, tribunal, or arbitrator prior to the hearing of the underlying dispute itself.)

In some cases, one of the parties might apply to the High Court or the County Court for an "interlocutory injunction" (to preserve the status quo pending the trial of the action).

If a defendant to a civil case wishes to pass all or some part of the liability on to a third party for the claim which has been made against him by the plaintiff (as, for example, in a motorway pile-up) he will be able to served a "third party notice" on that person. That person then becomes the defendant's defendant (but not the plaintiff's defendant unless the plaintiff also sues him). The third party may wish to serve a fourth party notice on another person and so on down the line of alleged participants in the plaintiff's loss or damage. Third party notices (and so on) are not commonly to be found in arbitration proceedings unless all the parties in question were originally parties to the same arbitration agreement. Once a third or subsequent party has been brought into civil litigation or arbitration proceedings, that party must then file his own pleadings in response to the notice which has been served upon him.

If the complexity of a case is such that the pleadings become voluminous and difficult to follow, as for example in many building contract cases, the parties will be expected to draw up a schedule, indexing and marrying-up all the claims and counter-allegations about each disputed item of work or other factual matter at issue between them. This document is known as a "Scott Schedule", after G A Scott QC (1862–1933) who popularised this procedure when he was an official referee of the High Court. (An official referee is a specialist demi-judge of the High Court, almost always being an expert in building and engineering contracts.)

Unlike "pleadings" which are filed and used in the courts of the USA, English pleadings do not contain arguments of law or socio-economic information. They are confined to allegations and counter-allegations of fact, in support of named causes of action or statutory sections. For this reason pleadings are not used in proceedings commenced by an originating summons in the High Court because (as above) these proceedings do not involve any significant disputes of fact – only disputes of law.

Witnesses

The general principle of civil procedure in common law countries is by oral testimony. (This is even more true in the case of criminal proceedings). Witnesses give their evidence and are then cross-examined by the other parties or their lawyers. The procedure is adversarial in nature, not inquisitorial, which means that the parties call the witnesses and present documentary and any other evidence to the judge or arbitrator, just as they – or their lawyers – think fit. The judge and, even more so, the arbitrator is not permitted to intervene with too many questions of his own or to "ferret out" additional evidence for himself.

There is some evidence that oral testimony is becoming more important in the legal systems of Europe than used to be the case before British and Irish membership of the European Union. By the same token, the English courts are becoming more willing to accept written evidence. The modern practice is for the parties to exchange copies of their own statements, and the statements of all the other witnesses, so that each party can judge the strength or weakness of the opposing party's case. If the case proceeds to trial, the parties and their witnesses will be cross-examined on the content of their statements without the need to give any prolonged evidence in chief.

This is a mixed blessing. It is intended to encourage out of court settlements and to save the court's time if the case proceeds to trial. However, it usually means that additional time and money has to be spent in drafting faultless witness statements and that the witness risks being pinned down and cross-examined about words which were drafted by his lawyer and not chosen by himself. From the point of view of the cross-examining party, it means that he will have to begin his cross-examination without having had an opportunity to spot any inconsistencies in the witness' evidence or to judge "the character who breathes through the sentences" .

After a witness has been cross-examined, it will be possible for him to be re-examined by his own lawyer in order to clarify any answers which he gave during cross-examination. When a lawyer is examining one of his own witnesses he should not ask leading questions on any matter which is in dispute between the parties. A "leading question" is one which suggests the answer for which the questioner is looking, or gives undue hints to a lazy or forgetful witness. This rule is less strictly enforced during the re-examination of a witness than it is during an examination-in-chief. There is no prohibition on leading questions during the cross-examination of a witness.

In cases where there are no significant disputes of fact (eg proceedings commenced in the High Court by way of an originating summons) any evidence which is necessary for those proceedings may be supplied by means of one or more sworn statements known as affidavits. Affidavits are also used in interlocutory proceedings (eg to support a claim for an interlocutory injunction). This is because any disputes of fact will have to be dealt with at the full trial of the action and the court will not have the time to resolve those disputes when an interlocutory application is being made by one of the parties. Therefore, an interlocutory injunction is usually granted or withheld according to where the balance of convenience lies, not according to a prior assessment of who is likely to win the case.

Where the outcome depends upon disputed questions of fact, the plaintiff is said to bear the burden of proving the facts alleged in his claim. The burden of proof – sometimes known as the onus of proof – means the responsibility of proving the facts in dispute. If the defendant makes any allegations of fact in his defence, or if he files a counterclaim against the plaintiff, he will have the burden of proving the facts which he is alleging. The maxim which applies here is "he who alleges, must prove". This also applies to any subsequent pleadings filed by the parties. The position is therefore different from criminal proceedings where, generally, the prosecution will have the burden of proving every disputed fact and the duty of disproving very defence which the defendant puts forward.

The "burden of proof" is a different concept from the "standard of proof". The standard of proof means the extent to which a fact must be proved. In civil cases, that standard will be proof on the "balance of probabilities" (or proof on the "preponderance of probability"). The standard resting upon the plaintiff and/or the defendant in a civil case is, therefore, less onerous than the duty which rests upon the prosecution in a criminal case, where guilt must be proved beyond reasonable doubt.

Decision

When a judge gives his decision it is known as a judgment, whereas the decision of an arbitrator is known as an award – even if he awards nothing. If there is a counterclaim, a separate judgment or award will have to be made relating to that claim also. If there is a monetary judgment (or award) in favour of the plaintiff on the claim, with a monetary judgment (or award) in favour of the defendant on the counterclaim, the smaller amount will be set off against the larger amount, leaving one party with a balance to pay to the other

It is not appropriate to uses phrases such as "verdict" or "guilt" in the context of civil proceedings. These terms relate only to criminal proceedings. Therefore, instead of referring to a defendant as being "guilty" of a tort or breach of contract, the correct phraseology would be that judgment had been given against him or that he had been held liable for the civil wrong in question. For the same reason, it is not appropriate to refer to an award of damages as a "fine" or as a "sentence" or as a "punishment". The only exception to this is if a civil court punishes a litigant for contempt of court, or awards "punitive damages" against an egregious wrongdoer – for example, a landlord who has harassed his tenants.

If an injunction is granted against a party in civil proceedings, this will either be an interlocutory injunction to preserve the status quo until the case has been fully heard or a final injunction which may be binding on him perpetually. Most injunctions are prohibitory in nature: they restrain the party in question from acting in a particular way. Some injunctions are mandatory in nature: they order the party in question to carry out a particular course of conduct, e.g. to repair a wall or to clear away rubbish. It will constitute contempt of court to infringe, or to fail to comply with, the order of the court.

The party in question is usually described as being in breach of the injunction, and his status is then that of a contemnor. As a final resort the court may send a contemnor to prison for contempt of court, but he may be released before he has served his sentence if he satisfies the court that he has purged his contempt.

Contributed by Leslie Blake.

CHAPTER 63

Payment-into-court, sealed offers and Calderbank letters

First published in Estates Gazette October 26, 1996

What do lawyers, surveyors and other professional advisers mean when they say that they have sent or received a "Calderbank letter"?

A Calderbank letter is one of the devices which a party to a legal dispute may use to put pressure on an opponent, exposing that person to the risk of having to pay substantial legal and other professional costs even if he succeeds in the main legal proceedings.

The risk of having to pay all or some of the other party's costs or of being left without an order for costs against them, is a constant worry to litigants. This risk has to be taken into account in all proceedings where the court, arbitrator, tribunal, or other decision-maker has a discretion to award costs against one party or the other. Almost all courts, and almost all arbitrators, have the power to do this.

Legal proceedings and commercial arbitrations usually operate under the rule that costs will "follow the event". The successful party can usually look forward to recovering most, but by no means all, of his costs from the unsuccessful party. Indeed, the peril of having to pay an opponent's costs, or of being denied the right to recover one's own costs, is often a powerful inducement to settle a case out of court. When the costs have mounted up so far that they may rival or even exceed the amount of money in dispute between the parties, there are few professional advisers who will encourage their clients to act like Macbeth when a possible settlement is put forward by the other party:

Though Birnam Wood be come to Dunsinane,
And thou opposed, being of no woman born,

Yet I will try the last. Before my body
I throw my warlike shield. Lay on, Macduff,
And damn'd be him that first cries "Hold, enough!"

If Macbeth's doom was foretold by the fact that Birnam Wood had upped its roots and by his new-found knowledge that Macduff was "of no woman born", the over-confident litigant can similarly be unnerved by the receipt of a Calderbank letter or by the knowledge that his opponent has made a "payment into court".

Accursed be that tongue that tells me so,
For it hath cow'd my better part of man!

Payment into court

A procedure is operated by the High Court and the County Courts whereby a defendant to a claim or counterclaim for damages may pay a sum of money into court: see Ord 22 of the Rules of the Supreme Court 1965, and Ord 11 of the County Court Rules 1981. (In the case of a counterclaim, the defendant is said to be "plaintiff to the counterclaim" and the plaintiff is said to be "defendant to the counterclaim".)

The plaintiff making the claim, or the defendant making the counterclaim, is informed of this payment but, if the case proceeds to trial, the judge is not told unless and until the question of costs arises.

A payment into court represents an offer to settle the claim for the amount in question, plus the opposing party's legal costs up to that date. If this offer is not accepted by the opposing party, the party who has made the payment may continue to deny liability and/or to argue that he should be ordered to pay only a lesser amount.

It is, of course, possible for the party defending the claim or counterclaim to make a small payment into court at an early date and then to increase that amount later by a further payment or payments. Obviously, the legal costs on both sides will have increased with the passage of time, but even a last-minute payment into court will avoid the costs of trial, if accepted.

A well-judged payment into court and a timely acceptance of it does not necessarily satisfy either party, but at least it allows both of them to go away appreciating the wisdom of the Spanish proverb: "a bad bargain is better than a good case" (*un mal acuerdo es mejor que un buen caso*).

Refusing a payment-in

The risk of not accepting a payment-in is considerable. If the trial is fought to the end and the claim or counterclaim for damages fails altogether, or succeeds only to the extent of bringing in no more than the amount already paid into court, the defendant, or the defendant to the counterclaim, will then make an application for costs. If his defence proved totally successful he would then ask for an order for costs in his favour, in accordance with the general rule that "costs follow the event".

If, however, he has been ordered to pay damages but the amount in question is less than or, at least, not more than the amount already paid into court, the judge would then be informed of the payment-in, the amount or amounts, and the date or dates. He would then be invited to make an order for costs in favour of the plaintiff, or the plaintiff to the counterclaim, up to the date of the relevant payment into court and not beyond it. He would also be invited to make an order for costs in favour of the defendant in respect of all the subsequent costs. This is the almost inevitable consequence of failing to beat a payment-in.

In many cases this leaves the plaintiff with a pyrrhic victory because the costs of the trial, and the immediate preparations for it, will usually be the largest item in the bill of costs on both sides. In addition to having to meet his own costs for this expensive exercise, he will also be ordered to pay his opponent's costs for the same period of time. He will have very little chance of persuading the judge not to make such an order, because payment into court is intended to be a powerful inducement to the settlement of disputes. The refusal of a payment which is subsequently vindicated as a reasonable sum is a significant event, which the judge must take notice of when he applies the rule "costs follow the event".

Sealed offers

Commercial arbitrations and certain other claims for financial sums, eg compensation claims in the Lands Tribunal, the facility for payment into court does not exist. Nevertheless, it is possible for either party to the dispute to make an unconditional offer in writing to pay a certain sum of money in settlement of the claim, or to accept a certain sum of money in substitution for the larger amount being claimed in the proceedings. If this offer is accepted by the opposing party, the agreement thus forged becomes a binding settlement. It becomes a contract which is binding on both parties.

The same rule applies if an offer is made (before or after litigation has commenced) in a "without prejudice" letter, or in a "without prejudice" conversation, and that offer has been accepted by the other party: *Tomlin* v *Standard Telephones & Cables Ltd* [1969] 1 WLR 1378.

In proceedings before the Lands Tribunal and in commercial arbitrations an unconditional offer, if refused, may be repeated in the form of a sealed offer. A copy of the offer is sealed up, and proof that the original offer was received by the other party is preserved, together with the date, and the sealed offer is delivered to the arbitrator or to the Lands Tribunal. The arbitrator or the member of the Lands Tribunal is not informed of the contents of the sealed envelope and he comes to open it only if the question of costs arises.

In the case of the Lands Tribunal, this procedure is given a statutory basis in section 4 of the Land Compensation Act 1961.

Ignoring a sealed offer

If the sealed offer is an offer to pay a sum of money in settlement of claim or a counterclaim, it will then have the same status as a payment into court in civil litigation. The claimant will have to beat the sealed offer or face the consequences of having costs awarded against him, wholly or in part. An over-greedy claimant in the Lands Tribunal will have to pay the legal costs of the acquiring authority, including the costs of expert witnesses, as well as his own costs "unless for special reasons [the Lands Tribunal] thinks it proper" not to make such an order: section 4(1) of the Land Compensation Act 1961. Most arbitrators will follow the same rule of practice.

If the sealed offer is an offer by the claimant to accept a lesser sum of money than the full amount of his claim or counterclaim, this is the opposite of a payment into court.

Nevertheless, an unrealistic refusal to settle the case on that basis will usually have the same consequences for the opposing party as the refusal of a payment-in usually has to an over-greedy plaintiff. Section 4(3) of the Land Compensation Act 1961 also deals with this situation:

Where a claimant has delivered a notice as required by subsection (1) of this section and has made an unconditional offer in writing to accept any sum as compensation, then, if the sum awarded to him by the Lands Tribunal is equal to or exceeds that sum, the Lands Tribunal shall, unless for special reasons it thinks it proper not to do so, order the acquiring authority to bear their own costs and pay the costs of the claimant so far as they were incurred after his offer was made.

Most arbitrators will follow this rule, eg in a building contract dispute or a rent review arbitration.

The phrase "sealed offer" is not used in ordinary civil litigation, but in those cases where a plaintiff wishes to make an offer to accept less than his full claim, or where either party wishes to make an offer which does not consist of the immediate payment of money, the offer in question is usually set out in a letter headed "Without Prejudice Except as to Costs". Such letters are known as "Calderbank letters", from the reported case of *Calderbank* v *Calderbank* [1975] 3 All ER 333.

Calderbank v *Calderbank* was a dispute about the division of matrimonial property after a divorce. Nevertheless, the principles recognised in that case are of considerable importance to valuers as well as to lawyers, eg in a rent review arbitration or a dispute about the terms of a new lease under the Landlord and Tenant Act 1954.

The existence of a "Calderbank letter" had an effect on the final order for costs in *BP Petroleum Developments Ltd* v *Ryder* [1987] 2 EGLR 233, a case on compensation for the exploitation of an oilfield.

However, in that case the landowners, who had rejected a generous "Calderbank" offer, were not ordered to pay the oil company's costs after the date of the letter. They were merely left to pay their own costs after that date.

Calderbank v Calderbank

In *Calderbank* v *Calderbank* the parties to a divorce were disputing among other things the ownership and value of the former matrimonial home. Mrs C claimed that the house was beneficially owned by her because she had bought it with her own money and she had put the legal title in her husband's name only for tax reasons. Nevertheless, in a "without prejudice" letter she offered to pay £10,000 to Mr C if he would agree to transfer the title to her. This offer was refused.

Mrs C then repeated this offer in an affidavit. The judge, having seen the affidavit but not the "without prejudice" letter, ordered Mr C to transfer the house to Mrs C in return for the sum of £10,000. He then ordered each party to pay his or her own legal costs.

On appeal, Mrs C argued among other things that she should not have been ordered to pay her own costs because of the terms of the offer which she had already made to her former husband. The Court of Appeal held that she could not rely on the "without prejudice" letter because, like all such letters, it was subject to privilege. Nevertheless, she was entitled to rely on the affidavit because this was not a privileged document.

In other words, there is no rule of law which stops a party from repeating a without prejudice offer in an affidavit or in an "open letter", sometimes known as a "with prejudice" letter. In such circumstances the court is entitled to know about the existence of the (open) offer, and to award the subsequent costs of the litigation against the party who rejected it. The Court of Appeal ordered Mr C to pay Mrs C's costs from the date of the affidavit.

In order to make a "without prejudice" letter admissible evidence on the question of costs, but privileged in every other respect, the text of the letter must make it clear that the writer is reserving the right to bring it to the attention of the court, arbitrator, tribunal etc, if the final decision shows that his offer should have been accepted.

The usual way to do this is to head the letter with such words as "without prejudice except as to costs". In such circumstances there is no need to send a separate open letter or to refer to the offer in any affidavit.

A "Calderbank letter" should be deposited in a sealed envelope with the court: see Ord 11 r 10 of the County Court Rules 1981; cf Ord 22 r 14, and Ord 62 r 9(d) of the Rules of the Supreme Court 1965. A court does not have to take account of a "Calderbank letter" if it was written at a time when the writer could have protected his position by means of a payment into court. Obviously some offers are incapable of payment into court, eg a future rent, and some Calderbanks are written before litigation has been commenced.

"Calderbank letters" can also be used in disputes about the taxation of costs. If C has obtained a judgment against D and has also been awarded his legal costs, D may wish to dispute the reasonableness of C's bill of costs. D may therefore insist on the bill being "taxed" by the court, ie scrutinised and, if appropriate, reduced. Normally D has to pay the costs of this "taxation", but he can protect his position by writing a "Calderbank letter" offering to pay C a specified sum in settlement of his bill.

If C refuses this offer, but the court afterwards "taxes off" so much of his bill that D's offer is shown to be equal to or more generous than the amount left owing to C, then C will have to pay all the costs of the taxation proceedings – D's costs as well as his own.

Contributed by Leslie Blake.

PROPERTY LAW AND THE ENGLISH LEGAL SYSTEM

CHAPTER 64

Customary rights

First published in Estates Gazette October 16, 1993

To what extent does English law recognise and enforce local customs?

The common law of England is said to originate from the "date of legal memory" (or "time immemorial"). The jurist Sir William Blackstone (1723–1780) defined this as being "time whereof the memory of man runneth not to the contrary".

Such a concept of aboriginal time is, of course, to be expected of a legal system based upon precedent, not upon a single historical event or any given code. Somewhat surprisingly, however, the "date of legal memory" does have a fixed day and date in English legal history – September 3 1189 – the coronation of King Richard I. This date was chosen by common lawyers in the reign of King Edward I and was incorporated in the Statute of Westminster I (1275).

This adoption by Parliament of a "date of legal memory" gives us the oldest historical source of English law, namely local customary law. If any local custom is found (even now) to be enduring in any particular place and is not uncertain in its scope or unreasonable in its nature, and not inconsistent with a statute of a fundamental principle of the common law, it will be enforced by the courts in the same way as they will enforce the general customs of the realm, now known as the common law.

Thus, prior to the Administration of Estates Act 1925, the courts enforced local customs as to intestate succession in the case of freehold land, even though these customs were different from the common law rule of "primogeniture" (succession by the eldest son or brother).

Kent maintained a custom known as "gavelkind", whereby all the sons (or brothers) inherited land equally and certain ancient towns (such as Nottingham and Bristol) maintained a custom known as "borough English" whereby land was inherited by the youngest son (or brother) to the exclusion of all others.

The effect of the Administration of Estates Act 1925 was to abolish not only the local customs of gavelkind and borough English but also to replace the common law rule of primogeniture with a statutory framework for intestate succession.

Many customary rights were rights relating to common land (village greens and so on). These have now been made the subject of compulsory registration by the Commons Registration Act 1965. If the rights were not registered before July 31 1970 they will, by now, have ceased to be exercisable.

Proof of antiquity

In practice it is almost impossible to demonstrate that a local custom, however well supported by ancient evidence, actually dates back to the coronation of Richard I. It is here that Blackstone's interpretation of the "date of legal memory" becomes useful. He defined this date as being simply a reference to time out of mind – "time whereof the memory of man runneth not to the contrary".

If there is sufficient evidence to show that the custom is of long uninterrupted usage and no evidence can be adduced to show that it must have commenced later than 1189, the court will apply a presumption that the custom in question dates back to that year.

The party who is relying on the custom will have been able to prove that it dates back to "time whereof the memory of man runneth not to the contrary".

This situation arose in *Fitch* v *Rawling* (1795) 2 Hy Bl 393. The court recognised that there was a right to play cricket on certain land, even though cricket did not exist as a game in the 12th century (and was illegal in the reign of Henry VIII). The custom was recognised to consist of the right to play all kinds of (currently) lawful games on the land. But in *Simpson* v *Wells* (1872) LR 7 QB 214 an alleged customary right to hold a market or fair on certain land was defeated by evidence that markets or fairs of the type in question had been authorised only by the Statute of Labourers 1349 and could not have been held before the passing of that statute.

Similarly, in *Mercer* v *Denne* [1905] 2 Ch 538 a claim by the fishermen of Walmer, Kent, to have a valid customary right to spread and dry their nets on the appellant's land would have been defeated but for the fact that the appellant was unable to adduce admissible evidence to show that the land in question had been under water in the 17th century and again in 1816. The appellant's documentary evidence was held to be inadmissible because it infringed the rule against hearsay evidence and did not come within any of the common law exceptions to that rule. Such a difficulty is unlikely to arise again, because the Civil Evidence Act 1968 has relaxed the rules of evidence in civil cases.

Nec vi, nec clam, nec precario

A local customary right can arise only if it has been exercised, at all times, "nec vi, nec clam, nec precario" (not by force, not by stealth, and not by mere permission). The persons asserting the right in question (and their predecessors) must have acted peacefully, openly, and for all the world as if they needed no one's permission to do as they were doing. Thus, there can be no customary right to a licence (eg a fishing licence) because the issuing of licences – however ancient in practice – is a form of giving permission, not a recognition of customary rights: *Mills* v *Colchester Corporation* (1867) LR 2 CP 476 (a case which related to oyster fishing).

In more recent times it has been held that the practice of beachcombing and the practice of taking sea-coal from the foreshore are no more than serendipity habits tolerated by the Crown. They are not local customary rights: *Beckett* v *Lyons* [1967] Ch 499.

Reasonableness

A claim to a local customary right will fail if it is shown to be unreasonable. Thus in *Bryan* v *Foot* (1868) LR 3 QB 497 a fee of 13 shillings for a marriage ceremony in a particular church was held not to be a valid custom because the sum in question would have been a grossly unreasonable fee in 1189. But, conversely, a toll of one shilling per cartload of vegetables was held to be a valid customary toll in 1868 because it was a reasonable sum at that date, whether or not it would have been so in earlier times: *Lawrence* v *Hitch* (1868) LR 3 QB 521. The court held that there was nothing wrong with a customary toll which imposed a reasonable sum, varying with the value of money. Even so, the court took the view that one shilling was probably not an unreasonable toll in 1189.

In *Goodman* v *Mayor of Saltash* (1882) 7 App Cas 633 the House of Lords held that a customary right to dredge for oysters in a tidal river (from February 2 to Easter Eve in each year) did not cease to be valid merely because continued usage by the inhabitants was tending to destroy the fishery itself.

Trade customs

Local customs must not be confused with trade and business customs. These arise from widespread usage in a particular trade, profession or business, but they do not have to be of ancient origin. They obtain their legal effect by being incorporated (impliedly) into business contracts. Accordingly, they form part of the law of contract and are not considered to be an independent source of English law.

While local customs are almost always connected with the use and enjoyment of land, there is no reason why trade customs should not also be relevant here. For example, in *Hutton* v *Warren* (1836) 2 Gale 71 it was held that a tenant of agricultural land was entitled to claim an allowance for seeds and labour when quitting in accordance with a notice given by the landlord. This was an agricultural custom in the area which had become an implied term in the tenancy agreement.

Contributed by Leslie Blake.

CHAPTER 65

Belgravia and Bermondsey

First published in Estates Gazette November 13, 1993

To what extent is the character of a neighbourhood important in the law of nuisance?

It is nearly 115 years ago that Thesiger LJ made the famous remark: "What would be a nuisance in Belgrave Square would not necessarily be so in Bermondsey." That remark was made in the course of an action for private nuisance brought by a doctor against a sweet manufacturer in the Wigmore Street/Wimpole Street area of London: *Sturges* v *Bridgman* (1879) 11 ChD 852. The doctor's action succeeded, even though the manufacturing of sweets (and the use of noisy machinery on the premises) had been a long-established practice in Wigmore Street. The activity did not, in fact, become a nuisance until the doctor built a consulting room in his garden in Wimpole Street, adjacent to the noisy premises. (This case is often cited as authority for the view that it is no defence for the author of a private nuisance to point out to the complaining party: "You have come to the nuisance".) Interestingly enough, the sweet manufacturer was not entitled to rely on a prescriptive right to carry on his noisy activities, because the 20-year period in the Prescription Act 1832 could not have begun to run until the consulting rooms had been built, cheek by jowl with the factory.

The comparison between Belgrave Square and Bermondsey has been used more often to suppress inappropriate activities in high-class areas than it has been to foist bothersome activities on disadvantaged ones. For example, in *Adams* v *Ursell* [1913] 1 Ch 269, an injunction was granted against a fish-and-chip shop in a well-to-do residential street because, even with the best means available, the smell of greasy cooking could not be suppressed.

In *Thompson-Schwab* v *Costaki* [1956] 1 All ER 652, an injunction was granted against a brothel in a residential area, even though the plaintiff could not point to any disorderliness, or noise, or to anything else except its fairly obvious nature as a brothel. (This case is the nearest example of the law of nuisance protecting the amenity value of a property and removing activities which offend the sense of sight.) In *Laws* v *Florinplace* [1981] 1 All ER 659, it was held that a sex shop could constitute an actionable nuisance in a residential area.

Some confusion has been introduced into the law by the decision of the Court of Appeal in *Miller* v *Jackson* [1977] QB 966. In that case, an action which (if successful) would have suppressed the playing of cricket on a village green, was disallowed by the Court of Appeal. It was held that the overflying of cricket balls on to neighbouring land was a long-established practice, going back nearly 90 years before the plaintiffs' houses were built on that land. Lord Denning MR expressly disapproved of the approach adopted in *Sturges* v *Bridgman*, and he took the view that the antiquity of the activity, compared with the recent erection of the complainants' houses, meant that playing of cricket on the village green could not be labelled a nuisance at all. The other two judges, however, merely confined their reasons to the inappropriateness of an injunction in all the circumstances of the case. They did not deny that the plaintiffs would have been entitled to damages if breakages had been caused by the cricket balls. (In fact, the cricket club had already made it clear that it would pay for such damage and it had already taken all reasonable precautions to safeguard the neighbouring properties.) *Miller* v *Jackson* is, therefore, better looked upon as a case which illustrates the discretionary nature of an injunction in the law of nuisance. In one sense, however, it does accord with Thesiger LJ's reference to the character of differing localities; for what might be a lawful sport in an isolated playing field might be a dangerous activity near a crowded thoroughfare.

In *Hilder* v *Associated Portland Cement Manufacturers Ltd* [1961] 1 WLR 1434, the owners of land 15 yds from a road and surrounded by a low wall were held liable for a fatal traffic accident after they allowed children to play football on that land, disregarding the risk that the ball might land in the road.

Planning considerations

Statutory authority is a defence to an action for nuisance, assuming that Parliament has authorised the nuisance in question at the precise place in question. In *Metropolitan Asylum District* v *Hill*

(1881) 6 App Cas 193, the defence of statutory authority failed because, although the defendants had been given authority to build a smallpox hospital, they had not obtained Parliament's authorisation for a particular location for that hospital. The House of Lords held that this meant that the statutory powers had to be used and a location had to be chosen in such a way so as not to cause a nuisance to neighbours.

However, in *Allen* v *Gulf Oil Refining Ltd* [1981] AC 1001, the same principle could not be used in the case of an oil refinery in South Wales because the promoters of the legislation in question had obtained Parliament's express consent to their chosen location. The House of Lords held that this meant that Parliament had implicitly authorised all the nuisances which would inevitably flow from siting such a refinery in that particular place. The plaintiffs would be able to proceed with an action for damages only if they could show (using expert evidence) that the refinery and its associated works were negligently designed, erected or operated, so as to cause more nuisance than inevitably necessary in the exercise of the statutory powers. This principle is sometimes paraphrased by stating that, although Parliament may authorise nuisance, it does not authorise negligence.

In so far as the authorised activities cannot be the subject of a private action for damages (still less for an injunction), the dissatisfied neighbours may have a statutory right to compensation under the Land Compensation Act 1973 if the activities in question cause noise, vibration, smell, fumes, smoke, artificial lighting, or solid or liquid discharges on to land (sometimes known as the "seven deadly sins"). Even if (as in the *Gulf Oil* case) the developer is a private enterprise, the works will be considered "public works" for the purposes of the Land Compensation Act if they were carried out or used "in the exercise of statutory powers": section 1(3).

The fact that claims to compensation under the 1973 Act are confined to depreciation caused by the use of "public works" may have been overlooked in *Gillingham Borough Council* v *Medway (Chatham) Dock Co Ltd* [1992] 1 PLR 113. In that case the High Court refused to grant an injunction against the running of lorries into and out of a private dock, 24 hours per day down residential streets, because the development of the dock (in the old Naval Dockyard at Chatham) had been authorised by the relevant planning permission. The trial judge took the view that the planning permission had authorised a change in the nature of the locality, rendering an increase in the traffic flow a vicissitude of urban life. Although the action was brought by the local authority (relying upon the law of public nuisance), the reasoning behind the division appears to have been wide enough to prevent the bringing of any actions for private nuisance by neighbouring landowners (even those closest to the dock). It certainly will not be open to anyone to argue that the redevelopment of the dock was an example of "public works" because planning permission alone does not achieve this transformation. However, perhaps a sounder basis for the decision in the *Gillingham* case is that an increase in passage of traffic along public highways does not (except when the most extreme forms of misuse are achieved) amount to an actionable nuisance, nor does it give a right to statutory compensation unless the road itself has been the subject of public works, for example, a road-widening or a new construction of a road junction.

Contributed by Leslie Blake.

CHAPTER 66

Restrictive covenants: assessment for compensation

First published in Estates Gazette October 15, 1994

I have come across a number of articles regarding restrictive covenants, but these are generally very brief when referring to assessment of compensation. It seems to me that many practitioners, let alone students, are under the misapprehension that the appropriate measure of payment to modify or discharge such covenants is a share of up to 50% of the difference in the resulting enhanced value, at today's prices.

The simple answer to this type of valuation problem – which is rather similar to the proverbial question concerning the length of a piece of string – is "by negotiation". Not very satisfactory! It is, however, a question of considerable importance because issues concerning restrictive covenants are more commonplace than is often thought.

Like many issues of practical valuation there are no right answers, but some of the principles which may lead to a possible answer can perhaps best be illustrated by reference to real examples, in which only peripheral details have been amended to protect the innocent.

At a recent RICS Assessment of Professional Competence (APC) a candidate had just completed his 10-minute presentation to the panel and was answering questions regarding the case. The discussion was about the freehold sale of an industrial property. The candidate answered the questions regarding the inspection, valuation and marketing in an acceptable manner. The next question, which concerned proof of title, was met with silence. The candidate had to admit that he had neither inspected the title nor received a report from the vendor client's solicitor, merely relying on what the client had told him. It subsequently transpired that the client's interest was, in fact, a leasehold interest and the option to purchase the freehold had not actually been exercised (this option having expired some months ago).

Setting aside the very important issues of property misdescription and negligence – which would be "Mainly For Students" articles in themselves – a review of title documents is most important when embarking on any type of valuation, be it the simplest house or a major investment property. As a valuer, discovery of facts will often save considerable time and problems at a later date. Issues such as freehold or leasehold, boundaries, planning and future planning policies, local road schemes, rights of way and restrictive covenants are all points that could have a material effect on the valuation. It is unwise to rely on the client, who is probably using the property as security for a loan and does not have access to the title deeds, probably last seeing them at the original purchase.

Restrictive covenants can take many forms and, as the name suggests, these amount to a restriction of use of the property to the benefit of another interested party. In legal terms they amount to a promise creating an obligation to refrain from doing something. They are binding in law and, provided they satisfy the normal legal requirements and are appropriate, they run with the land. While the Lands Tribunal has the power to modify or lift restrictive covenants (section 84 Law of Property Act 1925) this power is exercised sparingly and often only in circumstances where the covenant has become moribund. A good illustration of these difficulties can be found in *re Beechwood Homes Ltd's* application (1994) 28 EG 128.

One type of restrictive covenant experienced often by the practitioner is restriction of the use of a retail property by the former owner to protect nearby or relocated trade. An example of this may be a brewery moving a licence from one site to another nearby. Following the acquisition of the new site, they sell off the surplus property. The disposal may include a restrictive covenant to exclude the sale of alcoholic beverages. While this may have a theoretical restriction on the value of the surplus property, the effect is minimal. Generally there is a wide range of alternative retailers who would be prepared to pay the market price. The restrictive covenant would affect the valuation if the only other interested party was another off-licensee.

Central and local government are regular users of restrictive covenants for a variety of reasons. The local council may wish to reinforce planning restrictions with similar restrictive covenants.

Planning restrictions can be appealed against and removed, but, as explained earlier, restrictive covenants run with the land and can be enforced. The council may own adjoining land and may look at the disposal of a piece of land next to a school, for example, as sensitive, and they may wish to restrict the use of the land being disposed. Planning may not help them; a covenant will.

Since 1979 many former council houses have been disposed of under the right to buy schemes promoted by the Government. It is safe to assume that most of these sales will have included covenants among others to restrict the use of the land to the existing single dwelling.

In most cases this will not have an effect because former council houses, usually for construction economy, are built in semi or terraced form with limited width plots. However, certain wider or more substantial plots, particularly on corners or perhaps in semi-rural positions, are capable of further development by the building of one or more dwellings in the garden. In these cases the restrictive covenant comes into play.

At the time of the sale the tenant has a statutory right to buy often at below market value, the discount being linked to years occupied. At this time the valuer and legal adviser will seek to protect the vendor to ensure that any future development potential accrues to the benefit of the council. If at a later date the owner (former tenant) wishes to dispose of part of the garden for development, the covenant will come into play and, on application by the owner to the council for the restriction to be relaxed, will either fall on stony ground or result in a response demanding all the value attributed to the plot sale as fair payment for the lifting of the restriction. Stalemate!

Example 1

The subject property is one of several hundred houses on a large, modern estate comprising similar semi-detached and terraced houses, many of which have been sold under the right-to-buy scheme. The subject property adjacent to a recently completed private housing development is a semi-detached house with wide frontage and a very large garden. The office data base indicates that houses in the area have been selling as follows:

Inner terraced	£38,000

End terraced	£40,000
Semi detached	£42,000
Semi detached with large gardens	£45,000

The two parties' valuers may prepare very similar valuations:

Existing use valuation

By use of comparables	45,000
Add for extra large garden say	3,000
Existing Use Value as single dwelling	£48,000

The property owner now obtains outline planning consent for a single detached house with road frontage and vehicular access from the existing driveway. There are the normal costs but no abnormal items (see Table 1.)

Table 1. Valuation with the benefit of the planning consent

Value of house as before		£48,000
Less: allowance for large plot	3,000	
shared drive etc. say	2,000	5,000
Net Value after plot disposal		£43,000
Add Value of plot created say	15,000	
Less costs:		
planning, estate agent, architect,		
legal costs, say 20%	3,000	12,000
		55,000

Value of planning consent: £55,000 − 48,000 = £7,000

It can be seen that the marriage value or value of the planning consent is £7,000. The two valuers will seek a compromise and prob able share basis reflecting the *Stokes* v *Cambridge* (1961 13 P&CR 77) principle whereby the actual benefit arising from the lifting of the covenant is apportioned appropriately between the parties.

It is worth noting at this point that the apportionment in *Stokes* v *Cambridge* (a case concerning compensation for compulsory purchase) was subject to particular circumstances (the acquiring authority controlled the access to the land to be acquired but also owned additional land which would have benefited from the access) and there does seem to be a misapprehension about the way in which the net benefit was apportioned. It is surely the case that all the circumstances need to be taken into account and, at the end of the day, the parties will reach a bargain which reflects their respective positions including their particular anxiety to settle.

In practice the property owner may wish to agree principles of value and adjustment if the sale figure differs from that agreed, but defer the legal completion until a purchaser is found. This reduces the unknown and financial risk.

This is a simplistic approach to what can be a complex problem, as is the case if land previously sold for industrial use is subsequently rezoned in planning terms as out-of-town retail.

Example 2

A prime 8-hectare site fronting a main A road which is 3 miles from the city centre and in the centre of substantial residential development is sold in a single transaction to a developer for industrial use. The vendor, a government department which also retains adjoining land, has restricted the use of the land sold to B1 industrial and warehousing by means of an enforceable restriction.

The developer is approached by a number of out-of-town retail occupiers for units on this site. After appropriate planning negotiations, the developer obtains planning consent for retail on 6 hectares of the site, subject to highway improvements and screening of the residential properties at the boundary. The remaining 2 hectares retain the existing consent for industrial use. Six months after the completion of the purchase, the developer's valuer opens negotiations for the relaxation of the restrictive covenant on the 6 hectares that have received planning consent.

The developer then intends to sell the site. The valuations were agreed as shown below (see Table 2).

Table 2.

Existing Use Value

8 hectares of industrial land @ 250,000	£2,000,000
Purchase costs @ say 3%	60,000
Net Value	£2,060,000

Valuation with the benefit of planning consent for the development of 6 hectares retail and 2 hectares remaining as industrial

6 hectares retail land at say 937,500		£5,625,000
Less costs:		
Planning fee	£6,200	
Leading counsel	50,000	
Architect fee	125,000	
Legal fees	40,000	
Valuers fee	50,000	

Highway improvements	300,000		
Screening	25,000	596,200	
Holding costs:			
Finance (8 hectares @			
250,000 @ 10% for			
6 months)	97,618		
Risk and reward @ 10%			
of £5,625,000	562,500		
Selling costs @ 2.25%	127,000	764,500	1,360,700
Gain			4,264,300
Less original purchase cost 6/8 × 2,060,000			1,545,000
Net gain			2,719,300

In this case the developer has already received a risk and reward allowance of 10% of the value of the retail element as an assured payment. It follows that the covenantor should then suggest a split of 50/50 of the net gain, and this was actually agreed in practice.

Unsatisfactory as it may seem, the final apportionment comes down to the bargaining positions of the respective parties and it may well be the case that this will amount to some 50% of the net increase in value. Clearly there is no magic formula but, as the above example illustrates, it is obviously important to determine accurately what that true net increase might be.

As a final conclusion, although the *APC* case and both examples were lifted from practice life, it is unlikely that a student member would be faced with the second example. However, the principle of reviewing all legal documents prior to valuation is important to protect your client, your integrity and also your company's professional indemnity insurance.

Contributed by Stuart Carvell.

CHAPTER 67

Byelaws – their validity and scope

First published in Estates Gazette March 19, 1994

Who may draw up byelaws? What controls exist to prevent them being made for unreasonable purposes?

A byelaw is an example of a form of "secondary legislation" (sometimes known as "subordinate legislation"). When Parliament delegates a law-making power to a minister of the Crown, the resulting legislation is usually known as a "statutory instrument". When Parliament delegates such a power to a corporate body, such as a local authority, water authority, nationalised industry or a privatised utility, the resulting legislation is known as a "byelaw" or "by-law".

The origin of this terminology is possibly Scandinavian, from the old Norse word "byr" – a dwelling place or a town. Thus, historically, a byelaw would be a "town law" (as opposed to a national law). But now that transport undertakings and other utilities have been given the power to make byelaws, relating (for example) to the conduct of passengers on buses, trams and trains, the word "by" can be used in its ordinary sense, meaning "secondary" or "incidental". A modern example of such a statutory power is to be found in section 59 of the Leeds Supertram Act 1993 (a private Act of Parliament):

s.59(1) – The [West Yorkshire Passenger Transport] Executive may make byelaws regulating the use of, and working of, and travel on, the tramway system, the maintenance of order on the tramway system and on the Executive's premises or other facilities provided in connection with the tramway system, and the conduct of all persons, including officers and servants of the Executive, while on those premises.

s.59(2) – Without prejudice to the generality of subsection (1) above, byelaws under this section may contain provisions –
(a) with respect to tickets . . .
(b) with respect to interference with, or obstruction of, the working of the tramway system . . .

(c) for prohibiting or regulating the carriage of dangerous goods . . .

(d) with respect to the use of tobacco or other substances and the prevention of nuisances . . .

Whoever has been given the power to make byelaws, those byelaws have to be signed and approved by a minister of the Crown (usually the Secretary of State for the Environment). This is why (in the case of local authorities) the Department of the Environment publishes "model byelaws" for the guidance of those who will be drafting or voting upon draft byelaws.

Local authorities

So far as local authorities are concerned, the power to make byelaws is contained in section 235 of the Local Government Act 1972. The form of words used in this section is of some antiquity and reported cases on the validity (or otherwise) of byelaws date back to the 19th century. Section 235 states that a district council or a London borough council may make byelaws "for the good rule and government of the whole or any part of the district or borough, as the case may be, and for the prevention and suppression of nuisances therein".

One of the earliest cases is *R* v *Rose* (1855) 19 JP 676 where a local authority had a statutory power to make byelaws requiring occupiers to remove dust, filth, etc from the streets. It was held that a byelaw requiring occupiers to remove pure snow from the streets was beyond the powers of the local authority. Similarly, in *Strickland* v *Hayes* [1896] 1 QB 290 a byelaw was held to be *ultra vires* (beyond the powers of the law-maker) and contrary to the general law of the land because it purported to make the use of obscene language in public a criminal offence, whether or not it caused a nuisance or annoyance to anyone. But in *Mantle* v *Jordan* [1897] 1 QB 248 a byelaw was held to be valid (ie "*intra vires*" not "*ultra vires*") because the wording of the offence made it clear that it was limited to situations where annoyance was caused to persons in the street or a public place. This byelaw was not rendered invalid because it referred to language spoken and to gestures or conduct spoken or expressed in private premises abutting the street or public place in question.

The leading case on the validity of byelaws is *Kruse* v *Johnson* [1898] 2 QB 91 – a case heard by a specially constituted Divisional

Court consisting of the Lord Chief Justice (Lord Russell) and six other judges. The defendant conducted (and continued to conduct) an open-air religious service within 50 yards of a dwelling-house after being requested by the police to stop. He was prosecuted under a byelaw of Kent County Council which provided that:

No person shall sound or play upon any musical or noisy instrument, or sing in any public place or highway within fifty yards of any dwelling-house, after being required by any constable . . . to desist.

The Divisional Court held that the byelaws were to be interpreted benevolently and that there was a presumption in favour of them being valid and reasonable. The court therefore upheld the defendant's conviction. But important guidelines were laid down as to the circumstances in which a byelaw would be declared to be ultra vires for unreasonableness, namely if it were partial and unequal (in a discriminatory sense), manifestly unjust, tainted by bad faith, or oppressive and gratuitous in its interference with individual rights. Thus, byelaws containing a general prohibition on the playing of music or the holding of religious services in the streets of a town have been held to be *ultra vires* because they did not confine themselves to circumstances likely to cause a nuisance: *Johnson v Croydon Corporation* (1886) 16 QBD 708; *Munro v Watson* (1887) 51 JP 660.

Military lands

Very rarely Parliament may stipulate that certain byelaws will have to be made as a statutory instrument. In other words, the Secretary of State will not be the confirming authority, but will himself be the legislator (subject to the control of Parliament). An example is provided by the Military Lands Act 1892, which empowers the Secretary of State for Defence to make byelaws regulating the use of land appropriated for military purposes. Thus, in the case of the RAF base at Greenham Common, the Secretary of State for Defence made (in 1985) the Greenham Common byelaws (SI 1985 No 485). One of these byelaws made it an offence to enter without authority or permission the enclosed area within the perimeter fence and gates of the base. When the base began to be used for the stationing of cruise missiles, certain protestors entered the base without authority or permission. When they were prosecuted they claimed that the byelaws were *ultra vires* because Greenham

Common was common land and section 14(1) of the Military Lands Act 1892 contained the following proviso:

Provided that no byelaws promulgated under this section shall authorise the Secretary of State to take away or prejudicially affect any rights of common.

The defendants were convicted in the magistrates' court. They appealed to the Crown court (on mixed questions of law and fact). The Crown court held that the byelaws were ultra vires and quashed the conviction. The prosecutor appealed to the Divisional Court on a point of law. The Divisional Court held that the defendants were not entitled to rely on the proviso because they were not themselves "commoners" (ie persons locally resident and entitled to claim legal rights over the common land). Therefore, even if the byelaws had been ultra vires, the defendants were still liable to be convicted because it had been within the power of the Secretary of State to enact byelaws which were binding on outlanders (such as the defendants). The defendants appealed to the House of Lords: see *Director of Public Prosecutions* v *Hutchinson and Smith* (1991) 155 JP 71.

The House of Lords considered reported cases from USA and Australia, as well as from English and Irish courts. The earliest decision cited was *R* v *Company of Fishermen of Faversham* (1799) 8 Term 352, where Lord Kenyon CJ stated the law as follows:

. . . though a byelaw may be good in part and bad in part, yet it can be so only where the two parts are entire and distinct from each other.

The House of Lords held that it was not possible or permissible to speculate on what the Secretary of State would have enacted if he had applied his mind to the proviso in section 14(1) of the Military Lands Act 1892. Although it was permissible to delete the ultra vires part of a byelaw (or a statutory instrument) if that part was severable from the remainder of the enactment, it was not permissible for the courts to rewrite or to change the nature of such an enactment if it was worded too widely and could not be severed into two distinct parts. Accordingly, the House of Lords held the byelaw in question to be wholly void and quashed the convictions of the defendants.

Unreasonableness as a defence

When a defendant in a criminal trial claims that a byelaw is *ultra vires*, the criminal court (usually a magistrates court) must inquire into that aspect of the matter. It is neither necessary nor appropriate to adjourn the proceedings while an application is made to the High Court by way of judicial review: see *R* v *Reading Crown Court, ex parte Hutchinson* [1988] QB 384. This applies to allegations that the byelaw is unreasonable (in the limited legal sense of that word), not merely to allegations that it is outside the four corners of the statutory power given to the lawmaker.

The power of a magistrates court to rule on the reasonableness (or otherwise) of a byelaw (even one created by a statutory instrument) is in marked contrast to the role of such a court in the case of ordinary statutory instruments. It is not felt to be appropriate that a magistrates court should deal with arguments that a Secretary of State has acted unreasonably in making such a statutory instrument. This is an exercise which goes beyond statutory interpretation and it can only be undertaken by the High Court.

The reason for this diversity appears to be that magistrates have traditionally been vested with local Government functions (especially with regard to licensing, housing and environmental health). They are also allowed to take into account local knowledge when making their decisions. It is not considered unusual, therefore, that magistrates should be entitled to rule on the good faith, propriety and reasonableness of local byelaws. Yet where the conduct of the Secretary of State is directly challenged, on grounds that he is acting unreasonably or in bad faith, it is felt that the appropriate forum for such a challenge will be the High Court, either by way of judicial review or by way of a "case stated" when appealing from a decision of the magistrates.

Contributed by Leslie Blake.

CHAPTER 68

"Next step" agencies

First published in Estates Gazette October 1, 1994

To what extent have the functions of central Government been delegated to independent agencies in recent years? What constitutional or legal problems does this cause?

Executive agencies (or "Next step" agencies* were created following a report in 1988 by the then Prime Minister, Margaret Thatcher,'s Efficiency Unit, chaired by Sir Robin Ibbs. The report arose from a sense of frustration with existing managerial schemes, such as the Financial Management Initiative. The *Ibbs Report* made a number of findings:

- The Civil Service was too large to manage as a single organisation;
- "Ministerial overload" diverted attention from managerial matters;
- Middle management was intervening too much in minor matters;
- Senior management was concerning itself too much with policy issues at the expense of service delivery;
- There was too much emphasis on the control of expenditure and husbanding of resources and too little emphasis on the achievement of results.

To overcome these problems the *Ibbs Report* advocated radical changes in the way Government services were delivered (a function which was found to involve 95% of the Civil Service). It was felt that improved management could be achieved only if the work of each department was focused on results; if each department ensured that its staff had the relevant skills and experience; and if there was a real commitment within each department continuously to improve the value for money obtained in the delivery of services.

---

*Executive agencies are sometimes known as "Next step" agencies because, before this status is granted, the possibility of subsequent privatisation is always considered and often aimed at by the Government.

The report recommended that the executive branch of the state be reorganised so that its service delivery functions operated more effectively. To achieve this, the report suggested the establishment of agencies, each of which would be headed by a chief executive. These administrators would have considerable powers over pay, grading, recruitment and structure, within frameworks of policy and resources set by Government departments. They would be given the maximum freedom possible, consistent with central controls. Ministerial responsibility would remain, but would not extend to matters of detail. The role of the Government departments would be to set up the framework and to see that the agencies built properly upon it, leaving the managers to do the managing.

Ministerial responsibility

Clearly there is a contradiction between the "arm's length" distance of the Government from its new agencies (which the Ibbs Report wished to see established) and the convention of "ministerial responsibility" for the work of subordinates (which constitutional lawyers would wish to see preserved).

One of the main criticisms of civil servants was their tendency to be cautious – resulting from fear of repercussions should their minister be put in an awkward position in Parliament. Thus, the retention of the convention of "ministerial responsibility" was felt to go against the grain of the drive to develop a risk-taking enterprise culture within the Civil Service.

The Ibbs Report recommended a new constitutional convention, "managerial autonomy", which would make the minister responsible to Parliament for policy, but not for administration.

Policy and resources

It is notoriously hard to find the line which separates policy from administration. The experience of nationalised industries shows that management is likely to develop policy objectives of its own, with one of the main problems here being that ministers were far more short-sighted than management. The performance indicator which appealed to ministers was votes, not profits, and the forward planning of Governments was (under the Parliament Act 1911) limited to a maximum period of five years.

The criterion for distinguishing questions of policy from matters of mere administration has also been affected by the transient concept of political sensitivity. When a "live" issue arises, matters of administration may become the minister's most personal business, or an issue of policy may be described as an "operational" question to shield it from external scrutiny. So policy may become lost in administration and administration may contain some elements of policy.

A policy-and-resources "framework document" is essential in this context. It indicates a quasi-contractual relationship between ministers and chief executives and "sets out the policy, the budget, the specific targets, and the results to be achieved" (*Ibbs Report*, para 20). It is also important for the purposes of external scrutiny because it makes the relationships transparent by stating clearly the delegated powers and the division of responsibilities. Yet here, too, there is a contradiction: a detailed framework assists effective scrutiny, but it helps to defeat the whole rationale of executive agencies' flexible management.

Judicial review

Recent history offers an example of the possible consequences of imposing a too-rigid framework on a quasi-Governmental body. In the 1970s a policy guidance structure was used by the Department of Trade as a means of controlling the activities of the Civil Aviation Authority with regard to the licensing of airline services. But this system was too rigid, too difficult to adjust to changing economic and political circumstances and too vulnerable to challenge in the courts. (Sir Freddie Laker successfully challenged the policy guidance of the Secretary of State for Trade with regard to his "Sky-Train" service: *Laker Airways Ltd* v *Department of Trade* [1977] QB 643.) The system was subsequently abolished by the Civil Aviation Act 1980.

The need for flexibility in framework documents, and especially their vulnerability to judicial review, may lead to the abandonment (or non-publication) of such documents or, more probably, to their ambiguity. In any of these scenarios it will be impossible to discover what people are doing or what they are meant to be doing.

United Kingdom plc?

So far, "framework documents" for all the new executive agencies have been published. The Government has given repeated assurances that this practice will continue. More worrying than the prospect of a framework document not being published at all is the realistic suspicion that important information will be left out when it does appear. Obvious (and acceptable) omissions will be matters of national security and the public interest generally. But many corporate plans and business plans are now classified as "commercial in confidence": see House of Commons Paper: HC 496 [1990–91]: Appendix 3. It appears that framework documents are gaining a status analogous to such private-sector commercial documents. This creates a serious obstacle to parliamentary scrutiny. It also raises the question of whether the Government of a democratic state can be conducted along the same lines as a public limited company. (Such an analogy was certainly drawn in the case of 19th-century local authorities, which used to be known as "municipal corporations".)

In the commercial sector, the nearest equivalent of a Government's accountability to Parliament is the accountability of a board of directors to the shareholders of a company. But the general meetings of a company take place only annually (except in extraordinary circumstances), and no investigation takes place if profits are being made. Even in the event of a poor economic performance, the shareholders have no right to a critical examination of how the company has been run. They can sell their shares, but this does not alter the fact that the commercial affairs of business organisations are the epitome of secrecy.

The House of Commons, on the other hand, does not act in the name of shareholders. It represents the citizens of the United Kingdom in their dual capacity as electors and taxpayers. It claims a right to information because a citizen (in this dual capacity) has a right to make an informed democratic choice. Any trend towards the commercialisation of Government (sometimes known as the concept of "United Kingdom plc") will therefore have drastic consequences for the scrutiny of the executive branch of the state.

A scrutiny gap?

A further question mark over the "framework documents" is the ability of members of Parliament to understand them without assistance. Economics, finance and management are all very technical subjects. Members of Parliament, aware of their lack of expertise, now employ specialist advisers to help them in select committees. This practice will have to increase before any proper scrutiny can be given to executive agencies. This is another reason why Parliament ought to establish an expert secretariat.

Another problem is that executive agencies specifically discard the convention that (in both policy matters and administrative matters) civil servants act only on behalf of their ministers. Under the new system, ministers delegate authority to chief executives and these officials are personally responsible to the minister for "administration". But a minister will refuse to answer questions on administration and a chief executive will answer questions only "on behalf of the minister". This means that there can be no effective scrutiny of "administration".

In Sweden, which the British system of executive agencies superficially imitates, this problem has been recognised and chief executives are made directly accountable to the Swedish Parliament. The convention of individual ministerial responsibility does not exist there. In the United Kingdom, the only way this could be brought about, without a radical change to Parliamentary procedure, would be for chief executives to explain and justify their actions to select committees. Ultimate accountability would still rest with the minister, unlikely though it is nowadays for a minister to resign in a case where he is not personally at fault.*

Types of agency
Agencies are not generic. They come in all shapes and sizes. For example, in the field of social security law, the Benefits Agency has more than 65,000 staff. This is twice the size of the Foreign Office, the Department of Education, the Department of Health, the Department of Trade and Industry, the Department of Transport and the Welsh Office, including 20 agencies within those departments.

Agencies have varying characteristics. Some are fundamental to the mainstream policy of their departments, such as the Benefits Agency is to the Department of Social Security or the Employment

---

*The last example appears to be that of Lord Carrington, who resigned as Foreign Secretary in 1982, after the Argentine invasion of the Falkland Islands. No one has resigned over an injustice committed by civil servants in an environmental, agricultural or compulsory purchase matter since the much-honoured case of Sir Thomas Dugdale in the Crichel Down affair (1954).

Services Agency is to the Department of Employment. Some exercise statutory functions in a highly delegated way, such as the Vehicle Inspectorate. Some merely provide services to other departments and agencies, as does the Information Technology Services Agency (located within the Department of Social Security). Some are not linked to the main aims of a department at all, but simply report to a minister.

Agencies also maintain a diverse range of internal organisations, such as advisory boards or councils chaired by ministers, chief executives or civil servants. These may consist of private-sector managers, customers, representatives of professional bodies and members of other interest groups.

Civil Service disorganisation?

The growing financial autonomy of the executive agencies has caused problems within the Civil Service. Increasingly, agencies are bypassing their departments and establishing direct links with the Treasury in their negotiations for financing. Several agencies operate as "Trading Funds", benefiting from an amendment (made in 1989) to the Trading Fund Act 1973, which specifically allows agencies to achieve autonomy.

The long-term aim of these management reforms (explicitly stated in the *Ibbs Report*) is to give chief executives complete control over the organisation, pay and recruitment of their staff. Many agencies already have responsibility for the recruitment of their own junior staff and operate incentive schemes.

All this undermines the concept of a uniform Civil Service. Staff cannot easily be transferred to another agency if the employment policies there are different. (All chief executives are given fixed-term contracts and do not have the security of employment traditionally associated with public-sector posts.)

A rump Parliament?

For a system of parliamentary scrutiny that is dependent upon a concept of centralised Government, acting through departments, the dismantling of the Civil Service and the devolution of power to a variety of executive agencies is full of perils. If, as the Ibbs Report claims, 95% of executive functions can be categorised as administrative in nature (the delivery of policy and services), then

95% of what the executive does will escape examination by Parliament. All that will remain will be the core policy-making elements of the Government and Parliament may cease to be "a deliberative assembly for the redress of grievances". If select committees allow themselves to be confined to the scrutiny of policy, members of Parliament might as well go back to the chamber.

Contributed by Olu Popoola.

CHAPTER 69

The nature of the common law

First published in Estates Gazette October 29, 1994

What is meant by the phrase "the common law"? How does the common law of England differ from the jurisprudence of continental Europe?

The phrase "the common law" may be used in several different ways. It is like the word "home". The meaning differs upon the standpoint of the person using the word and, more particularly, the places, persons, or things he wishes to distinguish it from.

Thus, in one context, a lawyer in the USA will consider himself (quite justifiably) to be a "common lawyer" and, in another context, a Chancery lawyer practising in London's Lincoln's Inn (specialising, perhaps, in the law of trusts) will not want to be known by this name. This is because the American lawyer (even if he specialises in the law of trusts) will claim a kinship with English jurisprudence, its writings, its precedents and its essentially inductive nature, which he will not so readily see in the codified systems of continental Europe or in the deductive approach of its lawyers, whose ways will not be his ways nor their laws his.

But the Chancery lawyer in Lincoln's Inn will be at pains to emphasise that he is not specialising in "common law" subjects, such as negligence, nuisance or conspiracy to defraud, but in the unique contribution of the old Court of Chancery in developing new rights, new remedies, and new procedures, altogether known as the principles of "equity" in contra-distinction to the rules of common law, those somewhat older laws needing to be ameliorated by the Court of Chancery in the days before widespread statutory reforms.

"England"

The phrase "the common law" is used in its most poetic sense when it is conjoined with the name England ("the common law of England"). "England" is a geographical and legal expression, but it is not a nation state. It is part of the United Kingdom of Great Britain and Northern Ireland. England, Wales and Scotland together form "Great Britain". Jersey, Guernsey (and its dependencies) and the Isle of Man do not form part of the United Kingdom, nor do they constitute colonies. They are in an ambiguous legal position and are called "peculiars of the Crown". They have a legal and personal connection with the Crown, which antedates even the earliest days of British colonial history.

Within Great Britain the essential distinction is between the law of England and Wales on the one hand, and the law of Scotland on the other. The law of Northern Ireland (and, indeed, the Republic of Ireland also) is essentially a transplanted form of English law, but the same cannot be said of Scotland.

The law of Scotland is closer to the jurisprudence of continental Europe than English law is, although (like English law) it is an uncodified system and follows an adversarial mode of trial, rather than the inquisitorial system adopted in Europe. For this reason, and because of its respect for judicial precedent as a source of law, Scotland may be called a "common law" country. Many modern (statute-based) subjects, such as company law and revenue law, are applied uniformly throughout the UK. The essential nature of Scottish law, however, is protected by the Act of Union 1707, which expressly provides that no alteration shall be made "in the laws which concern private right except for evident utility of the subjects within Scotland".

It must be for Scottish lawyers to express a view on whether this bargain has been kept. To English lawyers, noticing (perhaps) the distinctive nature of Scottish property law and the continental flavour of its law of contract, the proviso in the Act of Union seems to have been respected well enough. Indeed, the influence of Scottish law lords (sitting in the House of Lords) has often been very influential in England and Wales. For example, the leading case on product liability in the tort of negligence (*Donoghue* v *Stevenson* [1932] AC 562) was a majority decision of two Scottish law lords and one Australian-born Welshman against the votes of two English law lords.*

---

*The Scottish law lords were Lord MacMillan and Lord Thankerton. The English law lords were Lord Buckmaster and Lord Tomlin. The Welshman (and, therefore, an English law lord) was Lord Atkin. The case was a Scottish case, but the tort of negligence is the same in both jurisdictions.

The "common law of England" may, therefore, be defined as the law which originated from the customs and judicial decisions of the people of England and Wales and was influenced to some degree (since the Act of Union 1707) by the common law of Scotland.

For the purposes of this definition it is not necessary to distinguish between the courts of common law and the courts of equity, although when using the phrase "common law" in a narrower sense it becomes essential to do so. Likewise it is not necessary to distinguish between those judicial decisions which constitute unwritten law in the fullest sense of that idea and those decisions which constitute judicial interpretations of statutes and other forms of legislation.

The "common law of England" in the sense that we are now regarding it (also being the sense in which the world at large regards it) means the particular approach to the discovery, interpretation, and (where necessary) the making of law was practised, to a greater or lesser extent, throughout the English-speaking world and in contra-distinction (particularly) to the jurisprudence of countries influenced by Roman Law and the later European codes (such as the Code Napoleon). We must now look at the characteristics of these two great systems of law.

Incremental approach

The common law is said to be "inductive" in nature because it proceeds (at first) in an incremental way, laying down its rules on a case by case basis, inferring a general principle only after a plentitude of precedents justifies that inference and showing always a marked reluctance to reason far beyond what actual experience has demonstrated to be wise. The common law is therefore deeply democratic in its origins (because it arises from popular need), acutely logical in its reactions (because it responds to the preponderance of legal argument), and disdainful of legal theory (because it looks backwards to its precedents, not forwards to hypothetical instances).

The traditional common lawyer, although he recognises the supremacy of Parliament, in fact holds no great reverence for statute law. He treats it as the transitory command of a sovereign superior, to be interpreted strictly and precisely because of this, in a way not greatly different from the interpretation of a contract or a lease signed by mutually suspicious parties who had negotiated that agreement at arm's length. He does not truly believe that statute law is a fitting place to enshrine the eternal verities of human experience.

Codification does not appeal to the traditional common lawyer. He is affronted by the platitudinous nature of most codes and believes that they shut off any further development of the law based upon unforeseen contingencies. He believes that they create problems of interpretation which can be cured only by a common law concept – the doctrine of binding precedent. To the common lawyer certainty in the law, more than abstract justice, is the pearl of great price.

Even equity, in seeking to ameliorate the harshness of the common law, has never sought (in modern times) to replace the doctrine of precedent and the rules of recorded discretion with unpredictable ad hoc decision-making. The traditional "common law" approach has seldom been better explained than by Bagnall J in a case about the equitable rights of a husband and wife in matrimonial property. After setting out the principles which he had derived from two previous decisions of the House of Lords, he went on to state:

In any individual case the application of these principles may produce a result which appears unfair. So be it; in my view that is not an injustice. I am convinced that in determining rights, particularly property rights, the only justice that can be attained by mortals, who are fallible and not omniscient, is justice according to the law; the justice which flows from the application of sure and settled principles to proved or admitted facts . . . This does not mean that equity is past childbearing; simply that its progeny must be legitimate – by precedent out of principle. It is well that it should be so; otherwise no lawyer could safely advise on his client's title and every quarrel would lead to a law suit.

Cowcher v *Cowcher* [1972] 1 All ER 943, at p948.

Deductive approach

In contrast with the common law of England, the continent of (Western) Europe has been directly or indirectly influenced by Roman Law. An alternative name for Roman Law is "the civil law" and the adjective "civilian" is sometimes used in this context. The origin of this usage is the Latin phrase *jus civile* ("civil law"). The word "civil" in this context should not, of course, be confused with the English (legal) uses of the word, ie "civil law" as opposed to "criminal law"; "civil law" as opposed to "military law"; and "civil law" as opposed to the law of the church.

Civil law (in the context we are now considering it) is said to be "deductive" in nature because it proceeds from an exhaustive code of propositions in accordance with which all subsequent experience must be judged. The civilian lawyers of Europe believe that accessibility, not certainty, is the pearl of great price in the law – "who may run may read" – the conception that the law should be available to all, easily understandable, and kept (so far as possible) out of the hands of a priestly class.

Precedent in civilian jurisdictions is not dispensed with (although it is more important in some countries than in others). But the idea that precedents should become strictly binding on future courts, or (still less) that an edifice of statutory interpretation should rise up out of a mound of case law to rival the code itself – these conceptions are considered to be fundamentally undemocratic because they usurp the function of the legislative power of the state. To avoid this state of affairs, judges are discouraged from giving reasons for their decisions, beyond a "legal logic [which] combines a certain wintry elegance with great brevity" (Bernard Rudden's comment in *Basic Community Cases*).

The horror of uncertainty in civilian jurisdictions is lacking because the fear of litigation is less strong. A career judiciary is provided so that there are more courts, including inexpensive tribunals (staffed by younger judges) who can informally hear disputes involving small amounts. A broad "purposive" approach is encouraged towards the interpretation of words and phrases, and consistency is considered less important than ad hoc justice. It is not uncommon for codes to be deliberately vague and general in the choice of language, the better to allow the individual cases upon their merits. The contrast between litigation in common law countries and civil law jurisdictions has never been better explained than by Christopher Hughes in his book *The British Statute Book* (1957):

Supposing one wants to find what the law is on a particular point – for example, if one's neighbours pigs invade the garden and eat the cabbages – how does one do it? In England the first step would certainly be to ask a lawyer, if one was in earnest about it, but failing that, if a good library was near, it would be possible to look it up in a legal textbook . . .

Then we look up the case, follow the references to other cases, and have some idea of the law. It is rather unlikely, on the whole, that we need to look at any statute.* And then we shall probably decide that the legal expenses will be so great that it would pay us to buy the neighbour half a dozen new pigs than to attack him on the subject of cabbages . . . But supposing the thing had happened in Germany or Switzerland or some Continental country . . . The Judge is not a great lord in wig and scarlet, he is probably a young fellow just down from university, a junior official. If we value the cabbages at ten shillings, that is by no means too small a sum to take to a court of law. The case is settled quickly and fairly, perhaps in the diametrically opposite way to which a similar case was settled a day or so ago. All this time there has been no mention of precedents, however. It is the Code which matters, and the Code is a little vague on the subject.

It is the belief of the civil law that codes create certainty and that the function of the judge is to make decisions which will be binding on the parties before him, but which will not attempt to supplement or to subvert the code in any way.

It is the belief of the common law that legislation (however precisely drafted it may be) always creates doubts and that it is the function of the judge to remove those doubts or (better still) to make legislation unnecessary in the first place. The common law judge attempts always to achieve the standards of the 17th-century Lord Chancellor, who intoned: "So let us decide cases here that they may be fit to stand with the wisdom of mankind when they are debated abroad."**

Both these beliefs are, to some extent, fictions, but it is true to observe none the less that there will be no other way in which the European Union can become a "union" in the truest sense of that word without developing further the system of case law which has already started to call itself "the common law of Europe".

Contributed by Leslie Blake.

---

*Nowadays the litigant (or his adviser) would have to look at a statute, although he would probably find it less helpful than the cases: see the Animals Act 1971.
**Lord Nottingham (1621–82), "the father of modern equity".

CHAPTER 70

Primary legislation

First published in Estates Gazette December 9, 1995

What is meant by the term "primary legislation"?

We may define "legislation" as "written, enacted law". Of all the forms of the law it is the type which most closely corresponds to the definition of law propounded by the jurist John Austin (1790–1859): "a command from a political superior backed by a sanction".

Leaving aside for present purposes the question of EC law, the ultimate political superior within the UK is the Queen in Parliament. Accordingly, any "Act" of the Queen in Parliament is entitled to be known as "primary legislation". Another name for an Act of Parliament is a "statute". It is written, enacted law originating from the highest law-making authority in the UK. The enacting words of every Act of parliament bear witness to this: "Be it enacted by the Queen's Most Excellent Majesty, by and with the advice and consent of the Lords Spiritual and Temporal, and Commons, in this present Parliament assembled, and by authority of the same, as follow . . ."

It is interesting to note that the enacting words embody the constitutional fiction of where power lies in the UK, not the constitutional reality. The Queen is mentioned first, as if she still had all the powers of a Tudor monarch. The House of Lords is mentioned next, as if it were the days when a duke could still be prime minister. The House of Commons is mentioned last, as if it were an afterthought. The constitutional reality, of course, is that royal assent to legislation is an automatic (but dignified) formality, and the House of Lords' powers are severely limited by the Parliament Acts of 1911 and 1949. It is votes in the House of Commons alone which will decide which party will form (or remain) the government of the day and which legislative programme will dominate the proceedings of parliament.

Public and general Acts

The Acts of Parliament which are usually found in most law libraries are known as "public and general Acts". They enact provisions which relate to the public at large, or to a section of the public at large, or deal with natural or legal persons in a way which cannot be said to be imposing purely personal or private obligations or bestowing purely personal or private rights.

Public and general Acts can be identified by a "chapter number", as if each Act was a separate chapter in a book of enacted laws. This dates from the days when Parliament was called together (by Plantagenet kings) for a short time and all the legislation passed in that session was treated as if it was a single statute, divisible into chapters. This sequence of chapter numbers nowadays starts anew in every calendar year, and the letter "c" is used to denote the chapter number after the year itself, eg "1990c.43" is the Environmental Protection Act 1990. Until 1962, Acts of parliament were identified by the regnal year of the reigning monarch (and the chapter number). The calendar year was used only in the short title, eg the Law of Property Act 1925 is dated and numbered as follows: 15 & 16 Geo.5, c.20. (1925 began as the 15th year, and ended as the 16th year, of the reign of George V). The new system of using the calendar year was introduced by the Acts of Parliament Numbering and Citation Act 1962.

Until 1896, Acts of Parliament did not have short titles. They were usually known by their regnal year and chapter number, or (if very famous) by the name of the government minister or other member of the House of Commons or House of Lords who introduced the Bill into parliament, eg the Act of Parliament which is dated and numbered 32 Geo.3, c.60 was always known (and is still known) as "Fox's Libel Act 1792". (It was introduced into parliament by Charles James Fox.) The 1896 Act took steps to give short titles to various pre-existing Acts of parliament. Unfortunately, this Act did not always bestow relevant or accurate titles. This was vividly illustrated by the recent case on expert evidence in arbitration proceedings: *London and Leeds Estates Ltd* v *Paribas Ltd (No 2)* [1995] 1 EGLR 102.

The question in that case was whether an expert's proof of evidence at a previous arbitration hearing could be put to him in cross-examination at a different arbitration hearing when (allegedly) he was giving evidence which was inconsistent with his previous views. The right to confront him with such a statement was upheld because of an Act of Parliament which had been passed in 1865: 28 & 29 Vict. c.18 (usually known as "Denman's Act"). In 1896 the Short Titles Act bestowed an inaccurate title on that Act, namely the "Criminal Evidence Act 1865". In fact (as the Paribas case shows), this legislation applies to civil cases (and to arbitration cases) with precisely the same effect on witnesses as would apply to them in a criminal trial.

Both before and after 1896, it has been the practice of Parliament to give long titles to its legislation, eg the Theft Act 1968 (short title) has a long title which reads as follows:

An Act to revise the law of England and Wales as to theft and similar or associated offences, and in connection therewith to make provision as to criminal proceedings by one party to a marriage against the other, and to make certain amendments extending beyond England and Wales in the Post Office Act 1953 and other enactments; and for other purposes connected therewith.

Acts which were repealed before 1896 were not given short titles by that Act. If they need to be referred to nowadays for historical reasons they have to be cited by their regnal year and chapter number or by their long title, eg 22 Hen.8, c.9. might be mistaken for an early statute on the law of food safety. (In fact, it is a law relating to the punishment for the criminal offence of poisoning.) It is entitled: "An Act for the boiling to death of the Bishop of Rochester's cook."

Private or local Acts

Private Acts relate to the interests of private persons or corporations, eg the Gulf Oil Refining Act 1965 gave statutory powers to an oil company to build and operate an oil refinery in South Wales. (This project gave rise to litigation for alleged nuisance: see *Allen* v *Gulf Oil Refining Ltd* [1981] 1 All ER 353.) Private Acts are sometimes called Local Acts because they may relate to the powers and interests of particular localities, eg the Canvey Island Improvement Act 1792.

Private Acts were very common in the 19th century because they were used to give compulsory purchase powers to railway companies and the promoters of other enterprises which the industrial revolution had made possible. They were also necessary in the days before local authorities were given wide powers under 18th-century local government legislation. Private Acts are numbered in a different sequence from Public and General Acts. Roman, instead of Arabic, numerals are used for the chapter numbers, so that, for instance, the Canvey Island Improvement Act 1792 is 32 Geo 3, c. xxxi, and the Gulf Oil Refining Act 1965 is 1965, c. xxiv. Private Acts are introduced into Parliament as Private Bills. "Private Bills" should not be confused with "Private Member's Bills". A Private Bill is promoted in Parliament by persons or corporations from outside Parliament, eg British Railways regularly promotes Bills in Parliament. A "Private Member's Bill" is one which is introduced by a back-bench MP (ie not by a minister of the Crown). If passed by Parliament (which is unlikely) it will be a Public and General Act like any other such Act. A recent example of such an Act, stemming from such a Bill, is the Criminal Procedure (Insanity and Unfitness to Plead) Act 1991 (1991, c.25).

Hybrid Bills

It is sometimes difficult to know whether a proposed item of legislation is "public" or "private" in nature. Christopher Hughes in his book (now sadly out of print) *The British Statute Book* (1957) put the matter this way:

. . . a Bill to give special powers of planning to the city of Bath, in view of its architectural beauty, would be a private Bill. A Bill to give such a power to all boroughs of more than a hundred thousand inhabitants, or to all beautiful towns even, would be a Public Bill. In borderline cases the boundary is an indeterminate or even a movable one: it may depend upon the words used rather than the functions performed, or it may shift with an alteration in the climate of opinion or with a different conception of the functions of Government.

If a Bill is largely "public" in nature, but contains provisions which adversely affect private rights, it will be said to suffer from "hybridity". (The Bill will be known as a "Hybrid Bill".) A recent example was the Channel Tunnel Bill (now the Channel Tunnel Act 1987). This Bill was introduced by the government (and was, therefore, a Public Bill), but it contained provisions which adversely affected the rights of landowners in Kent and the business interests of various enterprises (such as the ferry companies).

When they have received royal assent, Hybrid Bills become

Public and General Acts and they are numbered in the same series as other Public and General Acts. There is no such thing as a "Hybrid Act". It is important to know whether a Bill is Public, Private, or Hybrid because a quasi-judicial procedure applies to a Private Bill and to those provisions in a Hybrid Bill of an essentially "private" nature. This procedure consists of a hearing before a Select Committee of four members of the House of Commons which will hear evidence from the promoters of, and from objectors to, the Bill. These witnesses can be questioned by the committee and cross-examined by members of the Parliamentary Bar representing the opposing interests. The Select Committee can reject the Bill without giving reasons, as happened in the case of the CrossRail Bill in 1994. The House of Lords will also adopt a similar procedure when the Bill is considered in committee there. It is even open to the House of Lords to conclude that a Bill is a "Private" or a "Hybrid" Bill even though the House of Commons has decided to treat it as a Bill which is entirely "public" in nature, free from "hybridity".

Expert witnesses can (and often do) give evidence before Select Committees when Private Bills (or Hybrid Bills) are being considered by the House of Commons or the House of Lords. This was a particularly frequent occurrence in the 19th century, when many "railway bills" were being piloted through Parliament. This is the reason why the RICS and many firms of surveyors and engineers have grown up in the Westminster area. (Plans and specifications had to be taken to and from parliament, and to and from the nearby offices of "Parliamentary Agents".)

A select committee will not allow witnesses to raise any objections to a Private Bill (or to a Hybrid Bill) if those objections relate to public issues, not to private rights. For example, the committee which heard evidence relating to the Channel Tunnel Bill would not let landowners in Kent to raise the issue of rabies, because this was a risk of a public and general nature not directly relevant to their property rights.

Personal Acts

A "Personal Act" is now a rarity. It relates to the personal status, property, or other individual rights of one or more named individuals. Such Acts were common in the days when only Parliament could grant a divorce. Courts were not able to grant divorces until 1857. Parliament is sometimes asked to pass a

Personal Act to enable two people to marry each other who would otherwise would be unable to do so, eg people affected by the rule that "adoption imitates nature", so that (in law) they are brother and sister to each other, although they are not blood relatives. Personal Acts are numbered in a third series, separate from Public Acts and Private Acts. They are given chapter numbers in italic (Arabic) numerals, eg 1995 c.2.

Parent Acts

A "parent Act" is the name commonly given to a statute which empowers a minister of the Crown (or some other competent authority) to make delegated legislation, eg the Building Act 1984 can be described as the "parent Act" which empowers the making of the Building Regulations. A "parent Act" may be a Private Act (as where, eg various universities are empowered to make their own "statutes" or byelaws) or it may be a Public and General Act.

Another name for a "parent Act" is an "enabling Act". There is, however, a slight hint of disapproval in the term "enabling Act". It implies that too much power has been delegated, so that the minister of the Crown (or other law-maker in question) may exercise wide and insufficiently controlled legislative authority.

If a parent Act delegates a power which enables a minister of the Crown (or other person) to amend primary legislation, including, perhaps, the parent Act itself, this power is usually referred to (by critics) as a "Henry VIII clause". This refers to the fact that such clauses were commonly enacted by Parliament in the reign of Henry VIII, eg the Statute of Proclamations 1539 (31 Hen 8, c.8) contained the following enabling power: "The King [in council] . . . may set forth proclamations under such penalties and pains as to him and them shall seem necessary, which shall be observed as though they were made by Act of Parliament . . ." .

In 1929 the Lord Chief Justice, Lord Hewart, published a book, entitled *The New Despotism*, criticising the revived popularity of such clauses. One of the examples he gave was section 45 of the Unemployment Insurance Act 1920 (now repealed). This section contained the following words:

If any difficulty arises with respect to the constitution of special or supplementary schemes or otherwise in any other manner in bringing this Act into operation, the Minister, with the consent of the Treasury, may by order do anything which appears to him necessary or expedient for the constitution of such schemes or otherwise for bringing this Act into operation, and may modify the provisions of this Act so far as may appear necessary or expedient for carrying the order into effect.

Such practices are not a thing of the past. For example, the European Communities Act 1972, the Health and Safety at Work, etc Act 1974, and the De-Regulation and Contracting-Out Act 1994 all contain wide powers to bring about the repeal of Acts of Parliament (as well as delegated legislation).

Consolidation Acts

An Act which brings together a number of statutory provisions previously found in many different statutes is known as a "Consolidation Act" or a "Consolidating Statute". The purpose of such an exercise is mere convenience, not the bringing about of changes in the substantive law. When such a Bill is brought before Parliament, the only question which the House of Commons and the House of Lords can vote upon is: "Shall the law be consolidated"?

Other forms of legislation

Acts of Parliament are not only forms of law which fulfil our definition of "legislation" ("written, enacted law"). Even leaving aside the question of EC law, with its treaties, regulations, and directives, the English legal system is replete with orders-in-council, statutory instruments and byelaws, and with "quasi-legislation" (such as Circulars and Codes of Practice).

Contributed by Leslie Blake.

CHAPTER 71

Secondary legislation

First published in Estates Gazette January 20, 1996

What are the differences, if any, between statutory rules, orders, and regulations?

They are all forms of "secondary legislation". "Secondary legislation" may be defined as any written, enacted law made by any person in the exercise of a power delegated to him by Parliament. The "person" in question might not be an individual person or even a natural person. It might be a committee of law-makers, or a corporate body such as a local authority.

Secondary legislation is also known as "subordinate" or "delegated" legislation. It is convenient to subdivide this legislation into statutory instruments and byelaws.*

By section 1 of the Statutory Instruments Act 1946, a statutory instrument is defined as:

any order, rule, regulation or other subordinate legislation made, confirmed or approved by the Queen-in-council by means of a statutory order-in-council, or by a minister of the Crown using any statutory power conferred on him (if that power is expressed to be "exercisable by statutory instrument").

Orders-in-Council

An Order-in-Council is a legislative enactment made by the Queen-in-Council, rather than by the Queen-in-Parliament. The "Council" referred to is the Privy Council, members of which are denoted by the words "right honourable" in front their names and the initials "PC" after them. Orders-in-Council are enacted by a small group of privy councillors, usually government ministers, summoned by the Lord President of the council (a government minister).

---

*For a discussion of bye-laws, see pp465–467 of this book.

Although it is convenient to discuss Orders-in-Council as a form of delegated legislation (for most come within this category), there is a vestigial category of such orders which are "prerogative" in nature. In other words, they are a form of primary legislation, deriving their authority from the inherent powers of the Crown, not from the powers of parliament.

Prerogative Orders-in-Council

These are not statutory instruments. They do not need to recite any statutory authority for the rule-making powers which they exercise. The enacting words simply proclaim that Her Majesty "in the exercise of all her powers in that behalf hereby makes the following order".

Prerogative Orders-in-Council are rare because of the combined effect of three fundamental principles:

(1) Common law defines the scope of the royal prerogative, not vice versa. Bracton, in the 13th century, wrote that "the King should not be under a man, but under God and the law". This was affirmed by the courts in the 17th century when Sir Edward Coke (and three other judges) stated that "the King hath no prerogative but that which the law of the land allows him": *Case of Proclamations* (1611) 12 Co Rep 74.

(2) A prerogative power is incapable of existing in the face of a statutory power which expressly, or even impliedly, deals with the same subject-matter. This was the upshot of the famous case on the alleged power of the government to take land during time of war without paying compensation for it: *Attorney-General v De Keyser's Royal Hotel Ltd* [1920] AC 508.

(3) The royal prerogative is a closed book. It cannot give rise to new governmental powers. Unlike the torts of nuisance and negligence, it is not one of those concepts where a judge could ever lawfully say: "the categories of the royal prerogative are never closed". On the contrary, in *British Broadcasting Corporation v Johns* [1965] Ch 32, Diplock LJ rejected the argument that the BBC was the embodiment of a prerogative power to control broadcasting (and therefore exempt from income tax).

Scope for a prerogative Order-in-Council is very limited. The Court of Appeal's decision in *Post Office* v *Estuary Radio* [1967] 3 All ER

663 is a rare example of a prerogative Order-in-Council – the Territorial Waters Order 1964 – being interpreted by the English courts. This case related the precise metes and bounds of UK territorial waters in the Thames Estuary.

Statutory Orders-in-Council

Just as parliament may delegate rule-making powers to a minister of the crown, so may it also delegate such powers to the Queen-in-Council. This is usually done when it is desired to give the maximum amount of dignity, publicity, and moral force to the legislation in question, or when the government wishes to legislate as if it were an entity, rather than a collection of individual ministers and departments of state. An example might be the proclamation of a state of emergency under the Emergency Powers Act 1920 or the extension of British legislation to dependant territories.

Orders-in-Council of this sort are known as "statutory Orders-in-Council". They are classified as a species of statutory instrument and are given an "SI" number. The authority for such legislation comes from Parliament via a "parent Act", and the power of the Queen-in-Council is not then limited to the powers of the royal prerogative. Like all forms of delegated legislation, statutory orders-in-council are subject to the ultra vires rule if the rule-making power given by Parliament is exceeded or abused.

Even prerogative Orders-in-Council are subject to judicial review, because, as we have already seen, the royal prerogative itself exists only to the extent recognised by the common law and left unaffected by statute law. Even if a prerogative power to legislate on a certain matter exists, eg to regulate the terms and conditions of employment of civil servants, the manner of exercising that power may (sometimes) be open to judicial review: *Council of Civil Service Unions* v *Minister for the Civil Service* [1985] AC 374.

Rules, Orders and Regulations

The Statutory Instruments Act 1946 refers to "orders, rules, regulations, or other subordinate legislation". About 3,000 statutory instruments are brought into force every year. Some are called "rules"; some "orders" (although these are not usually Orders-in-Council); some "regulations"; and some are given other titles. Here are some examples from 1993.

Rules:
Asylum Appeals (Procedure) Rules 1993 (SI No 1661).
Employment Appeal Tribunal Rules 1993 (SI No 2854).

Orders:
A1 Trunk Road (Haringey) (Bus Lanes) Red Route Traffic Order 1993 (SI No 897).
East Kent Light Railway Order 1993 (SI No 2154).

Regulations:
Council Tax (Alteration of Lists and Appeals) Regulations 1993 (SI No 290).
Hill Livestock (Compensatory Allowances) Regulations 1993 (SI No 2631).

Other subordinate legislation:
Birmingham City Council (Grand Union Canal Bridge) Scheme 1991 Confirmation Instrument 1993 (SI No 2662).
Farm and Conservation Grant (Variation) Scheme 1993 (SI No 2901).

The terminology used in the naming of statutory instruments was investigated by the committee of ministers' powers, originally under the chairmanship of the Earl of Donoughmore (1875–1948). This committee had been established in 1929 as a result of Lord Hewart's book, *The New Despotism*, which had roundly criticised the over-wide bestowing of legislative powers on ministers of the crown. (Lord Hewart was Lord Chief Justice at the time.)

This committee's report was published in 1932 and, on the question of terminology, it recommended that the nomenclature should broadly reflect the three powers of government:

- *The legislative power of the state (or the power to control the purse):* True subordinate legislation, ie the enactment of rules intended to regulate future conduct, should be called "regulations". These might identify what forms of conduct would amount to a criminal offence, fall foul of certain standards, justify certain approvals or merit certain awards.
- *The executive power of the state (or the power to control the sword):* Executive and quasi-judicial decisions of an administrative nature should be called "orders". Examples are "commencement orders" (bringing an Act of Parliament, or part of it, into force) and "compulsory purchase orders" (authorising

the acquisition of land). Whereas true legislation is intended to be enduring, an executive act is often instantaneous in its nature, although it may be permanent, irreversible or long-lasting in its effects, eg the introduction of a traffic scheme.

- *The judicial power of the state (or the power to exercise judgment)*: Provisions of a procedural nature should be called "rules". For example, subordinate legislation is often used to set out the procedures to be followed by courts or tribunals, or by the parties to planning inquiries or compulsory purchase appeals. Such legislation is also used, on occasion, to impose time-limits or to set out rights of appeal to higher courts or tribunals. Examples of such statutory instruments are the Rules of the Supreme Court and the County Court Rules.

Difficulties with terminology

In some cases it is difficult to know whether a statutory instrument is legislative, executive or procedural in nature. For example, a statutory instrument is the usual method chosen by Parliament to publish the form and content of documents (notices and the like) which are required to convey specified statutory information or to comply with a particular pro forma.

Such documents are well known to estate managers and other general practice surveyors. The rights of a client may sometimes stand or fall according to whether the latest statutory instruments have been complied with. Such instruments could logically be entitled an "order". They embody the executive decision of a minister of the crown to insist on the use of a particular form or the giving of particular information in a specified way.

On the other hand, such forms or documents may often have a procedural importance. They may embody the notice which a landlord has to serve upon his tenant (or a tenant upon his landlord) in order to initiate the procedures relating to the termination or regranting of a tenancy.

In civil litigation or administrative law, the statutory instrument in question may contain the pro forma which has to be used in order to exercise a right of appeal. Accordingly, a good case could be made for calling such instruments "rules" (rather than "regulations" or "orders").

The view which seems to have been taken by the government is that these statutory instruments should be called "regulations". This is because they can be interpreted as a form of published information intended for the future guidance of persons who need to serve the notices in question, or to use the documentation or the form of words prescribed by law, or to assess the validity of notices or documents which have been served on them. Viewed in this way, such instruments can be described as legislative in character. Obvious examples are the Notices to Quit (Prescribed Information) Regulations and the Assured Tenancies and Agricultural Occupancies (Forms) Regulations.

The "Rule of law"

Lawyers have always been suspicious of subordinate legislation in all its forms because it creates the danger of executive law-making and the imposition of obligations without due process of law. This veneration of legality is reflected in *Magna Carta* 1215 (as reissued in 1297):

No freeman shall be taken or imprisoned, or be disseised of his freehold, or liberties, or free customs, or outlawed, or exiled, or any otherwise destroyed; nor will we pass upon him, nor condemn him but by lawful judgement of his peers, or by the law of the land.

Professor Dicey included an element of "due process" in his famous definition of the "rule of law" in his book *The Law of the Constitution* (1885):

. . . it [the rule of law] means, in the first place, the absolute supremacy or predominance of regular law as opposed to the influence of arbitrary power, and excludes the existence of arbitrariness, or prerogative, or even wide discretionary authority on the part of the Government.

Such sentiments are not outdated. In *Porter* v *Honey* [1989] 1 EGLR 189 the House of Lords had to consider the proper interpretation of the Town and Country Planning (Control of Advertisement) Regulations 1984. According to the literal interpretation of these regulations, an estate agent would have been guilty of a criminal offence if (without his knowledge or consent) another person added a second "For Sale" board to the land where the estate agent's own board was already lawfully displayed. The House of Lords refused to interpret the regulations in this way. Lord Griffiths observed:

The courts should surely be slow to impute to Parliament so harsh an intention as to impose criminal liability on a citizen acting lawfully because another citizen, over whom he has no control, acts unlawfully. We are dealing here with delegated legislation which does not receive the scrutiny of primary legislation.

Pre-legislative consultations

Although parliamentary control of subordinate legislation is almost non-existent, it would be a mistake to assume that such legislation always lacks due process of law. Modern government cannot be effectively carried out without the executive having rule-making powers. Parliament does not have time to discuss matters of precise detail and the legislative process is often very slow. One difference between primary and subordinate legislation is that Parliament can make amendments to a Bill, but it cannot propose an amendment to a statutory instrument even if, which is unlikely, it gets an opportunity to vote upon the proposal.

One safeguard often employed is to couple with the rule-making power an obligation to consult interested parties before finalising the wording of a statutory instrument. This obligation has to be expressly imposed by Parliament upon the minister in question. It will not be implied as a rule of common law. The rules of natural justice do not apply to the exercise of legislative powers: *Bates* v *Lord Hailsham of St Marylebone* [1972] 3 All ER 1019.

Where parliament imposes a duty to consult interested parties, a statutory instrument may be *ultra vires*, and therefore void, if the minister does not comply with this duty.

In the case of statutory instruments laying down procedural rules for certain tribunals, the minister concerned cannot validly exercise his rule-making power without first consulting the Council on Tribunals: see section 8 of the Tribunals and Inquiries Act 1992.

The tribunals in question are listed in Schedule 1 to the 1992 Act, and include industrial tribunals, the Lands Tribunal, rent assessment committees, social security appeal tribunals and many others.

Tertiary legislation

Many though the varieties of secondary legislation can be, students and chartered surveyors will also come across such documents as Codes of Practice, approved standards, Circulars and planning policy guidance notes. When referred to in court, the person doing so may have to answer the question from the judge: "Is this a rule-making document?"

The strict answer is that these documents are not legislative in nature – they are not, for example, statutory instruments.

Nevertheless, they are quasi-legislative in nature. They are referred to (expressly or impliedly) in Acts of Parliament and are said to constitute "material considerations" which must, as a matter of law, be taken into account before a statutory power is exercised or a relevant decision made.

Thus, such documents may be referred to as "tertiary legislation". More usually, however, they are called "quasi-legislation".

Contributed by Leslie Blake.

CHAPTER 72

Ending fixed-term leases early

First published in Estates Gazette April 13 1996

To what extent (if any) does a landlord have a duty to mitigate his loss if his tenant abandons a fixed-term lease before it has expired?

The relationship of landlord and tenant is complicated by the fact that a lease is not only a contractual agreement but also creates an "estate in land".

Leases in contracts

In recent years, the courts have had several occasions on which to consider the contractual nature of leases, particularly in the context of their termination. For example, in *National Carriers Ltd* v *Panalpina (Northern) Ltd* [1981] AC 675 the House of Lords held that a lease was capable of being determined by virtue of the occurrence of a "frustrating event". The decision removed the uncertainty which previously existed surrounding this area of law: see *Cricklewood Property & Investment Trust Ltd* v *Leighton Investment Trust Ltd* [1945] AC 221.

The significance of this decision was that the highest English appellate court decided that the fate of a lease could be determined by recourse to principles of pure contract law. The law lords therefore impliedly vindicated the contractual approach to analysing leasehold obligations.

Early examples of the application of a contractual approach to the analysis of leases can be seen in *Smith* v *Marrable* (1843) 11 M&W 5 and *Collins* v *Hopkins* [1923] 2 KB 617. In the case of *Hussein* v *Mehlman* [1992] 2 EGLR 87 assistant recorder Sedley (as he then was) further applied the logic of the contractual analysis of leases, holding that a lease could be terminated by virtue of the acceptance (by the tenant) of the landlord's repudiatory breach of a repairing covenant in the lease. (This decision was made in the county court, however, and it is not therefore a binding precedent.)

The above approach to analysing leases clearly stresses the contractual basis of the landlord and tenant relationship. But is it correct to view leases as contracts as well as proprietary rights (or conveyancers?)

Traditionally "property", to the lawyer, comes in three forms:

- personal property (such as chattels);
- real property (such as land and rights in relation to it, eg a freehold estate);
- real chattels (such as leases).

Leases have traditionally fallen between the first two categories, being seen as creatures of real property and, as a result of their contractual nature, personal property creations. Historically, those who possessed rights in real property could seek recovery of the res (the thing itself) by way of legal proceedings. But those who possessed only rights in real property could not do this. They could sue only for compensation.

It is because a lease generates both personal (contractual) rights and rights in relation to land that its exact nature has been a source of interest and debate. A lease is a hybrid form of property and has been (and probably always will be) simultaneously found in both the real property and personal property camps.

Abandonment of a fixed-term lease

The availability of a contractual analysis of the landlord and tenant relationship throws up many questions. One such dilemma arises where a tenant of a fixed-term lease abandons the premises and then fails, as from that date, to pay the rent and/or any other sums due.

Consider this simple scenario: A has granted a fixed-term 10-year legal lease to B of certain premises. B as tenant, takes up possession on January 1 1994. In early 1996, B encounters financial difficulties and abandons the premises. B clears the premises of all his possessions and forwards the keys to A. By abandoning the premises and handing back the keys to the landlord (A), B may have surrendered the lease. (Generally, surrenders must be made by deed – section 52(1) Law of Property Act 1925. However, section 52(2)(c) exempts implied surrenders or surrenders by operation of law from the requirement of a deed: where, for example, a landlord accepts a tenant's permanent and unequivocal abandonment of leasehold premises: see *Proudreed Ltd* v *Microgen Holdings Plc* [1996] 1 EGLR 89.)

But can A stick back and claim the remaining rent arrears and other costs as and when they fall due? Or is A under a contractual duty to mitigate his loss, for example, by attempting to reasonably relet the premises?

The answer is not clear. It is an accepted principle of the English law of contract that, where a contract has been breached, the innocent party will have a duty to take reasonable steps to minimise his loss. What is reasonable in any given situation is a question of fact. In this connection, *Brace* v *Calder* [1895] 2 QB 253 provides a good example; see also, *Shindler* v *Northern Raincoat Ltd* [1960] 2 All FR 239. Here the defendants – a partnership consisting of four members – agreed to employ the plaintiff as manager of a branch of the business for two years. Five months later the partnership was dissolved by the retirement of two of the members and the business was transferred to the other two. These two partners offered to employ the plaintiff on the same terms as before. The plaintiff rejected this offer. The dissolution of the partnership put the employers in breach of contract with the plaintiff. The plaintiff, in his action, therefore sought to recover the salary which he would have received had he served for the whole period of two years. It was held, however, that he was entitled only to nominal damages because it was unreasonable for him to have rejected the offer of continued employment. In short, the plaintiff had failed to mitigate his loss.

Failure to mitigate

If, after B's abandonment of the premises, A does nothing (except to seek to recover the remaining rent from B), can it be said that A is under a duty to make reasonable endeavours to find another tenant and thereby to mitigate his loss? If the logic of *Brace* (*supra*) is followed, A may be under such a duty.

However, what also complicates the position is the decision of the House of Lords in *White & Carter (Councils) Ltd* v *McGregor* [1962] AC 413. Here the appellants supplied litter bins to local councils throughout the UK. They were not paid by the councils, but by traders who hired advertising space on the bins. On June 26 1957 the respondent agreed to hire space on the bins for three years. Later on the same day the respondent wrote to cancel this contract. The appellants refused to accept this repudiation. Up to this moment the appellants had taken no steps to carry out the contract, but, despite the cancellation, they prepared advertisement plates, attached them to the bins and continued to display them for the following three years.

They made no attempt to minimise their loss by procuring other advertisers to take the respondent's place. In due course, they sued the apostate advertiser for the full contractual price. The House of Lords held, by a three to two majority, that the appellants were entitled to succeed. The majority seemed to take the view that there was no duty on the appellants to mitigate their loss. Perhaps a distinction can be drawn between *Brace* and *White & Carter*, on the basis that, in the latter case, there was an action for a specific sum of money rather than a recurring rent. However, the two authorities do not sit easily together.

Without doubt, *White & Carter* is controversial. One body of thought could support the basic outcome in favour of the appellants, viz why should the innocent contracting party be denied the expectations generated by the contract at the unilateral whim of the other? But, conversely, why should the innocent party to the contract, despite the repudiation, continue with an unwanted agreement and be absolved from all responsibility to mitigate his loss? Is it not economically inefficient for the law to condone an innocent party's performance in such instance? It comes as no surprise to note that *White & Carter* has been both criticised and justified by academics and judges alike.

What, therefore, is the position in relation to the similar situation described – where B has (in breach of contract) abandoned the demised premises? Like the law lords, academic opinion throughout several common law jurisdictions is also divided. In Ontario, Canada, the approach in *White & Carter* was adopted in *Ontario Inc* v *First Consolidated Holdings Corp* (1992) 26 RPR (2d) 298. It was held the landlord was entitled to sit back, do nothing and to sue to recover the arrears of rent owing to him. But it is noteworthy that, in British Columbia, Canada, a landlord is under a statutory duty to relet the premises at a "reasonably economic rent", when residential premises have been abandoned by his tenant: see c15, S48(b) Residential Tenancy Act SBS 1984.

It is also of interest that the rule in *White & Carter* seems to be subject to certain qualifications (suggested by Lord Reid). These are: first, where the innocent party cannot continue with performance without the co-operation of the defaulting party, he must accept the breach. Second, if it can be shown that a contracting party has no legitimate interest (financial or otherwise) in performing the contract, rather than in claiming damages, he ought not to be allowed to saddle the other party with an additional burden. The exact scope of this qualification is unclear. However, when faced with an abandonment, a landlord will obviously have a financial interest in carrying on with the contract because, by so doing, he will be able to hold the tenant liable for the rent as and when it accrues – thus reaping the expected return from his property, albeit as a debt.

Does the landlord have a choice?

So what is the preferred position? It is submitted that, when faced with a tenant's abandonment, the authorities of *Brace* and *White & Carter* are capable of reconciliation. In the event that a tenant abandons a fixed-term lease, it can be argued that the landlord has a genuine choice. He may either treat this breach as "repudiatory" in nature and accept the abandonment of the premises (whereupon the lease is terminated by surrender by operation of law) or he may choose not to accept the breach (the tenant's abandonment) and elect to treat the lease as continuing.

Brace dictates that, where a contract has ended by virtue of the acceptance of a repudiatory breach, it is at that time that the innocent party is under a duty reasonably to mitigate his losses. This would seem to apply where the landlord accepts a tenant's abandonment. Subject to this, the landlord will seek damages from the tenant. However, the landlord, following *White & Carter*, may choose not to treat the breach (abandonment) as being repudiatory and may decide to continue with the landlord and tenant relationship. In such instance, the lease will not have ended and no duty to mitigate will have arisen. The landlord will, in such an instance, be entitled to sit back and pursue the tenant for the rent as and when it falls due, even if this does give rise to "instalment litigation".

There are occasions when a tenant wants to end his letting arrangement with the landlord early. Two methods of managing this situation are popular: first, that (in return for the tenant supplying the landlord with fresh consideration) the landlord and tenant execute an express surrender of the lease by deed; second, the landlord and tenant agree at the outset to incorporate a tenant's break clause into the lease.

Perhaps, as both of these two methods of terminating the tenant's proprietary and contractual responsibilities in relation to the lease are open to lessees, it would be unfair to impose on a landlord (who is faced with a tenant's unaccepted premature abandonment), an automatic duty to mitigate his loss.

Contributed by James Brown.

CHAPTER 73

The doctrine of waiver

First published in Estates Gazette January 11, 1997

What do lawyers mean when they talk about "waiver"? In what circumstances may a landlord be said to have "waived" his rights?

According to the *Concise Oxford Dictionary* the verb to "waive" (from which the noun "waiver" is obtained) means "[to] refrain from insisting on or using, tacitly or implicitly [to] relinquish or [to] forgo, [a] right, claim, opportunity, legitimate plea, etc". The origin of the word is Norman French (and, perhaps, originally Scandinavian) and it is the same etymological root which gives us the word "waif" – an abandoned child or an ownerless animal or thing.

English law recognises a "doctrine of waiver", but it is uncertain how far this doctrine goes and the courts have been unable or unwilling to give a clear definition.

According to case law, the doctrine of waiver is significant when legal rights or legal remedies are "waived".

Waiver of rights

The waiver of legal rights is especially relevant in the context of the law of contract. As is, perhaps, well known, a variation to a contract is not binding if (not being executed as a deed) it is unsupported by consideration. This important principle was confirmed by the famous case of two seamen who deserted their ship at Kronstadt in the Baltic: *Stilk* v *Myrick* (1809) 170 ER 1168. The more recent case of *Williams* v *Roffey & Nicholls (Contractors) Ltd* [1990] 1 All ER 512 – a building contract dispute – purports to be a "refinement" of this common law rule, but it is unconvincingly reasoned and may be wrongly decided.

The doctrine of waiver recognises that a contracting party may promise to give up all or some of his contractual rights. For example, in *Hickman* v *Haynes* (1875) LR 10 CP 598 the parties entered into a contract for the sale and delivery of goods. The buyer then requested the seller to delay delivery. The seller agreed to do this and tendered delivery on the later date. Nevertheless the buyer refused to accept delivery, accusing the seller of delay. The seller therefore brought an action against the buyer for damages.

The buyer argued that the seller could not succeed in his claim because he had (for whatever reason) failed to meet the contract date for the delivery of the goods. The court held that the buyer had waived his right to demand delivery on the first-named date and that he could not subsequently reassert that date (if it had not yet passed) without giving reasonable notice that he had changed his mind.

Reasonable notice

An example of giving reasonable notice is *Charles Rickards Ltd* v *Oppenheim* [1950] 1 KB 616. In this case, early in 1947, the defendant ordered from the plaintiffs a chassis to a Rolls-Royce car. In July 1947 the plaintiffs agreed that a body should be built for that chassis "within six or, at the most, seven months". In fact the body was not completed within (or even after) seven months. Nevertheless the defendant agreed to wait another three months. At the end of this period the body was still not finished. The defendant then gave a final notice that, if the work was not finished within four weeks, he would cancel the order. Three months after the four-week time-limit had expired the body was completed and tendered to the defendant. The defendant refused to accept it. The plaintiffs then sued for damages.

It was not surprising that the court held that the defendant had given reasonable notice that "time was of the essence" when he had granted the final indulgence of four weeks and that the plaintiffs' claim therefore failed. However, it is interesting that it held also that the defendant had originally waived his right to insist on the first delivery date (however emphatically worded that obligation might have been) by agreeing to give the plaintiffs a further three months. If the plaintiffs had honoured that new date, the plaintiffs would have been prevented (by the doctrine of promissory estoppel) from arguing that that date was too late. "Call back yesterday, bid time return" would not have been a valid argument in those circumstances or at that time.

Promissory estoppel

The doctrine of waiver, as illustrated above, looks somewhat like the equitable doctrine of promissory estoppel as laid down in *Central London Property Trust Ltd* v *High Trees House Ltd* [1947] KB 130. The connecting theme is one of detrimental reliance.

Normally a lease (although it is an estate in land) will have its roots in the law of contract. Therefore, in so far as the doctrine of waiver can operate in relation to an everyday contract, so also can it be relevant to a landlord and his tenant. For example, in *Wallis* v *Semark* [1951] 2 TLR 222 a property was let to a tenant on a weekly tenancy. A rent book was provided by the landlord which contained the words "one month's notice each party". This was later crossed out and replaced by the statement (initialled by the landlord) "one month's notice from the tenant; two years' notice from the landlord".

The landlord's promise to give the tenant two years' notice was not supported by any consideration from the tenant. However, relying on this undertaking, the tenant remained in possession of the property and continued to pay his rent from week to week. It was held that the tenant was entitled to a full two years' notice from the landlord and that the landlord had waived his right to rely upon the original provision as to one month's notice.

Without doubt the concepts of waiver and promissory estoppel look similar in this context. The two concepts can sometimes produce the same result. For example, in *Brikow Investments Ltd* v *Carr* [1979] 2 EGLR 36, the landlords of four blocks of flats offered to sell 99-year leases to their sitting tenants. The leases in question contained undertakings by the landlords to maintain the structure of the buildings and, by the tenants, to contribute to the maintenance costs. At the time of these negotiations the roofs were in need of repair and the landlords made representations to the tenants' association (and to individual tenants) that they would repair the roofs at their own expense. Subsequently the landlords carried out these repairs, but they afterwards claimed contributions from the tenants.

The Court of Appeal decided in favour of the tenants, but the judges were not unanimous in their reasons for doing so. Lord Denning MR took the view that the doctrine of promissory estoppel applied. Roskill LJ and Cumming-Bruce J thought that the case was one involving the doctrine of waiver (in that the landlords had waived their contractual right to insist on a contribution from the tenants).

Leasehold renewals

The doctrine of waiver may also apply in the context of leasehold renewals under the Landlord and Tenant Act 1954. In *Kammins Ballrooms Co Ltd* v *Zenith Investments (Torquay) Ltd* [1971] AC 850 the tenants of business premises made a request for a new tenancy under Part II of the 1954 Act. The landlords served a notice of opposition indicating that they would oppose any such application.

The tenants filed an application for a grant of a new tenancy, but this application jumped the gun. (Section 29(3) of the 1954 Act lays down a proper timetable for such applications.) Nevertheless the landlords (when they filed their reply) made no objection to the timing of the tenants' application and they did not raise "prematurity" as an argument until a later stage.

On the facts, it was held that the landlords had not waived their right to object to the application. Lord Diplock took the view that, as no express representation of fact had been made, no waiver had occurred.

Waiver of legal remedies

The doctrine of waiver can be a bar to the operation of legal remedies. This can be very significant in contractual relationships.

A breach of contract may be a "breach of warranty" (a minor breach of contract) or it may be a "repudiatory breach". In the first case the innocent party will remain bound by the contract, although he may have a remedy in damages. In the second case, the innocent party will have a choice (known as a "right of election"):

- he may accept the breach as being repudiatory and treat the contract as at an end; this will release both parties from any further performance of their obligations, and will leave him (the innocent party) with his claim for damages if he has suffered any loss.
- he may "elect" to waive his right to terminate the contract: this will preserve the future rights and duties of both parties and it will also allow him to sue the other party for damages (unless he has waived this right also).

If the innocent party waives an opportunity to treat the contract as terminated he is said to have "affirmed" that contract. In such a case he will have waived a self-help remedy which was open to him, but he will not have waived his rights.

If, in addition to affirming a contract which the other party has broken in a repudiatory way, the innocent party also waives his right to sue for damages he will then be said to have made (or to have "granted") a "total waiver". This will be similar to a unilateral and gratuitous waiver of his legal rights (as discussed above).

Forfeiture of leases

Where a landlord is faced with a tenant who has broken a covenant in the lease (eg by failing to pay his rent or by failing to carry out his repairing obligations) that landlord will have the following choices open to him:

- he may seek to forfeit the lease (usually suing for debt or damages as well);
- he may sue for debt (or damages) while waiving his right to forfeit the lease;
- he may waive the breach totally.

A landlord who waives his remedy of forfeiture is not necessarily blessed with a saintly personality. He may do this thing without realising that he has done it.

In *Matthews* v *Smallwood* [1910] 1 Ch 777, Parker J held that, if (with knowledge of a breach) the landlord acknowledges to his tenant the continued existence of the tenancy, he will be taken to have elected not to forfeit the lease.

This rule still applies. In *Van Haarlam* v *Kassner Charitable Trust* [1992] 2 EGLR 59 a communist spy from Czechoslovakia adopted the identity of a long-lost child who had disappeared into night and fog. He came to England (on the basis that his "mother" lived there) and commenced his spying activities from a leasehold house, 35 Silver Birch Close, London N11. He was arrested and, in due course, he was sentenced to 10 years' imprisonment for doing acts preparatory to spying, contrary to the Official Secrets Acts.

The landlords of the house sought to forfeit the lease. They claimed (quite justifiably) that he had been using the premises for illegal or immoral purposes.

The High Court held that the landlords had waived this remedy by accepting the quarterly ground rent from the tenant (a purely nominal sum) after the date of his arrest. They knew that he had been arrested under the Official Secrets Acts and that the impedimenta of spying had been found in his house. In these circumstances it did not matter that the tenant had not yet been convicted of any criminal offence. (Although this is a perversion of the presumption of innocence, it operates in favour of the accused person's property rights, not against his interests.)

The High Court also held that, even if the landlords had not waived their remedy of forfeiture, the tenant would have been entitled to "relief against forfeiture" (an equitable dispensation) because his crime was a crime against the state, not against his landlords or against his neighbours, and he had already been sentenced to a lengthy term of imprisonment for that crime.

Landlord's knowledge

A landlord cannot be said to have "waived a breach of covenant" (ie waived his remedy of forfeiture in respect of that breach) unless: (1) he has knowledge of that breach; and (2) he acts in a way that indicates that he wishes the relationship of landlord and tenant to continue. But the test is not a subjective one. The landlord may have imputed knowledge of a fact without having actual knowledge of it, and his outward conduct may indicate an apparent intention which he does not truly attain or possess.

In *Central Estates (Belgravia) Ltd* v *Woolgar (No 2)* [1972] 1 WLR 1048 a tenant possessed a long lease of a house in Pimlico. The lease contained a covenant against causing a nuisance on the premises. The tenant was convicted of unlawfully keeping a brothel at the house. The landlords' agents (knowing of this conviction) then made arrangements that no further rent should be accepted or demanded. By a clerical error a demand for one quarter's rent was sent out and the tenant paid that rent. It was held that the landlords' demand for (and acceptance of) rent, made by the agents who knew the full facts, operated as a waiver of the remedy of forfeiture. (Indeed, if the *Van Haarlam* case is to be taken seriously, the agents should not have demanded or accepted rent after the date of the arrest, if they knew about that arrest, and what it was for, and what, if any, impedimenta of brothel-keeping had been found on the premises.)

Landlord's conduct

The state of the landlord's knowledge (or that of his agents) is a question of fact: see *Chrisdell Ltd* v *Johnson* [1987] 2 EGLR 123. The question of the landlord's conduct (does it amount to a waiver) is a question of law. He may still be held to have waived his remedy of forfeiture even if he accepted rent from his tenant "under protest" or on a "without prejudice" basis: see *Segal Securities Ltd* v *Thoseby* [1963] 1 QB 887; *Windmill Investments (London) Ltd* v *Milano Restaurants Ltd* [1962] 2 QB 373.

Consequences of waiver

Where a landlord has waived his remedy of forfeiture two different scenarios can arise. If the breach of covenant is a "continuing breach" (such as breach of "user covenant") the landlord's waiver will operate only until the date of his conduct in, for example, accepting the rent. The landlord will have a fresh right to seek forfeiture every day after the date of his waiver if the tenant's breach of covenant continues to occur.

If the breach of covenant is, or was, a "once and for all breach" (eg non-payment of rent), the landlord will lose forever his remedy of forfeiture if he waives that breach, for example by collecting rent for a period of the tenancy which has arisen after the date of the rent arrears.

Contributed by James Brown and Leslie Blake.

CHAPTER 74

The Arbitration Act 1996

First published in Estates Gazette April 5, 1997

Arbitration is about objectively assessing the arguments on both sides of a dispute. The 1996 Arbitration Act now strengthens its role.

From rent reviews to commercial documentation covering building contracts and international shipping disputes, arbitration has a role. It can also arise in a statutory context, such as the Agricultural Tenancies Act 1995, which uses arbitration to resolve the majority of tenancy disputes arising out of that legislation. There is also the county courts' "small claims" arbitration procedure, where a district judge can arbitrate in money claims up to £3,000.

The purpose of arbitration is always the same: to break deadlock in the quickest and most cost-effective way. In commerce, arbitration is an alternative to expensive and long-winded court proceedings. Without adequate procedures for resolving disputes, many agreements would be unworkable.

The essential ingredients common to all arbitration proceedings are:

- A written agreement to refer the dispute to arbitration; or a statutory provision to similar effect.
- Procedure for appointing an arbitrator.
- A well-drawn arbitration clause setting out the factors on which the arbitrator is to base his or her decisions.
- A defined procedure for the arbitration.

Written agreement
Section 5 Arbitration Act 1996, which came into force on January 31, requires arbitration agreements to be written if they are to be given the legal status which Part I of the Act provides for them.

Oral arbitration agreements are not outlawed, but they may be difficult to enforce. When a valid arbitration agreement is entered into, the courts will respect it. If legal proceedings are brought to decide any claim which is already covered by an existing arbitration agreement, section 9 of the Act allows either party to apply for a "stay" of the litigation. The court cannot refuse this application unless it is satisfied that the arbitration agreement is void, inoperative, or incapable of being performed.

Appointing an arbitrator

If agreement on a named individual cannot be reached, the decision has to be referred to an independent third party, usually the president of a named professional association. He or she will, upon payment of a fee, appoint an arbitrator when either party asks for one.

Matters to be decided

Most rent review arbitrations will require the arbitrator to make an assessment based on what a willing tenant might pay to a willing landlord for a hypothetical lease of the same property on terms, which in all other respects, are similar to the terms contained in the actual lease.

Normally the arbitrator must assume that the tenant has complied with repairs and other obligations under the lease (even if this is not the case). He or she must also ensure that the tenant's rent is not based on its own capital expenditure.

This means disregarding any enhancement of the rent due to the fact that the tenant is already in occupation of the property; any goodwill attached to the tenant's business; or any voluntary improvements which the tenant has lawfully made to the premises at its own expense. It must also be decided whether the person appointed to determine the dispute is to act strictly as an "arbitrator" or as an "expert".

An arbitrator must act judicially, taking account only of the arguments put forward by the claimant and the respondent. By contrast, an "expert" will have the freedom to reach decisions based on his or her professional experience, even if this is beyond what had previously been contemplated by the parties to the dispute.

In the High Court case of *British Ship Builders* v *VSEL Consortium plc*, *The Times*, February 4 1996, Lightman J said that the role of an expert had to be determined in accordance with the terms of the relevant agreement.

If that agreement gave an expert the exclusive right to decide a question, the court's jurisdiction was excluded, but if he or she went outside the terms of reference, the court could intervene and set the expert's decision aside.

Lightman J added that if there was manifest error the court could set an expert's decision aside so long as the agreement allowed for this. The court could also determine the limits of an expert's terms of reference and the conditions to which he or she had to comply. The courts, however, would normally decline to do this.

Defining procedure

Arbitrations may be decided purely on the basis of written representations from each party, or following a hearing at which each party gives oral evidence. So long as the procedures are fair and impartial, the law gives the parties freedom to agree the manner in which an arbitration is to be conducted.

Other issues might include: whether formal pleadings are to be used; requirements for the disclosure of documents; and whether strict rules of evidence should apply.

Arbitration agreements often do not set out sufficiently the procedures to be followed. The 1996 Act, however, fills in the gaps. Section 34 allows arbitrators to decide all procedural and evidential matters which have not been previously agreed between the parties. Unless otherwise agreed, arbitrators may consult their own legal and technical advisers and may also make provisional awards.

Sections 40 and 41 make it the duty of each opposing party to do everything necessary for the proper and expeditious conduct of proceedings. Arbitrators are empowered to impose sanctions on any party who does not do this.

To encourage each party to conduct a case economically, section 65 allows an arbitrator to limit the costs which the winner can recover from the loser.

How the 1996 Act limits the power of the Courts

Before the 1996 Act, arbitration was often no quicker, and often more expensive, than conventional court proceedings. In addition to their own costs in pursuing or defending claims, the parties had to pay the arbitrator's fees and the costs of hiring suitable premises.

The complexities and uncertainties of English arbitration law had also threatened London's future as a world arbitration centre, particularly given the competition from more "user-friendly" systems in France, Sweden, the Netherlands and the Far East.

The potential loss of international business prompted the government to overhaul arbitration law.

The 1996 Act's main advantage is that it brings together the legislation which had previously been contained in three Arbitration Acts (1950, 1975 and 1979) and in numerous decided cases. The Act also limits the power of the courts to intervene in an arbitration dispute, and there are now only four grounds for such judicial intervention:

1) Extending time

Many agreements contain strict time limits for referring disputes to arbitration and for taking steps during the course of the arbitration itself. A party who is late in commencing arbitration proceedings may be time-barred, unless the court extends time. Sections 12 and 79 of the Act allow courts to do this if:

- The particular circumstances were outside the reasonable contemplation of the parties at the time when the time limits were agreed, or
- one party's conduct makes it unjust to hold the other party to the strict time limit.

Once an arbitration is under way, the court may only extend a time limit if this cannot be done within the terms of the arbitration itself and to refuse to do so would cause substantial injustice.

The Court of Appeal has ruled that an inordinate and inexcusable delay by a party in applying for the appointment of an arbitrator was a proper ground for the court to refuse to extend time, even if the other party had not been prejudiced by the delay. The decision came in the case, *Frota Oceanic Brasileira SA* v *Steam Ship Mutual Underwriting Association (Bermuda) Ltd (The Frotanorte)*, *The Times*, August 13 1996, which concerned a dispute arising from a collision between two ships off Puerto Rico in 1978.

2) Challenging an arbitrator

Section 67 allows the judiciary to challenge an arbitrator if he acts outside their terms of reference. It should be noted that a party may lose this right if it has not made an objection known at the earliest opportunity.

3) In the event of irregularities

Section 68 gives judicial powers in the event of irregularities affecting the arbitrator, the conduct of the proceedings, or the arbitration award, if those irregularities cause substantial injustice. Section 68(2) sets out nine possible grounds on which such an irregularity may be alleged by the parties to an arbitration.

4) Appeal on a point of law

Section 69 says that, unless otherwise agreed, any party may appeal to the court on a point of law affecting an arbitration award. The parties may, however, choose to exclude the court's jurisdiction in this respect, in which case the arbitrator's award will be final both as to law and as to fact.

Appeals on points of law can only be made with the consent of the other parties or with leave from the court. Leave must be applied for within 28 days from the issue of the arbitration award. The court can only give leave if it is satisfied that the question substantially affects the rights of the parties; that the point of law was raised during the arbitration proceedings itself; that the arbitrator's decision was obviously wrong or that the question is one of general public importance; and that it is just and proper for the court to determine the question.

The "court" for any of these purposes is the High Court or the Business List of Central London County Court.

Current trends in commercial disputes are away from traditional court litigation and towards arbitration and other "alternative dispute resolution" procedures (ADR). In fact, judges in London's Commercial Court now ask litigants to consider resolving disputes through ADR in appropriate cases – and will temporarily halt proceedings for this to be considered.

Such trends have been reinforced by the emphasis which agricultural legislation places on arbitration to resolve tenancy disputes.

Contributed by V.C. Ward.

Index